Dreamweaver 4 | H·O·T
Hands-On Training

lynda.com/books

By Garo Green – Developed with Lynda Weinman

Design: Ali Karp

Dreamweaver 4 | H·O·T Hands-On Training

By Garo Green — Developed with Lynda Weinman

lynda.com/books | Peachpit Press
1249 Eighth Street • Berkeley, CA • 94710
800.283.9444 • 510.524.2178 •
510.524.2221(fax)
http://www.lynda.com/books
http://www.peachpit.com

lynda.com/books is published in
association with Peachpit Press,
a division of Pearson Education
Copyright ©2002 by lynda.com

ISBN: 0-201-74133-4

0 9 8 7 6 5 4 3 2

Printed and bound in the
United States of America

H•O•T | Credits

Original Design: Ali Karp, Alink Newmedia (`alink@earthlink.net`)

Peachpit Editor: Cary Norsworthy

Copyeditors: Paul Potyen, Rebecca Pepper

Peachpit Production: Lisa Brazieal

Peachpit Compositors: Owen Wolfson, David Van Ness, Jude Levinson

Beta testers: Victor Gavenda, Travis Amos, Dina Pielaet, Steve Perry, Chris Tegethoff, Chris Graham, Mary Ogle

Cover Illustration: Bruce Heavin (bruce@stink.com)

Indexer: Steve Rath

H•O•T | Colophon

The original design for *Dreamweaver 4 H•O•T* was sketched on paper. The layout was heavily influenced by online communication—merging a traditional book format with a modern Web aesthetic.

The text in *Dreamweaver 4 H•O•T* was set in Akzidenz Grotesk from Adobe and Triplex from Emigre. The cover illustration was painted in Adobe Photoshop 6.0 and Adobe Illustrator 9.0.

This book was created using QuarkXPress 4.1, Adobe Photoshop 6.0, Microsoft Office 2001, and Dreamweaver 4 on a Macintosh G3, running MacOS 9. It was printed on 50 lb. Lynx Opaque at Commercial Documentation Services, Medford, Oregon.

Dedication

To my father, James Joseph Doherty.

Thank you for teaching me how to give so much,
so freely. You are my inspiration.

Love, Garo

Dreamweaver 4 | **H•O•T** —————————————**Table of Contents**

Introduction

H•O•T

Dreamweaver 4

A Note from Lynda Weinman

In my opinion, most people buy computer books in order to learn, yet it is amazing how few of these books are actually written by teachers. Garo Green and I take pride in the fact that this book was written by experienced teachers who are familiar with training students in this subject matter. In this book, you will find carefully developed lessons and exercises to help you learn Dreamweaver 4—one of the most well-respected HTML editors on the planet.

This book is targeted toward beginning to intermediate level Web developers who are looking for a great tool to speed up production, offer workflow flexibility, and create great code and results. The premise of the hands-on exercise approach is to get you up to speed quickly in Dreamweaver while actively working through the book's lessons. It's one thing to read about a product and another experience entirely to try the product and get measurable results. Our motto is, "read the book, follow the exercises, and you will know the product." We have received countless testimonials to this fact, and it is our goal to make sure it remains true for all of our hands-on training books.

Many exercise-based books take a paint-by-numbers approach to teaching. While this approach works, it's often difficult to figure out how to apply those lessons to a real-world situation, or to understand why or when you would use the technique again. What sets this book apart is that the lessons contain lots of background information and insights into each given subject, which are designed to help you understand the process as well as the exercise.

At times, pictures are worth a lot more than words. When necessary, we have also included short QuickTime movies to show any process that's difficult to explain with words. These files are located on the **H•O•T CD-ROM** inside a folder called **movies**. It's our style to approach teaching from many different angles, since we know that some people are visual learners, others like to read, and still others like to get out there and try things. This book combines a lot of teaching approaches so you can learn Dreamweaver 4 as thoroughly as you want to.

This book didn't set out to cover every single aspect of Dreamweaver. The manual, and many other reference books are great for that! What we saw missing from the bookshelves was a process-oriented tutorial that taught readers core principles, techniques, and tips in a hands-on training format.

We welcome your comments at dw4hot@lynda.com. Please visit our Web site at **http://www.lynda.com**. The support URL for this book is **http://www.lynda.com/products/books/dw4hot/.**

It's Garo's and my hope that this book will raise your skills in Web design, HTML, JavaScript, and publishing. If it does, we will have accomplished the job we set out to do!

—Lynda Weinman

NOTE | About lynda.com/books and lynda.com

lynda.com/books is dedicated to helping Web designers and developers understand tools and design principles. **lynda.com** offers hands-on workshops, training seminars, conferences, on-site training, training videos, training CDs, and "expert tips" for Web design and development. To learn more about our training programs, books, and products, be sure to give our site a visit at **http://www.lynda.com**.

About the Author

Garo Green has been working with a wide range of computers since the tender age of 12. Those were the golden days of tape drives and 64K of RAM, when all you needed was a double-density floppy disk and a hole-puncher. ;-)

Garo has worked extensively in the development of custom curriculum and courseware for software training. He has over six years of teaching experience in both hardware and software applications. He is known worldwide for his enthusiastic, approachable, and humanistic teaching style.

Garo is the co-author of the upcoming Flash 5 H•O•T book and author of several Web design training CD-ROMs, including *Learning Dreamweaver 4* and *Learning Flash 5*. He has also been a featured speaker at the Web 99 and FlashForward2000 conferences.

In his spare time (he doesn't have much of that anymore, but that's OK), he has found that his passion for teaching and sharing what he knows is very fulfilling. He does sneak away, several times a day, to the local Starbucks for a double latte (to be honest it's usually a triple shot) with hazelnut. Of course, this might explain why he talks so fast!

Our Team

Lynda and Garo take a break from their busy schedules to smile at the camera.

*The lynda.com training center offers classes in Dreamweaver, Flash, Fireworks, Photoshop, ImageReady, GoLive, and Web-design principles. Visit **www.lynda.com/classes** for more information.*

Garo is learning the art of bonsai, and this is his first tree. Good thing you can't see the dozen that came before this one. ;-)

Acknowledgments

This book, and every other book you read, could not have been possible without a strong team of dedicated, enthusiastic, and talented individuals. I was fortunate enough to work with the best.

My deepest thanks and appreciation to:

You, the reader. There is nothing I enjoy more than sharing what I know with others. I really like what I do, and it's my highest hope that you like it too! ;-)

My dearest friend, **Lynda Weinman**; thank you for paving the way. Your friendship and support have helped me realize so many of my dreams! Gosh, I hope that doesn't sound like an epitaph!?

My **fellow instructors** at lynda.com, **Donna Casey, Garrick Chow,** and **Dina Pielaet.** Thank you for your help in developing many of the exercises in this book. Your knowledge and support were invaluable.

My **friends at Peachpit, Cary Norsworthy, Suzie Lowey,** and **Lisa Brazieal,** thank you for being there to make sure that I didn't cross my I's and dot my T's.

My **beta testers, Victor Gavenda, Travis Amos, Dina Pielaet, Steve Perry, Chris Tegethoff, Chris Graham,** and **Mary Ogle.** You guys did a great job of finding all the little mistakes. Of course, I left them there on purpose so that you would have something to do! Yeah right! ;-)

My **friends at Macromedia, Beth Davis, Eric Ott, Diana Smedley, David Morris, Mike Sundymeyer,** and all of the Dreamweaver engineers. How do you keep making a great product better? It's been great working with each of you.

The entire **lynda.com staff.** You guys make coming to work each day so much fun; what more could a person ask for?

How to Use This Book

Please read this section—it contains important information that's going to help you as you use this book. The chart below outlines the information we cover:

Dreamweaver 4 H•O•T
Information in this section:
The Formatting in This Book
HTML versus HTM
The Moon's Nest Inn, Again?
Macintosh and Windows Interface Screen Captures
Mac and Windows System Differences • "Open" for Mac and "Select" for Windows • "Open" in Mac System Is "Choose" in System 8.6
A Note to Windows Users • Making Exercise Files Editable on Windows Systems • Making File Extensions Visible on Windows Systems • Creating New Documents
Dreamweaver System Requirements
What's on the CD-ROM?

NOTE | The Formatting in This Book

This book has several components, including step-by-step exercises, commentary, notes, tips, warnings, and movies. Step-by-step exercises are numbered, and file names and command keys are shown in bold so they pop out more easily. Captions and commentary are in italicized text: *This is a caption.* File names/folders, command keys, and menu commands are bolded: **images** folder, **Ctrl+Click,** and **File > Open...** Code is in a monospace font: `<html></html>`. And URLs are in bold: **http://www.lynda.com**.

HTML versus HTM

All of the HTML exercise files on the CD-ROM end with an .html extension. Windows users might be more used to naming files with an .htm extension. You can name your files either way, and a Web browser will be able to read them. The choice to name them with the four-letter extension represents a personal bias of ours. The shorter .htm suffix is a throwback to the old days of DOS when file names were limited to the eight-dot-three convention. That meant that file names could be no longer than eight characters and had to end with a dot and a three-letter extension. Those days are history since the advent of Windows 95/98/2000, so we've named all the files with the more accurate four-letter extension. It does, after all, stand for **H**yper**T**ext **M**arkup **L**anguage, not HyperText Markup! Now you know why we chose to name the files this way, but the bottom line here is that you can use either naming method and your HTML files will still work, as long as they have been referenced this way in the links. We simply made a choice to use the four-letter extension because that's what we prefer.

The Moon's Nest Inn, Again?

If you have purchased other training material from lynda.com, you will already be familiar with the Moon's Nest Inn Web site. Some of you might be wondering why we are using this site, again, for the examples in this book. Well, for one, it has proven to be an effective site to teach you the basics of Dreamweaver 4. Second, and most important to us, and hopefully to you too, it has allowed us to produce this book much more quickly than if we were to develop an entirely new Web site. Like many of you, we are seeing the Moon's Nest Inn in our dreams and are ready for a change. So you can count on seeing a new Web site in the next edition of this book!

Macintosh and Windows Interface Screen Captures

Most of the screen captures in this book were taken on a Macintosh. The only time we used Windows shots was when the interface differed from the Macintosh. We made this decision because we do most of our design work and writing on a Macintosh. We also own and use a Windows system, so we noted important differences when they occurred and took screen captures accordingly.

Mac and Windows System Differences

Macromedia has done a great job of ensuring that Dreamweaver looks and works the same between the Macintosh and Windows operating systems. However, there are still some differences that should be noted. If you are using this book with one of the Windows operating systems, please be sure to read the following section, titled *"A Note to Windows Users,"* carefully.

WARNING | "Open" for Mac and "Select" for Windows

Throughout this book, you will be instructed to click the **Open** button. This is the correct way to do it on the Macintosh with OS 9. On a PC running Windows, you will instead see a **Select** button. The two buttons are interchangeable and do the same thing.

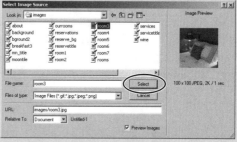

*Click **Select** in Windows.*

*Click **Open** on a Macintosh.*

WARNING | "Open" in Mac System 9 Is "Choose" in System 8.6

Since some of you will be using System 8 and others System 9, it is necessary to be aware of the following difference. When you **Browse for Files**, System 8 displays a **Choose** button, whereas System 9 displays an **Open** button. Both buttons perform the same function, even though they have different names.

*System 8 displays a **Choose** button.*

*System 9 displays an **Open** button.*

A Note to Windows Users

This section contains essential information about making your exercise folders editable, making file extensions visible, and creating new Dreamweaver documents from the document window versus the Site window.

Making Exercise Files Editable on Windows Systems

By default, when you copy files from a CD-ROM to your Windows 95/98/2000 hard drive, they are set to read-only (write protected). This will cause a problem with the exercise files, because you will need to write over some of them. When you define a site (you will learn to do this in Chapter 3, *"Site Control"*), you will notice that the files have a small lock next to them, which means they have been set to read-only. To remove this setting and make them editable, follow the short procedure below:

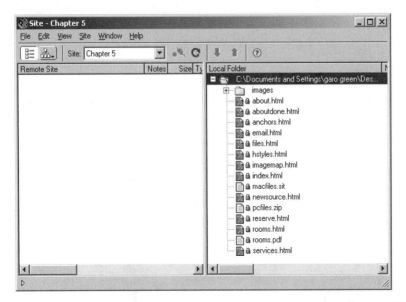

1. Define your site, using the folder you copied from the **H•O•T CD-ROM**. When the Site window opens, you will see little locks next to all of the files.

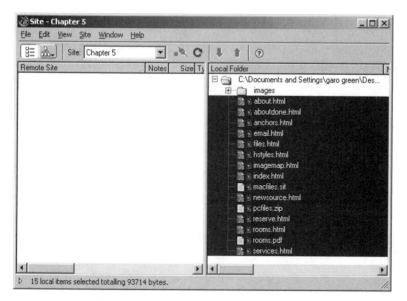

2. **Ctrl+Click** on each of the files that has a lock next to it.

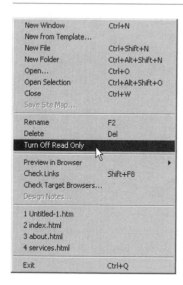

3. Once you have all of the files selected, select **File > Turn Off Read Only**.

Making File Extensions Visible on Windows Systems

In this section, you'll see three different examples of how to turn on file extensions for Windows 95, Windows 98, and Windows 2000. By default, Windows 95/98/2000 users cannot see file extensions, such as .gif, .jpg, or .html. Fortunately you can change this setting!

Windows 95 Users:

1. Double-click on the **My Computer** icon on your desktop. **Note:** If you (or someone else) have changed the name, it will not say **My Computer**.

2. Select **View > Options**. This opens the **Options** dialog box.

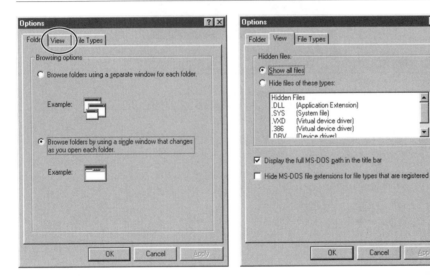

3. Click on the **View** tab at the top. This opens the **View** options screen so you can change the view settings for Windows 95.

4. Make sure there is no checkmark in the **Hide MS-DOS file extensions for file types that are registered** box. This ensures that the file extensions are visible, which will help you better understand the exercises in this book!

Windows 98 Users:

1. Double-click on the **My Computer** icon on your desktop. **Note:** If you (or someone else) have changed the name, it will not say **My Computer**.

2. Select **View > Folder Options**. This opens the **Folder Options** dialog box.

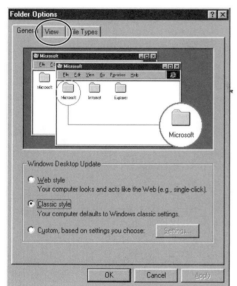 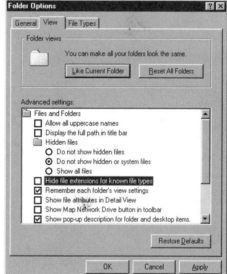

3. Click on the **View** tab at the top. This opens the **View** options screen so you can change the view settings for Windows 98.

4. Uncheck the **Hide file extensions for known file types** checkbox. This makes all of the file extensions visible.

Windows 2000 Users:

1. Double-click on the **My Computer** icon on your desktop. **Note:** If you (or someone else) have changed the name, it will not say **My Computer**.

2. Select **Tools > Folder Options**. This opens the **Folder Options** dialog box.

3. Click on the **View** tab at the top. This opens the **View** options screen so you can change the view settings for Windows 2000.

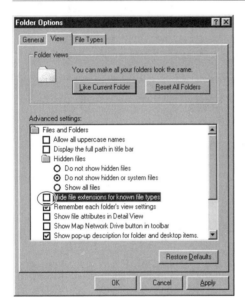

4. Make sure there is no checkmark next to the **Hide file extensions for known file types** option. This makes all of the file extensions visible.

Creating New Documents

Creating a new document in the Windows version of Dreamweaver can vary a little, depending on whether you are in the document window or the Site window.

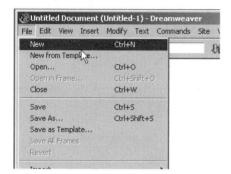

• To create a new document with the document window open, select **File > New** or press **Ctrl+N**.

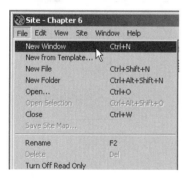

• To create a new document that opens as a blank document window from the Site window, select **File > New Window**. If you were to select **File > New File**, the document would appear only in the Site window, and not as a new untitled document.

Dreamweaver System Requirements

This book requires that you use either a Macintosh operating system (Power Macintosh running System 8.6 or later) or Windows 95, Windows 98, Windows 2000, or Windows NT 4.0. You also will need a color monitor capable of 800 x 600 resolution and a CD-ROM drive. We suggest that you have at least 64 MB of RAM in your system, because that way you can open Dreamweaver and a Web browser at the same time. More RAM than that is even better, especially on Macintosh computers, which do not dynamically allocate RAM, as Windows does. Here's a little chart that cites Macromedia's RAM requirements, along with our recommendations:

Dreamweaver System Requirements		
	Dreamweaver Requires	**We Recommend**
Mac	32 MB	64 MB
Windows 95/98/NT	32 MB	64 MB

What's on the CD-ROM?

Exercise Files and the H•O•T CD-ROM

Your course files are located inside a folder called **exercise_files** on the **H•O•T CD-ROM**. These files are divided into chapter folders, and you will be instructed to copy the chapter folders to your hard drive during many of the exercises. Unfortunately, when files originate from a CD-ROM, the Windows operating system defaults to making them write-protected, meaning that you cannot alter them. You will need to alter them to follow the exercises, so please read the "Note to Windows Users" on pages xxii and xxiii for instructions on how to convert them to read-and-write formatting.

Demo Files on the CD-ROM

In addition to the exercise files, the **H•O•T CD-ROM** also contains free 30-day trial versions of several software applications for the Mac or Windows. All software is located inside the **software** folder on the **H•O•T CD-ROM**. We have included trial versions of:

- Macromedia Dreamweaver 4.0 + (4.01 update)

- Macromedia Extension Manager 1.2

- Macromedia Fireworks 4.0

- Netscape Navigator 3.0 • Netscape Navigator 4.7 • Netscape Navigator 6.01

- Internet Explorer 3.0 • Internet Explorer 4.5 • Internet Explorer 5.0

We also have included several plug-ins on **the H•O•T CD-ROM**. If you don't have these plug-ins installed already, you should do that before working with any exercise in this book that calls for one of them. All of the plug-ins are located inside the **software** folder. We have included the following:

- Flash 5.0 plug-in

- Shockwave 8.5 plug-in

- QuickTime 5.0 plug-in

I.

Background

What is Dreamweaver?	Roundtrip HTML
Do You Need To Know HTML?	HTML Resources	What Does HTML Do?
What Does HTML Look Like?		HTML Deconstructed
File Naming Conventions	File Name Extensions
Extending Dreamweaver	What Is DHTML?
What Is XML?	What Is JavaScript?

H·O·T
———————————————
Hands-On-Training

We could start this book with lots of exercises, throwing you right into working with Dreamweaver without any preparation. But then you would be flying blind, without understanding basic Web-design fundamentals such as HTML, DHTML, XML, and JavaScript. Instead, we are starting you off with some definitions, concepts, and guidelines to help with your hands-on Dreamweaver training. Feel free to scan this chapter for information if you already know some of what is here or want the instant gratification of getting started.

What Is Dreamweaver?

Dreamweaver is a WYSIWYG (**W**hat **Y**ou **S**ee **I**s **W**hat **Y**ou **G**et) HTML generator. This means if you change something on the screen inside Dreamweaver, it will show you the results instantly. In contrast, if you were to code the HTML by hand, you would have to look at the code inside a Web browser to see the results. The instant feedback of a live design environment such as Dreamweaver speeds up your workflow tremendously, because you can see whether you like the results while you are working.

Roundtrip HTML

Dreamweaver has gained a lot of great reviews and customer loyalty because of its invention of roundtrip HTML. Roundtrip HTML means you can alter the code that Dreamweaver automatically writes. Most other WYSIWYG HTML editors today do not let you alter the code they produce. That's because they need to work with code that's written in a specific way, so they can offer all the WYSIWYG features. In other words, the code is self-serving to help the program, not to create the HTML.

Why is roundtrip HTML important? Because you can alter the code that Dreamweaver writes, and it will leave your changes alone, even if it doesn't understand them. This respect for your changes is key, because the program doesn't assume it knows what you want better than you do. Don't you wish all programs were so respectful?

Roundtrip HTML is especially important because HTML isn't yet a stable standard. If you have been watching the development of HTML, you might have noticed that it's changed a lot since it was first introduced in 1993. The inventors of the markup language didn't really expect that the Web would catch on as it has or that people would want to do full-scale multimedia with HTML.

To put it politely, HTML was extremely limited when it was first released. Browsers, such as Mosaic, Netscape Navigator, and Microsoft Internet Explorer, pushed the early boundaries of developing HTML without the consent of the Web's formal standards committee (the **W**orld **W**ide **W**eb **C**onsortium, or W3C). This meant that if you were using a WYSIWYG editor that didn't allow you to write your own code, you were prevented from trying some of the new markup that wasn't officially part of HTML. So many people who started building pages with visual HTML editors, such as Claris HomePage, NetObjects Fusion, and Microsoft FrontPage, couldn't always take advantage of the latest features that were supported by browsers.

It was like having a tool that handcuffed you in time to whatever was possible at the moment it was released. Roundtrip HTML, on the other hand, allows you to try things that aren't even invented yet. That's pretty cool.

Programmers have looked at HTML editors with dubious eyes because of the inflexibility of these tools and their inclusion of nonstandard HTML code. Dreamweaver is the first HTML editor to win the approval of programmers and designers alike. Programmers like the product because they are not tied to writing code in a rigid manner. Designers like Dreamweaver because it writes clean code without a lot of proprietary and self-serving tags, and it allows them to do a lot of great visual layout without under-standing even a line of code. Hard to believe there could be a tool to please both of these divergent groups, but there is, and Dreamweaver is the tool.

Do You Need to Learn HTML to Use Dreamweaver?

For most people, HTML is quite intimidating at first glance—your first reaction may be to avoid it at all costs. After all, when you design pages using Photoshop, QuarkXPress, or PageMaker, it isn't necessary to look at raw PostScript code anymore. However, the early pioneers of desktop publishing had to know how to program in PostScript just to create a page layout! Most of the early Web developers were programmers, not artists, and it was necessary to write the raw code to create a Web page.

HTML has come a long way since its inception, and many of its features have become standardized while others have not. In the past, if you didn't know some HTML, you were at the mercy of a programmer who might have more control over your design than you liked. Today, with Dreamweaver, you can get by without understanding or writing a single line of code. Attractive though it might be, we recommend that you do understand basic HTML so that you aren't afraid of it. No one likes to work in fear, and we find that most people who don't take the time to learn a little HTML are at a disadvantage in the workplace. When you don't understand HTML, it's sort of like having a secret that you hope no one will discover, or feeling like a fake and worrying that you will be found out.

How do you learn HTML? The best way is to view the source code of pages that you like. Most of the HTML jocks we've met have taught themselves in this way. One of the best things about HTML is that "learning by doing" is possible. It would be very difficult to learn other computer languages this way, because the code would be compiled and hidden from your view. In HTML, the code is visible to everyone and is parsed on-the-fly by the Web browser itself. To view the source code of a page, look under your browser's **Edit** menu and choose **View > Page Source** (Netscape) or **View > Source** (Explorer). This will show you the raw HTML, and once you get comfortable with some of the tags, you will likely be able to deconstruct how these pages were made.

HTML Resources

There are many great resources, online and off, for learning HTML. Here are some online sites that are worth checking out.

World Wide Web Consortium
`http://www.w3.org/MarkUp/`

HTML: An Interactive Tutorial for Beginners
`http://www.davesite.com/webstation/html/`

Webmonkey: HTML Tutorial
`http://www.hotwired.lycos.com/webmonkey/teachingtool/index.html`

NCDesign: HTML Design Guide v5.0
`http://www.ncdesign.org/html/`

Index DOT HTML: The Advanced HTML Reference
`http://home.webmonster.net/mirrors/bloo-html/`

The HTML Writers Guild: A Resource List
`http://www.hwg.org/resources`

What Does HTML Do?

HTML stands for **H**yper**T**ext **M**arkup **L**anguage. It is a derivative of SGML (**S**tandard **G**eneralized **M**arkup **L**anguage), an international standard for representing text in an electronic form that can be used for exchanging documents in an independent manner.

When Lynda first touched computers, (way) back in 1980, people had to use a form of mark-up in word processor documents. If you wanted something to have a bold face, for example, you had to tag it with the symbol <B> in order to create that formatting. You would never see the actual boldfaced text until the file was printed; back then, bold type could not even be displayed on the computer screen!

We've come a long way since then, and so has HTML. That's why programs such as Dreamweaver have become viable alternatives to writing all the tags by hand. With maturity and established standards, HTML in its raw form will likely become as hidden as the markup behind word processors is today.

At its heart, HTML allows for the markup of text and the inclusion of images, as well as the ability to link documents together. Hyperlinks, which are at the core of HTML's success, are what allow us to flip between pages in a site, or to view pages in outside sites. These hyperlinks are references that are contained within the markup. If the source of the link moves or the reference to the link is misspelled, it won't work. One of the great attributes of Dreamweaver is that it has site-management capabilities, which will help you manage your internal links so they are automatically updated if the links are changed.

What Does HTML Look Like?

HTML uses a combination of tags, attributes, and values to generate its results. Here is a sample line of code that uses a tag, an attribute, and a value.

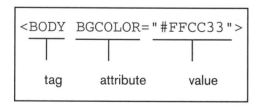

In this line of code, the tag is **<BODY>**, the attribute is **BGCOLOR**, and the value is **FFCC33**. When put together, this collection of items within the brackets **< >** is called an **element.**

Many tags require **opening** and **closing containers**, as marked here for the **<BODY>** element.

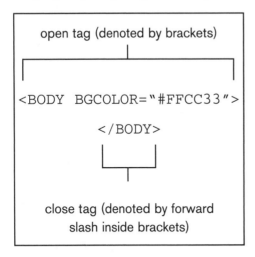

HTML Deconstructed

All HTML pages follow a basic structure. Each page must contain the **HTML**, **HEAD**, **TITLE**, and **BODY** tags. Whenever you open a new untitled document in Dreamweaver, this framework is already written. It is deconstructed for you below. Fortunately, you don't have to worry about getting this structure right. It is automatically built in to any page you create in Dreamweaver.

```
1. <HTML>
2. <HEAD>
3. <TITLE>Untitled Document</TITLE>
4. <META HTTP-EQUIV="Content-Type" CONTENT="text/html; charset=iso-8859-1">
5. </HEAD>
6. <BODY BGCOLOR="#FFFFFF">
7. </BODY>
8. </HTML>
```

1. Notice how the **<HTML>** tag is at the beginning of the document? It signifies that this is an HTML page. Without this tag, a browser cannot read the page. See line 8, the close **</HTML>** tag? This tag requires an open and a close tag. Both tags are required for most HTML tags, but not all.

2. The **<HEAD>** element of the document contains the **HEAD** information, or the URL and hidden information about your page. For example, the **TITLE** tag and the **META** tag are contained within the **HEAD**.

3. The **<TITLE>** is what appears at the top of the page inside a browser. If you leave the title **Untitled Document**, as in the example above, that is exactly what will appear! Dreamweaver has a setting for easily changing this title. We will get to this setting in Chapter 4, *"Basics."*

4. META tags are **HEAD** elements that are invisible when viewed in the browser, but contain information about the current page, such as the character encoding, author, copyright, and keywords. Many properties can be set here, which you will learn about in Chapter 4, *"Basics."*

---

5. Here's the close tag for the **HEAD** element. Notice that the **TITLE** and **META** tags were nested within the **HEAD** tag.

---

6. The **BODY** tag is specifying that this page will be white, instead of the default gray. If you don't enter a **BGCOLOR** value here, the page will defer to browser defaults.

---

7. This is the close tag for **BODY**.

---

8. This is the close tag for **HTML**.

File-Naming Conventions

Working with HTML is much more restrictive than working with other types of computer media. The strictest part about HTML is its file-naming conventions.

Don't use spaces: It's best if you save your files using no spaces in between the file name elements. For example, the file name **about lynda.html** would be considered illegal because of the space between the words **about** and **lynda**. Instead, you would write this file name as **about_lynda.html** or **aboutlynda.html**.

Avoid capital letters: It is best to avoid capitalization in your file names. Although **AboutLynda.html** will work as a file name, anytime you link to the file you will have to remember the correct capitalization because many UNIX servers are case sensitive. It is far easier to simply use all lowercase letters.

Avoid illegal characters: The chart below contains a list of characters to avoid when naming files.

File-Naming Conventions	
Character	**Usage**
.(dot)	Periods are reserved for file name extensions or suffixes, for example .gif and .jpg.
"	Quotes are reserved for HTML to indicate the value of tags and attributes.
/ or \	Forward slashes (/) indicate that the files are nested in folders. If you include a forward slash in your file name, HTML may lose your references, thinking you are specifying a folder. A backslash (\) isn't allowed on MS-Windows servers.
:	Colons are used to separate certain script commands on Macs and Windows. Avoid them in your file names so as not to confuse a file name with a script command.
!	Exclamation marks are used in comment tags.

File Name Extensions

You may be curious about the many extensions used after the dot at the end of file names. Below is a chart which lists the meaning of some extensions you'll commonly run across.

File Name Extensions	
Extension	**Usage**
.html, .htm	These two extensions are commonly used to denote an HTML file. The three-letter extension works just as well as the four-letter version. Older DOS systems didn't allow for four-letter extensions, which is why you sometimes see .html abbreviated as .htm. Dreamweaver defaults to using .htm.
.gif	GIF images
.jpg	JPEG images
.swf	Flash files
.mov	QuickTime movie files
.avi	AVI movie files
.aif	AIFF sound files

Extending Dreamweaver

One of the neatest things about the Dreamweaver community is the way people share **Objects**, **Commands**, and **Behaviors**. These pre-built elements can be shared and distributed, much the way Photoshop plug-ins work. If you visit the Dreamweaver section of the Macromedia site, you'll find numerous listings for shared resources. Here are a few of our favorites.

Dreamweaver Depot
`http://www.andrewwooldridge.com/dreamweaver/`
This is one of the largest repositories of Dreamweaver Objects, Commands, and Actions on the Internet. Many of them were developed by the site's owner, Andrew Woodbridge.

Dreamweaver Extensions Database
`http://www.idest.com/cgi-bin/database.cgi`
Features an extensive database, which includes all of the Dreamweaver extensions.

Yaromat

`http://www.yaromat.com/dw/index.php`

A personal home page that contains several very useful Dreamweaver extensions, including a great one for importing Fireworks-created rollovers.

Massimo's Corner of the Web

`http://www.massimocorner.com`

A great resource for Dreamweaver extensions, Objects, Commands, and Behaviors. It has an interesting DHTML interface, too!

What Is DHTML?

DHTML (**D**ynamic **HTML**) is a collection of different technologies. This can include any combination of HTML, JavaScript, CSS (**C**ascading **S**tyle **S**heets), and DOM (**D**ocument **O**bject **M**odel). By combining these technologies, you can author more dynamic content than what basic HTML affords.

Some of the things possible with DHTML include animation, drag-and-drop, and complicated rollovers (buttons that change when a mouse moves over them). Dreamweaver uses DHTML to enable you to create pages with buttons that change in more than one place on the screen at the same time.

Just like HTML, DHTML effects in Dreamweaver are coded behind the scenes. There are, however, some serious cross-platform issues with DHTML, because it is supported quite differently by Netscape and Explorer (the two leading browsers). Fortunately, Dreamweaver lets you target specific browsers, as well as test the cross-browser compatibility of your DHTML effects.

DHTML uses a combination of HTML, JavaScript, CSS, and DOM. Below is a short description of each.

DHTML Terms	
Technology	**Explanation**
HTML	(**H**yper**T**ext **M**arkup **L**anguage) The default markup for basic Web pages and the root of DHTML
JavaScript	A scripting language that extends the capabilities of HTML
CSS	(**C**ascading **S**tyle **S**heets) A page-layout system supported by newer Web browsers, which allows for better control over the appearance and positioning of elements on a Web page
DOM	(**D**ocument **O**bject **M**odel) A hook to outside scripting protocols, such as ActiveX, or external Plug-Ins, such as Shockwave or Flash. It allows scripts and programs to address and update documents.

What Is XML?

XML stands for **Ex**tensible **M**arkup **L**anguage. The specifications for XML are still in development, but many people are looking to XML as a solution to improve interactivity between Web sites and databases. XML would make it possible, for example, to sort a list of names alphabetically online. It would also enable much more sophisticated searching of data, making it a boon to many Web-based forms and databases.

Dreamweaver supports templates, covered in Chapter 17, *"Templates and Libraries."* One of the advanced features of Dreamweaver is the ability to import XML databases through a template. Because XML is so new, and the use of databases is outside the scope of this book, we don't include any XML exercises in any of the chapters. But you can investigate XML extensibility at the developer's area of the Dreamweaver site.

Macromedia Developer's Site
http://www.macromedia.com/support/dreamweaver/

World Wide Web Consortium
http://www.w3.org/xml/

What is JavaScript?

JavaScript was developed by Netscape in 1996 and has become almost as popular as HTML. It actually has nothing to do with the Java programming language, but Netscape licensed the name from Sun Microsystems in hopes of increasing acceptance of the new scripting protocol. We're not sure if it was the name that did the trick, but JavaScript has become almost as widely adopted as HTML itself! The most common uses of JavaScript allow for rollovers, resizing of browser windows, and checking for browser compatibility.

Most of the JavaScript routines are accessed by Dreamweaver's Behaviors palette, which you will learn about in Chapter 13, *"Rollovers & Navigation,"* and Chapter 16, *"Behaviors."* This is one area of Dreamweaver's product that must be previewed in a browser to be visible. This book covers many JavaScript techniques, including rollovers (Chapter 13, *"Rollovers & Navigation"),* browser-sniffing (Chapter 7, *"Cascading Style Sheets"),* and launching external browser windows (Chapter 15, *"Forms").*

You will not have to learn to write JavaScript by hand in order to use it within Dreamweaver. This is very fortunate for those of us who are not programmers, because JavaScript programming is more complicated than HTML. For those of you who are JavaScript programmers, however, Dreamweaver 4 offers a JavaScript Debugging feature. This feature is outside the scope of this book, but you will find documentation on it in the Dreamweaver manual or online Help system.

2.

Interface

| Interface Tour | Objects Panel |
| Launcher and Mini-Launcher |
| Property Inspector |
| Document Window | Preferences |

H•O•T

Hands-On-Training

We are big fans of the Dreamweaver interface. Other HTML editors that we've used require that you open a lot of different sized windows and panels in order to reach all of the features. Instead, Dreamweaver uses a system of fixed panels and windows that stay in one place and change setting options depending on the context of what you are doing. This saves screen real estate and makes learning the interface a lot easier. Although you might believe at this point that learning Dreamweaver represents a big learning curve, understanding the interface is probably one of the easier challenges ahead of you.

This chapter will take you through the basic concepts of the program's interface. In addition, we'll also share how to set up our favorite Dreamweaver **Preferences** settings and configurations.

You might be antsy to start in on some of the step-by-step exercises contained in later chapters, but you should review this chapter first to identify the toolbars, panels and windows that you'll be using.

A Tour of the Interface

The features that Dreamweaver offers are very sophisticated, but its interface is actually quite simple. There are six main parts to this program, the Toolbar, Launcher, Objects Panel, Document Window, Mini Launcher and Property Inspector.

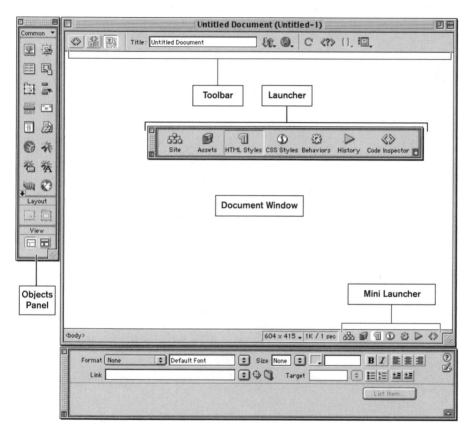

The six main features include the Objects Panel, Property Inspector, Launcher, Mini-Launcher, Toolbar, and Document Window. Whenever you open Dreamweaver, it defaults to opening a new blank Untitled Document, as shown here.

The Objects Panel

The Objects panel contains rows of object icons and is used as a one-click stop for many operations. If you move your mouse over the Objects panel and pause for a moment, you will see what each one of the icons stands for. You may alter the appearance of this panel in your Dreamweaver Preferences, if you want to see the object names in addition to, or instead of, their icons.

 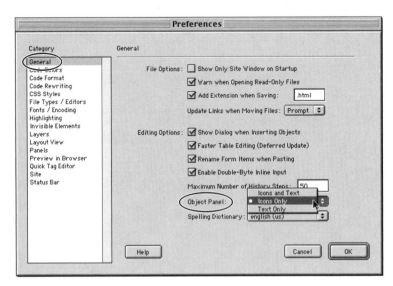

The Objects Panel shown above is in its default mode (Icons Only.) To change the appearance of the Objects Panel, select Edit > Preferences... > General > Object Panel. The Objects Panel's setting can be changed to Icons and Text, Icons Only, or Text Only.

Icons and Text   **Icons Only**   **Text Only**

The three versions of the Objects panel shown above are the choices available in the Preferences. As you examine the Objects panel, you'll see that it allows you to access essential functions, such as inserting an image, a table, a horizontal rule, which are otherwise known as "objects."

Many items that exist as objects are also found under the Insert menu in the top menu bar. The Objects panel provides a one-click alternative to using that menu bar. Some people are more comfortable clicking the icons, and others prefer the menu access. There is no right or wrong way to do this; it's just a matter of personal preference.

Important Note: Windows users—the underlined letters in the menu names and command names represent the **Alt+key** shortcuts you can use. For example, to insert an image, you can first hit **Alt+I** (for the **Insert** menu) and then press **I** again for the Image command. The **I** is underlined for both the menu and command. Sadly, Mac menus cannot be accessed using this method.

Types of Objects

Like many of the toolbars in Dreamweaver, the Objects panel is context sensitive. It defaults to showing what Dreamweaver calls the **Common** objects. You can change the Objects panel to show other categories of objects when you need them.

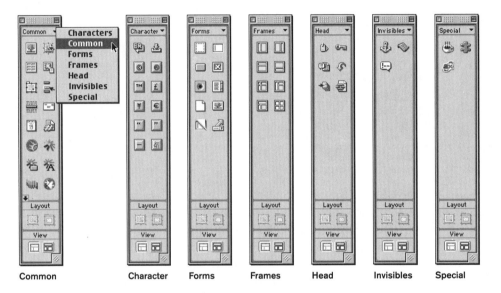

| Common | Character | Forms | Frames | Head | Invisibles | Special |

When you hold your mouse down on the arrow at the top of the Objects panel, notice that it says Common. That tells you you're looking at the Common elements on this toolbar. To show the other types of objects, click and hold the mouse on the pop-up menu arrow. You'll see a list of the other panels called Characters, Forms, Frames, Head, Invisibles, and Special. Throughout the book, you'll get to learn how and when to use each kind of Object panel setting. For now, this is just a sneak peek to show you that they're hidden inside this interface.

Objects Panel Types	
Panel	**Description**
Characters	The Characters panel contains frequently used character entities, such as the ®, ©, and ™ symbols, so you no longer have to memorize tricky keyboard commands.
Common	The Common panel contains the most frequently used objects in Dreamweaver, including Images, Tables, Layers, simple Rollovers, Insert Fireworks HTML, etc. You will use this panel a lot. This panel has been updated for Dreamweaver 4.
Forms	The Forms panel contains all of the objects essential for creating Forms for your Web page. These objects include text boxes, buttons, menus, etc. You'll learn about these items in Chapter 13, "Forms."
Frames	The Frames panel contains several preset framesets. With a click of the mouse, you can add any number of different framesets.
Head	The Head panel contains objects that are inserted in the HEAD tag of your Web page. These elements, even though not visible on the page, can be an important part of your pages, as they include META tags, such as Keywords and Descriptions. Many of these tags are used for search operations.
Invisibles	The Invisibles category contains objects such as Named Anchors, Server-Side Includes, Non-Breaking Spaces, etc. You will get a chance to work with some of the invisible elements in exercises later in the book.
Special	The Special category is probably the least used, but it does still contain some important objects, such as Java applets, plug-ins, and ActiveX objects.

The Property Inspector

Like the Objects panel, the Property Inspector is context sensitive, meaning it constantly changes depending on what type of element is selected. The Property Inspector controls many settings, including those for text, tables, alignment, and images. Because Dreamweaver defaults to opening a blank page with the text-insertion symbol blinking, the Property Inspector defaults to displaying text properties, as shown below.

The Property Inspector changes depending on what is being edited on screen.
Because these elements change depending on context, future chapters will
cover the various properties on this bar in depth.

The Launcher and Mini-Launcher

The Launcher allows you to access several aspects of Dreamweaver with a single click. It basically "launches" the **Site**, **Assets**, **HTML Styles**, **CSS Styles**, **Behaviors**, **History**, and **Code Inspector** areas of the interface. Go ahead and try clicking each of the buttons to see what they do. You can't hurt anything, we promise! Click the button again, and the feature will go away.

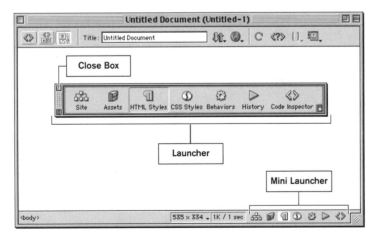

The Mini-Launcher at the bottom of the screen works identically to its larger counterpart. Try clicking each of its buttons to see what we mean. If you can train yourself to understand what the icons on the Mini-Launcher represent, then you can close the larger Launcher (by clicking its close box) to make more room on your screen. You can open the larger Launcher at any time by selecting Window > Launcher.

Launcher and Mini-Launcher Features	
Site	Opens the Site panel, where you will control Dreamweaver's powerful site-management features. This window is covered in detail in Chapter 3, "Site Control."
Assets	This panel lets you manage the assets for your site, such as images, colors, external links, movies, scripts, libraries, templates, etc. You can even organize your assets as "Favorites" so they can be renamed and accessed quicker.
HTML Styles	HTML Styles are similar to Cascading Style Sheets (CSS) in function, except that they work on any browser, including really old ones.
CSS Styles	CSS Styles are an advanced feature of Dreamweaver. They allow you to automate the application of layout and text styles to multiple pages in your site. This feature will be covered in Chapter 11, "Cascading Style Sheets."
Behaviors	This feature allows you to add JavaScript to your pages, even if you are not a programmer. Some of the Behaviors features will be covered a lot more in Chapter 14, "Behaviors."
History	The History panel is used to orchestrate animation using Dynamic HTML. You will learn about this feature in Chapter 15, "DHTML."
Code Inspector	The Code Inspector is where you can view the actual code generated by Dreamweaver. You can even watch the HTML code being generated as you create objects on your page! You will learn about this feature in Chapter 4, "Basics."

Customizing the Launcher

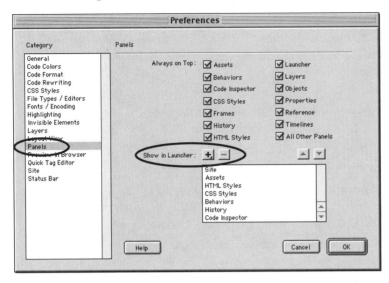

When you open Dreamweaver, the Launcher contains default options. If you find that you aren't working with some of the choices, or crave different ones, you can change the options that appear in both the Launcher and Mini-Launcher by selecting **Edit > Preferences... > Panels > Show in Launcher**. You can remove existing options by highlighting them and clicking on the minus sign (–). Clicking on the plus sign will display a list of options that can be added to both launchers. The selected options can be easily reordered by highlighting and option then clicking the up or down arrows.

Launcher Shortcuts

All of the Launcher features are available as items under the **Window** menu. In addition, the following function-key shortcuts are available for both Mac and Windows users.

If you memorize the F-keys for the Launcher items, you'll probably never need the large Launcher panel again. For example, we use the Site window and Code Inspector more often than the others, so we have memorized **F8** and **F10** as keyboard shortcuts. Below is a handy chart of the Launcher shortcuts.

Launcher Shortcuts			
Key	**Function**	**Key**	**Function**
F2	Layers	F10	Code Inspector
F4	Hide Panels	F11	Assets
F8	Site Files		

> ## WARNING | Redundancy in the Interface
>
> Truth be told, there is some redundancy in the Dreamweaver interface. For example, you can insert an image by clicking on the Objects panel or by choosing the Insert Image command from the Insert menu. You can often align objects using the Property Inspector or using a command on a menu. Though it's convenient at times to have different options, it can be confusing to learn a program that has two or three ways to accomplish the same task. Throughout the book, we'll be citing our favorite ways to access features, but if you prefer an alternate method, don't let us stop you!

The Toolbar

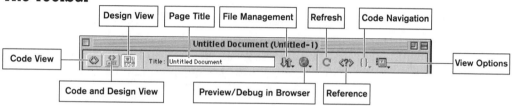

You can now access many of the options you need directly from the **toolbar**, a new feature in Dreamweaver 4. The toolbar contains a series of buttons and drop-down menus that let you do things like change the document view, set the page title, preview the page in a browser, and access the new Reference panel. The table below will give you a more detailed explanation of each feature.

Toolbar Features	
Code View	The Code view will display the code that creates your page. You can use this to edit the code directly and make changes without having to use a separate text editor, such as BBEdit or HomeSite. This Code view is helpful if you are comfortable coding your pages or need to create/modify custom code, such as JavaScript, ASP, etc. You'll have numerous opportunities throughout the book to learn to work with the Code View.
Code and Design View	The Code and Design view will split your document in half, displaying both the code and the actual page layout. This view is helpful if you want to make some minor changes to the code and want to immediately see the visual effect they have on your page.

continues on next page

Toolbar Features *continued*	
Design View	The Design view is the default view for your document window. This view will display your page in WYSIWYG (What You See Is What You Get) mode, which means you will see images, text, and other media as you add them to your page. This view is helpful if you aren't familiar with HTML or just don't want to take the time to type all of the code in yourself, plus it gives you a pretty accurate preview of what your page will look like a browser as it's being designed. Cool.
Page Title	This text field lets you specify the title for your page. This text will appear at the top of the browser window, and is used by some search engines to describe your site listing. It is also the name that identifies the page when you save it in a list as a bookmark or favorite in your browser. You can also set the title inside the Page Properties dialog box. You'll learn how to set a Page Title in Chapter 4, *"Basics."*
File Management	This drop-down menu lets you manage the files of your site by letting you upload/download files, unlock them, check them in or out, and work with design notes. It is great to have access to all of these options directly from the document window. You'll learn how to upload/download files in Chapter 20, *"Get it Online."*
Preview / Debug in Browser	This drop-down menu lets you choose a browser to preview your page or debug the JavaScript. You can also access the Define Browsers dialog box, which will let you define new or change reference to existing browsers that have already been defined. We won't get into debugging JavaScript in this book, but at least you know where to find it should the mood strike you!
Refresh Design View	This button will let you refresh the contents of the Design view. This can be helpful if you make changes to your page in the Code view and don't immediately see the changes.
Reference	This button lets you quickly access the new Reference panel in Dreamweaver 4. This is especially helpful in the Code view, where you can highlight some code, click this button, and have refer to the Reference panel for a complete explanation of the selected text. This is a great way to learn HTML, CSS, and even JavaScript. You'll learn more about this feature in Chapter 12, *"Code."*
	continues on next page

Toolbar Features *continued*	
Code Navigation	This option is for use in the Code view and lets you quickly select code for adding JavaScript functions. You probably won't use this feature unless you have a pretty good working knowledge of JavaScript.
View Options	This drop-down menu lets you control several options that modify the appearance of the Code view. You can set the Code view to word wrap, display line numbers, display syntax coloring, etc. You can also set the Design view to be on the top of the Code and Design view. You'll get to put this view into practice in Chapter 12, "Code."

The Document Window

The **Document** window is where all the action happens. This is where you assemble your page elements and design your pages. The document window is similar in appearance to the browser window when viewed from Netscape or Explorer. On both the Mac and Windows, Dreamweaver will create a blank Untitled Document each time you open the application. By default, the Document window will be in the Design view.

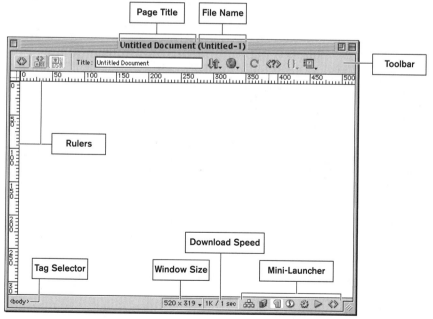

Document Window Features

Feature	Description
Title Bar	Contains the name of your Web page (for instance, "My Web Page") and the file name of your document (for example, webpage.html).
Toolbar	This is a new feature in Dreamweaver 4. This portion of the document window lets you quickly modify the page title and contains several buttons and drop-down menus for several frequently used options.
Rulers	You can show or hide rulers by selecting View > Rulers and checking Show on or off.
Tag Selector	If you select visual elements on your screen, the Tag Selector highlights the corresponding HTML code. It's a fast and easy way to select different items on your page.
Window Size	This pop-up menu lets you resize your window to various preset or custom pixel dimensions.
Download Time	This gives you the approximate size (kilobytes) and download time for the current page.
Mini-Launcher	A small version of the Launcher toolbar, it gives you access to various key features within Dreamweaver.

WARNING | PC Users and Document Window

Dreamweaver is a bit different between the Mac and PC. If you are using Dreamweaver on the PC, you should know that you will be prompted to quit the program when you close the last open document window. This occurs only on the PC.

Document Window Views

Code View   **Code and Design View**   **Design View (default)**

Dreamweaver 4 gives you the added control and flexibility of viewing your pages in one of three different views, Code view, Code and Design view, and Design view. By default, all new documents will open in the Design View. The three buttons in the upper-left corner of the document window let you change between the 3 different views.

Preferences

There are many different Preferences that you can change to make Dreamweaver your very own custom HTML editor. These settings can be changed at any time. To access the Preferences dialog box, select **Edit > Preferences...** Under the **General** category are settings that determine the appearance and operation of Dreamweaver as a whole. For example, you might consider changing the Objects panel's appearance setting to **Icons and Text**, as described earlier in the chapter, until you become more familiar with the icons representing the various Dreamweaver objects. The next few pages will explore Preferences that may be set for external editors, preset window sizes, and browser choices.

External Editors

You can specify **External HTML Editors**. This means that another HTML editor like BBEdit or HomeSite can be specified to edit the code Dreamweaver generates. This book does not cover the use of external HTML editors; as they are mostly used by experienced programmers who want to more tightly control the code that Dreamweaver automatically generates. Dreamweaver 4 ships with BBEdit (for Mac) and HomeSite (for Windows), so these will be preset as the default external HTML editors. In addition, you can specify **External HTML Editors**. If you set your preferences for an image editor, you can launch Fireworks or other image-editing applications from Dreamweaver by double-clicking an image file in the Site window, in the Assets panel, or on the page.

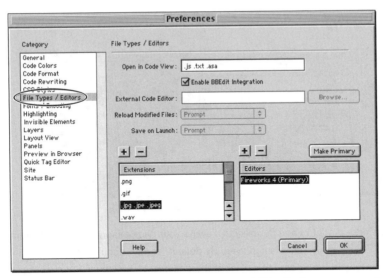

You can specify an External Editor by choosing Edit > Preferences... and clicking the External Editors category. A separate editor can be specified for different types of files. For example, a .gif or .jpg file can be edited in Fireworks or Photoshop, while a .mov file could be opened in Adobe Premiere or Apple's QuickTime Player.

Preset Window Sizes

One of the pitfalls of Web design is that your page's look will change depending on the size of the monitor that displays it. Dreamweaver has a handy feature—the **Window Sizes** option—to help you design more accurately for a specific monitor size.

The Window Sizes menu offers a variety of preset sizes for the Document window. For example, if you want to design for a **640 x 480** pixel screen, you can select this setting, and Dreamweaver will automatically resize the Document window to reflect this size setting. This helps you visualize how your designs will look in browser windows of various sizes, but it doesn't physically change the browser window size for your end user. You will learn how to restrict the size of the HTML window for your end user, should you choose to do so, by using a Behavior in Chapter 14, "Behaviors."

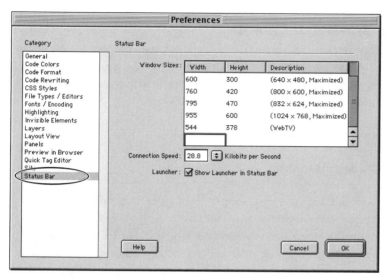

You can set your own window sizes settings by choosing Edit > Preferences... and clicking the Status Bar category.

You can click the Window Sizes menu on the Status Bar to access the various default dimensions. If you choose Edit Sizes... you can add your own size presets.

How to Define Your Browser of Choice

Netscape 4.7 was used in all the screen captures for this book, and has been provided for you on the **H·O·T CD-ROM**. You are welcome to use the browser of your choice for the exercises in this book. **Warning:** A few exercise steps will not work in earlier browser versions. To set up your browser preference, follow the steps below:

1. Choose **Edit** > **Preferences**…

2. Under **Category**, click on **Preview in Browser**.

3. Click the plus sign, minus sign, or **Edit…** to add, remove, or change a browser from the list of choices. **Note**: The Primary Browser defines which browser will launch using the **F12** shortcut key. The Secondary Browser defines which browser can be launched using **Shift+F12**. Many designers like to preview in both Netscape and Explorer. Using a primary and secondary setting will allow you to easily do so.

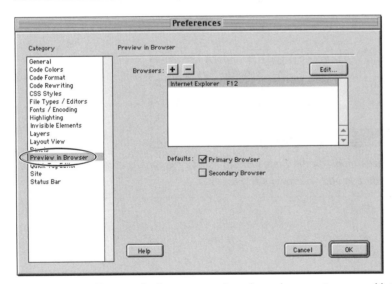

The Preview in Browser Preference sets the primary browser to open with the F12 shortcut key.

Shortcut Keys

There are lots and lots of shortcut keys in Dreamweaver, and all of them are listed in your manual. Below is a chart that lists our favorite ones.

Shortcuts in Dreamweaver		
Command	**Mac**	**Windows**
New Document	Cmd+N	Ctrl+Shift+N
Line Break	Shift+Return	Shift+Enter
Page Properties	Cmd+J	Ctrl+J
Select a Word	Double-click	Double-click
Check Spelling	Shift+F7	Shift+F7
Find and Replace	Cmd+F	Ctrl+F
Layers	F2	F2
Objects	Cmd+F2	Ctrl+F2
Frames	Shift+F2	Shift+F2
Property Inspector	Cmd+F3	Ctrl+F3
Behaviors	Shift+F3	Shift+F3
Switch to Standard View	Cmd+Shift+F6	Ctrl+Shift+F6
Switch to Layout View	Cmd+F6	Ctrl+F6
Site Window	F8	F8
Timelines	Shift+F9	Shift+F9
Code Inspector	F10	F10
Frames	Shift+F2	Shift+F2
History	Shift+F10	Shift+F10
HTML Styles	Cmd+F11	Ctrl+F11
CSS Styles	Shift+F11	Shift+F11
Preview in Primary Browser	F12	F12
Preview in Secondary Browser	Shift+F12	Shift+F12

TIP | Customized Keyboard Shortcuts

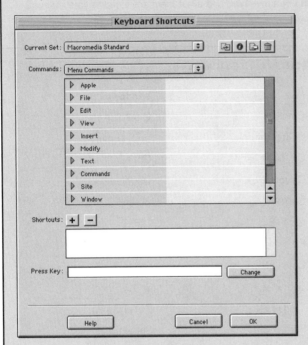

If you are a keyboard shortcut junky, like we would frankly categorize ourselves, then you will be happy to know that Dreamweaver 4 gives you the ability to easily and create, save, and modify custom sets of keyboard shortcuts. In previous versions of Dreamweaver, you had to edit a huge and complex XML file to do this, but not anymore! There are even predefined sets of keyboard shortcuts set up for other programs you might already be familiar with, such as BBEdit, HomeSite, and Dreamweaver 3. You can access this feature by selecting Edit > Keyboard Shortcuts.

3.

Site Control

| Defining a Site | Relative and Absolute Links |
| Understanding Paths | Site Maps |

chap_3

Dreamweaver 4 HOT CD-ROM

Those of you who have already built Web pages will likely agree that file management is one of the greatest challenges of this medium. So what is file management? File management is the organization, folder structure, and naming conventions of all the pages and graphics in your Web site. Few other disciplines require the creation of so many documents at once, because Web pages are usually comprised of numerous text and image files.

To compound the difficulty of managing numerous files, most people build Web sites from their hard drive, and when they're finished they upload these files to a Web server so that the files can be viewed from the WWW. Let's say that you created a folder on your hard drive and called it **HTML** and created another folder called **graphics**. If you put your HTML and graphics files inside those two folders, you would have to replicate this exact folder hierarchy when you uploaded those files to your Web server, or your links to those files would break. In this chapter, you will learn how to avoid such misfortune, by building your Dreamweaver site management skills.

What is a Local Root Folder?

Dreamweaver has a site management scheme that requires that you keep all your files within one main local root folder, so you can easily duplicate the folder hierarchy that's on your hard drive when you upload to a Web server. A **local root folder** is no different from any other kind of folder on your hard drive, except that you have specified to Dreamweaver that this is where all HTML and media files for your site reside.

If you think of the local root folder as the folder from which all other files stem, just like the roots of a tree, then you will understand its function. A local root folder can contain many subfolders, but Dreamweaver cannot keep track of elements unless they are stored inside the local root folder.

Taking the concept further, let's say that you decide midstream to change the folder hierarchy of your site by adding a folder or changing a folder name. If you were hand-coding the pages, it would be a hassle to make these changes. Dreamweaver makes this process painless, as long as you work within its site-management structure.

By the time you are through with these exercises, you will have learned to define a site and a local root folder, create a site map, and reorganize files and folders. Not bad for a day's work!

WARNING | Site Management

You might think that site management in Dreamweaver is a neat but optional feature, and that you would rather skip it now to return later when you're in the mood. Don't do it! Site management is actually integral to Dreamweaver, and the program kicks up quite a fuss if you don't use it properly. This book will ask that you define a site with each new chapter, because if you have files outside your defined area, you will be constantly plagued by warnings. If you choose to ignore this, you will not be using Dreamweaver properly and will run into problems.

NOTE | Mac and Windows Differences

For the most part, Dreamweaver has the identical interface for both Mac and Windows platforms. The one case where this is untrue is with site management. For this reason, this chapter sometimes contains different directives for the Mac and the Windows user.

I. Defining a Site

This exercise will show you how to define sites in Dreamweaver. You'll be working with a folder of HTML and image files from the **H•O•T CD-ROM** that you transfer to your hard drive. Once you've finished this exercise, Dreamweaver's site management feature will catalogue all the files inside this folder by building a site cache file—a small file that holds information about the location and name of all the files and folders in your site.

This exercise teaches you how to define a site from an existing Web site. You would use this identical process if you wanted to use Dreamweaver on a site that you or someone else had already created outside of Dreamweaver. At the end of the chapter, you'll complete an exercise that will show you how to define a site from an empty folder, which will more likely simulate your approach when you are starting a new site from scratch.

1. Copy the contents of the **chap_03** folder to your hard drive. For clarity, it's best if you leave this folder named **chap_03**.

The folder contains images and HTML files that are requested throughout this chapter. You will be asked to add and change files, which requires that you have all of the files on your hard drive.

WARNING | Windows Users

If you are working on a PC using any of the Windows operating systems, make sure that, after you have copied the files to your hard drive, you refer to the instructions in the beginning of the book. The Windows operating systems will automatically lock the files that you copy from the CD-ROM, so you will have to manually unlock these files in order to work with them in this and other chapters. If you don't already know how to unlock files, the procedure is documented in the front of this book, and will walk you through the whole process. Thank goodness. ;-)

2. Open Dreamweaver and press **F8** to bring up the Site window. On the pop-up menu, select **Define Sites...** This will open the **Site Definition** window. **Note:** If you've worked in Dreamweaver before, and have already defined other sites, you will see the **Define Sites** dialog box. In this event, click **New...** in order to define a new site. As an alternative, you can use **Site > New Site**.

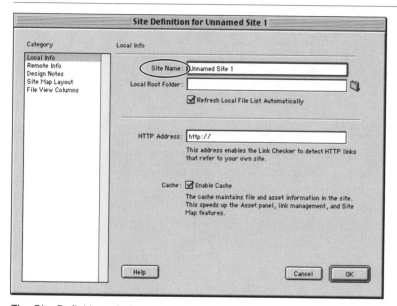

The Site Definition window.

3. Type **Chapter 3** in the **Site Name** field.

This is an internal naming convention, so you can use any kind of name you want without worrying about spaces or capitalization. Think of it as your own pet name for your project, just like you give a folder or hard drive a custom name.

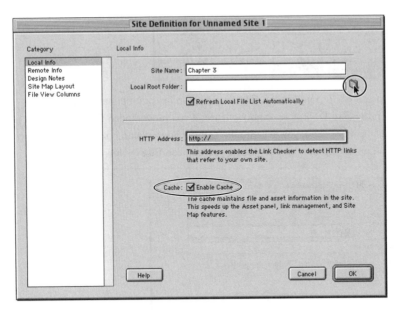

4. Click the small folder icon to the right of the **local root folder** text box. Browse to the **chap_03** folder that you copied to your hard disk and click **Choose** (Mac) or **Open > Select** (Windows). Make sure there is a check in the **Enable Cache** checkbox. This will increase the speed with which Dreamweaver performs its link-management features.

5. Click **OK**.

A message box will appear, indicating that the initial site cache needs to be created. You can choose to not have this message displayed in the future by clicking the checkbox (highly recommended!).

6. Click **OK**. After the site cache has been created, you will be brought back to the **Define Sites** dialog box.

7. Click **Done**.

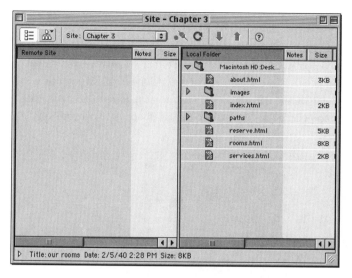

The site is now defined as Chapter 3. The right side of the window displays the local root folder. This is the folder on your hard disk that contains all of your HTML files and images. The list represents all the files on your hard drive within the chap_03 folder. The left side of the window displays the Remote Site or the Site Map information. Nothing is displayed right now because you haven't gotten to that exercise yet. **Windows Users Note:** *If you see locks next to the file names, refer to Chapter 1, "Introduction."*

NOTE | Local Root Folder, Root Folder, Root

As you work through Dreamweaver, you will notice references to a local root folder, a root folder, and root. All these terms are interchangeable. Each refers to a folder on your hard drive that contains all of the HTML, images, etc. for your Web site. This can be any folder on your computer. It can be empty, or it can have an entirely completed Web site. We did not want this slight difference in terminology to cause any unnecessary confusion.

2. _____Relative and Absolute Links

This exercise will help you understand two different types of links—those that are **relative** and those that are **absolute**. Relative links reference files that are part of your site. All the files that you see in the Local Folder of your **Site** window are internal files and can be referenced as relative links. If you want to link to an external file, such as someone else's site, you have to use an absolute link. If you don't understand the difference between these two types of links, read on.

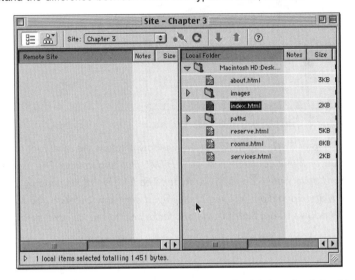

1. If your Site window isn't still open, press **F8**. Look on its right side to the Local Folder and double-click **index.html** to open it. Alternately, you could choose **File > Open** and browse to the **chap_ 03** folder to locate **index.html**.

We suggest that you train yourself to open HTML files from the Site window instead of your hard drive. If you do, it will ensure that you have successfully defined a site and that Dreamweaver's site management features are being enforced. Believe us, this will save you a lot of potential pain, since the alternative of not working within a defined site can cause your HTML code to produce broken links and images!

2. Click the "**about the inn**" (**about.gif**) image at the bottom of the screen to select it.

3. With the image selected, look at the **Property Inspector** and notice that this image links to **about.html**. **Tip:** If your Property Inspector doesn't show as many features as the one shown here, click the arrow at the bottom-right corner to expand it. The link **about.html** is a relative link. It does not have additional information in front of it, such as **http://www.moonsnestinn.com/about.html**. The file does not need that information because the file name is relative to other internal files in the site.

4. Highlight the word "**ojai**" at the bottom of the document window. **Tip:** You can double-click the word to select it!

5. In the Property Inspector, notice that this image links to **http://www.ojai.org**. This is an external link to another site on the Internet. This type of link is referred to as an absolute link. It needs the additional information to specify its location because it is not relative to any internal documents, and it exists on its own server, separate from the **moon's nest inn** site.

6. Close the file.

NOTE | Absolute and Relative URLs

The term URL stands for **U**niform **R**esource **L**ocator. In plain English, URLs are the addresses you use when you go to a Web site. Some are simple, such as `http://www.lynda.com`, while others are very complicated and hard to remember, such as `http://www.lynda.com/dw4hot/lessons/chapterone`. Regardless of whether a URL is short or long, there are two different types: absolute and relative.

An absolute URL looks like this:

`http://www.lynda.com/index.html`

An absolute URL is a complete URL that specifies the exact location of the object on the Web, including the protocol that's being used (in this case, `http`), the host name (in this case, `www.lynda.com`), and the exact path to that location (in this case, `/index.html`). Absolute URLs are always used when you want to link to a site outside your own.

You can use absolute URLs within your own site, but it's not necessary, and most Web publishers opt to use relative URLs instead. If you use relative URLs for internal documents, it's easier to move them if you change your domain name.

A sample relative URL looks like this:

`index.html`

If we were linking from pageone.html of our site to pagetwo.html of our site, we wouldn't need to insert the entire `http://www.lynda.com` URL anymore.

3. _____File and Folder Management

From within Dreamweaver's Site window, you can create new folders and files, as well as move them around from one directory into another. When you do this, you're actually adding folders and files to your hard drive, as this exercise will demonstrate. Accessing your hard drive from within Dreamweaver is essential to site management practices because Dreamweaver can then keep track of where the files have been moved or added. This exercise will show you how to add folders and files to the Chapter 3 site.

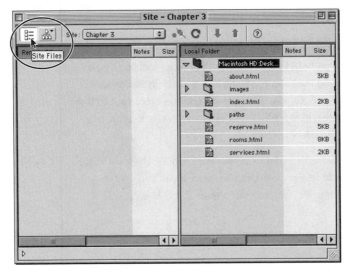

1. Make sure the Site window is open (**F8**) and click the **Site Files** button located in the upper-left corner.

2. Select the folder at the top of the Local Folder view.

3. Choose **Site > Site Files View > New Folder** (Mac) or **File > New Folder** (Windows). This will add a new folder to the Local Folder and your hard disk.

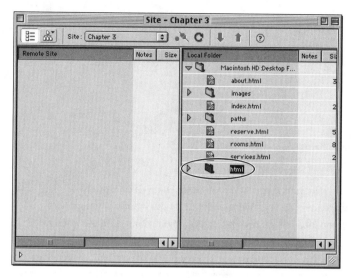

4. Type **html** for the folder name and press **Return** (Mac) or **Enter** (Windows).

5. Next, you'll learn to select files to move them into the folder you just created. Additionally, you'll learn how to select discontinuous files—files that are not adjacent to one another.

 •**Mac:** Click **about.html**, then **Cmd+Click reserve.html**, **rooms.html**, and **services.html**. *(Hold down the Cmd key as you click the last three file names.)*

 •**Windows:** Click **about.html**, then **Ctrl+Click reserve.html**, **rooms.html**, and **services.html**. *(Hold down the Ctrl key as you click the last three file names.)*

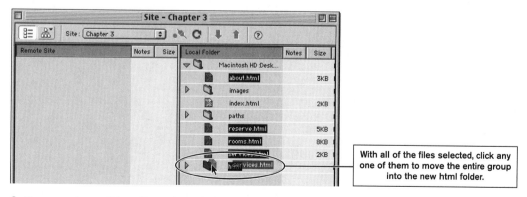

With all of the files selected, click any one of them to move the entire group into the new html folder.

6. Once you have all four files selected, drag them to the **html** folder that you just created. This will move all four files into this new location.

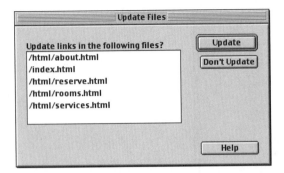

7. When you move files, Dreamweaver will prompt you to update their links. Click **Update**. Dreamweaver will list all the different files whose links were affected by the files you just moved. Once you click the Update button, these files will be rewritten automatically to reflect the change in file structure.

WARNING | Use the Site Window

If you want to add, modify, move, or delete files or folders in your Web site, do it inside Dreamweaver's Site window, as shown in Exercise 3. If you make these folder changes on your hard drive without opening Dreamweaver, you'll have to go in and repair the links manually by re-linking each page. If you make your changes inside the Site window, then Dreamweaver will keep track of them and automatically update your pages.

4. ———————Understanding Path Structure

This next exercise shows how path structures are created and altered when you move files inside the local root folder. A path structure is how HTML represents the path to different files in your site, depending on where they are located. Relative and absolute URL paths can result in a variety of different path structures. In this exercise, you will move files around the local root folder in three distinct ways, each demonstrating a different type of path structure you might encounter.

In this first example, you will simply insert a file that is within the same folder.

1. Make sure the Site window is open (**F8**).

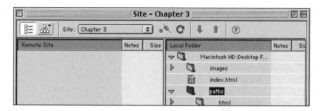

2. Under the Local Folder column, double-click the **paths** folder. This will cause the arrow to turn down (Mac) or the plus sign to change to a minus sign (Windows) and you'll see the contents of the paths folder inside the **Site** window

3. Open **path1.html**, by double-clicking it in the Site window.

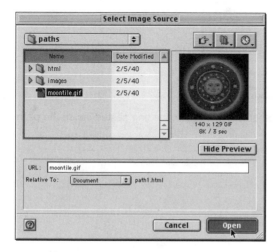

4. Choose **Insert > Image**. Select the **moontile.gif** from the **paths** folder, and click **Open**.

5. Once you have inserted this image, look at the Property Inspector. Notice that the **Src** is set to **moontile.gif**. As you become more experienced with building Web pages, you will begin to notice that a file name with no slash in front of it means that the file is in the same folder as the HTML that referenced it.

In this second example, you will insert an image that is inside another folder.

6. In the document window, delete the image that you just inserted by selecting it (clicking it once) and pressing the **Delete** key.

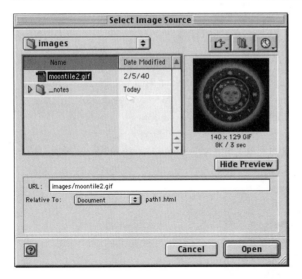

7. Choose **Insert > Image** and open the other **images** folder, the one nested inside the **paths** folder, to select **moontile2.gif**. Click **Open**.

8. Once you have inserted this image, look at the Property Inspector again. Notice that the **Src** is now set to **images/moontile2.gif**. The slash means that the file is nested inside another folder.

9. Select **File > Save** to save your changes. Close **path1.html**.

In this example, you will open an HTML document that is inside a folder and insert an image that is outside a folder.

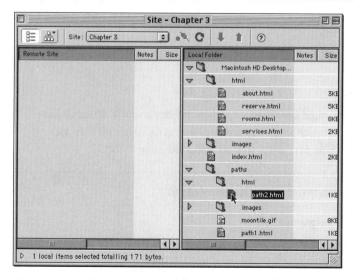

10. From the Site window (**F8**), open **path2.html** from the **html** folder nested within the **paths** folder.

11. Choose **Insert > Image** and navigate outside the **html** folder to find **moontile.gif**. Click **Open**.

12. Once you have inserted this image, look at the Property Inspector again. Notice that the **Src** is now set to **../moontile.gif**. The two dots before the slash indicate that the image was one folder up from the HTML document that referenced it.

13. Save and close the file.

This point of this last exercise was simply to point out how different path structures are generated depending on how your files and folders are situated within the Site window. Path structures are something you'll encounter as you build HTML pages in Dreamweaver, and this hopefully made them a bit less mysterious!

Different Path Notations

When you reference files in HTML, you must specify exactly where the document is. Dreamweaver writes the HTML for you, and inserts different path structures depending on where the files are located. Below is a chart to reference how path structures are specified within HTML.

Path Notations in Dreamweaver	
Path Notation	**Description**
document.gif	No slash (/) or dots (..) indicates that the file is inside the same folder as the referring HTML file.
images/document.gif	The forward slash (/) indicates that the file is inside the images folder or the file is located one level down from the referring HTML file.
../images/document.gif	The two dots (..) indicate that the folder is one level up from the referring HTML file.

5. ————————Creating a Site Map

Creating a **site map** is a great way to examine the structure of your Web site because it allows you to see the different levels of your Web site and what is contained within those levels. Many people use site maps to show their client how the site looks from a structural viewpoint. It's handy that Dreamweaver can easily create site maps, and even render them as PICT or JPEG (Mac) or BMP or PNG (Windows) files. If you change the structure of the site, the site map will change as well. There is no right or wrong time to make a site map, it is simply a convenience to have this feature available when you want one. This exercise will show you how easy it is to create and save a site map.

1. Press **F8** to open the Site window, if it's not already open.

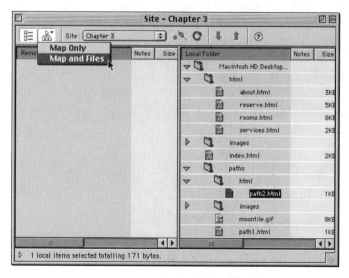

2. Click **Site Map** in the upper-left corner of the Site window. A pull-down menu lets you choose between two options, **Map Only** or **Map and Files**. Select **Map and Files**.

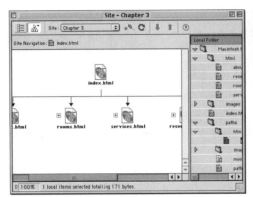
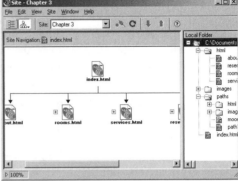

The Macintosh Site Map   **The Windows Site Map**

The site map view, set to Map and Files, will open in the left side of the window. The site map view is great if you want to see the overall structure of your Web site and how the different pages link to each other. The site maps appear slightly different between the Macintosh and Windows operating systems.

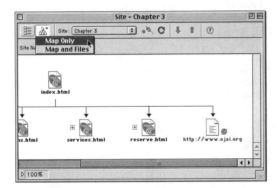

Here in the Map Only view, you can see the absolute and relative links displayed side by side. The absolute links are in blue and have a small globe to their right. The relative links have a small plus sign on their left.

3. Save this view as an image file.

> **•Mac:** *Select* **Site > Site Map View > Save Site Map > Save Site Map as PICT... Note:** *On the Macintosh, if you wanted to save this image in a compressed format, you could* **choose Save Site Map as JPEG***.*

> **•Windows:** *From the Site window, select* **File > Save Site Map...** *A* **Save As** *dialog box will appear so you can name the map.*

4. Close the Site window.

6. ————————**Creating a Site from Nothing**

So far, you've had a chance to work with Dreamweaver's site management window by defining a site based on folders and files from the **H•O•T CD-ROM**. What about when you finish this book and go to create your own Web site? You might know how to define a Web site that already exists, but not know how to go about creating a site from scratch. We wouldn't want that to happen to you, so this next exercise will walk you through the steps of defining a site before you have any content to put in it.

1. Leave Dreamweaver open, but go to the desktop of your computer. Create a new empty folder on your desktop and name it **website**.

2. Return to Dreamweaver and choose **Site > Define Sites...** from the top menu. In the **Define Sites** dialog box that will open up, click **New...**

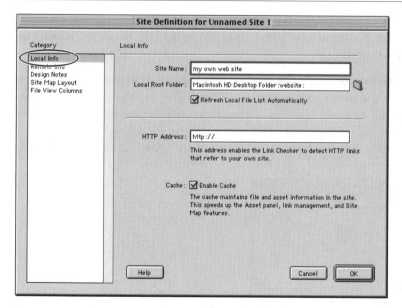

3. Fill in the **Site name** (we chose **my own web site**, but you may name it what you want). For the local root folder, click the folder icon and navigate to the empty folder you created on your desktop called **website**. Click **Choose** (Mac) or **Open > Select** (Windows), then **OK**.

4. If a dialog box pops up, indicating that the initial site cache needs to be created, check **"Don't ask again,"** and click **Create**.

5. Click **Done**.

6. This is what your Site window will look like now that you have created a new site based on an empty folder. Notice there's nothing in the Site window. Dreamweaver is doing an accurate job of displaying the contents of an empty folder.

7. You can add files and folders directly from within the Site window of Dreamweaver. This ensures that the files are automatically saved within the current local root folder (website), which is where they should be saved. To do so, make sure you highlight the local root folder at the top of the Site window first, then:

- **Mac:** *Choose* **Site > Site Files View > New File**. *The file will appear inside the Site window as* **untitled.html**

- **Windows:** *From the Site window (***F8***), choose* **File > New File**. *The file will appear inside the Site window as* **untitled.htm**

Note: You can name the file from the Site window, just as you can rename an untitled document on your hard drive. Once a file has been created in the Site window, its name will be highlighted and ready to be named. You can do it now, or later by opening the untitled.html and selecting File > Save As

8. Leave Dreamweaver open. Look on the desktop of your computer and open the **website** folder.

Lo and behold, there is an HTML document called **untitled.html** in there! The same HTML file that appeared in the Site window is also on your hard drive.

TIP | What is the "_notes" folder for?

You might have noticed that a folder called **_notes** mysteriously appeared inside the empty folder you created on your desktop. Don't panic and don't delete this folder; it's supposed to be there. In fact, this folder will be created inside every folder you define as a local root folder. It is used to store information about Design Notes, and integration between Fireworks and Flash. You will learn more about Design Notes in Chapter 20, *"Online."*

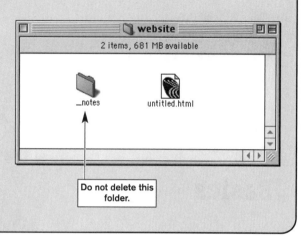

Do not delete this folder.

9. Try creating some more files and moving them into this folder. When you return to Dreamweaver, these other files will appear in the Site window. The Site window is simply a mirror of what exists on your hard drive.

10. When you are finished, close all open files. It doesn't matter if you save your changes; you won't be using any of these files for the rest of the book.

In summary, Dreamweaver allows you to create files and folders directly from its Site window. Some Web designers create a lot of images first and throw them into a folder and define that as a site inside Dreamweaver. Others might start with an empty folder and build empty HTML files first, then create and add images later. There is no right or wrong way to start a Web site, but Dreamweaver is flexible enough to work from scratch with an empty folder or to create a site around existing files.

4.
Basics

Defining the Site	Creating a Document
Inserting Images and Text	Centering Images and Text
Page Properties	Links	META Tags
Background Images	Looking at HTML

chap_4

Dreamweaver 4
H•O•T CD-ROM

If you're the impatient type (as we would frankly characterize ourselves), this is the chapter you've been waiting for. The following exercises are going to teach you how to create and save a page, insert and align images and text, link images and text, color text links, add a background image, insert META information (such as keywords and descriptions for search engines), and view the HTML that Dreamweaver created. Covering this much material may seem overwhelming, but fortunately Dreamweaver makes most of these operations as simple as accessing a menu or property bar.

By the time you are done with this chapter, your Dreamweaver feet will finally be wet, and you will be well on your way to understanding the program's interface for creating pages and sites. The exercises here will be your foundation for building more complex pages in future chapters.

I. —————————Defining the Site

In each new chapter, we will request that you copy files from the **H•O•T CD-ROM** to a folder on your hard drive. In this exercise, you will revisit how to define a site based on the contents of the folder. Since each chapter of this book features different files, each chapter will be defined as its own distinct site, so you will go through the process of this exercise many times. Normally, if you were working on a single site, you would most likely define your site once. If you switched projects, however, you would need to define a new site. Dreamweaver allows you to manage multiple sites, which is helpful if you have multiple clients or projects for which you plan to use the program.

1. Copy the contents of the **chap_04** folder to your hard drive.

2. Make sure the Site window is open. If it's not, press **F8**.

3. Select **Site > Define Sites...**

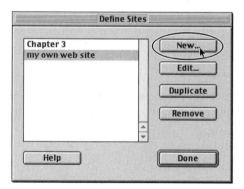

4. Click **New...**

5. In the Site window, type **Chapter 4** for the **Site Name**.

6. Click the small folder and then select **chap_04** as the local root folder.

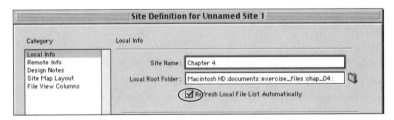

The **Refresh Local File List Automatically** option is checked by default to automatically refresh the Site window when files are copied. To ensure that you see your changes as you make them, we suggest you leave this option checked.

7. Make sure the **Enable Cache** checkbox is checked. Click **OK**.

8. If the **Create Site Cache** dialog box opens, click **Don't show me this message again**. Then click **OK**. Since you will always want to create a site cache, this dialog warning will get annoying if you see it every time you create a Web site with Dreamweaver.

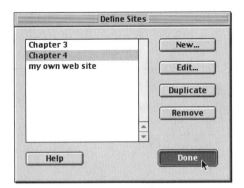

9. When the **Define Sites** dialog box opens, click **Done**. You will not need the Site window right now, so press **F8** to close it. The shortcut key **F8** will toggle the Site window open and closed, and is a useful keyboard command to memorize since this is a function you will likely perform often.

2. —————————**Creating and Saving a Document**

This next exercise teaches you how to create and save a document in Dreamweaver. You will be naming this document **index.html**, which has special significance in HTML, and almost always means that it is the beginning page of a site. Additionally, you will learn to set the title of this document to **Moon's Nest Inn**.

> **1.** A blank document should be visible; if not, select **File > New**. **Note:** Windows users can create a new blank document by selecting **File > New** from a document window or by selecting **File > New Window** from the **Site** window.

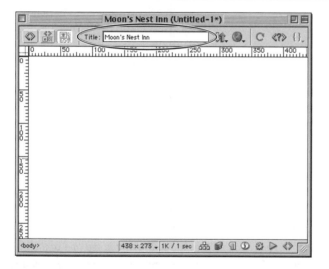

> **2.** In the document window's **Title** option, type **Moon's Nest Inn**. Press **Return/Enter**.

> **3.** Type **Title: Moon's Nest Inn.** Leave the other options at their default values. Click OK.

> *You will be returned to the document window. The page is blank, but you're going to turn it into a cool and functional Web page in a jiffy.*

Before you get started, it is very important that you save your file first. All of the site management benefits introduced in the last exercise depend on Dreamweaver knowing the name of your file. With this ability, the program constantly notifies you if you are working on an unsaved document. Besides, no one wants to unexpectedly lose work, and this practice is good insurance against system crashes and/or a power outage.

4. Select **File > Save**. Name the file **index.html** and save it inside the **chap_04** folder on your hard disk. Leave this file open; you will be using it in the next exercise.

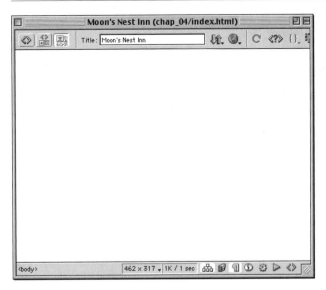

There are two names in the title bar of your document window. The first is the title of the document (**Moon's Nest Inn**). *The second name is the file name* (**index.html**), *which shows up to the right of the title. The title can be different from the file name, as in the example shown above.*

File Names Versus Titles

As you create Web pages with Dreamweaver, you will need to specify various names for your files, folders, sites, etc. This might not seem tricky at first glance, but there are actually two different names associated with HTML files: the file name and the title.

When you save a document, you will be assigning its file name. The file name must always end with the .htm or .html extension. There is also another name associated with the document, and it is called the title. The file **index.html** here, for example, has the title of **Moon's Nest Inn**.

It is essential that file names do not contain spaces or special characters. Page titles, however, are much more flexible and should be more descriptive than the file name. A title can contain spaces and special characters, while file names should not. When the page is viewed from a Web browser, the title will be much more visible to your end user than your file name. Also, when end users bookmark this page, the title will appear in their bookmark list.

In the above example (which you will build in this chapter), note that the title appears in the browser's title bar, while the file name appears in the URL. The file name is essential in that it allows the browser to understand that this is an HTML file, and to display the page properly. Titles are also important, because they are sometimes used as the description for your site in search engines.

The Significance of index.html

You just created a document called **index.html**. What you may or may not appreciate is that this particular file name has special significance. Most Web servers recognize the index.html as the default home page. If you type the URL **http://www.lynda.com**, for example, what you will really see is **http://www.lynda.com/index.html**, even though you didn't type it that way. The Web server knows to open the index.html file automatically without requiring the full URL to be typed. Therefore, if you name the opening page of your Web site with the file name index.html, the Web server will know to automatically display this file first.

Taking this concept one step further, you can have an opening page to each section of your Web site, not just to your home page. This feature has definite advantages—among them, your users won't find themselves looking at a generic index like the example below.

This is why the file name index.html is so significant. It's also the reason most professional Web developers use it as the **root file** name, although on some servers a different name is used, such as **default.html**. What you may not realize is that you are not limited to just one index.html on your site. You can have an index.html inside each folder that represents a category for your site, such as **Company**, **Services**, **Store**, and **Products**.

If you do not have an index.html, browsers will display a general list of your files, such as the above example.

3. ————————Inserting Images

In this exercise, you will continue working with the **index.html** file and learn to insert images for your page's headline, logo, and navigation bar.

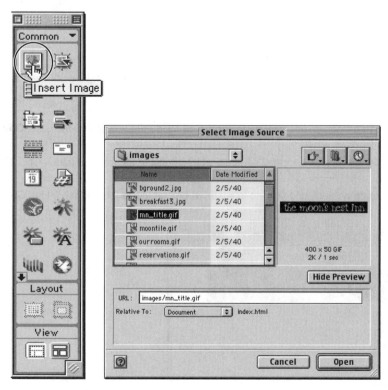

1. Click the **Insert Image** object in the **Objects** panel. **Note:** You may also choose **Insert > Image** from the menu bar, or use the shortcut key combination **Opt+Cmd+I** (Mac) or **Alt+Ctrl+I** (Windows).

---

2. Browse to **mn_title.gif** inside the **images** folder. Click **Open**. If you are not familiar with the extension **.gif**, refer to Chapter 1, "*Background.*"

---

3. In the Document window, click off the image to deselect it, and press **Return/Enter** to create a paragraph break, causing a space to form between the headline graphic and the next image.

4. Click the **Insert Image** object in the Objects panel again. Browse to **moontile.gif** inside the **images** folder. Click **Open**.

5. Click off the image to deselect it, and then press **Return/Enter** twice. This inserts two paragraph breaks into the formatting of the page.

6. Click the **Insert Image** object in the Objects panel, and browse to **about.gif** inside the **images** folder. Click **Open**.

7. Click the **Insert Image** object, and browse to **rooms.gif** inside the **images** folder. Click **Open**.

8. Click the **Insert Image** object, and browse to **services.gif** inside the **images** folder. Click **Open**.

9. Click the **Insert Image** object, and browse to **reservations.gif** inside the **images** folder. Click **Open**.

This is what your page should look like at this point.

10. Save your file and leave it open for the next exercise.

4. —————————Inserting Text

Adding text to your Web page is simple in Dreamweaver. Just like your favorite word processor, you can simply start typing text on your page and the text will appear.

In this exercise, you will add some text at the bottom of your page as an alternative navigation system, which is useful to users who might have their images turned off in their browser settings or be browsing in a non-graphical browser (such as sight-impaired audiences).

1. Click to the right of the reservations.gif you inserted in the last exercise and press **Return** to create a paragraph break. Type **home**, press the **spacebar**, press **Shift+Backslash** to insert a small vertical line (|), or "pipe," and press the **spacebar** again.

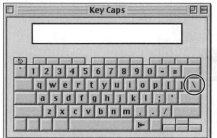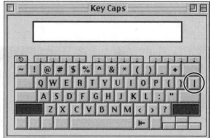

Without the Shift key pressed   **With the Shift key pressed**

Note: The Backslash key is located in different spots on different keyboards.

2. Type **about the inn**, press the **spacebar**, press **Shift+Backslash** to insert a pipe, and press the **spacebar** again.

3. Type **our rooms**, press the **spacebar**, press **Shift+Backslash** to insert a pipe, and press the **spacebar** again.

4. Type **guest services**, press the **spacebar**, press **Shift+Backslash** to insert a pipe, and press the **spacebar** again.

5. Type **reservations**.

6. Press **Shift+Return** to create a line break. This puts your type-insertion cursor on the next line without introducing a two-line paragraph return.

7. Type **want to learn more about ojai?**

8. Save your file.

> home | about the inn | our rooms | guest services | reservations
> want to learn more about ojai?

This is the result you should get at the end of typing in the items.

This is what your page should look like now.

NOTE | Paragraph Versus Line Breaks

You may have noticed that each time you pressed the **Return** or **Enter** key, Dreamweaver skipped down the page two lines. Pressing this key inserts a single paragraph break. The HTML tag for a paragraph break is **<P>**. This is useful when you want to increase the space between different paragraphs. However, there will be times when you just want to go to one line directly below the one you are working on without introducing extra space. Pressing **Shift+Return** (or **Shift+Enter**) inserts a line break instead. The HTML tag for a line break is **
. Knowing the difference between a **<P> and a **
** will allow you to control the spacing between lines of text.

Note: If your screen looks different from ours, that's because we changed a setting in the Code View window called **Word Wrap**. You will learn to do this in Chapter 12, "*HTML*."

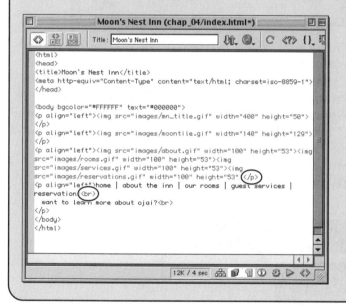

5. ——————Centering Images and Text

Now that you have added the images and text to your page, it's time to learn how to center them. The next section shows you how to use centering procedures with text and images.

1. Select the "**moon's nest inn**" logo image from the previous exercise (**mn_title.gif**) at the top of the screen.

2. Click the **Align Center** button in the Property Inspector. This will snap the "**moon's nest inn**" logo to the center of the screen.

3. Hold down the **Shift** key and click on the images **moontile.gif** (the round image), **about.gif** "**about the inn,**" **rooms.gif** "**our rooms,**" **services.gif** "**guest services,**" and **reservations.gif** "**reservations.**" With the **Shift** key still depressed, select the text at the bottom of the screen. Holding down the **Shift** key allows you to select multiple items at once.

4. Click the Align Center button in the Property Inspector.

Your page should look like this at the end of the exercise.

5. Save the file and leave it open for the next exercise.

6. ——————**Modifying Page Properties**

This exercise will walk you through changing the colors of your page, using the **Page Properties** window. The Page Properties feature controls many important attributes of your page, including the document title (which we looked at in Exercise 2), and the colors you set for your text and links.

1. Select **Modify > Page Properties...** or use the shortcut to access Page Properties, **Cmd+J** (Mac) or **Ctrl+J** (Windows).

2. Move this window to the side so you can see the Page Properties and your document at the same time.

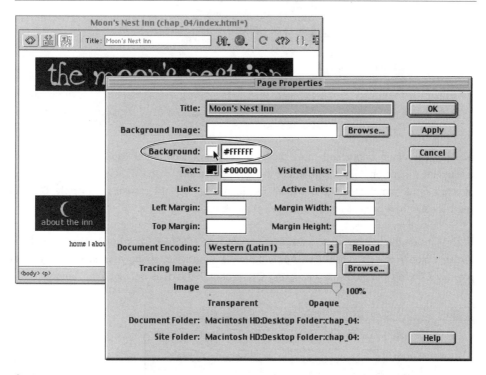

3. Click the small box to the right of the word **Background**. This will open the Dreamweaver Color picker.

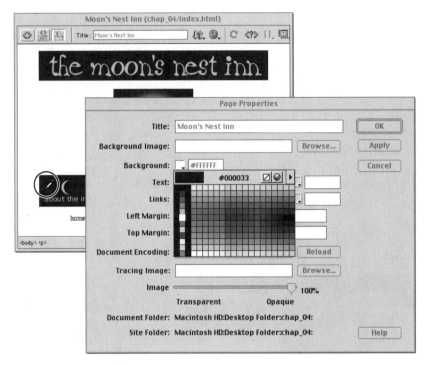

4. With your mouse depressed, move the Eye Dropper outside of the Page Properties window to release the mouse on the background of the "**about the inn**" image. This will set the background color of your page to match the edge of this image. To instantly see the results, click **Apply**. **Don't** click **OK** yet, because there are still more colors to set in the upcoming steps.

---

5. Click inside the text box next to the **Text** option. Type **#CCCCFF**. Click **Apply**. You just colored all your text light blue in this document. The **Apply** button is actually accepting your changes; it is not merely a preview. Clicking it is the same as clicking **OK**, except that it does not close the window.

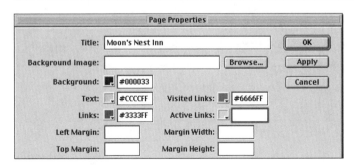

To set other colors, you can insert your own values.

---

6. Type **#3333FF** for the **Links** option. All the text in this document that contains a link will be bright blue. Type **#6666FF** for the **Visited Links** option. After someone has visited a link it will turn blue, letting him or her know that that link has already been viewed.

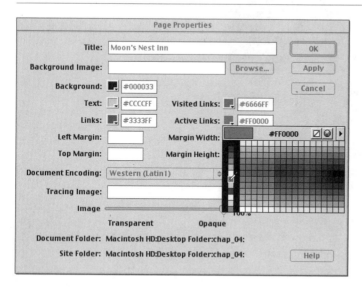

7. You could also choose a color by sight, instead of typing in a hexadecimal value. Click the box to the right of the words **Active Links** and the **Color** picker will open. Select a red color. This will set the active link color to red. The only time an active link color shows is when the mouse is depressed on the link.

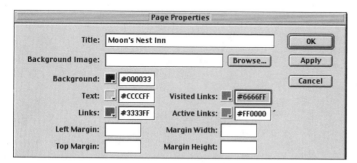

The Page Properties window should look something like this. **Note:** *You might have a different red for Active Links than shown here, since you selected this color by sight, not numeric value.*

8. Click **OK**.

This is what the results of this exercise should look like.

9. Save the document and leave it open for the next exercise.

The Page Properties Window

The Page Properties window does more than just set the colors of the links and your document title. See the chart below for an explanation of all its features.

Page Properties	
Properties	**Description**
Title	The title of your page is what will appear in the title bar of the Web browser and when your page is bookmarked. This name can contain as many characters as you want, including special characters, such as %(#*!.
Background Image	If you want a background image for your Web page, you would specify it here. A background image can be any GIF or JPEG file. If the image is smaller than the Web browser window, then it will repeat (tile).
Background	Sets the background color. The values can be in hexadecimal format or by name, for example red, white, etc.
Text	Sets the default text color. It can be overwritten for specific areas of text.
Links	Sets the color for links. This option can be overwritten for specific links.
Visited Links	A visited link color specifies how the link will appear after a visitor has clicked it.
Active Links	The active link color specifies how the link will appear while someone clicks it.
Document Encoding	Specifies the language for the characters and fonts used in the document.
Tracing Image	Tracing images are used as guides to set up the layout of your page. They can be any GIF, JPEG, or PNG file.
Transparency	Sets the transparency level of your tracing image.
Left Margin	Sets the left margin value in pixels. This attribute is only supported in Internet Explorer 4.0 or later.
Top Margin	Sets the top margin value in pixels. This attribute is only supported in Internet Explorer 4.0 or later.
Margin Width	Sets the margin width value in pixels. This attribute is only supported in Netscape Navigator 4.0 or later.
Margin Height	Sets the margin height value in pixels. This attribute is only supported in Netscape Navigator 4.0 or later.

The Dreamweaver Color Pickers

From the Page Properties dialog box, Dreamweaver gives you access to five different color pickers, from which you can select the colors for your pages. Two of the color pickers, Color Cubes and Continuous Tone, are browser-safe, and they're arranged in a manner that makes is easy to select pleasing color combinations. To understand each function of the Color picker drop-down menu, see the color picket options chart.

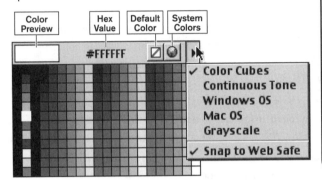

NOTE | What Is Browser-Safe Color?

Browser-safe colors are the 216 colors supported by browsers across platforms (Mac and Windows). If you use the browser-safe colors inside the Page Properties settings, you reduce the risk of having your colors shift when people view your Web pages.

Color Picker Options	
Color Preview	Gives you a preview of the color that is currently selected or the color that the eyedropper is picking up.
Hex Value	Displays the hexadecimal value of the current color or the color that the eyedropper is picking up.
Default Color	Removes any colors you have selected. If you do not specify a color in the Page Properties, the user's browser will determine what colors are used for the different text options.
System Colors	Opens the system color options for your computer—these options will vary between the Macintosh and Windows operating systems.
Color Options:	This drop-down menu lets you choose from five different color arrangements. The Color Cubes and Continuous Tone options contain only Web-safe colors. The Windows and Mac options contain the system colors for the Windows and Macintosh operating systems. The Grayscale option contains grays ranging from black to white.
Snap to Web Safe:	Automatically switches non Web-safe colors to their nearest Web-safe value.

7. ——————————Creating Links with Images and Text

The ability to link to pages and sites is what makes the Web dynamic. This chapter will show you how to set up links using Dreamweaver's Property Inspector.

1. Select the **moontile.gif** image in the center of the screen.

2. Click the **Browse for File** icon, next to the **Link** option, in the Property Inspector.
Note: If your Property Inspector window is smaller than what is shown here, click the arrow at the bottom right corner to expand it.

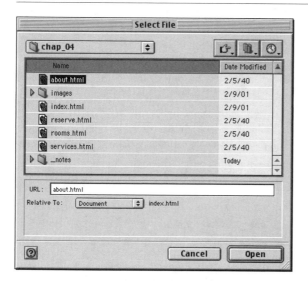

3. Browse to **about.html** and click **Open**. Congratulations, you have just created your first relative image link. Why was it relative? It is relative simply because it linked to a document within this site, not to an external Web site.

4. Highlight the **about.gif** ("about the inn") image at the bottom of the screen.

5. Click the small folder next to the **Link** option in the Property Inspector.

6. Browse once again to **about.html**. Click **Open**. Now **moontile.gif** and **about.gif** are linked to **about.html**.

7. Repeat this process for the remaining navigation icons. Select the **rooms.gif** ("our rooms") image and link it to **rooms.html**. Click **Open**. Select the **services.gif** ("guest services") image and link it to **services.html**. Click **Open**. Select the **reservations.gif** ("reservations") image and link it to **reserve.html**. Click **Open**.

You have just successfully added links to the images on this page! If you want to preview the links in a browser, press F12 and click any of the images. **Note:** *If a browser does not launch when you press F12, refer to Chapter 2, "Interface", to learn how to specify a browser to preview your pages.*

Next, you will create some links using text. The process is almost identical, except you will be selecting text instead of images.

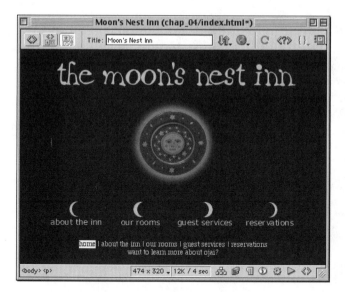

8. Highlight the word "**home**" at the bottom of the page.

9. Click the small folder next to the **Link** option in the Property Inspector.

10. Browse to **index.html**. Click **Open**.

11. Repeat this process for each word in the text navigation bar at the bottom of the screen.
(You can select each word easily by double-clicking it). Once selected, link the "**about the inn**" text
to **about.html**, the "**our rooms**" text to **rooms.html**, the "**guest services**" text to **services.html**, and
the "**reservations**" text to **reserve.html**.

*As you create the text links, you will notice the color of the text change. This happens because you
set the Links color option in the Page Properties to blue, and Dreamweaver is previewing that setting
for you.*

12. Highlight the word "**ojai**" at the bottom of the page.

13. Type **http://www.ojai.org** into the **Link** option in the Property Inspector. Congratulations, you just created your first absolute link. It's an absolute link because it begins with an **http** header and includes the full address.

14. Select **File > Save**. You don't want to lose any of your work!

15. If you want to preview all of your links, press **F12** to launch a browser and try them out.
Note: Only the links you created on the **index.html** page will be working. You will learn some effective and fancy ways to work with linking in Chapter 5, "*Linking.*"

8. ————————META Tags

One of the big challenges (aside from building a Web site) is letting the search engines know that your site exists. There are two steps to getting your site listed: the first is to list it with all the various search engines out there, and the other is to insert META tags into your HTML so the search engines can find you on their own and correctly index your site. Many search engines send robots (also called spiders) out to search the Web for content. When you insert certain META tags into your document, you make it much easier for the search-engine robots to understand how to categorize your site. This exercise will show you how to enter META tags with specific attributes, so you can make your Web page more search-engine friendly.

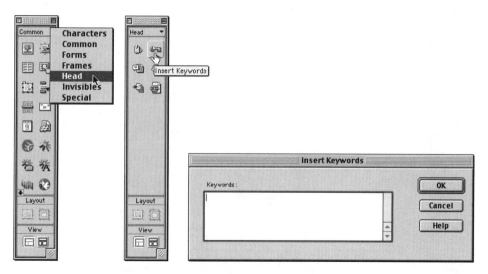

1. Click the arrow at the top of the Objects panel. This will reveal a small pop-up menu, which contains the following options: **Characters**, **Common**, **Forms**, **Frames**, **Head**, and **Invisibles**. Select the **Head** option. You are going to work with it, because it contains the META elements.

2. Click the **Insert Keywords** object. A dialog box will be displayed for you to enter in the keywords for your page.

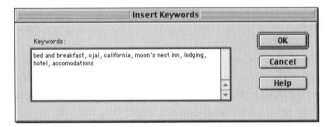

3. Type **bed and breakfast, ojai, california, moon's nest inn, lodging, hotel, accommodations**.
Basically, you're listing words that someone might use in a search engine to bring up your site.

4. Click **OK**.

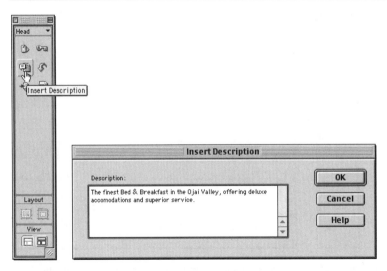

5. Click the **Insert Description** button. A dialog box will appear in which you can enter the description of your Web page.

6. Type **The finest Bed & Breakfast in the Ojai Valley, offering deluxe accommodations and superior service.**

7. Click **OK**.

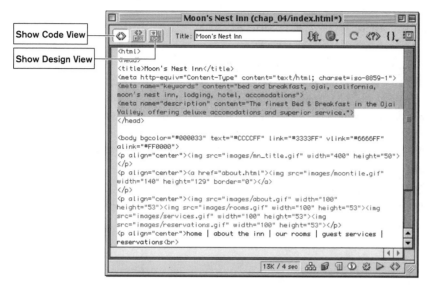

8. Click the **Show Code View** button to view the HTML in this document. See the META information inside the HEAD tag? Visitors to your site won't be able to see the META tag information because it's only visible inside your HTML. It's a part of authoring the page that has nothing to do with appearance—and everything to do with helping the search engines find your site.

9. Save and close this document.

WARNING | Keyword and Descriptions

Keywords are META tag values that specify certain words to help Internet search engines index your site. Many search engines limit the number of keywords you can use. Choose your words wisely and use no more than 10 to 15 keywords that best describe your site's contents.

Descriptions are META tag values that also help various search engines index your site. Some search engines will actually use in their directory the very descriptions you specify to describe your site. Again, some search engines limit the number of characters indexed, so keep it short and simple! If you would like more information about META tags, check out these URLs:

Web Developer—META Tag Resources
http://www.webdeveloper.com/html/html_metatag_res.html

META Builder 2
http://vancouver-webpages.com/META/mk-metas.html

Background Images

Instead of using a solid color for a background, as you learned to do in exercise 6, you can alternatively place an image into the background of your page. This kind of image is no different from any other JPEG or GIF, except that you insert it via the Page Properties interface instead of the Insert Image method that you learned about earlier. The end result is that a background image will appear behind foreground images and HTML. The source art for your background images can be small or large in dimensions. The file you'll work with in this exercise is large in dimensions, but small in file size.

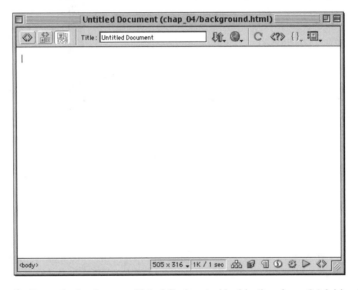

1. Open the **background.html** file located inside the **chap_04** folder. This is nothing more than a blank file that we created and saved for you. Hey, at least we gave it a name. ;-)

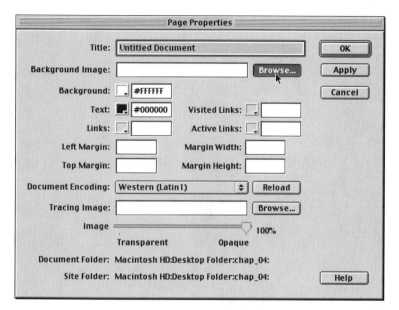

2. Select **Modify > Page Properties** to open the Page Properties dialog box. You can also use the keyboard shortcut of **Cmd+J** (Mac) or **Ctrl+J** (Windows) to open the Page Properties. Click the **Browse** button next to the Background field to open the **Select Image Source** dialog box. As you learned earlier, this dialog box lets you locate an image on your hard drive to insert onto your page.

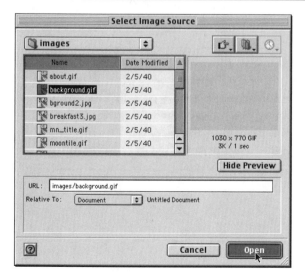

3. Browse to the **chap_04** folder and locate the **background.gif** file. This is a large image we created for you, but in the future you could use any GIF or JPEG file that you created.

4. Click **Open**. This will select that image and return you to the Page Properties dialog box.

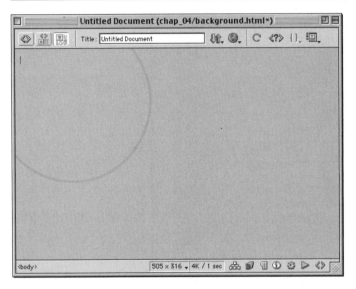

5. Click **OK** to accept this image and return to your page. You will now see a light brown background image on your page. Yes, it's that simple, can you believe it?

6. Select **File > Save** to save the changes you made to this file. You can go ahead and close this file; you won't need it any longer.

TIP | Removing Background Images

There are bound to be times when you will add a background image to a page, then decide you don't want it there anymore. You are, after all, entitled to change your mind. Removing a background image is as easy as adding one. In the Page Properties dialog box, simply remove the information inside the Background Image text field with the **Backspace** or **Delete** key, and click **OK**.

10. _____Looking at the HTML

You briefly looked at raw HTML code in the last exercise. This exercise will help you understand the relationship between the images and text on your page, and the HTML code that Dreamweaver generated. The **Code View** and **Design View** buttons are new in Dreamweaver 4. They are a welcome addition to the program, as these buttons help you easily toggle between the visual layout of your page, and the code that is being generated as a result.

1. Open the **index.html** page inside the **chap_04** folder. You can view the HTML generated in Dreamweaver by clicking the **Show Code View** button in the Toolbar.

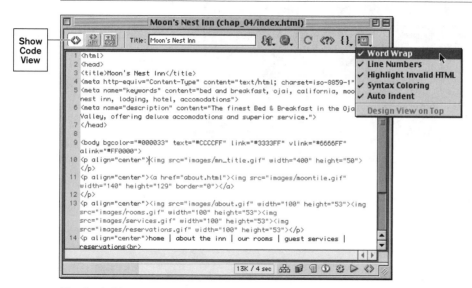

The Code View, new to Dreamweaver 4, is somewhat self-explanatory. However, there are a few options you should know about that definitely make it easier for you to view the code. The View Options drop-down menu, which you can access from the top Tool bar as shown above, gives you options to control the appearance of the Code View. The Wrap option causes the text to wrap to the next line based upon the size of the window. This eliminates the need to scroll to the right to view all the code. The Line Numbers option displays a number next to each line of code. This is helpful when you are troubleshooting errors in specific lines of your code. These line numbers only appear in Dreamweaver, not in the final code.

2. Make sure there is a check next to the **Word Wrap** and **Line Numbers** options.

Show Design View

3. Click the **Show Design View** button to change back to the visual authoring mode of Dreamweaver.

4. Select the **moontile.gif** image, in the middle of the page, by clicking it.

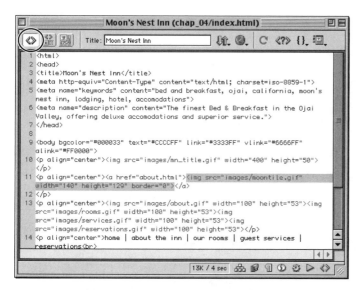

5. Click the **Show Code View** button to return to the HTML view of your page. Notice that the HTML code for the image is highlighted. This is very helpful when you want to look at specific HTML code in your page! You can actually teach yourself HTML by deconstructing your code in this way.

6. Close and save your changes. You won't be working with this file any longer.

Onward ho! You just built a page, colored it, set links, and looked at the code in one chapter. Future chapters will reveal more of Dreamweaver's powers, so keep on reading!

5.
Linking

| Linking with Point to File |
| Browse for File and Link History |
| Linking to New Source Files | Email Links |
| Named Anchors | Image Maps | Linking to Files |

---

chap_5

Dreamweaver 4
H•O•T CD-ROM

In Chapter 4, "Basics," you learned how to create links by clicking the **Browse for File** button and browsing to the HTML file on your hard drive. There are a few other ways to create links as well, and this chapter covers them.

For example, in this chapter you'll learn about **Point to File**, which allows you to point to a file inside your Site window and create the link based on your selection. This is helpful because it forces you to select files only within your local root folder, which ensures better link integrity. In addition to creating links to HTML files, you can also use Point to File to select new image files and replace ones already on your page.

Another type of link is an email link. This special type of link launches your end user's email program and automatically enters a recipient address. You will also learn how to use the **Link History** to quickly replicate links across your site, which can save you time and effort. Another new type of link you'll work with here is called **Named Anchors**, which work in conjunction with links to allow you to jump to different sections of one page. This can be very helpful when you have a large amount of text or information to navigate through.

We will also be looking at image maps in this chapter. Image maps are useful when you want a single image to contain multiple links. The final type of link this chapter demonstrates is a file link. File links let you link to files, such as PDFs, .sit and .zip archives, etc. If this all sounds abstract, dive into the chapter so you can get the hands-on experience that will make these new concepts understandable.

I. —————————Linking with Point to File

The Point to File feature is an alternate way to create links on your Web pages. This feature forces you to select files that are within your local root folder, which eliminates the unwanted possibility of linking to files that are located outside of your defined site. Here's how it's done.

1. Copy **chap_05** to your hard drive. Define your site for Chapter 5 using the **chap_05** folder as the local root folder. If you need a refresher on this process, visit Exercise 1 in Chapter 3, *"Site Control."*

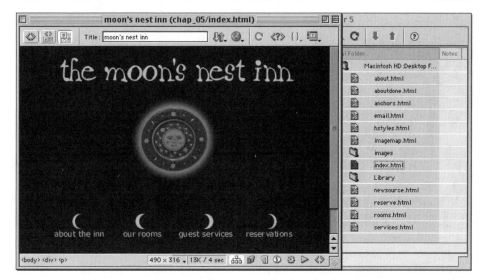

2. Open **index.html**. This file is complete except that it does not contain any links. You will create them using the Point to File feature.

3. The Site window does not have to be in the foreground; just open and visible in the background or side-by-side with your document on your screen. Click **index.html** to make it active.

4. Click the **about.gif** image so that it is highlighted. Before you can create any link, you must first have the image or text selected.

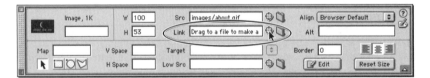

5. In the Property Inspector, click and hold the **Point to File** icon next to the **Link** field. When you click on the icon and hold the mouse button down, the **Link** field will fill in with some text, telling you to point to a file to create a link.

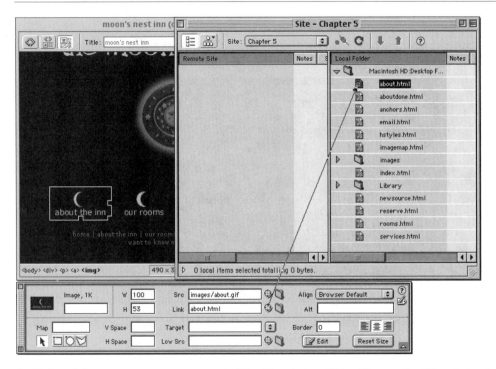

6. Click and drag your cursor over any part of the Site window. This will cause the Site window to come to the front on top of the document window. Move your mouse over **about.html** so that it is highlighted, and release the mouse button. This will create a link to **about.html**.

7. The **Link** field will display the file you are linking to. This is a good place to look if you forget what file you linked to.

8. Click your document window to bring it forward.

9. Click the **rooms.gif** ("**our rooms**") image so that it is highlighted.

10. In the Property Inspector, click and hold the **Point to File** icon again. When you click and hold the mouse button down, the **Link** field will fill in with some text.

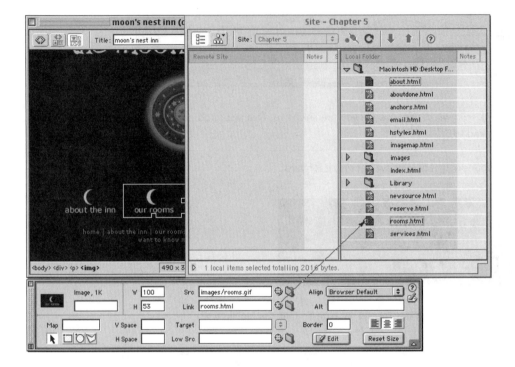

11. Click and drag your cursor over any part of the Site window. This will cause the Site window to come to the front, on top of the document window. Move your mouse over **rooms.html**, so that it is highlighted, and release the mouse button. This will create a link to **rooms.html**.

---

12. Using the Point to File feature, create a link for the **services.gif** ("**guest services**") image to **services.html** and a link for the **reserve.gif** ("**reservations**") image to reserve.html.

---

13. Press **F12** to preview the page in a browser. Click any of the images you linked to see if they work. When you are finished, return to Dreamweaver.

---

14. Choose **File > Save** to save the changes you've made, and leave it open for the next exercise.

MOVIE | point_to_file.mov

To learn more about Dreamweaver's Point To File feature, check out **point_to_file.mov** located in the **movies** folder on the Dreamweaver 4 **H·O·T** CD-ROM.

2. ───────────Linking to New Source Files

So far you have learned how to use the Point to File feature to create links on your pages. While this is the most common use of this feature, there are other ways to use it. You can use the Point to File feature to quickly replace images or placeholders on your page. In this context, Point to File is an alternate method to using the **Insert Image** object on the **Objects** panel, which you learned about in Chapter 4, "*Basics*." Sometimes there is more than one way to do the same thing in Dreamweaver. You'll find that you will develop your own preferences for which method to use as you gain experience in the program.

1. Open **newsource.html**. This HTML file contains a background, a table, and placeholders.

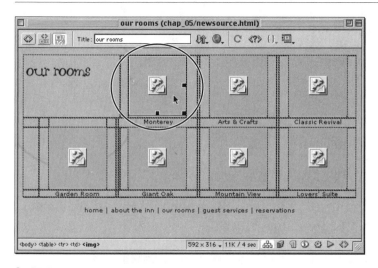

2. Click the placeholder in the upper-left corner of the page to highlight it.

NOTE | What Is a Placeholder?

A placeholder is an object that you can add to your page to represent where final images will be inserted. You can add a placeholder by holding down the **Option** (Mac) or **Ctrl** (Windows) key while clicking the Insert Image object in the Objects panel. Then, you can resize the placeholder by selecting it first and then changing its height and width values in the Property Inspector. Placeholders are helpful in a workgroup where one person designs the page and another adds the content. You can resize the placeholder so that it matches the dimensions of the image that will replace it. This will give you a more accurate preview of your page layout and positioning.

3. In the Property Inspector, click the **Point to File** icon next to the **Src** option and drag it over the corner of the Site window. This causes Site window to come to the front of the document window.

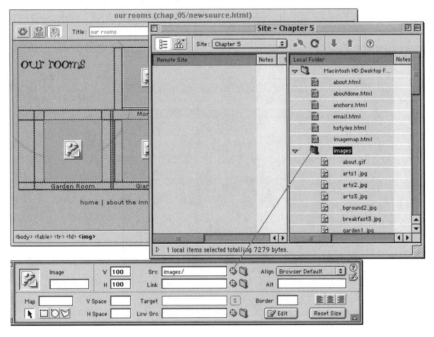

4. Hold the cursor over the **images** folder until it expands to reveal all the images inside.

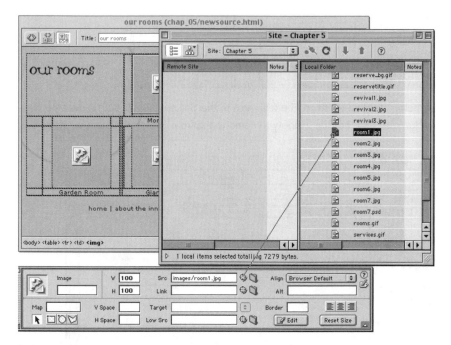

5. Move your cursor over the **room1.jpg** image and release the mouse button. This will select that image to replace the placeholder currently on your page.

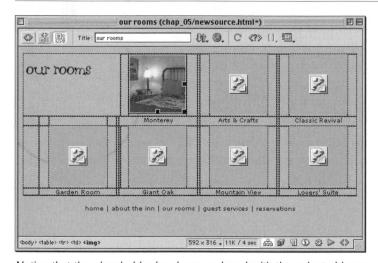

Notice that the placeholder has been replaced with the selected image.

6. Click to select the placeholder to the right of the image that you just replaced.

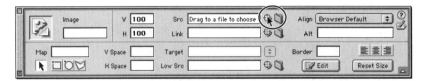

7. In the Property Inspector, click the **Point to File** icon next to the Src option and drag it over the corner of the Site window, causing the Site window to come to the front of the document window.

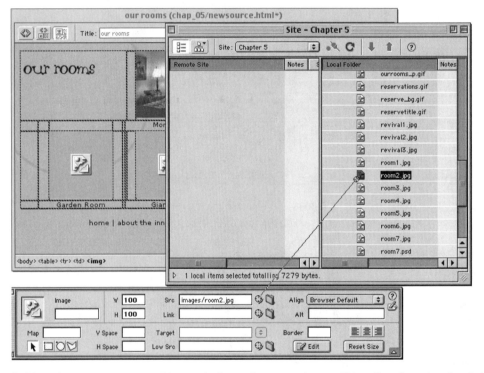

8. Move the cursor over **room2.jpg** and release the mouse button. This will replace the placeholder with **room2.jpg** on your page. **Tip:** If you can't see **room2.jpg**, hold your cursor over the images folder until its contents are revealed.

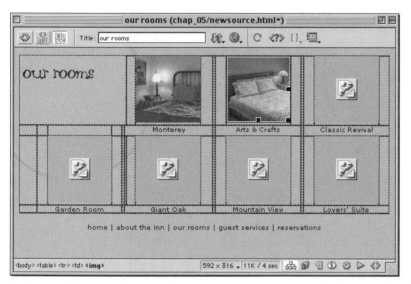

Notice that the second placeholder has now been replaced with the room2.jpg image.

9. Replace the other five images on this page, using the **Point to File** feature (and the image above as a guideline). When you are finished, your page should look like the one in Step 10.

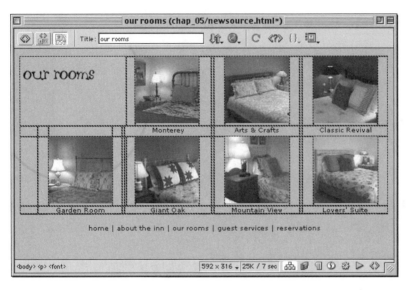

10. Choose **File > Save** to save your work. You can close this file, as you won't need it for any other exercises in this book.

3. —————————**Browse for File and the Link History**

The **Link History** is one of those features that you probably are not aware of, but it can save you time and ensure that links are entered properly throughout your site. It will not remember links that you attach to images using the Point to File feature. If you want to enjoy the convenience of the Link History for both image and text links, you should create your links using the Browse for File feature.

This exercise will show you how to use the Link History to reproduce links throughout many pages in your site.

1. Make sure you have **chap_05/index.html** file open.

2. Highlight the words "**about the inn**" at the bottom of the page. You are going to start with this text rather than "home" because you are already on the home page, so you don't need to create a link to that page.

3. In the Property Inspector, click **Browse for File**.

4. Browse to **about.html** and click **Open**. This will create a link to that HTML file.

5. Highlight the words "**our rooms**" at the bottom of the page.

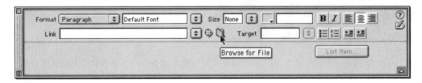

6. Click **Browse for File** again.

7. Browse to **rooms.html** and click **Open**. This will create a link to that HTML file.

8. Using the Browse for File method, create a link for the words "**guest services**" to **services.html** and for "**reservations**" to **reserve.html**.

Now that you have created the links for your site, you are ready to begin using the Link History.

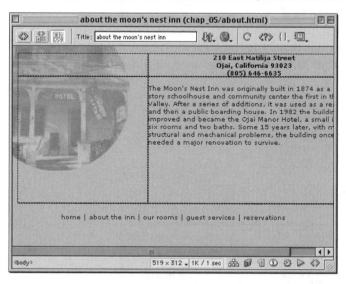

9. Open **about.html**. The text at the bottom of the page needs to be converted to links. In the following steps, you will use the Link History to do this very quickly.

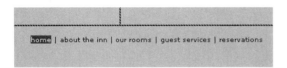

10. Highlight the word "**home**" at the bottom of the page. Because you didn't create a link for this on the **index.html** page, let's do that now so it will be in the Link History for later use.

11. In the Property Inspector, use the Browse for File method to browse to **index.html**, inside the **chap_05** folder, and click **Open** to create a link to **index.html**.

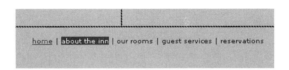

12. Highlight the words "**about the inn**."

*You have already created a link to this file on the **index.html** page, so it is recorded in the Link History.*

13. In the Property Inspector, click the **Link History** pop-up menu and choose **about.html**. This will create a link to that HTML file. Notice that each link you created using the Browse for File method is listed in the Link History.

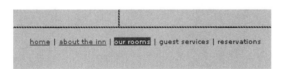

14. Highlight the words "**our rooms**."

15. Click the **Link History** pop-up menu and choose **rooms.html**. This creates a link to that HTML file.

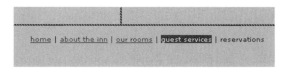

16. Highlight the words "**guest services**."

17. Click the **Link History** pop-up menu and choose **services.html**. This will create a link to that HTML file.

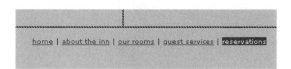

18. Highlight the word "**reservations**."

19. Click the **Link History** pop-up menu and choose **reserve.html**. This will create a link to that HTML file.

*By now, you should be able to see how much time you can save by using the Link History. If you want more practice using the Link History, open **rooms.html**, **services.html**, and **reserve.html** and create links for the text at the bottom of each page.*

20. Press **F12** to preview your page in a browser. Make sure you check the links you created at the bottom of each page.

21. Return to Dreamweaver and save and close the file.

You did all that work in just a few minutes and no typing, browsing, or pointing was needed. Sweet!

4. —————————**Creating Email Links**

An **email** link will launch your end user's email application and insert the recipient's address into the **To:** field. This is convenient and doesn't require the end user to remember complex and lengthy email addresses. This exercise will show you how to create an email link.

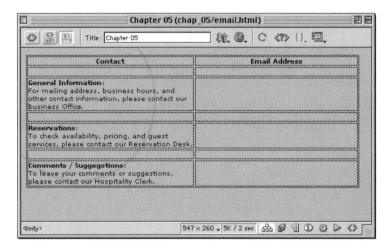

1. Open **email.html**. This file contains a table with some text and spaces for some email links. You will create those links in this exercise.

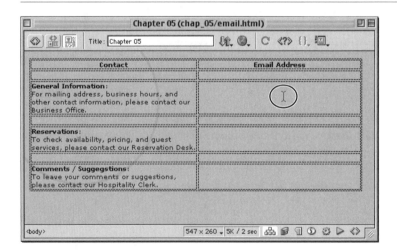

2. Click inside the cell to the right of the "**General Information**" column.

3. Click **Insert EMail Link** in the **Objects** panel. This will open the **Insert EMail Link** dialog box.

4. Enter **Text: General Information** and press **Tab**. Enter **E-Mail: information@moonsnestinn.com**. Click **OK**.

5. Click anywhere on the email link you just inserted on the page. In the Property Inspector, notice that the **Link** field reads **mailto:information@moonsnestinn.com**. This is the correct format for creating email links.

NOTE | Text versus Email

The Text field determines what text will be displayed on the page, whereas the E-Mail field sets the actual email address for the recipient. Sometimes, you might want to put the email address in both fields, to allow someone to copy and paste the actual email link into another document or email application.

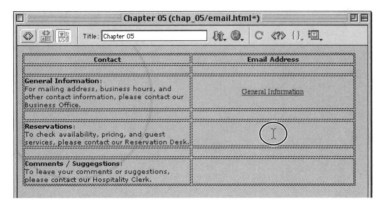

6. Click inside the cell to the right of the "**Reservations**" cell.

7. Click **Insert EMail Link** in the Objects panel.

8. Enter **Text: reservations@moonsnestinn.com** and press **Tab**. **Enter E-Mail: reservations @moonsnestinn.com.** Since Dreamweaver will automatically insert any email address that you used previously, **information@moonsnestinn.com** will appear in the **E-Mail:** field. Click **OK**. This will insert an email link into the empty cell.

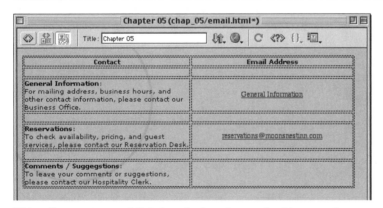

This will create an email link that displays the email address on the page.

9. An alternate way to create an email link is to avoid the **Insert EMail Link** object and do it manually. To do this, first click inside the cell to the right of the "**Comments/Suggestions**" cell.

10. Type **comments@moonsnestinn.com** inside the empty cell.

11. Click and drag over **comments@moonsnestinn.com** to highlight the text.

12. In the Property Inspector, type **mailto:comments@moonsnestinn.com** in the **Link** field and press **Return/Enter.** This will create an email link from the selected text.

*You see, once again there are two ways to do the same operation. You learned how to create the email link using the **Insert EMail Link** object and how to manually insert an email link. Again, as your skills build in Dreamweaver, you will develop your own personal preferences for creating email links, just as you will develop your own preferences for assigning links.*

13. Press **F12** to preview this page in your default browser. You can click each of the email links to make sure they work.

14. When you are finished, return to Dreamweaver so you can save and close this file.

WARNING | Browser Email Settings

Not all site visitors use a browser for their email, as they sometimes use other programs, such as Eudora, Entourage, etc. If visitors to your site click an email link and do not have their email preferences set in their browser, they will get an error message asking them to do so. This is true for both Internet Explorer and Netscape Navigator. There's not a lot you can do about this, and it's a good reason to include email addresses in your email links, as was shown in Step **8** of the above exercise.

Named Anchors

Named Anchors are a type of link. They are used infrequently, but when they're appropriate there's no other link quite like them. Named Anchors have two components—the **anchor** and the **link**. The time to use them is when you want to link to sections within a long page of content. Working together, they make it easy to jump to specific areas of your page. This exercise will show you how to set up anchors on your page.

1. Open **anchors.html**. This file has a table with some images that extend down the page.

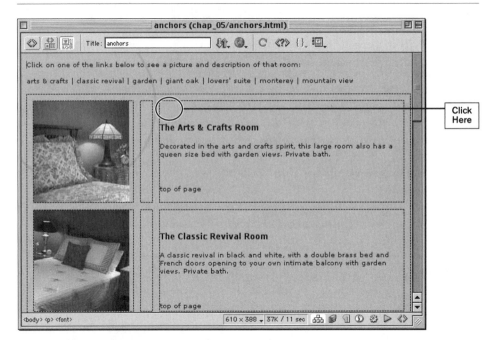

2. Click above the words "**The Arts & Crafts Room**." You will learn next how to insert a Named Anchor here, so users can easily jump to the photo and description of this room.

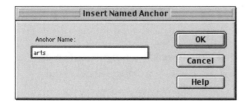

3. Choose **Insert > Invisible Tags > Named Anchor**. This will open the **Insert Named Anchor** dialog box. Type **arts** and then click **OK**.

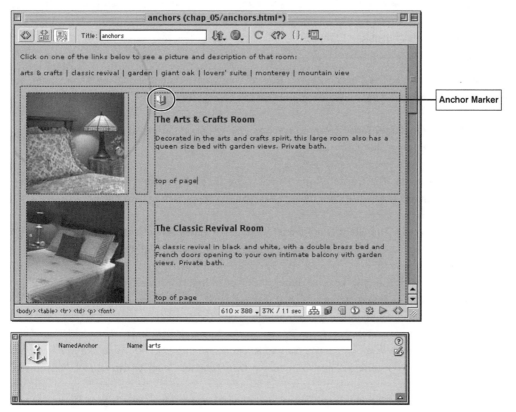

Notice the small yellow Anchor Marker that appears on your page where you inserted the Named Anchor tag? If you ever want to change the name that you've set for your Named Anchor, click this **Anchor Marker** *to access its name in the Property Inspector in order to modify it.*

TIP | What Does This Dialog Box Mean?

If you have the **View Invisible Elements** option disabled, you will get the error message shown here when you try to insert a Named Anchor on your page. This just means that you won't see the little yellow Anchor Marker for your Named Anchor. However, the Named Anchor will still work. We prefer to work with the View Invisible Elements option on when we work with Named Anchors so we can see the Anchor Marker tags on the page. You can disable/enable this option by choosing **View > Visual Aids > Invisible Elements**.

---

4. Click above the words "**The Classic Revival Room**." You will insert another Named Anchor here, so users can easily jump to the photo and description of this room.

---

5. Choose **Insert > Invisible Tags > Named Anchor**. This will open the **Insert Named Anchor** dialog box. Type **classic** and then click **OK**.

---

6. Click above the words "**The Garden Room**" and choose **Insert > Invisible Tags > Named Anchor**. This will open the **Insert Named Anchor** dialog box. Type **garden** and then click **OK**.

---

7. Click above the words "**The Giant Oak Room**" and choose **Insert > Invisible Tags > Named Anchor**. This will open the **Insert Named Anchor** dialog box. Type **giant** and then click **OK**.

---

8. Click above the words the "**The Lovers' Suite**" and choose **Insert > Invisible Tags > Named Anchor**. This will open the **Insert Named Anchor** dialog box. Type **lovers** and then click **OK**.
Note: Named Anchors cannot contain special characters like apostrophes.

---

*Since you are going to be inserting several Named Anchors, we thought you would like to know that the keyboard shortcut for inserting Named Anchors is **Opt+Cmd+A** (Mac) or **Ctrl+Alt+A** (Windows).*

---

9. Click above the words "**The Monterey Room**" and choose **Insert > Invisible Tags > Named Anchor**. This will open the **Insert Named Anchor** dialog box. Type **monterey** and then click **OK**.

---

10. Click above the words "**The Mountain View Room**" and choose **Insert > Invisible Tags > Named Anchor**. This will open the **Insert Named Anchor** dialog box. Type **mountain** and then click **OK**.

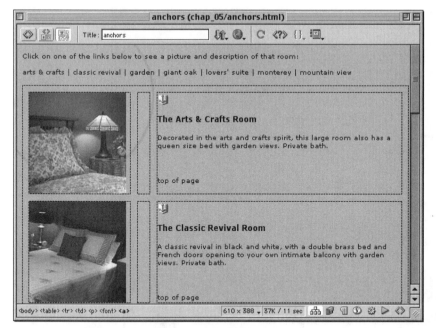

When you are finished, your page should look something like this. There should be a small Anchor Marker near each room title.

---

11. Click and drag to highlight the words "**arts & crafts**" in the navbar at the top of the page. Now that you have set up all of your Named Anchors, you need to create links to each of them.

 MOVIE | anchor.mov

To learn more about using Named Anchors, check out **anchor.mov** located in the **movies** folder on the Dreamweaver 4 **H•O•T CD-ROM**.

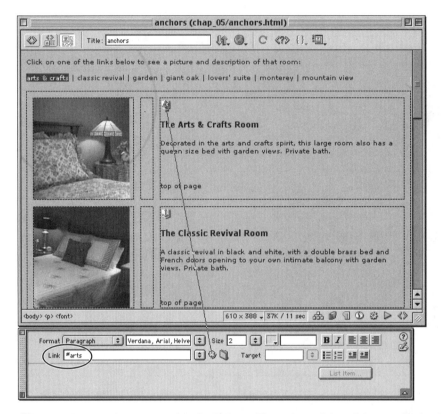

12. In the Property Inspector, using the Point to File option, click and drag to the Anchor Marker above the text "**The Arts and Crafts Room**." Release the mouse button to create the link.
Note: Links to anchor points always begin with a **#** sign.

13. Click and drag to highlight the words "**classic revival**" at the top of the page.

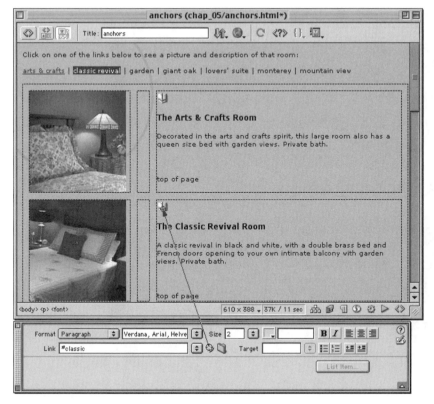

14. In the Property Inspector, using the Point to File option, click and drag to the Anchor Marker above the text "**The Classic Revival Room**." Release the mouse button to create the link.

15. Click and drag to highlight the word "**garden**" at the top of the page.

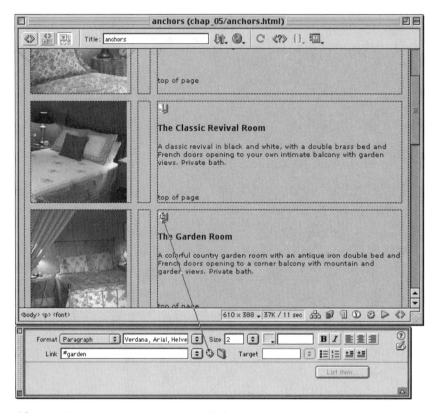

16. In the Property Inspector, using the Point to File option, click and drag to the Anchor Marker above the text "**The Garden Room**." Release the mouse button to create the link.

17. Using this same process, go ahead and finish the other links at the top of the page.

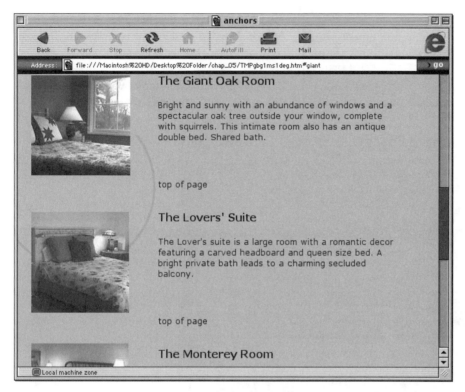

18. Press **F12** to preview your page in a browser. Click each of the links at the top to see how the Named Anchors work.

As you can see, this is a nice way to jump to different sections within a single page. Once you are at the bottom of the page, wouldn't it be nice if you had a link to a Named Anchor that would take you back to the top of the page? Well, you will create just that in the next few steps.

19. Return to Dreamweaver and click just to the left of the word **"Click"** at the top of the page.

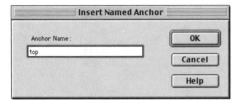

20. Choose **Insert > Invisible Tags > Named Anchor**. Type **top** for the name and click **OK**. This will insert an Anchor Marker at the top of your page.

21. Highlight the words "**top of page**" under the description of the "**The Arts & Crafts Room**."

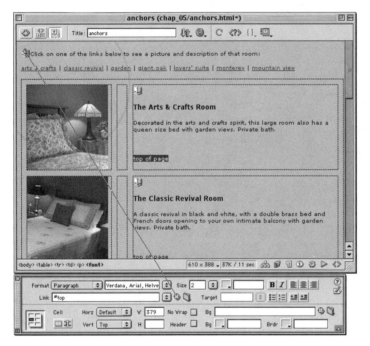

22. In the Property Inspector, using the Point to File option, click and drag to the Anchor Marker next to the word "**Click**" at the top of the page. Release the mouse button. This will create a link to the top Anchor Marker.

23. Repeat this process for each block of text that reads "**top of page**." This will create a link to the top Anchor Marker, so users have a quick and easy way to get back to the top of your page. **Note:** If you find it difficult to use the point-to-file method, you can simply type **#top** in the **Link** field of the Property Inspector. There is no right or wrong way to do this; it's a matter of personal preference.

24. Press **F12** to preview your page in a browser. Click the "**monterey**" link. This will take you to the bottom of the page. Next, click the "**top of page**" link. This will take you back up to the top. Pretty slick!

25. Return to Dreamweaver. Save and close all the work you've done in this file.

6. _____Image Maps

An image map contains invisible coordinates that allow you to assign multiple links to a single image. With image maps, you can specify multiple regions of a single image and have each of those areas link to a different URL. This exercise will show you how to create an image map.

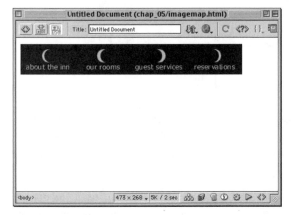

1. Open **imagemap.html**. This file contains a single image that will serve as a navigation bar for the site. In the following steps, you will create an image map so this single image can link to multiple pages.

---

2. Click the image so that it is selected.

With an image selected, the Property Inspector changes to reflect options for images, which include the image map settings.

3. In the **Map** field, enter **navbar**. By doing this, you are assigning a name to the image map, which is required and becomes even more important if you have multiple image maps on a single page.

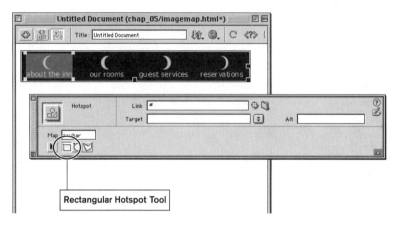

Rectangular Hotspot Tool

4. Click the **Rectangular Hotspot Tool**. Click and drag a rectangle around the words "**about the inn**" and the image of the crescent moon. By doing this, you are defining what area of the image you want to serve as a link. When you release the mouse, you will notice a light blue box around the image and the options in your Property Inspector will have changed.

*Note: The # mark in the **Link** field is used as a temporary link for the real link. If you don't remove this or add your own link, the users will still see the link icon—the little hand—when they move their cursor over the image map. It won't link to anything, though! It's just a stand-in for the real thing.*

5. With the light blue rectangle selected, click **Browse for File** and browse to **about.html**. Click **Open**. This will create a link for this specific area of the image map.

6. With that image map still selected, type **about the inn** in the **Alt** field in the Property Inspector and press **Enter/Return**. In some browsers this will display a small help tag when the user hovers over the hot area of the image map. You don't have to put anything here if you don't want to.

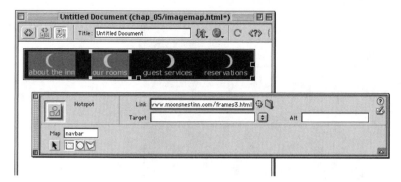

7. Click the **Rectangular Hotspot Tool** again. Click and drag a rectangle around the words "**our rooms**" and the image of the crescent moon.

8. In the **Property Inspector Link** field, type **http://www.moonsnestinn.com**. This will create an external link in this part of the image map.

9. Press **F12** to preview the links in a browser. Like other links, they cannot be previewed from within Dreamweaver; they must be viewed through a browser.

10. When you are finished, return to Dreamweaver. Save and close this file.

TIP | Help Tags

Have you ever held your mouse over an image map only to discover that a little tag pops up with some text inside it? This type of effect can be easily created by using the **ALT** attribute of the **HREF** tag being displayed. If you want to  add an **ALT** tag to your image map, simply give each link a message inside the **ALT** field of the Property Inspector, as shown in Step 6. However, this does not work in all browsers. :-(

7. ————————————Linking to Files

In addition to creating links to HTML pages, there might come a time when you want or need to link to a file. For example, maybe you have a PDF brochure for users to download or you want to let them download an entire folder of stuffed or zipped images. The possibilities are endless. The good news is that linking to files is just as easy as linking to other HTML pages and this exercise will show you how.

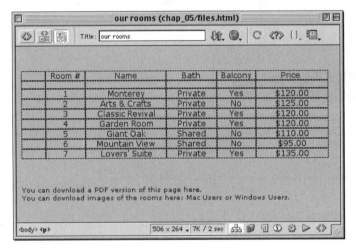

1. Open the **files.html** file located inside the **chap_05** folder. This page contains a table with information about each of the rooms at the inn. You are going to create a link that will let the end user view this same content in PDF (**P**ortable **D**ocument **F**ormat), which is great for printing.

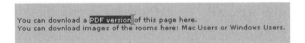

2. At the bottom of the page, click and drag to select the words "PDF version." Like other text links, you need to select your text before creating the link.

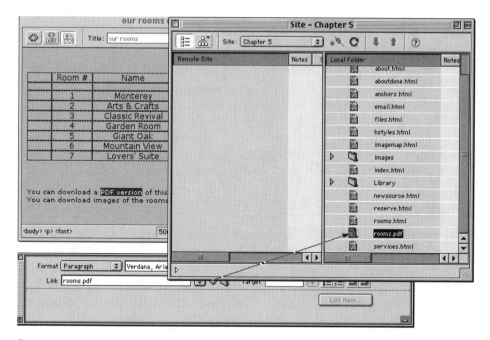

3. With the text selected, in the Property Inspector, click the Point to File icon and drag to select the **rooms.pdf** inside the Site window. As before, the Site window will need to be partially visible in the background to use this method of linking. Honestly, any linking method will work; it's simply a matter of which one you prefer.

4. Press **F12** to preview this page in a browser. Click the link you create at the bottom. Because the file you linked to is a PDF file, the browser will automatically launch the Adobe Acrobat Reader plug-in for your browser.

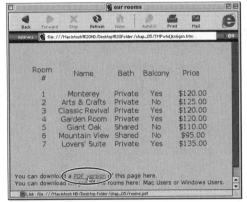
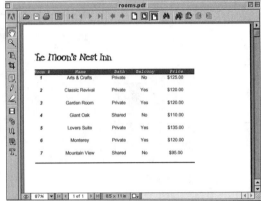

Clicking on a link that points to a PDF file will automatically launch the Adobe Acrobat Reader plug-in if it's installed in your browser. If it's not installed and you get an error when you click on the link, you'll need to go to the Adobe site to download it. The Adobe Acrobat Reader plug-in is a free download and is available at http://www.adobe.com/products/acrobat/readermain.html. You should also consider adding a link to the Adobe PDF download area to your page so users can download the plug-in if they don't already have it installed.

TIP | How do you create PDF files?

In this exercise, you learned how to create a link to a PDF file and then view that link in a browser, but you did not learn how to create the PDF file we supplied for you. Creating PDF files is now a pretty easy process; you just need the right software. If you think you'll create PDF files often, you might want to purchase the full version of Adobe Acrobat. This is a PDF authoring tool that Adobe sells, and will give you the ability to create PDF files from almost any application. Alternatively, you can now create PDF files online for free at Adobe's web site at **http://createpdf.adobe.com**. Pretty neat.

In the following steps, you will learn how to create a link to a file of compressed images. Using a compressed file format lets you transfer large amounts of data, like images, with a smaller file size. We have created two files—one for Mac users and one for Windows users. Why? Because each operating system uses different file formats to compress files. The most common format on the Mac is the .sit (StuffIt) format and the most common format on Windows is the .zip format.

You can download a <u>PDF version</u> of this page here.
You can download images of the rooms here: **Mac Users** or Windows Users.

5. At the bottom of the page, click and drag to select the words "Mac Users."

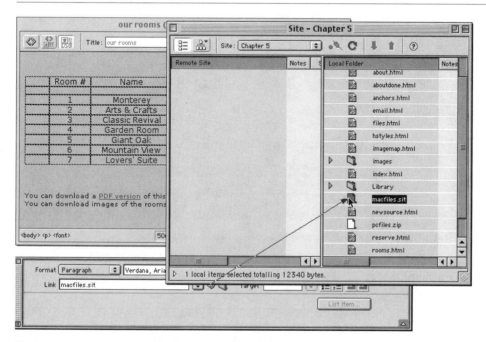

6. Using one of the linking methods you learned earlier, create a link to the **macfiles.sit** file located inside the **chap_05** folder. This file was compressed in the .sit format specifically for Mac users.

You can download a <u>PDF version</u> of this page here.
You can download images of the rooms here: <u>Mac Users</u> or **Windows Users**.

7. At the bottom of the page, click and drag to select the words "Windows Users."

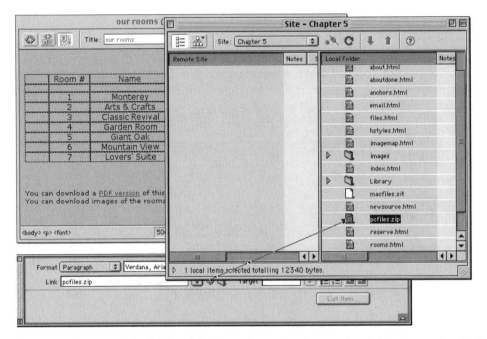

8. Again, using one of the linking methods you learned earlier, create a link to the **pcfiles.zip** file located inside the **chap_05** folder. This file was compressed in the .zip format specifically for PC users.

TIP | How do you create .sit and .zip files?

When you have a large file or a collection of files that you want to let people download, it's a good idea to compress those files so the download goes as quickly as possible. There are different file formats on the Mac and PC for compressing files, .sit and .zip. The .sit (StuffIt) format is the most common on the Macintosh and the .zip format is the most common on the PC. There are several programs that let you create these formats. For example, on the Macintosh you can use StuffIt (**http://www.aladdinsys.com**) to create .sit files, or MacZip (**http://www.sitec.net/maczip/**) to create .zip files. On the PC, you can use WinZip (**http://www.winzip.com**) to create .zip files.

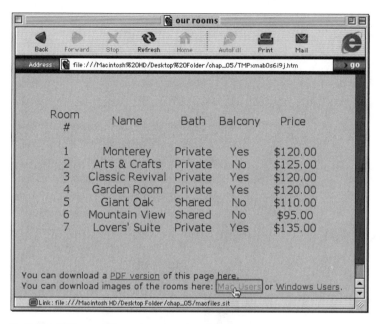

9. Press **F12** to preview your page in a browser:

•**Mac Users:** *Click on the "Mac Users" link; your browser will automatically download and save the file to your desktop. In order to open this file, you will need a program capable of opening .sit files, such as Stuffit Expander.*

•**Windows Users:** *Click on the "Windows Users" link; you will be promoted to save this file someplace on your hard drive. Save the file on your desktop. In order to open this file, you will need a program capable of opening .zip files. WinZip is a great program to do just this and they offer a free trial version at http://www.winzip.com.*

10. Close and save the **files.html** file; you won't be working with it any longer.

Phew, another chapter under your belt. Congratulations! When you are ready, you can move on to the next chapter. ;-)

6.

Typography

| Creating and Formatting Text | Font Lists | Aligning Text |
| Ordered, Unordered, and Definition Lists |
| Color Schemes | Formatting Text in Tables | Repeat Last Action |
| Applying HTML Styles | Character Entities | Flash Text |

chap_6

Dreamweaver 4
H•O•T CD-ROM

Most professional typographers cringe when they look at Web pages because type that appears on the Web, for lack of a better expression, sucks. It sucks for many reasons. It sucks because Web browsers default to Times Roman, and most sites use the default font. It sucks because type appears differently on Macs, Windows, and UNIX platforms.

It sucks because browsers rely on whichever fonts are installed in the end-users' systems, so you can't freely use any font you want. It sucks mostly because your choices for formatting type are limited, and that's guaranteed to frustrate the best of us.

Dreamweaver gives you many hooks and handles for making the best of this situation. This chapter will cover how to set font styles (such as **bold**, *italics*, and <u>underlined</u>), font sizes, font colors, and font faces (such as Times Roman, Helvetica, Arial, etc.). It will also cover making bullet lists, definition lists, and unordered lists. If you haven't heard those terms before, they will also be explained here. A most exciting enhancement has occurred in Dreamweaver 4: the ability to add Flash text. This feature allows you to use any font or style you want without concern about how it will appear on other platforms. By the end of this chapter, your Web-based type education should be quite complete!

A Word about FONT FACE

The **FONT FACE** element in HTML allows you to specify a typeface other than the end user's default font. You can apply the attribute in Dreamweaver by creating **font sets**, which are described in the following exercise. The caveat is that the typeface must be installed in your end user's system, or the browser will not be able to display it. It is therefore helpful to know which fonts ship in the systems of Macintosh and Windows machines. Below is a chart that lists them for you.

Default System 9.1 Macintosh	Default Windows 2000 Fonts
Apple Chancery	Arial
CAPITALS	**Arial Black**
Charcoal	Arial Narrow
Chicago	**Arial Rounded MT Bold**
Courier	Book Antiqua
Gadget	Bookman Old Style
Geneva	Calisto MT
Helvetica	Century Gothic
Hoefler Text	**COPPERPLATE GOTHIC BOLD**
Monaco	COPPERPLATE GOTHIC LIGHT
New York	**Comic Sans MS**
Palatino	Courier
Sand	Courier New
Skia	Franklin Gothic Book
Σψμβολ (Symbol)	Garamond
Techno	**GOUDY STOUT**
Textile	*Harlow Solid Italic*
Times	Helvetica
VT102Font	**Impact**
	Lucida Console
	Lucida Handwriting
	Lucida Sans
	Lucida Sans Unicode
	□□ ✓ ✗ ⌐ ⌐ ▲ ▲ □ (Marlett)
	Mistral
	OCR A Extended
	Palatino Linotype
	STENCIL
	Tahoma
	Times New Roman
	Trebuchet MS
	TW Cen MT
	Verdana
	▶ 🏠 ⚘ ♥ ⓘ ●◼ ? (Webdings)

TIP | HTML Default Text Size

It might come as a surprise that HTML text uses different sizing conventions from traditional print type sizes. Actually, all HTML text has a default size of 3, with a total range from 1 to 7.

To change HTML text to a size other than the default of 3, you can either specify a number from 1 through 7, or + or -1 through + or -7 relative to the **BASEFONT** size (which is 3). For example, if you want your HTML text to be size 6, specify the font size to be 6 or +3. Either setting produces an HTML type at size 6. Some browsers let you set the **BASEFONT** for a page by using <**BASEFONT** size = "4">. You can specify any size you want, using one of the above-mentioned methods.

This is an example of the **FONT SIZE** settings in Dreamweaver. The top example, None, is the equivalent of **FONT SIZE** 3. Notice how the type does not look different in **FONT SIZE** +4 through +7, or **FONT SIZE** -2 through -7? There is no difference between these settings.

FONT SIZE None
FONT SIZE 1
FONT SIZE 2
FONT SIZE 3
FONT SIZE 4
FONT SIZE 5
FONT SIZE 6
FONT SIZE 7
FONT SIZE +1
FONT SIZE +2
FONT SIZE +3
FONT SIZE +4
FONT SIZE +5
FONT SIZE +6
FONT SIZE +7
FONT SIZE -1
FONT SIZE -2
FONT SIZE -3
FONT SIZE -4
FONT SIZE -5
FONT SIZE -6
FONT SIEZ -7

I. _____Creating and Formatting HTML Text

In this exercise you will learn how to add HTML text to a Web page. You will also learn how to format this text by modifying the typeface, size, style, and other attributes. As you will see, creating and formatting HTML text with Dreamweaver 4 is just as easy as working with any word processing application.

1. Copy **chap_06** to your hard drive. Define your site for Chapter 6 using the **chap_06** folder as the local root folder. If you need a refresher on this process, visit Chapter 3, *"Site Control."*

2. Open the **text1.html** file.

3. Type **About the Inn** and press **Return/Enter**.

4. Type **Our Rooms** and press **Return/Enter**.

5. Type **Guest Services** and press **Return/Enter**.

6. Type **Reservations** and press **Return/Enter**.

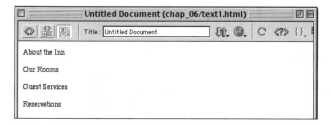

7. Select the words **"About the Inn."**

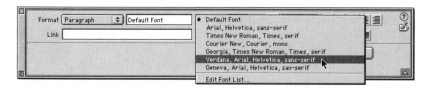

8. In the Property Inspector, choose the **Font List** pop-up menu and select the **Verdana, Arial, Helvetica, sans-serif** option. This will change your text to Verdana if you have that font installed; if you do not, Dreamweaver will display the next font in the list.

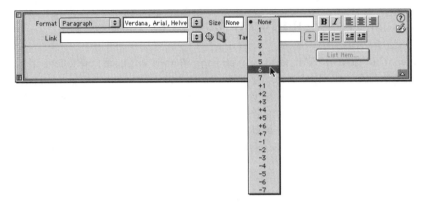

9. With "**About the Inn**" still selected, in the Property Inspector, choose the **Size** pop-up menu and select **6**. This will change the size of your type.

10. Go to the **Size** pop-up menu again and select **+3**. Notice how the type size stays at 6. That's because all HTML text has a basefont size of 3, from which you add or subtract to make your type larger or smaller.

11. Select the words "**Our Rooms**."

Text Color Box

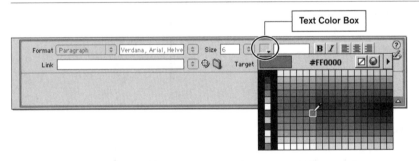

12. From the Property Inspector, choose the **Text Color Box**. Select a bright red color. Your text color is now red. This setting will override any text color that you might have specified under **Modify > Page Properties...**

13. Select the words "**Guest Services**."

14. In the Property Inspector, click the **Bold** button. This will make the selected text bold.

15. In the Property Inspector, click the **Italic** button. This will make the selected text italic.

16. Select the word "**Reservations**."

17. From the **Format** pop-up menu, select **Heading 2**. For more information about headings, see the tip on the next page.

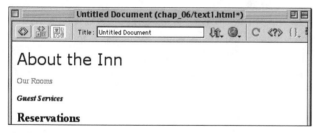

At the end of this exercise your page should look like this.

18. Save and close the file.

TIP | What Are Headings?

HTML text can also be formatted using **Heading** tags. The tags look like this: **<H1>**. They range from **1** to **6** and change the size of the HTML text. Here's a tricky thing that you might want to remember: The smaller the number next to the **H**, the bigger the text will be. For example, **<H1>** will produce the largest text, while **<H6>** will produce the smallest text. Generally, the (**<H1>-<H6>**) tags insert a line break before and after the text without requiring additional code. **Heading** tags can be useful for formatting large text.

Why might you use a **Heading** tag instead of a **FONT SIZE** element? If sight-impaired end users access your Web page, they might not "see" your Web page, but will instead have a reading device "read" it aloud. **Heading** tags can be "read" by HTML readers as headlines, whereas large type, formatted with the size attribute, is given the same emphasis as body copy. You might not imagine that your site has much of a sight-impaired audience, and perhaps do not think this information applies to your site design strategy. Many Web design and HTML authorities, ourselves included, believe there will come a day where the Federal Disabilities Act will apply to Web pages and all of us will have to give consideration to our sight-impaired audience. Our advice is to use **Heading** tags instead of large font sizes for headlines.

H1

H2

H3

H4

H5

I6

This image shows the range of how **Heading** *tags display in a browser.*

2. _____Font Lists

In this exercise you will learn how to add and modify the **font lists** that come with Dreamweaver. By specifying multiple fonts using a font list, the likelihood of visitors seeing the page in one of the typefaces you specified is higher, because you're offering more than one choice. If you base the font list on fonts that are likely to be installed in their system, the chances are even higher. You will learn how to modify what typefaces are in the existing font lists and how to create your own custom font list. Learning and using this technique will allow you to break out of the Times Roman mold a little bit, which is a welcome enhancement to the bland Web type landscape we all see every day.

1. Open **text2.html**.

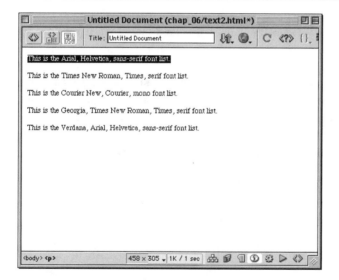

2. Select the words **"This is the Arial, Helvetica, sans-serif font list."**

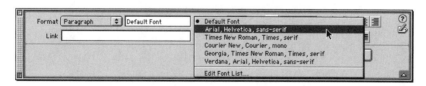

3. From the **Font List** pop-up menu in the Property Inspector, choose **Arial, Helvetica, sans-serif**. This will change your text to Arial if you have that font installed; if you do not, it will go to the next font in the list.

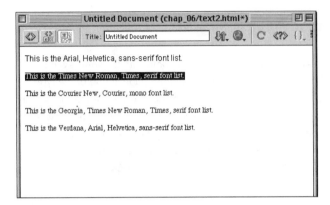

4. Select the words "**This is the Times New Roman, Times, serif Font List.**"

5. From the **Font List** pop-up menu, choose **Times New Roman, Times, serif**. This will change your text to Times New Roman if you have that font installed; if you do not, it will go to the next font in the list.

6. Select the words "**This is the Courier New, Courier, mono Font List.**" From the **Font List** pop-up menu, choose **Courier New, Courier, mono**. This will change your text to Courier New if you have that font installed; if you do not, it will go to the next font.

7. Select the words "**This is the Georgia, Times New Roman, Times, serif Font List.**" From the **Font List** pop-up menu, choose **Georgia, Times New Roman, Times, serif**.

8. Select the words "**This is the Verdana, Arial, Helvetica, sans-serif Font List.**" From the **Font List** pop-up menu, choose **Verdana, Arial, Helvetica, sans-serif**.

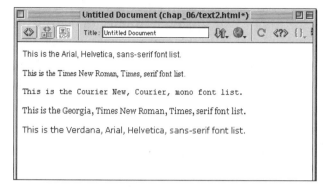

This is what your page should look like now.

9. Click off the text to deselect it, and press **Return/Enter**. Below the last sentence on the page, type **This is my very own Font List.**

10. From the **Font List** pop-up menu, choose **Edit Font List**.

NOTE | How Font Lists Work

Font lists are a very useful way of ensuring that the HTML text on your Web page is viewed the way you intended. A Web browser will search for each font in the list until it finds one that is installed on the end user's system. Once it finds a font in the list, it will use that font to display the HTML text on your Web page. For example, if your font list were Arial, Helvetica, sans-serif, the browser would try to use Arial first to display text. If the end user did not have Arial installed, the browser would then try to display Helvetica. If it could not find Helvetica, it would then display the first sans-serif font it found. The goal of font lists is to create sets of fonts that have similar structure and characteristics, so that there is minimal change from viewer to viewer.

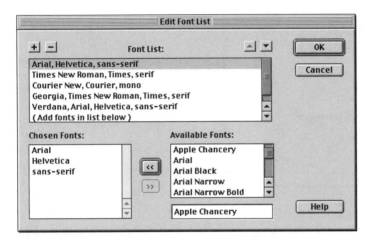

11. In the **Edit Font List** dialog box that will appear, select **Arial, Helvetica, sans-serif** from the **Font List** option. Select **Arial** under **Chosen Fonts:**, then click the **>>** button to remove Arial from this font list. Select **Arial Black**, under the **Available Fonts** option.

12. Click the **<<** button in the **Edit Font List** dialog box to add this to the current font list. You have just modified what fonts will be used for this font list.

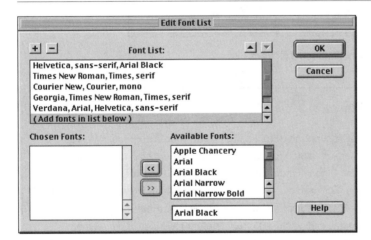

13. Select (**Add fonts in list below**) from the bottom of the **Font List** field.

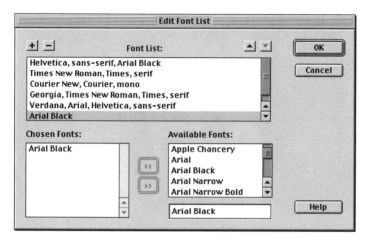

14. Select **Arial Black** under **Available Fonts** and press the ≪ button to add this to your list.

15. Select **Verdana** under **Available Fonts** and press the ≪ button to add this to your list.

16. Click **OK** to add your new list to the font list.

17. In the **text2.html** file, select the words "**This is my very own font list.**"

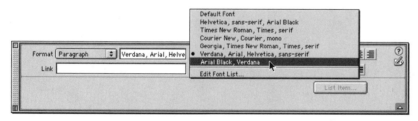

18. From the **Font List** pop-up menu, choose **Arial Black, Verdana.** This will change your text to Arial Black if you have that font installed; if you do not, it will go to Verdana.

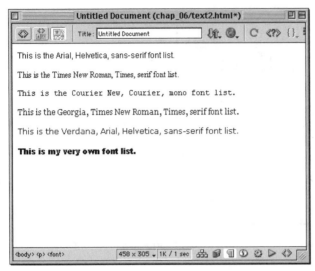

This is what your screen should look like now. This exercise gives you an example of how these font lists will display on your computer system. What you see might appear differently on other people's browsers, because they might have different fonts installed in their systems than you do.

19. Save and close the file.

NOTE | Type Size: Mac versus Windows

Unfortunately for all of us well-intentioned Web publishers, HTML type appears much larger on Windows than it does on the Mac. While they both display images at 72 dpi (dots per inch), Windows displays type at 96 dpi while the Mac displays it at 72 dpi. This deceptively small technical difference results in much larger type on Windows.

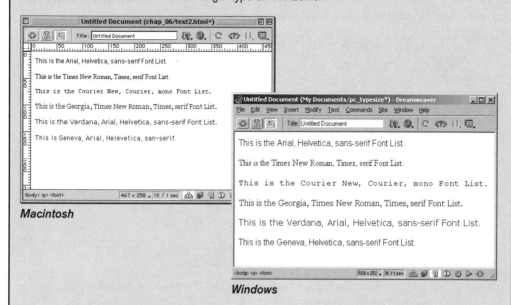

Macintosh

Windows

The images above illustrate the difference in size between the two platforms. Pretty scary, huh? There is no solution to this, except to turn to **Style Sheets** (see Chapter 10, "*Cascading Style Sheets*") to size your text by using pixels, but that only works on 4.0 version and later browsers.

To compensate, we often make type smaller at -1 or -2 when we are developing pages, but it only results in a more appealing Windows version, and a less appealing Mac version. Ugh! The theory is that there are more Windows users than Mac users, so we've taken the tack to make the type on our pages look acceptable on Windows, and slightly small on Macs.

One other solution to the size difference issue is to use images of text instead of HTML text. Because images display at 72 dpi on either Mac or Windows, the type will look identical on either platform. Later in this chapter, you'll learn to make Flash Text, which generates an image using the SWF file format. The downside is that images are larger in file size than corresponding HTML text, and are not searchable by search engines. It's always one gotcha or another, right?

**Aligning Text**

In this exercise you will learn how to align text on the page. Unfortunately, HTML does not give you much control aligning text. You have three basic options: **Left Align**, **Center Align**, and **Right Align**. You do have some extra options when you align text next to images, which you will also explore in this exercise. If the limitations of HTML alignment features frustrate you, that's understandable. You'll learn about more exact layout techniques in the following chapter.

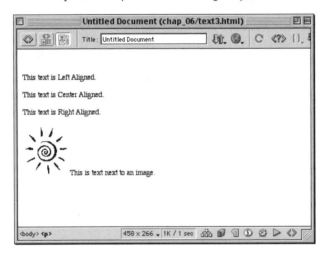

1. Open **text3.html**. Notice that the three lines of text at the top are left aligned. This is the default alignment setting for text.

2. Select the words "**This text is Center Aligned.**"

3. In the Property Inspector, click the **Align Center** button. This will center your text on the page. **Note:** The centering of the text is relative to the width of the browser window.

4. Select the words "**This text is Right Aligned.**"

5. In the Property Inspector, click the **Align Right** button. This will place your text on the right edge of the page.

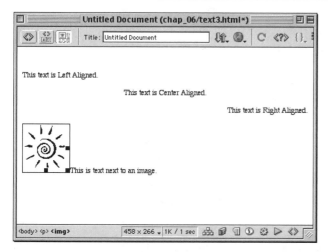

6. Click the **burst.gif** image. Notice when you select an image to align with type, you have different alignment options available in the Property Inspector.

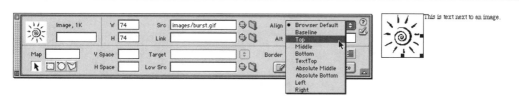

7. In the Property Inspector, choose the **Align** pop-up menu and select the **Top** option. Notice that the text moves to the top of the image.

8. Save and close the file.

Aligning Text and Images

Dreamweaver offers many alignment options for text and images. Below is a chart defining all the alignment terms, so now you will know what you are requesting when you select one:

HTML Text and Image Alignment Definitions	
Alignment	**Description**
Browser Default	Varies between browsers, but usually uses the Bottom option (see below).
Baseline	Aligns the baseline of the text to the bottom of the image.
Bottom	Aligns the baseline of the text to the bottom of the image (same as Baseline).
Absolute Bottom	Aligns text, including descenders (i.e., j), to the bottom of the image.
Top	Aligns the image to the tallest part of the object (image or text).
TextTop	Aligns the image with the tallest character in the line of text.
Middle	Aligns the baseline of the text to the middle of the image.
Absolute Middle	Aligns the middle of the text to the middle of the image.
Left	Left-aligns the image and wraps text to the right.
Right	Right-aligns the image and wraps text to the left.

4. —————— Ordered, Unordered, and Definition Lists

In this exercise you will learn how to create a variety of lists—**an Ordered List**, an **Unordered List**, and a **Definition List**. These are HTML terms that refer to whether the list is formatted with a bullet, an indent, or Roman numerals. These lists can be generated from existing text or from scratch.

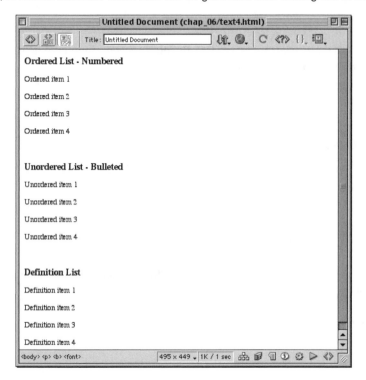

1. Open **text4.html**.

2. Select the four lines of text under the **Ordered List - Numbered** section (**Ordered item 1, Ordered item 2, Ordered item 3, Ordered item 4**).

3. Choose **Text > List > Ordered List**.

```
Ordered List - Numbered

  1. Ordered item 1
  2. Ordered item 2
  3. Ordered item 3
  4. Ordered item 4
```

This is what an Ordered List looks like.

4. Select the four lines of text under the **Unordered List - Bulleted** section (**Unordered item 1**, **Unordered item 2**, **Unordered item 3**, **Unordered item 4**).

5. Choose **Text > List > Unordered List**.

```
Unordered List - Bulleted

  • Unordered item 1
  • Unordered item 2
  • Unordered item 3
  • Unordered item 4
```

This is what an Unordered List looks like.

6. Select the four lines of text under the **Definition List** section (**Definition item 1**, **Definition item 2**, **Definition item 3**, **Definition item 4**).

7. Choose **Text > List > Definition List**.

```
Definition List

Definition item 1
       Definition item 2
Definition item 3
       Definition item 4
```

This is what a Definition List looks like.

8. Save the file and close it. You'll find that knowing how to set up these different types of lists will come in very handy as you create your own Web pages and sites.

5. ————————Color Schemes

Color schemes are preset groups of colors that Dreamweaver provides for your background, text, links, active links, and visited links colors. You can apply a color scheme to a page at any time. They are useful when you are not sure which colors to use. Why is this exercise in the "Typography" chapter? Because color schemes affect the color of type and links on your page, that's why!

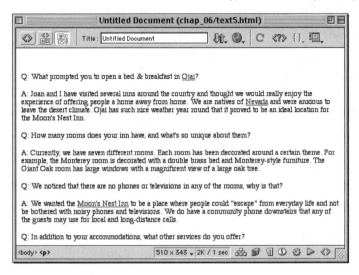

1. Open **text5.html**.

2. Choose **Commands > Set Color Scheme...**

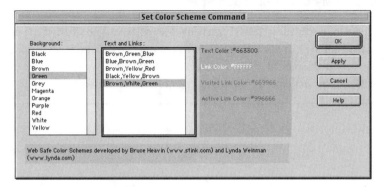

3. In the **Set Color Scheme Command** dialog box, select **Green** under the **Background** option. Select **Brown, White, Green** under the **Text and Links** option. Click **OK**.

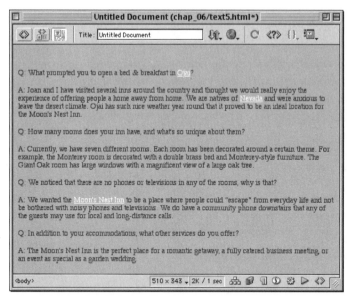

This is what the page looks like with the color scheme applied. If you do not like it, go ahead and choose another!

---

4. Choose **Commands > Set Color Scheme...** again. Pick a different combination of colors and click **Apply**. Knock yourself out! (In other words, enjoy yourself.)

---

5. When you're done having fun with colors, click **OK** and save and close the file.

NOTE | Can I Create My Own Color Schemes?

One question our students always ask is, "Can I create my own color schemes?" Well, the answer is yes and no. You can't do it through this dialog box; however, you can do it by using templates, and we will show you how in Chapter 11, "*Templates/Libraries*." We think it would be great if you could do it from the **Set Color Scheme Command** dialog box—maybe someday... ;-)

6. ————————Formatting Text in Tables

In this exercise you will learn to change a **table's** type, style, color, alignment, and more. In the old days, which weren't so long ago, you would have had to edit each individual cell, one at a time, and it could have taken hours to edit a large table. Not any more! With Dreamweaver, you can do it with a few deft clicks and drags.

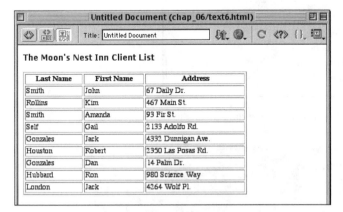

1. Open **text6.html**.

2. Click in cell 1 in row 2 ("**Smith**") and drag down to the last cell in the column ("**London**").
Note: You must be in Standard View to select a range of table cells.

3. In the Property Inspector, choose the **Font List** pop-up menu and select the **Verdana, Arial, Helvetica, sans-serif** option. All the text in the selected column will update before your eyes. If you've ever hand-coded this sort of thing, you will be gasping in delight right now.

4. Highlight cell 1 in row 1 ("**Last Name**") and drag across to cell 3 ("**Address**").

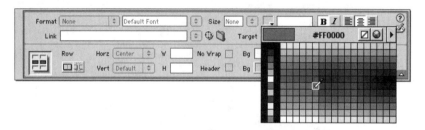

5. Using the Property Inspector's **Color Box**, change the text color to a bright red.

6. Press **F10** to see the HTML. Look at all those **FONT** tags! Aren't you glad you didn't have to insert each one by hand? Press **F10** again to close the **HTML** panel.

7. Save the file and leave it open for the next exercise.

7. ————————Repeat Last Action

Often you want to apply the same formatting to different blocks of text on your page. This is pretty easy to do if the words are adjacent. But what can you do when the words are in different places on the page? Well, Dreamweaver 4 has a new feature that will let you replay the last action you completed. This exercise will show you how to use that feature to format text easily and quickly.

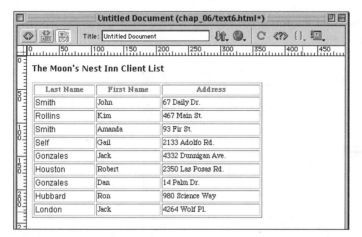

1. Make sure you have **text6.html** open from the previous exercise.

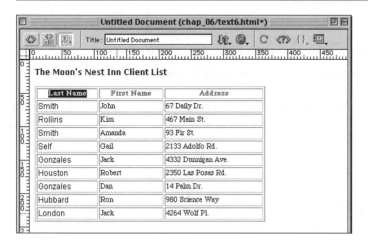

2. Select the text "**Last Name**" in the upper-left cell of the table.

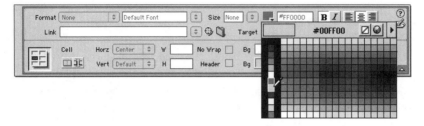

3. In the Property Inspector, click the **Text Color Box** and select a bright green. This will change the color of the selected text to green.

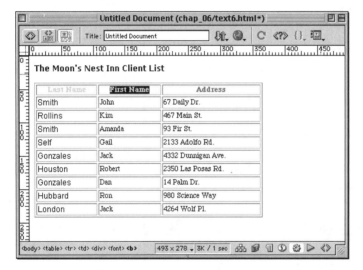

4. Select the words "**First Name**" in the cell to the right of "**Last Name**."

5. Choose **Edit > Repeat Font Color**. This will repeat the last step you completed, which in this instance was applying green to text. You can also use the keyboard shortcut for this menu command, **Cmd+Y** (Mac) or **Ctrl+Y** (Windows).

6. Select the word "**Address**" in the cell to the right of "**First Name**."

7. Choose **Edit > Repeat Font Color**. This will repeat the last step you completed, which in this instance was applying green to text.

8. In the second row, select the words "**67 Daily Dr.**"

9. Using the Property Inspector, click the **Italics** button to format the selected text with italics.

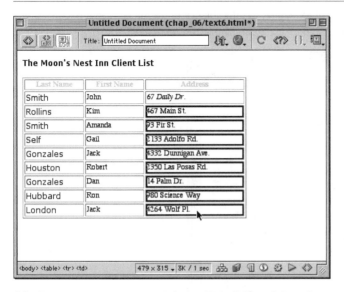

10. Click in the cell underneath ("**467 Main St.**") and drag down to the bottom of the column. This will select multiple blocks of text inside the table.

11. Choose **Edit > Repeat Apply Italic**. This will apply the italics to all of the text you have selected. Try formatting some more text and using this feature to repeat your actions.

12. When you are finished, save and close this file. You won't need it for the rest of this chapter.

TIP | Repeat Last Action

You might have noticed that the **Repeat** menu command changes as you perform different tasks. In the first example, it said **Repeat Font Color**, and in the second example it said **Repeat Apply Italic**. This type of dynamic menu is designed to give you feedback so you know what action you are going to repeat. This subtle addition makes this feature much easier to use.

8. —————————Applying HTML Styles

HTML Styles are a great way to quickly format text in a document. You can save specific text formatting attributes and then apply them to any text on a page or within an entire site. Unlike cascading style sheets, which require a 4.0+ browser, HTML Styles will work in earlier browsers, which makes them an attractive option. In this exercise, you will format some text and create an HTML Style based on that formatting. Then you will apply that formatting to other blocks of text on the same page. You will quickly begin to see how HTML Styles can help automate simple text formatting.

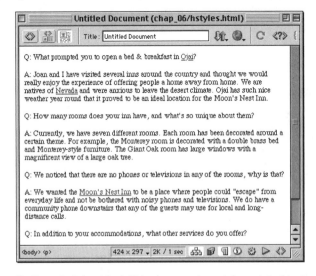

1. Open **hstyles.html**. This document contains a lot of text, and it provides a good example of when you might want to use HTML Styles to apply formatting across large amounts of text.

NOTE | The Library Folder and HTML Styles

As you begin working with HTML Styles, you might notice a small addition to your local root folder. When you create your first HTML Style, Dreamweaver automatically adds to your local root folder a Library folder, inside which you will see a **styles.xml** file. All of your HTML Styles will be saved in that file. The file is important to Dreamweaver's internal workings, but it is not necessary to upload it when you publish your site to the WWW. The folder does not hurt anything by residing in your Site window. In fact, it is a needed element to ensure that HTML Styles will work properly.

2. Make sure your **HTML Styles** panel is open. If not, choose **Window > HTML Styles**. The shortcut keys are **Cmd+F11** (Mac) **or Ctrl +F11** (Windows).

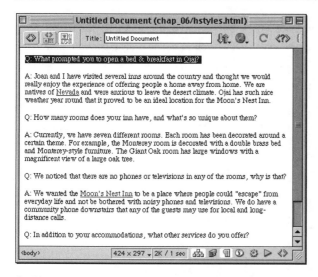

3. Click and drag to select the first line of text.

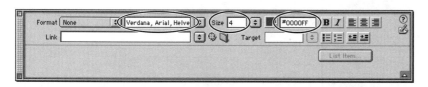

4. Using the Property Inspector, change the font to **Verdana, Arial, Helvetica, sans-serif**, the **Size** to **4**, and the color to blue (any color of blue is fine).

5. With your text still selected, click the **New Style** icon at the bottom of the **HTML Styles** panel. This will open the **Define HTML Style** dialog box, which allows you to define a style based on the selected text.

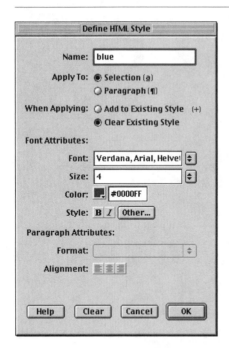

6. For **Name**, enter **blue**.

Tip: *We recommend that you name your HTML Styles relative to something that describes how they look. Because this text is formatted with a blue color, we named it* **blue**.

7. You can leave the rest of the options at their default values. Click **OK**. For an explanation of the options in the **Define HTML Style** dialog box, refer to the handy chart on page 155.

8. You should see your new style, **blue**, listed in the **HTML Styles** panel.

NOTE | Managing Your HTML Styles

As you begin working with HTML Styles, you will no doubt want to go back and make changes to them. You might also want to delete ones that are no longer needed, make duplicates, and/or apply your styles. You can complete all of these tasks from the pop-up menu in the HTML Styles panel. This handy menu is your quickest path to managing your HTML Styles. In addition, you can use the **New Style** and **Delete Style** buttons to make quick changes.

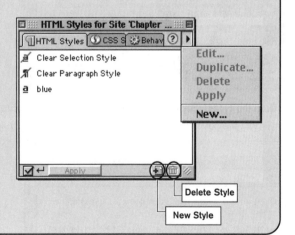

9. Select the third paragraph of text in the **hstyles.html** file by clicking and dragging.

10. In the **HTML Styles** panel, click the style named **blue**. This will format the selected text using the style you previously defined. Now, that is what we call quick formatting ;-).

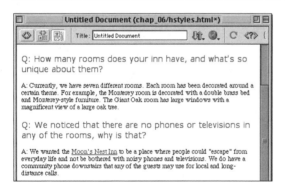

11. Go ahead and repeat this process for the fifth and seventh paragraphs. When you are finished, your page should look like the one above.

12. Now the only real way you are going to learn this is by doing it on your own. So, see if you can make another HTML Style and then apply that to the other paragraphs. Don't worry; if you get stuck, just refer to the beginning of this exercise.

13. When you are finished exploring this feature, save and close the file. It will not be needed for future exercises.

HTML Styles Options

Here is a quick definition for each of the options in the Define HTML Style dialog box:

HTML Styles	
Option	**Description**
Name:	This is the name of your style that appears in the HTML Styles panel.
Apply To: Selection	With this option selected, the formatting will only be applied to the text you have selected.
Apply To: Paragraph	With this option selected, the formatting will be applied to everything within the paragraph <p> tag.
When Applying: Add to Existing Style	With this option selected, the formatting will be added to any formatting that has already been applied to the selected text.
When Applying: Clear Existing Style:	With this option selected, the formatting will replace any formatting that has already been applied to the selected text.
Font Attributes: Font:	This allows you to specify what font is used with the style.
Font Attributes: Size:	This allows you to specify what font size is used with the style.
Font Attributes: Color:	This allows you to specify what font color is used with the style. You can choose from the swatch or enter in a hexadecimal value.
Font Attributes: Style:	This allows you to specify which font styles (bold, italic, etc.) are used with the style. The Other... pop-up menu displays less frequently used options.
Paragraph Attributes: Format	Only available if Apply To: Paragraph is selected, this lets you choose formatting options such as Heading 1, Paragraph, etc.
Paragraph Attributes: Alignment	Only available if Apply To: Paragraph is selected, this lets you specify the alignment settings for the style.

9. —————————**Character Entities**

Character Entities are text elements such as the © **Copyright** symbol, ® **Registered** symbol, and the ™ **Trademark** symbol. Inserting these types of common symbols used to be quite a bear to hand code in HTML. Luckily, Dreamweaver includes a **Characters** Object panel, which lets you easily add several of the most frequently used character entities. This exercise will show you how to use this easy feature.

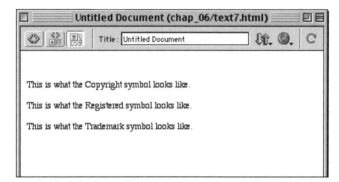

1. Open **text7.html** and click to the left of the capital "**C**" in "**Copyright**."

2. Open the **Characters** Object panel by clicking the arrow at the top of the **Objects** panel and choosing **Characters** from the pop-up menu.

3. Click the **Insert Copyright** icon. This will insert the copyright symbol where your cursor is placed.

4. Click to the left of the capital "R" in "**Registered**."

5. Click the **Insert Registered Trademark** icon. This will insert the registered trademark symbol where your cursor is placed.

6. Click to the left of the capital "T" in " **Trademark**."

7. Click the **Insert Trademark** icon. This will insert the trademark symbol where your cursor is placed.

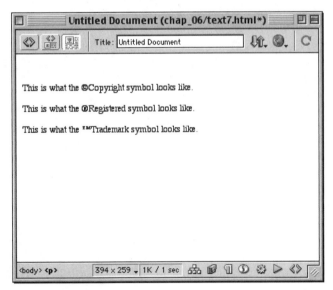

This is what your page should look like when you are finished.

8. Save and close the file.

Macintosh and Windows Character Entities

The chart below outlines some of the more frequently used character entities, their Macintosh and Windows keyboard shortcuts, and the HTML code for each. **Note:** If you are using Windows, you must use the keypad (not the keyboard) to enter the numbers or this will not work.

Character Entities in Dreamweaver			
Entity	**Macintosh**	**Windows**	**HTML**
©	Option+G	Alt+0169	&copy;
®	Option+R	Alt+0174	&reg;
™	Option+2	Alt+0153	&#153;

What is Flash Text?

It's pretty hard to be involved in Web design today and not hear the word "Flash"—it has become the buzzword du jour in the industry. Macromedia Flash is a vector-based drawing, animation, and interactivity program. It can be used to create something as simple as a button for a Web page or as complex as an entire video game that can be played on the Web. Flash uses a proprietary file format called SWF (pronounced SWIFF). Flash content that gets uploaded to the Web always ends in the .swf suffix.

In order to view Flash content on the Web, you must have the Flash plug-in installed in your browser. If you don't have this plug-in, you can download the it for free at **http://www.macromedia.com/software/ flashplayer/**

The **Flash Text** feature in Dreamweaver lets you create text and text rollovers for your Web pages, using any font on your system, in the SWF file format. Flash Text is a good feature for creating text rollovers and small lines of text, such as headlines for your body text. It is not searchable by search engines and should not be used for large bodies of text. Before you move on to the exercise and learn the nuances of Flash Text, here's a handy list that outlines some of the pros and cons of this feature.

Using Flash Text	
Pros	**Explanation**
Font Integrity	With Flash Text, you can use any font installed in your system and the visitors to your page don't need to have that font installed, as they do with regular HTML text. This gives you much more flexibility when you are designing your pages.
Text Rollovers	Creating text rollover usually requires that you use a separate image editing program to create the necessary images. With Flash Text, you can create text rollovers without ever leaving Dreamweaver.
Cons	**Explanation**
Plug-In Required	All Flash content on the Web requires a plug-in in order to be viewed properly. Flash Text is no different and requires that the Flash plug-in be installed in the browser.

10.——————————**Creating Flash Text**

In this exercise you'll get to use Flash Text—a new feature in Dreamweaver 4 that's easy to use. Flash Text lets you use any font you want without fear of whether the visitors to your site will have it installed in their system. It also lets you easily create rollovers without using any JavaScript. It's really easy to learn and use—read on and try it out to see what we mean!

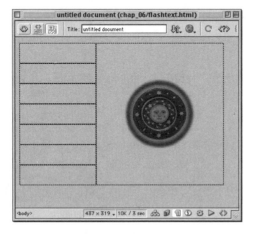

1. Open **flashtext.html**. This page contains a simple layout that was created using tables to control the position of the images on this page. You will learn more about tables in the next chapter, we promise!

2. Click inside the first cell at the top. This will place a blinking I-beam cursor in that cell and lets Dreamweaver know that this is where you want to place your object, which is Flash Text in this case.

WARNING | Flash Plug-In Required

One of the greatest advantages of Flash Text is that you can use any font you want and your end users do not need to have that font on their computer. Because of the way Flash works, it will embed the necessary font information in the SWF file. This is a plus anytime you want to use a unique font that most people don't have. But, there is a price to pay for this increase in design freedom. All Flash content on the Web requires that the end user have the Flash plug-in installed in their browser. According to Macromedia, about 330 million people have a version of the plug-in installed. That's a lot of people. We will talk about ways to detect if users have this plug-in installed in Chapter 14, "*Behaviors.*"

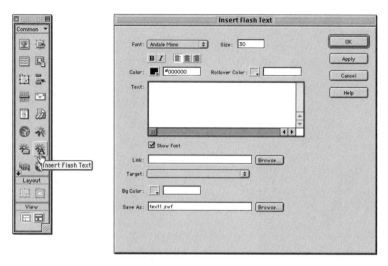

3. From the **Common** Objects panel, click the **Insert Flash Text** icon. This will open the Insert Flash Text dialog box.

4. Select a font for your text from the **Font** drop-down menu. You can use whatever font you want. We used Buglight, a great font designed by our friend Don Barnett. Don sells this font for $25 from his Web site at **http://www.donbarnett.com**. What a deal! If you don't have this font and have a favorite font of your own, use that one instead. The point is to use a font that isn't common to that many people.

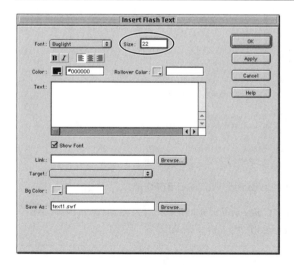

5. Set the **Size** option to **22**. This option sets the size of your text in points.

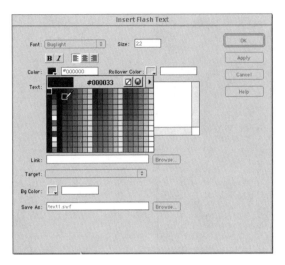

6. Click the **Color** option and select a dark blue color. We used **#000033**, but you are welcome to use any color you like.

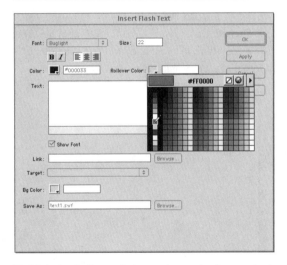

7. Click the **Rollover Color** option and select a shade of red. We used **#FF0000**.

Note: *You only have to set a color for the Rollover Color option if you want to create a text rollover. If you do not specify a color, no rollover will be created. It's that simple!*

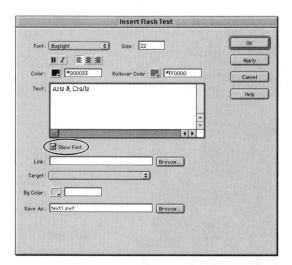

8. In the **Text** field type "**Arts & Crafts**." By default, the **Show Font** checkbox is checked, this will give you a preview of the text in the font you selected. If the font you selected is not being displayed, make sure the **Show Font** checkbox is checked.

Warning: *This dialog box will not give you a preview of the size you specified; the actual size can only be seen in the document itself. We do think that it would be nice if the next version let you preview the size of your text in this dialog box.*

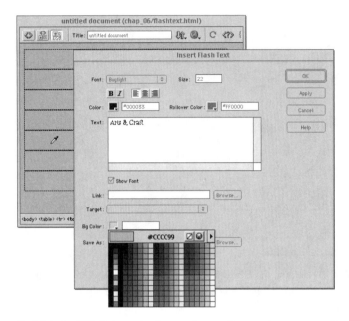

9. Click the **BG Color** color box and move the eyedropper over the background of the document window and click. This will let you sample and select the background color of your page so that it matches the background color of your Flash Text.

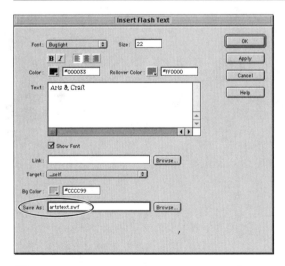

10. In the **Save As** field, type "**artstext.swf.**" Good file management principles dictate that you give your files names that reflect their content.

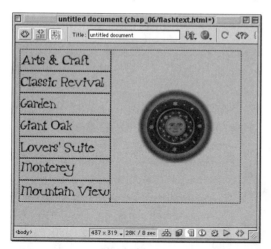

This is what your page should look like when you are done. Remember, we used the Buglight font, so yours will display whatever font you selected.

11. Repeat step 4 though 10 to create Flash Text for **"Classic Revival,"** **"Garden,"** **"Giant Oak,"** **"Lovers' Suite,"** **"Monterey,"** and **"Mountain Room."** When you're finished, your page should look similar to the one shown above.

12. Press **F12** to preview this page in a browser. Move your cursor over the text to preview the rollovers.

13. Select **File > Save** to save the changes to this file. You can close this file: you won't be working with it any longer.

Woo-hoo! You are done with another chapter; you can take a nap or keep on moving to the next chapter!

7.

Tables

| Creating, Sorting, and Modifying a Table |
| Using Tables to Align Images and Text |
| Assembling Seamless Images |
| Combining Pixels and Percentages |
| Inserting Tabular Data | Nested Tables and Borders |
| Rounded Corner Tables |

chap_7

Dreamweaver 4
H•O•T CD-ROM

HTML tables were introduced back in Netscape 1.2 as a way to display and organize charts and data. They were commonly used in financial or database spreadsheets because they provided defined columns and rows. The HTML engineers who created tables for the Web did not predict that developers would use tables to align images, not just to display text and numbers. You'll learn about both uses for tables: a formatting device for data, and a layout device for custom positioning of images.

This chapter shows you how to create custom tables, insert rows and columns, come up with color schemes, and handle formatting and sorting tasks. You will also learn how to use tables to align and position images. Tables are a critical item in your Web design toolbox, and Dreamweaver gives you great control and techniques for mastering them. Towards the end of this chapter, we will show you two table tricks: one for creating custom table borders and another for making rounded table corners. Don't worry, the fun doesn't stop there; you will get to work with tables some more in Chapter 8, "*Layout.*"

What Is a Table?

A table is a highly versatile feature in HTML. It can be useful for organizing data or positioning images. What does a table look like under the hood of Dreamweaver? It is comprised of a combination of HTML tags.

A table in the browser.

```
<table width="75%" border="1">
  <tr>
    <td> </td>
    <td> </td>
    <td> </td>
  </tr>
  <tr>
    <td> </td>
    <td> </td>
    <td> </td>
  </tr>
  <tr>
    <td> </td>
    <td> </td>
    <td> </td>
  </tr>
</table>
```

*Here's the HTML for the table above. Tables always begin with a **table** tag. The **width** and **border** elements are attributes of the **<table>** tag. **<tr>** stands for Table **R**ow, and **<td>** stands for Table **D**ata.*

Anatomy of a Table			
	Column		
Row			
			Cell

A table contains rows, columns, and cells. If these terms are unfamiliar to you, this diagram should help.

I. ————Changing the Border of a Table

This first exercise helps you build your table formatting skills on a premade table. It also alerts you to a common HTML problem relating to empty table cells. You see, even if a table cell is empty, you've got to put something in it to preserve the table formatting. That "something" can be a single-pixel transparent GIF. This is a small image file that has been set to be fully transparent, or invisible. It serves as a placeholder to keep the table formatting from collapsing with empty cells. You'll learn how to add a transparent GIF in a few moments, once you get going with this exercise.

1. Copy **chap_07** to your hard drive. Define your site for Chapter 7 using the **chap_07** folder as the local root folder. If you need a refresher on this process, visit Exercise 1 in Chapter 3, *"Site Control."*

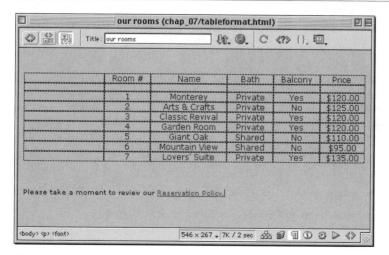

2. Open **tableformat.html**. The dotted lines that you see around each cell are just formatting guides, and will not show up inside the browser.

3. Click **F12** to preview this file in your Web browser. Notice how the dotted lines don't appear in the browser? In this file, the **border** setting was changed to **0** in order to make the formatting guides disappear, because Dreamweaver uses a default setting of **1** for table borders. Next you'll learn how to control the weight of the lines with the **border** property.

4. Return to Dreamweaver and select the entire table. You can do this by using the **Tag Selector** at the bottom left of the document window. Click your mouse anywhere inside the table. You should see the word **<table>** appear as a Tag Selector. Click the **<table>** element in the Tag Selector and the entire table should become selected.

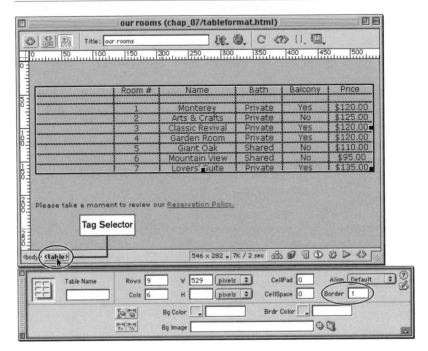

5. With the table selected, in the Property Inspector enter **Border: 1**.

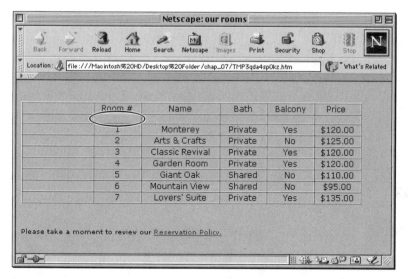

6. Click **F12** to preview the results. See how the border value affected the appearance? This is one of the many controls that you have over the appearance of tables.

Note: Some browsers display the cell underneath "Room #" in a different way from the other table cells. In every other row there is content, but the row without content looks different, or "bloated" because it is empty. The following steps will show you how to correct this problem.

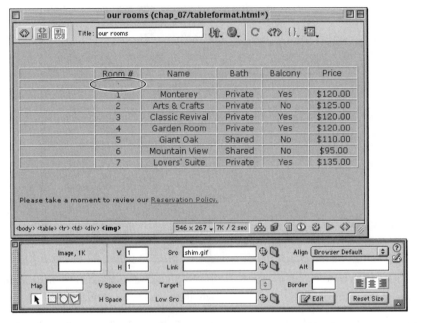

7. In Dreamweaver, click inside the cell below the "**Room #**" cell (column 2, row 2). Choose **Insert > Image**, browse to **shim.gif** located inside the **chap_07** folder, and click **Open**. Be careful to deselect the image after you insert it. If you hit **Return** or **Enter** with it selected, it will disappear!

The file that you just inserted (shim.gif), contains a single-pixel transparent GIF, which is invisible to your end user. By placing it inside the empty table cell, you fool the browser into thinking there is content, even though your audience will never see that content. The sole purpose of inserting the graphic is to fix the appearance of the empty table cell.

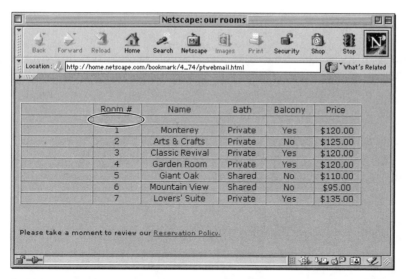

8. Choose **File > Save** to save the changes to the border. Click **F12** to preview the results. See, no more funky pixels, Mom! The empty cell looks like every other cell, which is just the way it should look! Return to Dreamweaver and leave this document open for Exercise 2.

> ### NOTE | What Is a Transparent GIF?
>
> The GIF file format supports a feature called transparency, which is a term for a mask. Transparency makes it possible to specify areas in a GIF graphic to disappear in a Web browser. A single-pixel transparent GIF is a graphic that only contains a single pixel that has been instructed to disappear. You can create transparent GIF files in Fireworks, Photoshop, ImageReady, or a host of other graphics applications. Methods for making them vary in each program, so consult the user manual of whichever graphics application you own. If you like, you can store the file shim.gif for Web projects other than this book, and that way you will always have a single-pixel transparent GIF on hand.
>
> **Note:** Shim is a term used in carpentry to hold things in place. You may name your single-pixel transparent GIF anything you like. Shim was just a name we chose.

2. ———Sorting the Table

In version 2.0, Macromedia introduced the ability to sort the content of tables both alphabetically and numerically in Dreamweaver. Before this feature existed, if you wanted to sort a table, you had to copy and paste each row or column manually. Thankfully, sorting table content in Dreamweaver is only a simple dialog box away.

1. The document **tableformat.html** should still be open. If not, go ahead and open it again.

2. Make sure that the table is selected and choose **Commands > Sort Table...** The **Sort Table** dialog box will open.

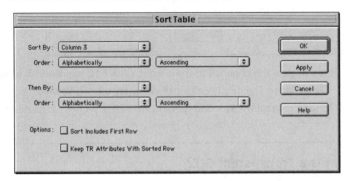

3. Change the settings to **Sort By: Column 3, Order: Alphabetically Ascending**. Click **OK**.

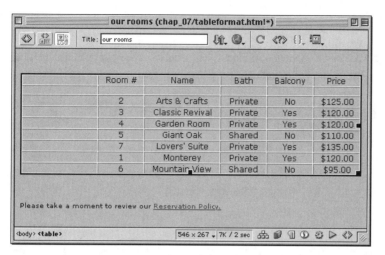

Notice that the file has been sorted differently from when you first opened it? The third column is now in alphabetical order. You can arrange table contents through this kind of command. Try doing this manually, and you'll really appreciate this feature!

4. Save the file and keep it open for the next exercise.

The Sort Table Dialog Box

The **Sort Table** dialog box has a variety of options to help you modify the appearance of tables. See the chart below for an explanation of all its features:

Sorting Features	
Feature	**Definition**
Sort By	Use this option to select which column you would like to use to sort the table.
Order	Use these two pull-down menus to choose Alphabetically or Numerically and Ascending or Descending.
Then By	Use this option to sort multiple columns in your table.
Options: Sort Includes	If this box is checked, the first row in your table will be sorted. This option is off by default because most often the first row is used as a header for the table.
Options: Keep TR Attributes	If this box is checked and a row is moved around due to sorting, all the attributes for that row will also move (i.e. color, font, etc.). **<tr>** stands for **T**able **R**ow in HTML.

Changing the Color Scheme

Next on the list of table building skills is learning how to apply color formatting. This exercise will show off Dreamweaver's color-picking features for tables. Dreamweaver offers a variety of ways to get the job done. When it comes to coloring your tables, you may use Dreamweaver's automatic color features or set whatever custom colors you desire.

1. With **tableformat.html** still open from the last exercise, make sure that the table is selected. Choose **Commands > Format Table...** to open the **Format Table** dialog box.

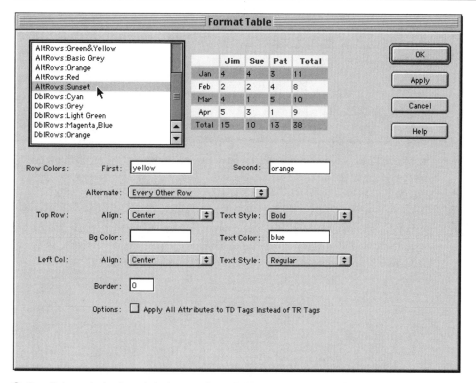

2. Scroll through the list of choices and try clicking some of them. See how the table preview in the middle changes colors as you click on different formatting schemes? These color combinations are part of Dreamweaver and can be applied to any table. Select **AltRows: Sunset** and click **OK**.

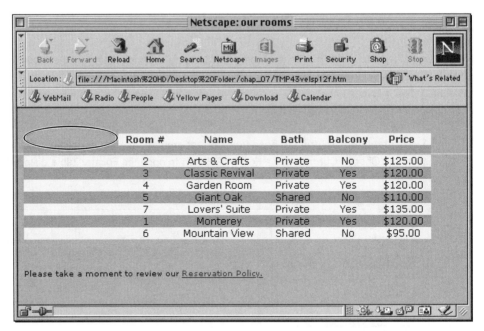

3. Click **F12** to preview the results. If you are using Netscape, the top left row will be missing color information. You can correct this by once again inserting **shim.gif** in the offending cell.

4. Return to Dreamweaver. Click inside the top left cell. Choose **Insert > Image**, browse to **shim.gif**, and click **Open**. There's that teeny single pixel again, so teeny yet so capable, because when you preview in your browser, the mistake is corrected.

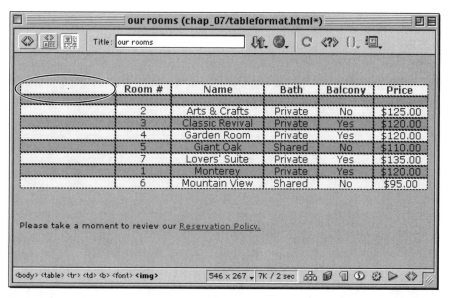

5. Click **F12** to preview the results. The table should appear as it does in the above image, nice and colorful all the way to its top-left corner.

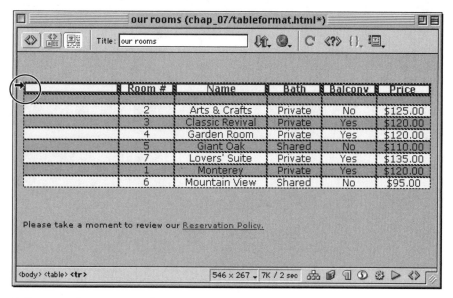

6. Return to Dreamweaver. Select the top row by positioning your mouse in the left-hand corner of the row—until it becomes an arrow—and click once, to select the whole row.

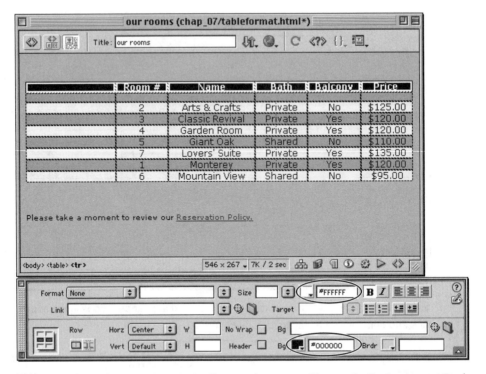

7. With the top row selected, go to the Property Inspector. Change the **Text** color and **Bg** (as in background) color, as shown above. You can enter the values, or click the color well to the left of the values, to select colors from the built-in Dreamweaver color box.

8. Save your changes and close this document. Congrats, you've just combined automatic color features and custom color settings in one table.

NOTE | An Alternative to Transparent GIFs

The last exercise showed you how to insert transparent GIF files to correct empty table cells, but there is another way to do this as well. If you change your Objects panel to show Characters, you can insert a non-breaking space ** ** tag into an empty cell, and then the table will render correctly.

The advantage to transparent GIF files is the fact that their **WIDTH** and **HEIGHT** attributes can be stretched to move table cells around (as you will learn first-hand in Exercise 5). If all you want to do is insert content, and you don't care about changing the shape of an empty table cell, insert ** ** and it will work just as well as a single-pixel transparent GIF.

Creating and Modifying a Table

This exercise will show you how to create your own table from scratch and how to modify it. You will learn to work with a combination of the **Insert Table** object, the **Modify > Table** menu, and the Property Inspector. You won't be building a finished page yet. Instead, you'll have a chance to explore many of the different table options first.

1. If an untitled document isn't already open, choose **File > New**. Save this file into the **chap_07** folder and name it **firsttable.html. Note**: Windows users can create new documents from the Site window by selecting **File > New Window**.

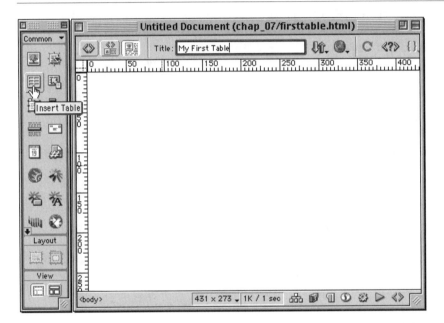

2. Enter **Title: My First Table**. Click the **Insert Table** object in the **Common Objects** panel or choose **Insert > Table**. The **Insert Table** dialog box will appear.

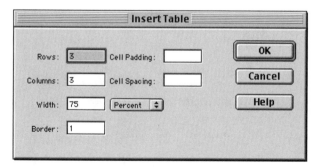

3. Make sure your settings match the settings above, then click **OK**.

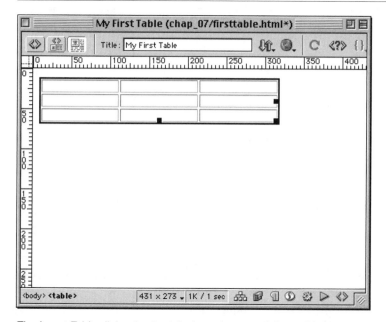

The Insert Table dialog box's default settings result in a table that is three rows high and three columns wide.

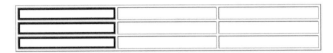

4. Select the left column, by clicking your mouse inside the top-left cell and dragging down to the bottom row with your mouse button still depressed.

5. Choose **Modify > Table > Merge Cells.** This will result in a table with three columns, with the left column made of only one cell and the other two columns containing three rows of cells.

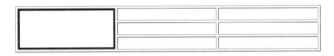

6. Select the middle row by clicking your mouse inside the left-middle cell and dragging over to the right-middle cell while leaving your mouse depressed.

7. In the Property Inspector, click the **Merge Cells** button. This achieves the same effect as the Modify menu did in Step 5. As with many things in Dreamweaver, there are multiple ways to accomplish the same task. We prefer to use the Property Inspector to merge cells, though you may prefer to use the Modify menu method.

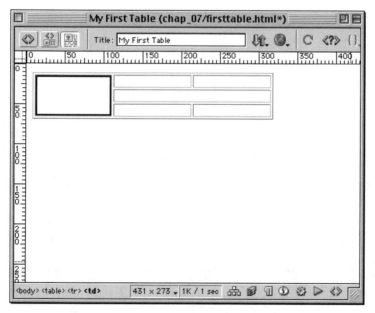

8. Put your cursor inside the left cell and click the **<td>** element on the **Tag Selector** at the bottom of the document (**<td>** stands for Table Data).

Just as you can merge cells in rows and columns, you can also add and delete entire rows and columns. However, selecting rows and columns can be tricky at times. For example, to select the column on the far left, you will find that you can no longer click and drag inside it because now it is only a single cell.

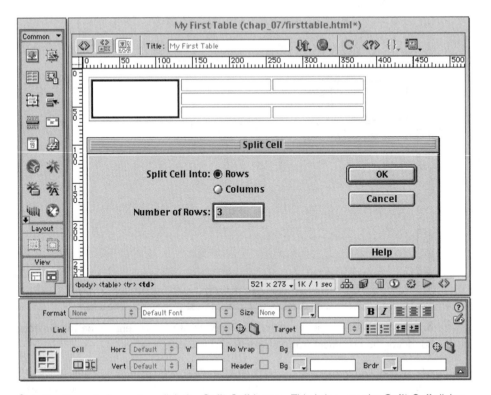

9. In the Property Inspector, click the **Split Cell** button. This brings up the **Split Cell** dialog box. Enter **3**, if it's not already entered, and make sure the **Rows** radio button is selected, then click **OK**.

You just added back to this table the three cells that you merged in Step 5. See how flexible this table editor is?

10. To delete the left column completely, select it again and choose **Edit > Cut**. The shortcut keys for this are **Cmd+X** (Mac) and **Ctrl+X** (Windows). You can delete rows or columns by selecting them and cutting them out at any time. **Note:** Sometimes (and we're not sure why), **Cut** will not work, but hitting your **Delete** key will.

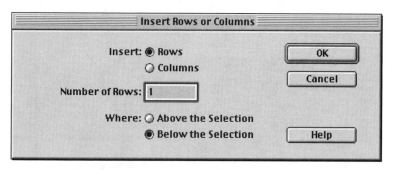

11. Add a new row by clicking inside the upper-right cell and choosing **Modify > Table > Insert Rows or Columns...** Select Insert: **Rows, Number of Rows: 1** and **Where: Below the Selection**. Click **OK.**

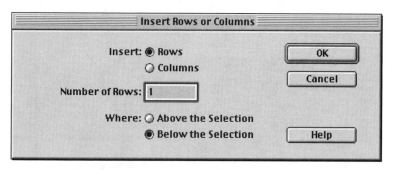

12. Here are the results of that action. You can also select other options, of course. Dreamweaver offers a lot of flexibility when it comes to formatting tables, which you'll likely find useful for the variety of table-related tasks that will arise over the course of your future Web-design projects. **Save** and close the file.

NOTE | Contextual Table Menus

Time and again, Dreamweaver lets you accomplish the same task in many different ways. For example, Exercise 4 showed you how to merge and split cells using the **Modify > Table** menu or the Property Inspector. Alternately, you could select the column as you did in Step 8 and **Ctrl+Click** (Mac) or **right-click** (Windows) to access the **Contextual** menu. There you will a handy list of everything you'd ever want to do to a table.

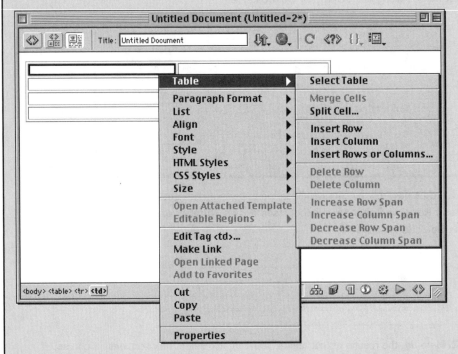

You can use any of three ways to access this same information (Property Inspector, Modify menu, or contextual menu), depending on your preference.

5. ———————Aligning Images and Text with Tables

Many people use tables to align images and text because they offer the ability to position artwork freely on a page. This next exercise will show you how to work with a page layout and modify the alignment through adjusting the height and width of table rows and columns.

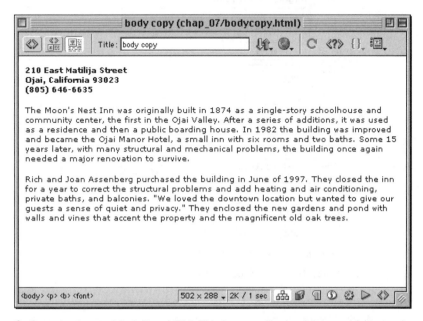

1. Open **bodycopy.html**. Press **F12**. This is a text file that has no table formatting. See how the width of the text within the document extends to the width of the browser? This is default alignment behavior, and the problem with it is that it can create very wide layouts on large monitors.

Most design experts agree that column widths should be limited in order to make reading text easier. You don't see books that are 21 inches across with text stretching side-to-side. That's because it's hard for people to read lines of text that extend more than 3–4 inches across the screen. In order to create a narrower column, you will need to learn how to create a table with fixed-pixel widths.

2. Return to Dreamweaver. Create a new document by choosing **File > New**. Save this file into the **chap_07** folder and name it **align.html**.

```
┌─────────────────────────────────────────────────────────────┐
│                       Page Properties                         │
│                                                               │
│         Title: [Alignment with Tables        ]    [   OK   ]  │
│                                                               │
│  Background Image: [about_bg.jpg     ] [ Browse... ] [ Apply ]│
│                                                               │
│     Background: [▢] [#FFFFFF ]                    [ Cancel ]  │
│                                                               │
│          Text: [▢][    ]   Visited Links: [▢][    ]           │
│                                                               │
│         Links: [▢][    ]    Active Links: [▢][    ]           │
│                                                               │
│    Left Margin: [    ]      Margin Width: [    ]              │
│                                                               │
│     Top Margin: [    ]     Margin Height: [    ]              │
│                                                               │
│ Document Encoding: [Western (Latin1)    ◆] [ Reload ]         │
│                                                               │
│  Tracing Image: [                    ]     [ Browse... ]      │
│                                                               │
│          Image ═══════════════════◁ 100%                     │
│              Transparent        Opaque                        │
│                                                               │
│ Document Folder: Macintosh HD:Desktop Folder:chap_07:         │
│                                                               │
│    Site Folder: Macintosh HD:Desktop Folder:chap_07:  [ Help ]│
└─────────────────────────────────────────────────────────────┘
```

3. Choose **Modify > Page Properties** and enter **Title: Alignment With Tables**. Click **Browse...** to the right of the **Background Image** field and browse to **about_bg.jpg**. Click **Open**. You will be returned to the **Page Properties** dialog box. Click **OK**.

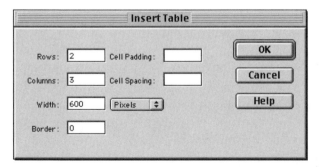

4. Choose **Insert > Table** and change the settings to **Rows: 2, Columns: 3, Width: 600 Pixels** (make sure you change this to **Pixels**, not **Percent**), **Border: 0**. Click **OK**.

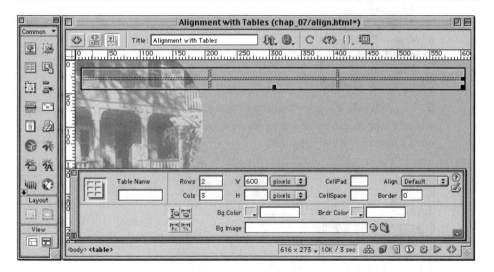

The result of those settings should look like this. You're laying the framework for a fixed-pixel table that is suitable for aligning objects.

5. Choose **Window > bodycopy.html** (located at the bottom of the Window menu, which lists all the open documents). If for some reason **bodycopy.html** is not open, go ahead and open it from the Site window (F8).

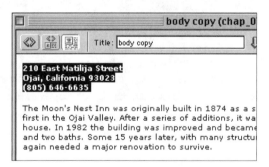

6. Select and **copy** just the text that contains the address information.

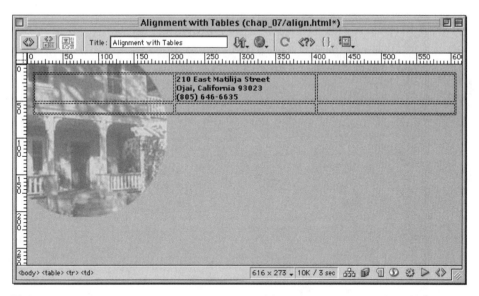

7. Choose **Window > align.html** to bring forth the other open document. Click inside **column 2**, **row 1** and paste.

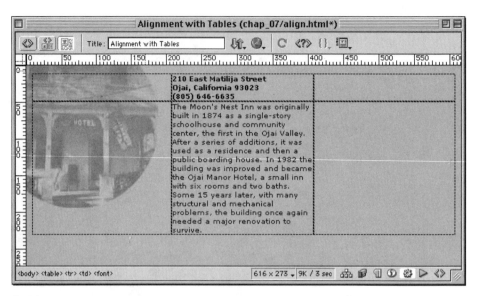

8. Switch back to the **bodycopy.html** document by choosing **Window > bodycopy.html**. You could also go back and forth between these two documents by clicking them on the screen if you have a large enough monitor. Select and copy the first paragraph. Switch back to the document with the table in it by choosing **Window > align.html**. Click inside **column 2**, **row 2** and paste.

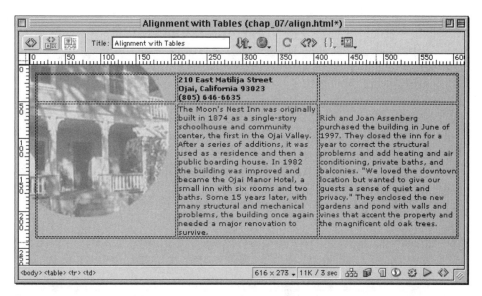

9. Switch between the two documents, using the **Window** menu, to copy and paste the second paragraph into column 3, row 2 of the table, as shown above. **Close bodycopy.html.** You're finished with copying and pasting.

Notice that the top of column 2, row 2 does not align with the top of column 3, row 2? This is an example of default table formatting, which vertically centers the text in a table cell unless otherwise instructed. In order to fix this, you'll need to adjust the table-alignment settings. The next step will show you how.

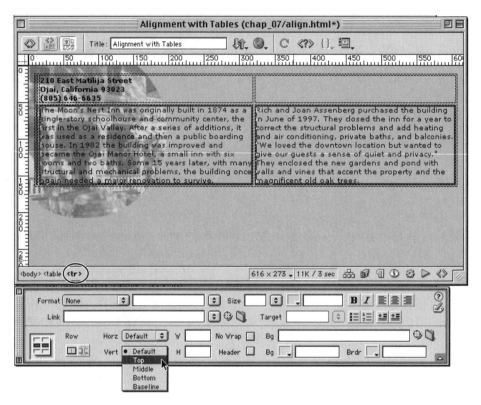

10. Click anywhere in the second row of the table. Click the **<tr>** tag in the Tag Selector to select the entire second row. Change the **Property Inspector's Vert** setting to **Top**. As you can see, this corrects the irregular alignment, but it also collapses the empty cell on the far left.

Empty cells in Dreamweaver and in browsers are certainly problematic, aren't they? The only solution is to insert a transparent GIF again, which you'll do in the following step.

11. If your rulers aren't visible, choose **View > Rulers > Show**. The visible ruler helps you see the page's pixel dimensions.

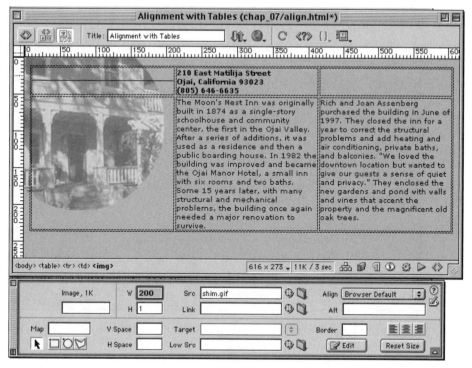

12. Click inside the cell with the address and press **Shift+Tab**. This will move your cursor into the collapsed cell. Choose **Insert > Image**, and browse to **shim.gif**, then click **Open**. The **shim.gif** will be selected, and you should see its settings inside the Property Inspector. **Hint:** If the **shim.gif** accidentally gets deselected, click inside its table cell and select the **<img>** element in the Tag Selector to reselect it. In the Property Inspector enter **W: 200**. This should stretch the single-pixel GIF to hold the left-hand cell's dimension open.

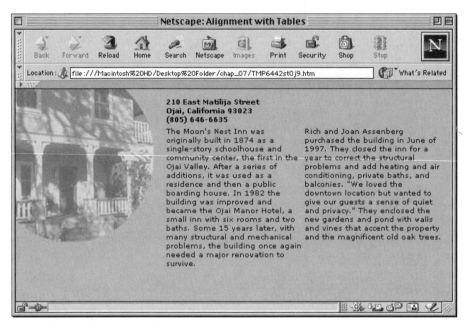

13. Press **F12** to preview the results. This layout is starting to look good, but the space between the table cells feels a little cramped, doesn't it?

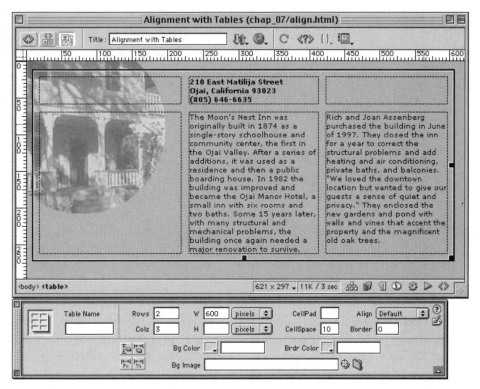

14. Return to Dreamweaver and select the table by clicking anywhere inside it and choosing the **<table>** element inside the Tag Selector. In the Property Inspector, enter **CellSpace: 10**. As you will see, CellSpace controls the amount of space between cells. Click **F12** to preview the results.

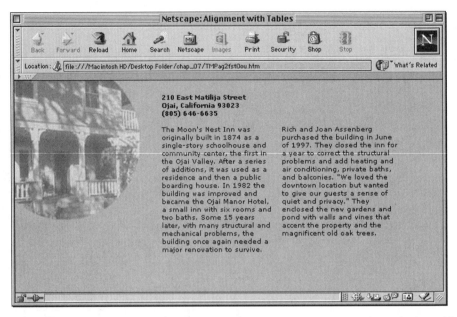

Here are the results of changing the CellSpace attribute. Want to experiment further with this file? Try changing the dimensions of the shim.gif or the CellSpace or CellPad settings. You are in total control over the alignment of this page. By leaving the rulers turned on, you can get a better idea of what values to enter into the settings.

15. Save and close all the open documents before you begin the next exercise.

NOTE | Using Rulers

Rulers in Dreamweaver are helpful for getting a sense of scale. You can access rulers by choosing **View > Rulers > Show**.

NOTE | Fixed Pixels Versus Percentages in Tables

You can size your tables in two ways: by percentages or by pixels. A percentage-based table will stretch with the width of the browser, meaning that its size will vary depending on the shape of the browser window. If you specify that a table uses a width of 75%, for example, it will stretch to fill three-fourths of the horizontal space regardless of the browser window size. This can be a great thing in some cases, but not in others. When you want to restrict the size of a table, regardless of the browser window size, pixel-based tables are the way to go. When you want the table to stretch to the size of the browser window, percentage-based tables are best. To complicate matters, it's possible to nest a pixel-based table inside a percentage-based table or vice versa. By the time you've finished the exercises in this chapter, you will have some concrete examples as to why and when to choose which type of table, and how to combine the two for more complex formatting.

NOTE | CellPad Versus CellSpace

Using CellPad and CellSpace settings alters the amount of space between table cells. CellPad adds room inside the cell, whereas CellSpace adds to the border width. When used with table borders set to **0**, CellSpace and/or CellPad achieve the identical result, by interjecting more space between the data and the edge of each cell.

The top table uses neither CellPad nor CellSpace, the middle table uses a CellPad setting of **10**, and the bottom table uses a CellSpace setting of **10**.

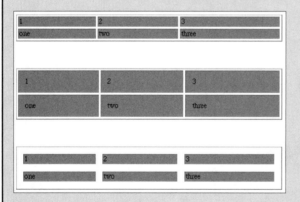

With colored table cells, the differences between CellPad (middle) and CellSpace (bottom) are more noticeable.

6. _____ Percentage-Based Table Alignment

In the last exercise, you worked with a table that was fixed at 600 pixels. When you want to control your alignment precisely, fixed pixels are the way to go. There's another way to achieve alignment with tables that is based on percentages. This next exercise will use percentage-based tables to ensure that the page elements will be centered on any size browser window.

1. Create a new document and save it into the **chap_07** folder and name it **center.html**.

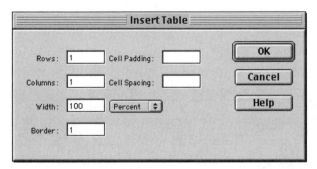

2. Choose **Insert > Table** and change the settings to **Rows: 1, Columns: 1, Width: 100 Percent, Border: 1**. For this exercise to work, it's imperative that the width be set to Percent and not Pixels. Click **OK**.

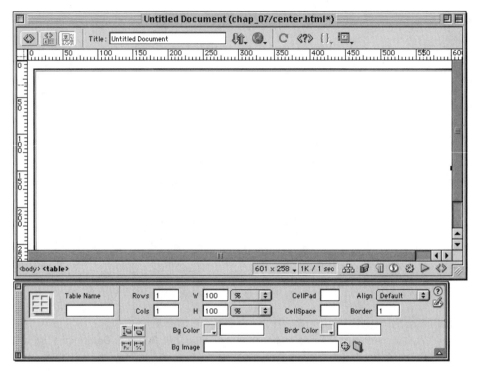

3. Select the **<table>** tag at the bottom of the document and change the Property Inspector's height setting (**H**) to **100%**. The Property Inspector's width setting (**W**) should already be set to **100%**. Press **F12** to preview this page in a browser.

Note: *When you press F12 to preview this page right now, you can move the browser window size around and you'll see the table stretch. What's happening? You specified that the width and height of this table would fill 100% of the browser's shape, regardless of its size. This is critical to the success of this exercise, because you are now going to align an image to this table, and the image will be aligned in relationship to the size of the browser, regardless of its shape.*

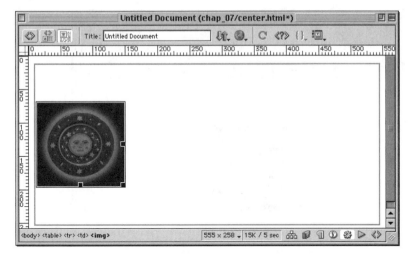

4. Return to Dreamweaver. Click inside the giant table cell. Choose **Insert > Image**, browse to **tilelogo4.jpg**, and click **Open**.

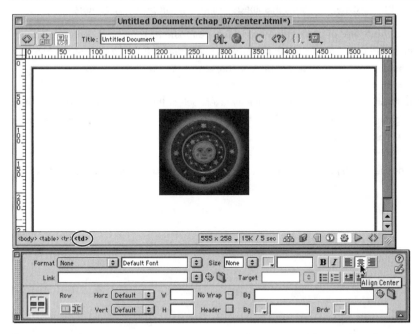

5. In the Tag Selector, click on the **<td>** tag to select the table cell, and then in the Property Inspector click the **Align Center** button. The image will pop into the center of the large table.

6. Press **F12** to preview and try stretching the browser to different positions. No matter how you set the browser window, this image will always be perfectly centered!

This is the power of percentage-based table alignment. You could center an image to a pixel-based table, but because the table wouldn't stretch to the size of the browser window, the image would center to the table's shape, not the browser's shape.

7. To finish the effect, return to Dreamweaver. Select the table by clicking inside it and highlighting the **<table> Tag Selector**. Change the Property Inspector **Border** setting to **0**. This will turn off the border.

8. Choose **Modify > Page Properties**, enter **Background: #000033**, and click **OK**.

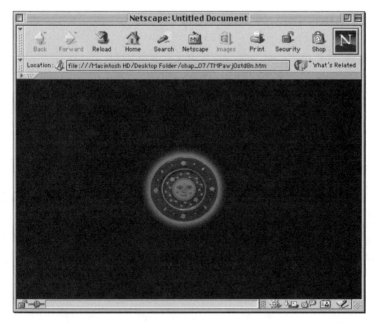

9. Press **F12** to see the results. People who view this page will never know you used a table, yet the image will always be centered.

What's so great about hiding the table from viewers? Because you've just created a layout that is centered regardless of the size or shape of the browser window, and people who view this page won't be distracted by a table border at the edge of the browser screen.

10. Return to Dreamweaver. Save and close this file.

Seamless Image Assembly

If you've looked around the Web much, you've probably noticed that tables are sometimes used to assemble multiple images so that they look like a single image. Why would anyone want to do this? Tables can ensure that artwork stays aligned and grouped, whereas HTML without tables can be subject to movement depending on the size of the browser window. This exercise will show you how to reassemble multiple images into a pixel-based table so that they won't be misaligned.

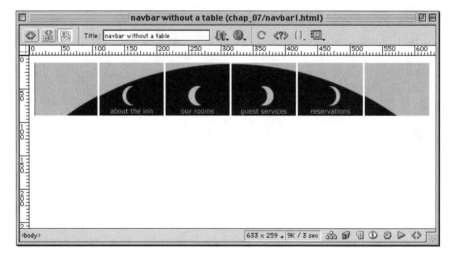

1. Open **navbar1.html**. Notice the gaps between each of the images? This can be the result of putting images next to each other without a table.

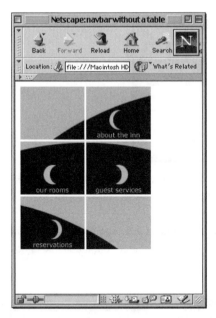

2. Press **F12** to preview this document, then make your browser window smaller. Notice how the row of images gets disrupted? By placing them inside a table, they will become grouped, and won't be able to move around like this.

3. Return to Dreamweaver. Click each image once (don't double-click!), and you'll see its dimensions inside the Property Inspector. You have six images, which are each 100 pixels wide. If you add that number together, it's 600, so you'll need to create a 600-pixel-wide table in order to assemble these as one seamless-looking image.

4. Position your cursor after the last image and hit the **Return** or **Enter** key, so your insertion cursor appears below the images on the screen and on the left.

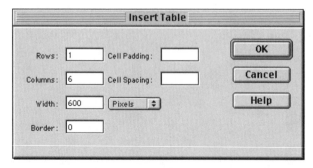

5. Choose **Insert > Table** and change the settings to **Rows: 1**, **Columns: 6**, **Width: 600 Pixels** (not Percent!), **Border: 0**. Click **OK**.

6. Click inside the far-left bottom cell, and choose **Insert > Image**. Browse to **navbar1.gif** and click **Open**. The table formatting between cells has shifted, but the image is now inside the appropriate cell.

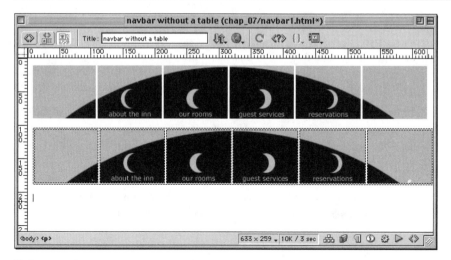

7. Once you insert all the other images into the appropriate cells, the table should appear like this. The names of the files, from left to right, are: **navbar1.gif**, **navbar2.gif**, **navbar3.gif**, **navbar4.gif**, **navbar5.gif**, and **navbar6.gif**.

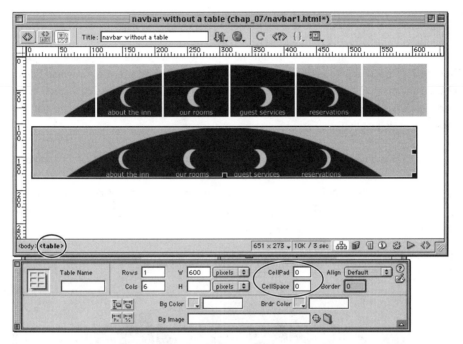

8. To get rid of the gaps between the cells, select the entire table by clicking inside any cell and selecting the **<table>** Tag Selector. Once you've selected it, change the Property Inspector setting to read **CellPad: 0** and **CellSpace: 0.** The table will come together seamlessly.

9. Press **F12** to preview your seamless table. Now that is what a navigation bar ought to look like!

10. Save this file and leave it open for the next exercise.

8. ——————Combining Pixels and Percentages

This next exercise demonstrates how to combine a pixel-accurate table, like the one you just created in Exercise 7, with a percentage-based table like you created in Exercise 6. Why would this be important? Let's say that you had a navigation bar, like the one you just built, that you wanted to be center aligned regardless of whether it was seen on a small or large monitor. Combining the last two techniques lets you do just that.

1. Create a new document and save it into the **chap_07 folder** and name it **navbar2.html**.

2. Choose **Insert > Table** and change the settings to **Rows: 1**, **Columns: 1**, **Width: 100 Percent** (not Pixels!), **Border: 0**. Click **OK**. By using percent for width, the table will always be horizontally centered on the page.

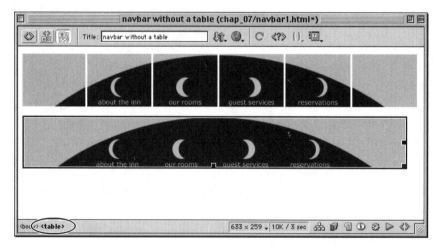

3. Return to **navbar1.html** (use the **Window** menu and look at the bottom to locate it) and select the bottom table. Remember that you can click anywhere in the table to access the Tag Selector in order to select it. With the table selected, choose **Edit > Copy**.

4. Now switch over to **navbar2.html** and click inside the centered table. Choose **Edit > Paste**.

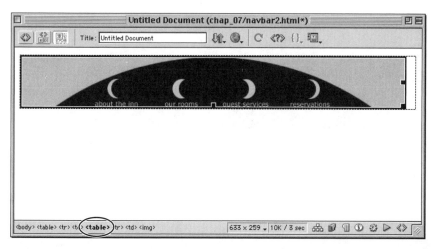

5. Select the table that you just pasted. Again, if you click inside it you can use the **<table>** Tag Selector to select it. Notice there are two **<table>** tags in the Tag Selector now. This happens because you've got one table nested inside another.

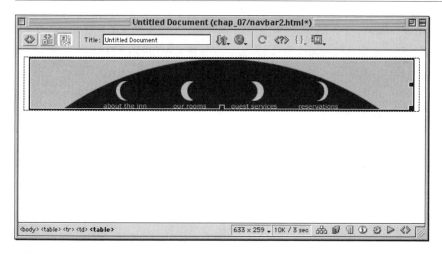

6. With the nested (navigation bar) table selected, change the Property Inspector **Align** setting to **Center**.

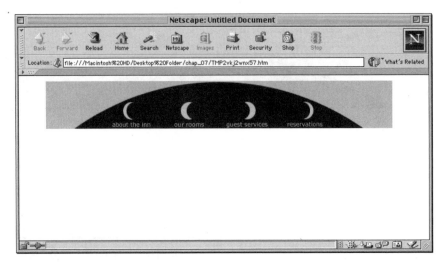

7. Preview in the browser (**F12**), and you should see that the navigation bar remains centered regardless of how wide you drag your browser window out. Congratulations again, you've just made a nested table using a combination of pixels and percentages. Sounds impressive, but even better than that—it's useful!

8. Return to Dreamweaver. Save and close the **navbar1.html** and **navbar2.html** files.

9. ——————Inserting Tab-Delimited Data

As you just learned, creating tables from scratch can be quite a chore. So anything that helps stream-
line the process is a dream. Dreamweaver gives you the ability to easily insert delimited text files. This
is great for people who use Excel and other office applications, because now it's simple to get that
data into Dreamweaver. This exercise will show you how to import a delimited text file into a table.

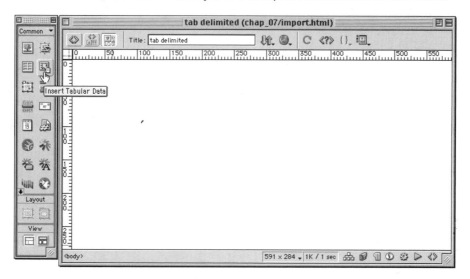

1. Open **import.html**. This is just a blank file that we created for you. Click the **Insert
Tabular Data** object in the **Common Objects** panel to open the **Insert Tabular Data**
dialog box.

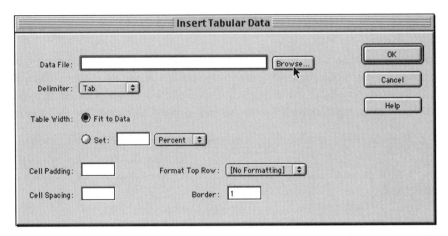

2. Click **Browse…** and navigate to **tabdelimited.txt** located inside the **chap_07** folder. Click **OK** to select that file.

Insert Tabular Data Settings

You won't be changing most of the default settings in this exercise, but you should know what those options mean. Here's a handy chart that explains what you can do in the **Insert Tabular Data Settings** dialog box.

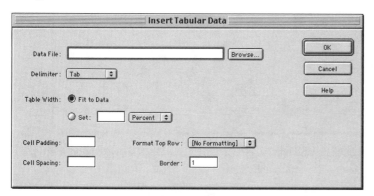

Insert Tabular Data Settings	
Setting	**Function**
Data File	Use this option to browse to the delimited file on your hard drive.
Delimiter	This option specifies the type of Delimiter used in the imported file, such as tabs or commas.
Table Width: Fit to Data	This option will create a table large enough to fit the data in the imported file.
Table Width: Set	This option lets you specify how wide to make the table that holds the imported data. You can choose either percent or pixel widths.
Cell Padding	Controls the CellPad value for the table that holds the imported data.
Cell Spacing	Controls the CellSpace value for the table that holds the imported data.
Format Top Row	You can apply a number of different formatting options to the first row of data in your table.
Border	Controls the table's border width.

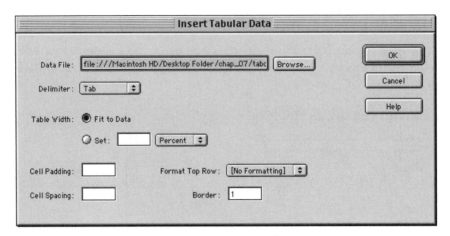

3. Leave the rest of the settings at their default settings. Click **OK**. This will import the data into Dreamweaver inside a custom table.

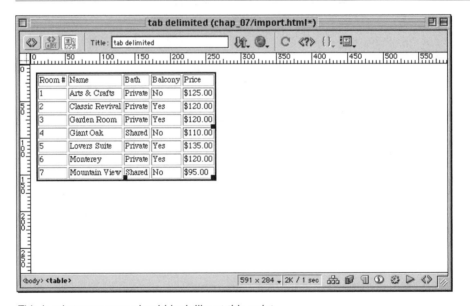

This is what your page should look like at this point.

4. Save and leave this file open for the next exercise.

IO. _____ Nested Tables and Borders

As you learned earlier, it is possible to modify the size and appearance of table borders through changing the width and border in the Property Inspector. In this exercise, we will show you how produce an
outline appearance around the border of the table. This technique isn't accomplished through the
Property Inspector; it's created instead through nesting tables. If you like this technique, don't forget to
share this trick with someone you know. ;-)

The table on the left uses standard table properties to create its appearance. The table on the right
uses nested tables to create the appearance of a stroked outline around the border of the cells and
outer table. This technique offers an attractive alternative to the boring old tables we see everywhere.

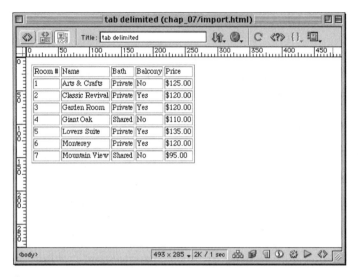

1. The file from the previous exercise should be open, if it's not, go ahead and open the **import.html** file located inside the **chap_07** folder.

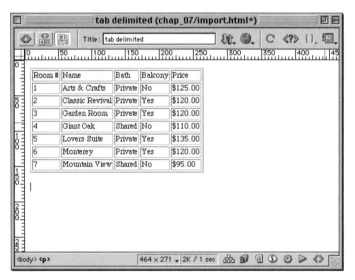

2. Click to the right of the table to place your blinking cursor outside the table. Press **Return/Enter** to move your cursor down.

3. Click the **Insert Table** object in the Common Objects panel. This will open the **Insert Table** dialog box.

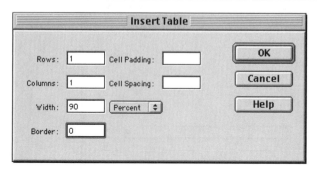

4. Create a table with **1 Row**, **1 Column**, **90% Width**, and **0 Border**. Your dialog box should look just like the one shown above. Click **OK**.

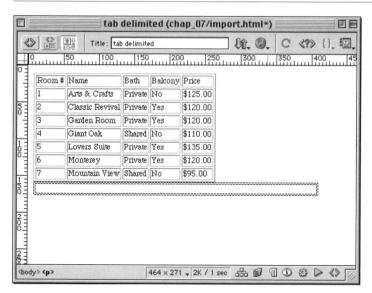

This is what your page should look like after the new table has been added. Don't worry, you are going to make it look much better than this!

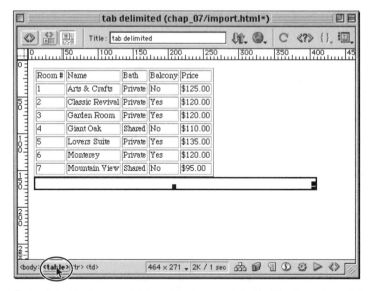

5. Click inside the new table you just created. In the Tag Selector, click on the **\<table\>** to quickly select the entire table.

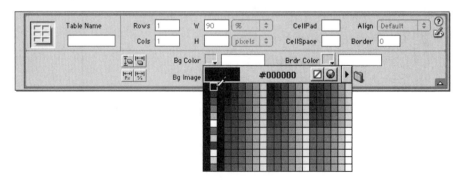

6. In the Property Inspector, click the **Bg Color** option and select **black**. The color you select for the background will also be the color of your table borders.

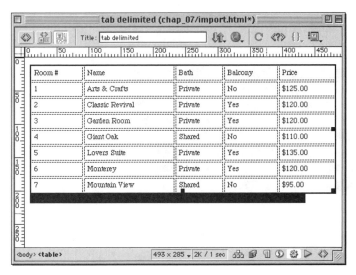

7. Select the top table using the Tag Selector, just like you did in step #5. In the Property Inspector, change the **Width** to **100%**, **CellPad** to **5** and the **Border** option to **0**.

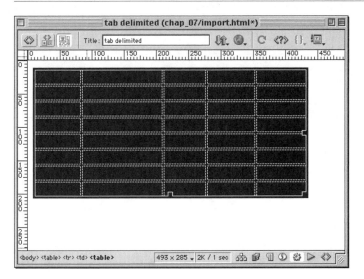

8. Move your cursor to the upper-left corner of the table until it turns into a small hand (Mac) or a four-headed arrow (Windows). Then, click and drag the upper table into the lower table.

Your nested tables should look like the one shown above. Everything will turn black! Don't worry, you'll fix this soon.

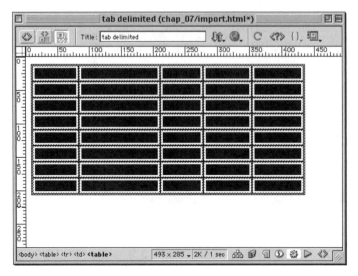

9. Click inside the upper left cell and drag to select all of the cells in the table.

10. In the Property Inspector, set the **Bg Color** option to White. This will change the background of each individual cell to white so you can see your text and the black table borders.

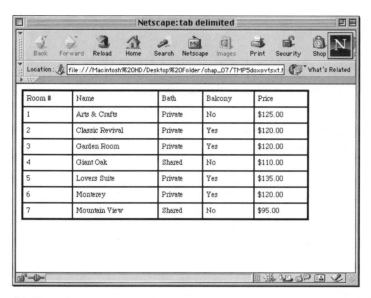

11. Press **F12** to preview this page in your default browser. Here, you can clearly see how the inner table is used to color the border of the outer table. Pretty neat, huh?

12. Click anywhere inside the table so the Tag Selector looks like what you see here. In the Tag Selector, click the second instance of the **<table>** tag to select the inner table.

13. Try setting the **Cell Padding** and **Cell Spacing** of the inner table to **0**. Then preview the page again in a browser. Another cool effect. Go ahead and experiment with other settings. You can't break anything, so just have some fun.

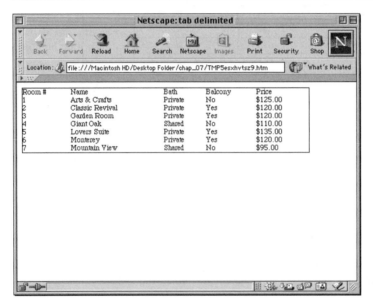

Room #	Name	Bath	Balcony	Price
1	Arts & Crafts	Private	No	$125.00
2	Classic Revival	Private	Yes	$120.00
3	Garden Room	Private	Yes	$120.00
4	Giant Oak	Shared	No	$110.00
5	Lovers Suite	Private	Yes	$135.00
6	Monterey	Private	Yes	$120.00
7	Mountain View	Shared	No	$95.00

This is what the page looks like with the Cell Padding and Cell Spacing set to 0. As you can see, by adjusting these two options you can dramatically change the appearance of the table border.

14. Return to Dreamweaver. Save and close this file.

II. ————Rounded Corner Tables

Tables, like most things on the Web are square. Images are square, frames are square, the browser window is square; it seems like almost everything on the web is square. It's no wonder web designers are always looking for ways to make things look less square. This handy little trick is one way to make your tables look less boxy. This is another one of those custom tricks you might want to share with your friends, or perhaps not share with your competitors!

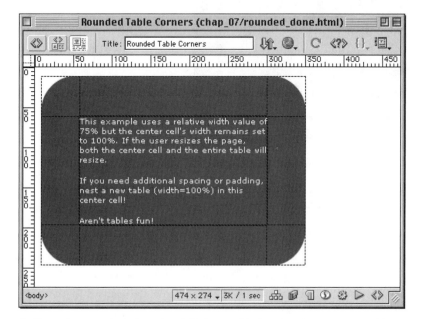

1. Open the **rounded_done.html** file located inside the **chap_07** folder. This is the completed file for this exercise, so you can see the effect you're aiming for in this exercise.

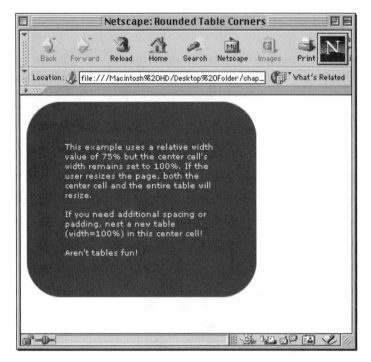

This is what the finished table looks like in the browser. Notice that as the browser window changes size, so does the table.

2. Press **F12** to preview this page in a browser. Go ahead and resize the window of your browser, notice how the table size adjusts with the size of the window. This occurs because the table is set to a percentage width, in this case 75%.

3. Return to Dreamweaver.

Now you know where this exercise is going, it's time to get started. The following steps will walk you through the whole process of creating this same table.

4. Create a new document and save it inside the **chap_07** folder as **round.html**.

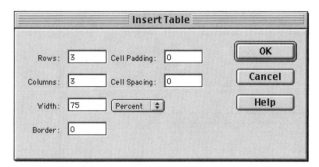

5. Create a new table that has **3 Rows**, **3 Columns**, **Width 75%**, **Borders 0**, and **Cell Padding** and **Cell Spacing** of **0**. Your dialog box should look just like the one shown above.

6. Click inside the upper-left cell. In the Property Inspector, set the **Horz** option to **Left** and the **Vert** option to **Top**. This will ensure that the images you insert into this cell are aligned in the upper-left corner of the cell.

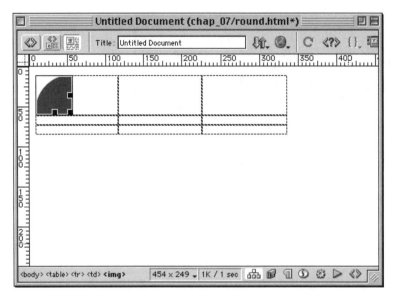

7. Click the **Insert Image** object on the Objects Panel and browse to the **chap_07** folder. Click to select the **topleft.gif** file and click **Open**. This will insert that image into the table cell.

8. Click inside the upper-right cell. In the Property Inspector, set the **Horz** option to **Right** and the **Vert** option to **Top**. This will ensure that the images you insert into this cell are aligned in the upper-right corner of the cell.

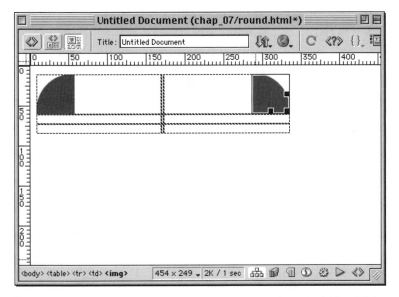

9. Click the **Insert Image** object and browse to the **chap_07** folder. Click to select the **topright.gif** file and click **Open**. This will insert that image into the table cell.

10. Click inside the lower-left cell. In the Property Inspector, set the **Horz** option to **Left** and the **Vert** option to **Bottom**. This will ensure that the images you insert into this cell are aligned in the lower-left corner of the cell.

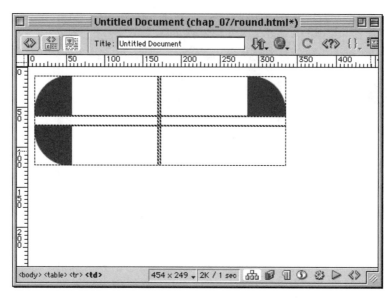

11. Click the **Insert Image** object and browse to the **chap_07** folder. Click to select the **bottomleft.gif** file and click **Open**. This will insert that image into the table cell.

12. Click inside the lower-right cell. In the Property Inspector, set the **Horz** option to **Right** and the **Vert** option to **Bottom**. This will ensure that the images you insert into this cell are aligned in the lower-right corner of the cell.

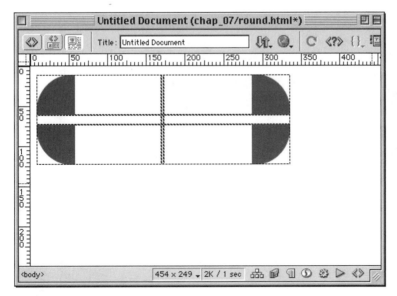

13. Click the **Insert Image** object and browse to the **chap_07** folder. Click to select the **bottomright.gif** file and click **Open**. This will insert that image into the table cell.

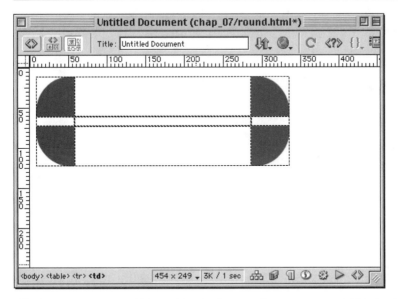

14. Click in the upper-middle cell. In the Property Inspector, enter **100%** for the **Width** option. This will cause the center cell to expand with the width of the table.

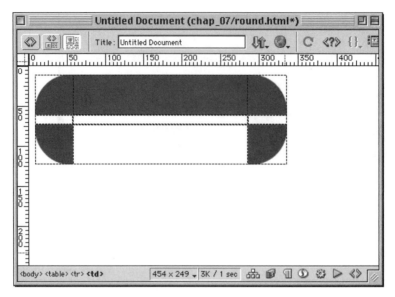

15. Use the **Bg** color option to sample the color of one of the blue images. This will change the background color of that cell so that it matches the corner images.

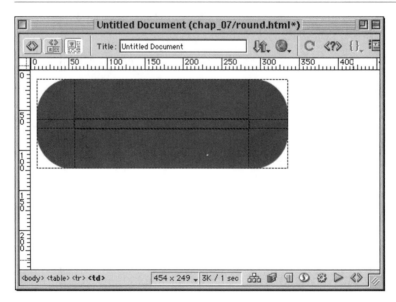

16. Use this same process to color the other cells. When you are finished, your table should look like this.

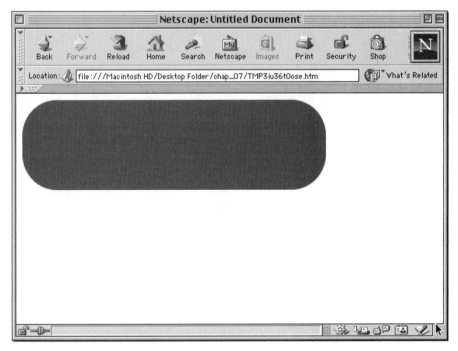

17. Press **F12** to preview this page in a browser. Resize the browser window. Notice how the table changes size and the corners all stay in their correct positions.

18. Return to Dreamweaver. If you want to experiment, try adding some text to the middle cell. There are lots of variations on this technique. Save and close this file. Phew, you made it again, another chapter under your belt! You deserve a break; this was a long chapter!

8.

Layout

Tracing Images	Using Layers
Converting Layers to Tables	Converting Tables to Layers
Using Margin Tags	Using Layout Cells and Layout Tables

---

chap_8

Dreamweaver 4
H•O•T CD-ROM

In traditional layout programs, such as Adobe PageMaker and QuarkXPress, most people take it for granted that they can move blocks of text and images around almost anywhere on the screen. Unfortunately, standard HTML doesn't have any tags to easily position elements. You've learned how you can use tables to position your elements both horizontally and vertically on your Web pages, but creating a basic table still doesn't give you the precision that you get in traditional print layout programs. This has caused considerable frustration among Web page designers.

Fortunately, Dreamweaver has built-in functions that help you work in a visual mode to create precise alignment for your text and images. You'll learn how to align your images using tracing images and layers, which you can then convert into tables that can be viewed on nearly any browser. And Dreamweaver 4 has an even newer alignment feature—layout cells—that give you the freedom of absolute positioning while still conforming to strict HTML guidelines!

In this chapter, you'll learn several techniques that allow you to position elements anywhere on your Web page, such as tracing images, layers, converting layers to tables, and working with layout tables and layout cells. After completing these exercises, you can decide for yourself which method you prefer when building your own pages.

What are Tracing Images, Layers and Tables?

The following chart outlines the concepts behind tracing images, layers, and tables, which you will learn about in the proceeding exercises:

Tracing Images, Layers, and Tables Defined	
Item	**Definition**
Tracing Image	An image (GIF, JPEG or PNG) that can be loaded into the background of your Web page to serve as a reference for layout. Consider this the blueprint you follow to build your pages.
Layer	This is where you put your text and images so you can move them around freely. The downside to using layers is that they only work on 4.0 browsers and above.
Table	Tables can hold images and text in place, but they are not intuitive or flexible when it comes to positioning them on the screen. However, Dreamweaver offers some helpful features that give you more flexibility, including the ability to convert layers to tables, and new innovative table drawing tools.

I. _____Applying a Tracing Image

Imagine that you have mocked up a wonderful layout for a Web page in Photoshop, Fireworks, Illustrator, or any drawing or painting program of your choice. Wouldn't it be great if you could take that mock-up and put it up on the Web? Dreamweaver's **Tracing Image** feature allows you to place any GIF, JPEG, or PNG into a Tracing Layer on your page, which can then be used as a reference for you to use to align your HTML elements to match up to it perfectly.

In this exercise, you will learn how to apply a tracing image to your Web page, as well as how to change its transparency and position on the page. You'll work with a tracing image that is supplied from the **H•O•T CD-ROM**. If you were to create your own tracing image, you would create a composite of your Web page in a graphics application of your choice, such as Photoshop, Fireworks, Illustrator, or whatever, and save it as a GIF, JPEG, or PNG. You would then specify your design as a tracing image, so that you could use it in Dreamweaver as your guide to re-create your page design.

A tracing image is visible only in Dreamweaver. Visitors to your site cannot see it. Keep in mind that when you are viewing the tracing image in Dreamweaver while building your page, you cannot see the background image or background color that you are setting, unless you decrease the tracing image's transparency setting. You'll learn to do this in the following exercise.

1. Copy **chap_08** to your hard drive. Define the site for Chapter 8 using the **chap_08** folder as the local root folder. If you need a refresher on this process, visit Exercise 1 in Chapter 3, "_Site Control_."

2. Open **index.html**. This page is blank, but it won't be for long! Choose **Modify > Page Properties...**. The shortcut keys for this are **Cmd+J** (Mac) and **Ctrl+J** (Windows).

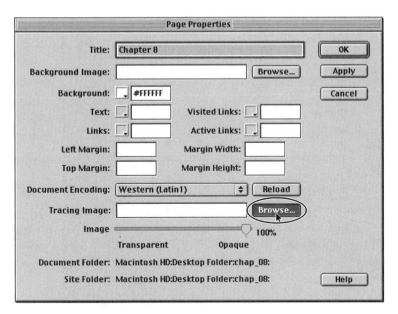

3. Click **Browse** next to the **Tracing Image** field.

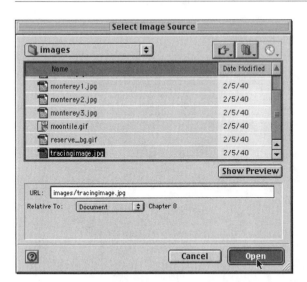

4. Browse to **tracingimage.jpg** inside the **images** folder and click **Open.**

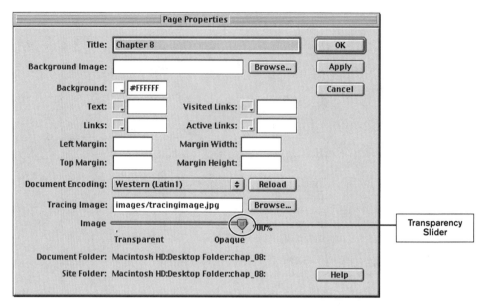

5. For this exercise, make sure the **Image Transparency Slider** is at 100%. This will enable your tracing image to be visible in the Document window of Dreamweaver.

6. Click **OK** in the **Page Properties** dialog box.

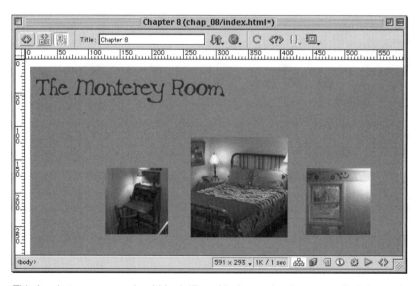

*This is what your page should look like with the tracing image applied. It was inserted at 100% opacity in the **Page Properties** dialog box, which makes it opaque.*

NOTE | Browser Offset

The white space you see above and to the left of the tracing image is the result of an offset that Dreamweaver created. You can control this offset by choosing **View > Tracing Image > Adjust Position…**

Why would Dreamweaver introduce such an offset? The program is emulating what would happen in a Web browser. For some dumb reason, browsers do not display foreground images flush top and left, but that's exactly how they display background images—flush top and left. This means that any image in the foreground (meaning it is not a background image) will always be displayed in the browser with this offset. Dreamweaver allows you to get rid of the offset; however, the offset is intentionally there to show you how the foreground artwork will align in a Web browser.

Dreamweaver offsets tracing images from the top-left corner to emulate an offset that exists in Web browsers. You can get rid of this offset if you like. We usually leave the offset alone, because it represents what will happen in a browser, anyway. If you have not accounted for this offsite in the design of your tracing image, we suggest you don't change this setting.

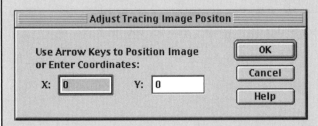

*You can use the **Adjust Tracing Image Position** dialog box to fix the offset. To bring up this dialog box, choose **View > Tracing Image > Adjust Position…** and enter **X: 0** and **Y: 0**.*

7. Press **F12** to preview this page in a Web browser (if you have not defined a browser yet, this is explained in Chapter 2, "*Interface*"). When you do this, notice that the page appears as a blank screen. This is supposed to happen! The tracing image only appears in Dreamweaver, and it won't be visible to your end user.

8. Return to Dreamweaver and choose **Modify > Page Properties...** to access the tracing image settings again.

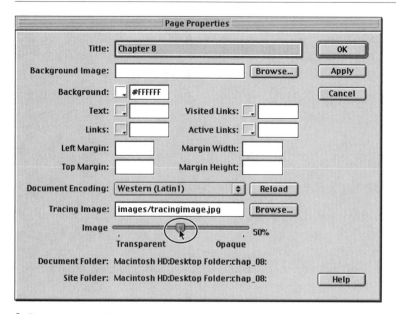

9. Drag the Image **Transparency Slider** down to **50%** and click **OK**.

10. Choose **File > Save** and leave this file open for the next exercise, in which you'll add images to match this layout.

WARNING | Tracing Image Dilemma

Occasionally Dreamweaver will not allow you to insert a tracing image when your **Image Transparency Slider** is set to **50%**. You can troubleshoot this problem by dragging the slider up or down the scale in any direction.

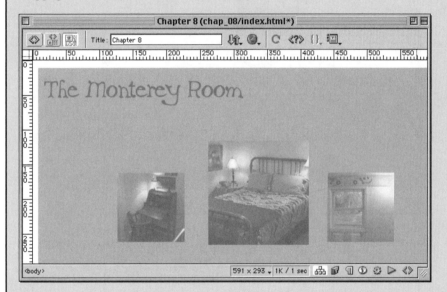

With the opacity reduced, it's much easier to use the tracing image as a guide because it doesn't compete with foreground images and text that are by default set to full opacity.

Tracing Images, Background Colors, and Images

Once you apply a tracing image to your page, it will hide the background color and background images while you are editing the document inside Dreamweaver. However, if you view the page that contains the tracing image from a browser, the background color and/or background image will be visible and the tracing image will not. In other words, tracing images are only visible to you while you're working in Dreamweaver. This is a good thing, because you don't want people seeing your blueprint—you want them to see the final results.

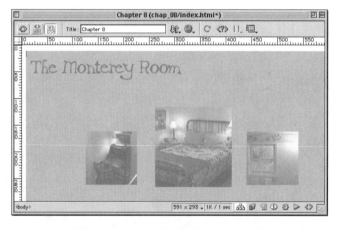

The tracing image is an internal function of Dreamweaver to help you follow a preconceived layout. When you preview the Dreamweaver file on the left in a browser, it appears empty because there is no placed artwork yet.

2. Adding Layers

In past chapters, you have been putting artwork and text directly on your page or inside tables. With that method, you can right-, left-, or center-align elements, and that's the end of the story. This frustrates most people because it would be a lot nicer if you could stick that artwork or text anywhere you wanted on the page and have it stay there. Layers are your friends, as they can be positioned anywhere without restriction. Rather than simply placing artwork and text on a page, as you have been doing so far, you can put your content into layers and move it anywhere you want.

In this exercise, you will learn how to create layers on your page and insert images and text inside them. Then—presto, you'll be able to move everything around. Ahh, the beauty of layers!

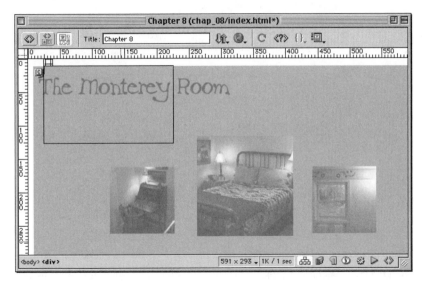

1. With **index.html** still open from the last exercise, choose **Insert > Layer**. This will insert an empty layer in your document, in the form of a rectangle on the top left of your screen.

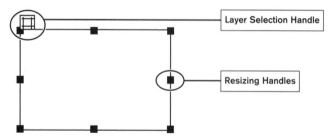

2. Click the white **Layer Selection Handle**. This will cause eight resizing handles to appear around the layer.

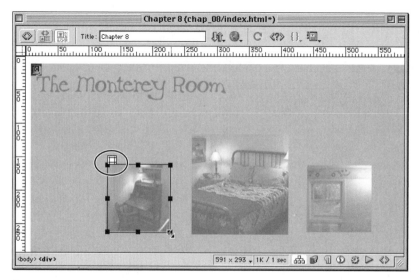

3. Using the layer selection handle, move the layer so its upper-left corner aligns with the photo of the desk that is visible in the tracing image. Using the bottom-right resizing handle, resize the layer so that it fits around the edge of the desk image.

Notice the blue thingie in the upper-left corner? It's called an **invisible element** in Dreamweaver. If you deselect the layer by clicking outside its boundaries, you'll see that the invisible element is deselected as well. For more on invisible elements, see the note later in this chapter.

4. Click inside the layer. You should see a blinking I-beam cursor inside the layer.

5. Choose **Insert > Image**.

6. Browse to **monterey3.jpg** inside the **images** folder. Click **Open**.

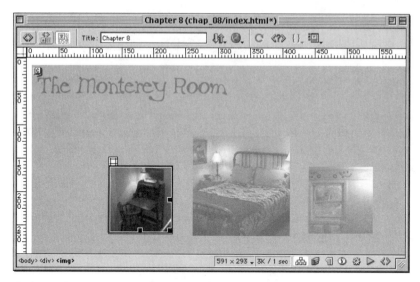

*An image is now inside the layer. Notice how this image is darker, while the tracing image is screened back? That's because you set the tracing image's opacity to **50%** in the last exercise. This makes it easy to distinguish between the layout and the final artwork, doesn't it?*

WARNING | Invisible Element Markers

When you create a layer in Dreamweaver, a small yellow icon appears at the top of your page. This is referred to as an invisible element marker. Each time you create a layer, a yellow marker will be inserted. By selecting these markers, you can easily select the associated layers. When the yellow icon is selected, it becomes a blue icon, by the way!

You will see these markers in the **index.html** document after you have completed Exercise 2. If you find that these markers get in your way, choose **View > Visual Aids > Invisible Elements** to hide/show them all. You can turn off invisible elements permanently if you want, by choosing **Edit > Preferences... > Invisible Elements**.

 This is what an invisible element marker looks like in Dreamweaver.

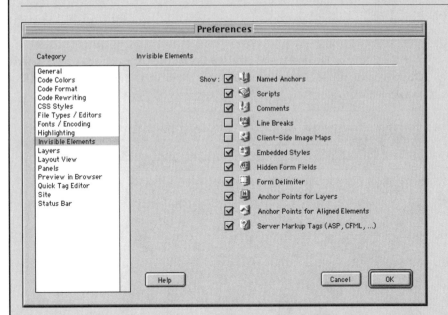

You can turn invisible elements on or off permanently in Dreamweaver's Preferences, available under the Edit menu.

7. In the **Common Objects** panel, click the **Draw Layer** object. If you have a different Objects panel visible, click on the small arrow at the top of the panel and select **Common** to switch back to it.

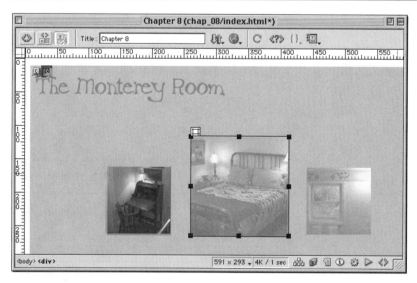

8. With the **Draw Layer** tool selected, draw a layer around the large center image of the bed.

You've just inserted a layer by using the Objects panel instead of the Insert menu. Either way works fine, and you have now been exposed to both.

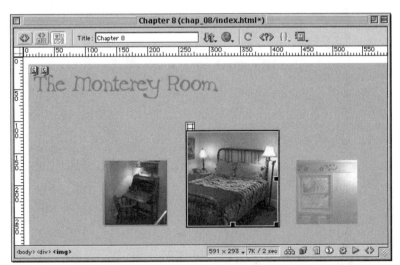

9. Make sure your blinking cursor is inside the layer and click the **Insert Image** object in the Objects panel.

10. Browse to **monterey1.jpg** inside the **images** folder. Click **Open**.

11. Add another layer around the small image of the window. You can use either the Objects panel or the **Insert** menu to accomplish this.

12. Choose **Insert > Image** and browse to **monterey2.jpg** inside the **images** folder. Click **Choose**.

13. Add another layer around the words "**The Monterey Room**" at the upper-left corner of the page.

14. Click inside the layer around the words "**The Monterey Room**," then choose **Insert > Image** and browse to **monterey.gif** inside the **images** folder. Click **Choose**. If you have trouble aligning the image, select it by using the layer selection handle and use the arrow keys on your keyboard to nudge it into place. **Note:** Make sure that the edge of your layer does not extend off the edge of the document window; this will cause an error when you try to convert the layers into a table.

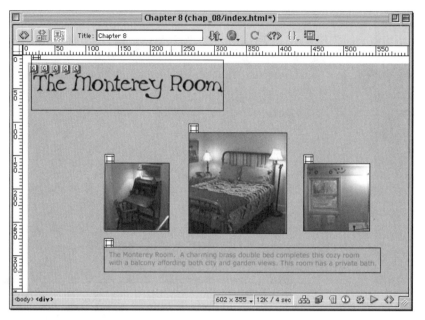

15. So far you have inserted images into layers. Inserting text is just as simple. Add another layer around the two lines of text at the bottom of the screen.

16. Click inside the layer and type **The Monterey Room. A charming brass double bed completes this cozy room with a balcony affording both city and mountain views. This room has a private bath**. For the purpose of this exercise, don't worry about matching the type of the original layout. If you need a refresher on type, revisit Chapter 6, "*Typography*."

17. Press **F12** to preview this page in a browser. Notice once again that the tracing image disappears. Only this time, you've recreated the layout using layers. When you are finished marveling at this accomplishment, return to Dreamweaver and save the file. Leave this document open for the next exercise.

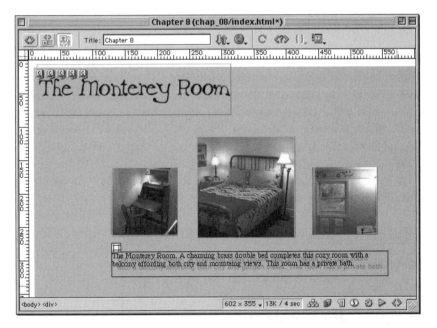

This is what your page looks like now. Most likely your text won't perfectly match the tracing image. That's all right—the tracing image is there only as a guide.

MOVIE | layers.mov

To learn more about using layers, check out **layers.mov** located in the movies folder on the Dreamweaver 4 **H•O•T CD-ROM**.

3. —————Converting Layers to Tables

You've just positioned artwork precisely to match a specific layout. As you may recall from the introduction to this section, layers only display on version 4.0+ browsers. People using earlier browsers will see the content of the layers all jumbled up along the left side of your page, which, of course, is not cool at all! We're guessing that you want the luxury of freely positioning artwork with layers, but still want people with older browsers to view your site. This exercise will show you how to convert layers to standard HTML tables so anybody can see your perfect layout, no matter what browser they're using.

1. With **index.html** still open from the last exercise, choose **Modify > Convert > Layers to Table...** The **Convert Layers to Table** dialog box will open.

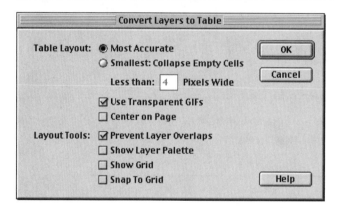

2. Click **Table Layout: Most Accurate**. Check the **Prevent Layer Overlaps** checkbox. This setting is required because layers can overlap, but tables cannot. Leave the **Use Transparent GIFs** option selected. This will insert a transparent GIF into your layout as needed to ensure that your table doesn't collapse in some browsers. Click **OK**.

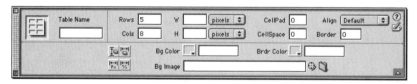

Note: *When you convert your layers to tables, by default Dreamweaver will set the table borders to* ***0****, shown above in the Property Inspector. Why? You do not want to advertise that you are using tables. The* ***0*** *gives you an invisible border, creating the illusion of floating background images and text on your Web page.*

*You can access the table properties by clicking anywhere in the table, and then selecting the **<table>** tag at the bottom of the document. The Property Inspector will reveal the different table settings.*

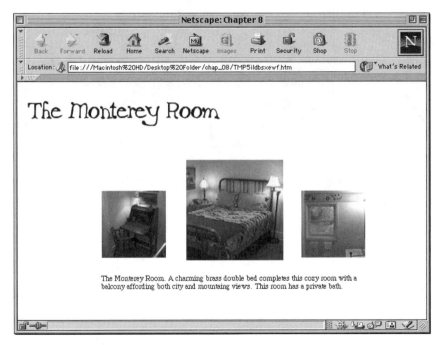

3. Preview the results in a browser by clicking **F12**. Notice that in the browser you can't tell whether layers or tables were used. Converting layers to tables affects the compatibility of the HTML document, not the appearance.

4. Return to Dreamweaver. Save the file and leave it open for the next exercise.

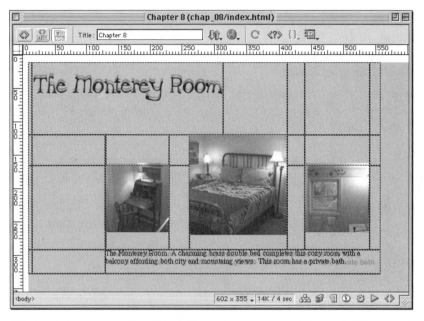

This is what your page should look like in Dreamweaver at the end of this exercise.

Convert Layers to Table Options

The **Convert Layers to Table** dialog box has several options to help you control how your layers are converted. The chart below explains how these features work:

Convert Layers to Table Options	
Option	**Desciption**
Most Accurate	This default option creates a table cell for each layer and all the cells necessary to maintain the layer structure. More information about tables and cells can be found in Chapter 7, "*Tables*."
Smallest: Collapse Empty Cells	This option sets the edges of the layers to align if they are within a certain pixel range of each other. This typically results in fewer columns and rows. This can be a good thing, because fewer columns and rows equate to faster downloading; or it can be bad thing, because it can potentially disrupt your layout's appearance. We recommend experimenting to see which suits your needs best.
Use Transparent GIFS	This option inserts transparent GIFs in each of the empty cells. This helps maintain the table structure across browsers. Tables can collapse in some browsers if they don't contain content, and transparent GIFs can fill in as content, though they are invisible.
Center on Page	This option centers the table on the page.
Prevent Layer Overlaps	Table cells cannot overlap. This option prevents you from overlapping your layers by warning you about which layers, if any, overlap.
Show Layer Panel	This opens the Layer panel, which allows you to rename or reorder your layers. This exercise didn't require that you view the Layer panel, but you'll get a chance to learn about this in Chapter 15, "*DHTML*."
Show Grid	If it's not already visible, this will turn on the grid for the page.
Snap To Grid	This snaps the layer to the nearest snapping point on the grid. This can be useful for aligning objects.

Converting Tables to Layers

In this exercise, you will convert the table version of your page back to layers, modify the layout, and then convert it back to tables for browser compatibility. You will turn the tracing image off and be encouraged to modify the page's layout however you want. When you are finished, you should definitely appreciate how powerful these features are in helping you create and modify the layout of your pages.

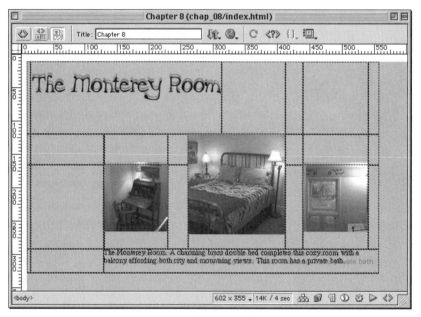

1. With **index.html** still open from the last exercise, choose **Modify > Convert > Tables to Layers...** The **Convert Tables to Layers** dialog box will open.

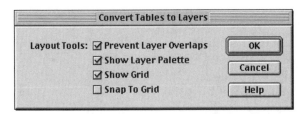

2. Remove the check in the **Snap To Grid** checkbox. If checked, this option will force your layers to snap to a grid, sometimes causing unwanted shifting of page elements. For this reason, we prefer to not use this option. Make sure that your settings are like those shown above and click **OK**.

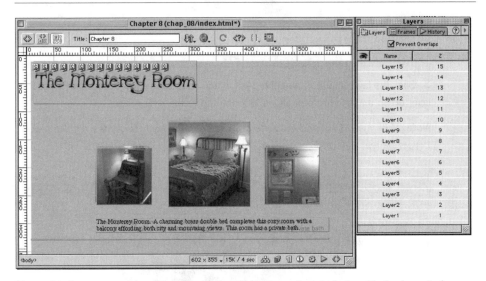

*Your table is converted into layers, and the grid is turned on to help with the layout of your page. If you want to change the layout, you'll find that it's much easier to do so with layers than with tables! If the grid bothers you, turn it off by choosing **View > Grid > Show Grid**.*

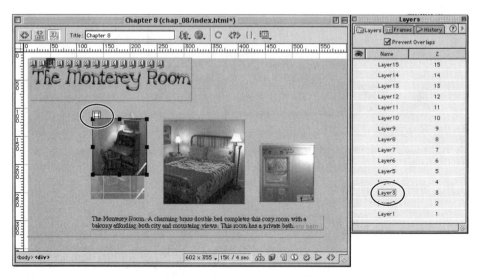

3. Click the layer that contains the desk image. Use the **Layer Selection Handle** to drag this layer up so that the top of it aligns with the top of the bed image.

Note: When you click and drag the desk image, that layer becomes highlighted in the Layers panel.

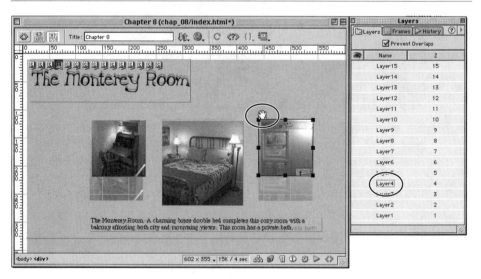

4. Select the layer with the image of the window. Use the layer selection handle to drag this layer up so that top of it aligns with the top of the image of the bed.

5. Choose **Modify > Convert > Layers to Table...** Click **OK**.

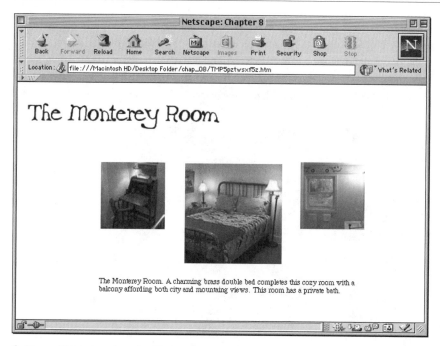

6. Press **F12** to preview the file in a browser.

7. Save and, finally, close the file.

You can start to see how easy it is to change the layout of your pages by converting back and forth between layers and tables. On the left is the original page and on the right is the new page, with the artwork aligned with the top of the center image.

Using Margin Tags

Standard HTML has always produced an offset between the way foreground and background images are displayed in Web browsers, and this made it impossible to perfectly register a foreground image element to the background. However, both Explorer and Netscape introduced **MARGIN** tags in the version 4.0 browsers and above. This exercise shows you how to specify **MARGIN** settings in Dreamweaver that will remove the offset in Netscape and Explorer versions 4.0 and above.

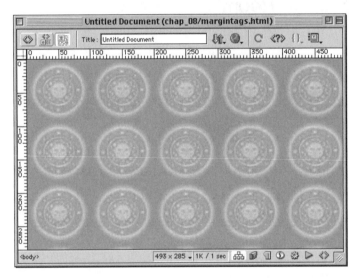

1. Open **margintags.html** located inside the **chap_08** folder. This page already contains a background image. **Note:** if you still have the grid visible select **View > Grid > Show Grid** to turn this feature off.

2. Click the **Insert Image** object in the **Common Objects** panel.

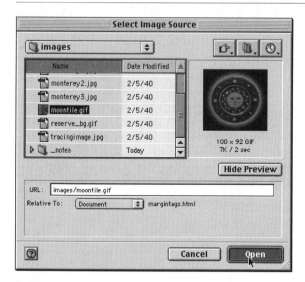

3. Browse to **moontile.gif** inside the **images** folder and click **Open**. Since this image is the exact same size as the background image, it will help to demonstrate how to perfectly align foreground and background images.

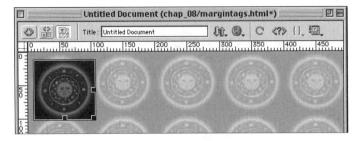

When the image is inserted, you can see a gap from the left edge of the document and the top of the document. In some designs, this can be really annoying. You'll fix this next.

Browser-Specific Margin Tags

It's important to know that specific tags work only in Netscape, while others only work in Explorer. Just to be safe, we recommend that you use both tags, to ensure that your page displays without an offset in either browser. The chart below outlines which tags work in which specific browser.

Browser-Specific Margin Tags	
Browser	**Tag**
Netscape Navigator 4.0 or later	MARGIN WIDTH
	MARGIN HEIGHT
Internet Explorer 4.0 or later	LEFT MARGIN
	TOP MARGIN

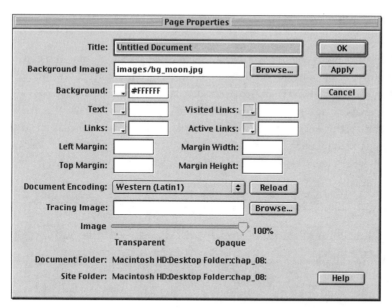

4. Choose **Modify > Page Properties...** This will open the **Page Properties** dialog box.

5. Type **0** for the **Left Margin**, **Top Margin**, **Margin Width**, and **Margin Height** options. This will eliminate the offset on the browser and align the foreground image perfectly with the background image. Click **OK**.

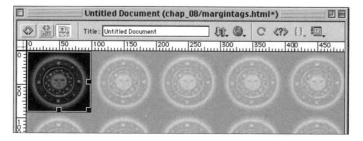

This is what your page should look like when you are finished.

6. Save and close this file.

What is the Layout View?

Dreamweaver 4 has introduced a completely new way to create the layout for your Web pages. A new **Layout View** feature allows you to create layout cells and tables by drawing them exactly where you need them, at exactly the size that you want. This technique has been introduced as a more visual way to design your layouts while creating clean and optimized table code behind the scenes. While converting from layers to tables is convenient and easy, it does not write nested tables (tables that are within other tables). Instead, it must produce table code that is not as "clean" or optimized as possible. Layout cells and tables, on the other hand, are written in a very clean manner and can included nested tables.

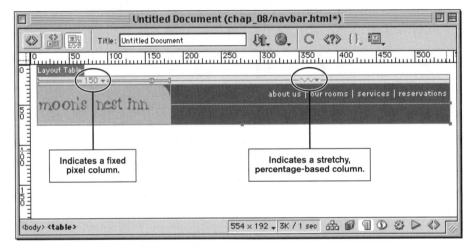

Layout tables and cells are indicated by different symbols to describe what kind of table cell (fixed pixel or percentage based) is being used.

Layers to Tables versus Layout View

During the course of this chapter, you were shown how to create Web-page layouts using two different methods; first, with layers and then converting layers to tables. Next you'll learn how to create layouts with the new **Layout View** using layout cells and layout tables. At this point, you might be scratching your head and wondering which one should you be using for your page layouts. While there are some pros and cons to both, much of it boils down to a matter of preference. We always suggest that you find a workflow that makes you comfortable and stick with it. Just because there are many ways to accomplish the same thing doesn't mean you have to use them all.) The table below outlines some of the pros and cons of each workflow.

Item	Pros	Cons
Layers to Tables	Easy to use and do not require knowledge of table behaviors and restrictions.	The table code generated in this process is often overly complex.
	Easy to save a layer-based and table-based version of your page. Helpful if you intend to work with DHTML, which you will learn more about in Chapter 15, "*DHTML*."	More difficult to create layouts with percentage based designs.
Layout View	Easy to create layouts with percentage-based designs.	Requires knowledge of table behavior and restrictions.
	Table code is optimized and very clean.	
	Will automatically create and insert spacer.gif into your layout.	

6. ———Layout Tables and Layout Cells

This exercise will show you how to use layout cells and layout tables to create a navigation bar that stretches with the width of the browser window. It combines the use of fixed table cells and percentage-based table cells using the **Layout Cell** editor.

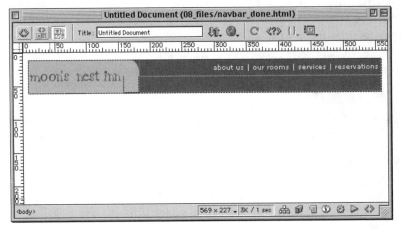

1. Open the **navbar_done.html** file located inside the **chap_08** folder. This is the finished version of the file you will create in this exercise.

2. At the bottom of the Toolbar panel, click the **Layout View** button. This will switch the view of your document to the Layout View.

Layout View vs. Standard View

A page as it appears in Standard View.   **A page as it appears in Layout View.**

You learned earlier that Dreamweaver has three different views for your Document window: the *Design View* (default), *Design and Code View*, and *Code View*. In addition to this, there are two ways to view the Design View: the *Standard View* (default) and the *Layout View*. You can use the two buttons at the bottom of the Toolbar panel to switch between these two views.

The Standard View is where you will do most of your work, such as inserting objects, text, and links. The Layout View is an alternative, flexible mode to constructing the layout of your page. However, while in the Layout View, you cannot use the Insert Table object or create layers. Despite these few limitations, the Layout view lets you design your pages in a visual manner while creating clean and optimized table code behind the scenes.

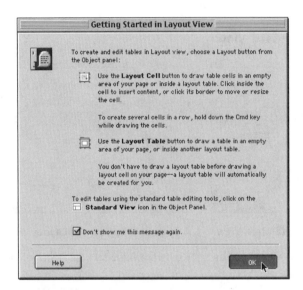

3. The **Getting Started in Layout View** dialog box will appear. This is just a simple introduction and explanation of the Layout View, layout tables, and layout cells. Once you've read this, you probably won't want to read it again, so we suggest you select the **Don't show me this message again** checkbox.

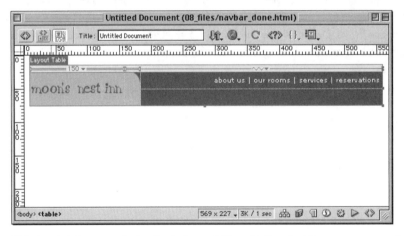

This is what the page looks like in Layout View. Notice that the appearance of the table has changed quite a bit. By the end of this exercise, you will know what this change in appearance means and how to work in this mode.

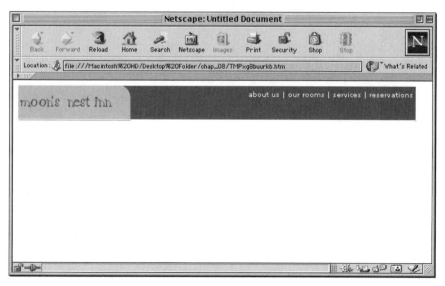

1. Press **F12** to preview this page in a browser. Resize your browser window. Notice that the text content stretches with the size of the browser window. This design is effective because it can accommodate almost any resolution.

2. Return to Dreamweaver.

The following steps will walk you through the process of creating this page using layout tables and cells in the Layout View.

1. Create a new document and save it inside the **chap_08** folder as **navbar.html**.

2. At the bottom of the Toolbar panel, click the **Layout View** button.

3. Click the **Draw Layout Cell** icon in the Objects panel. This will let you draw a table cell in your document window.

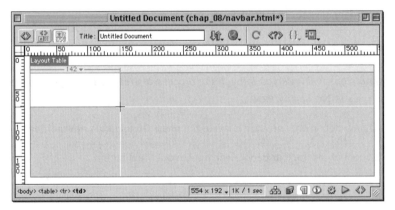

4. Click and drag to create a cell that is approximately **150 x 50** pixels. Hey, don't stress yourself out trying to get it exact. You will learn how to adjust the size in a few steps—just get as close as you can.

Table cells cannot exist without a table—that's a fact of Web design. So, when you create a table cell, Dreamweaver will automatically create a table to hold the cell, as dictated by HTML guidelines. That's exactly what happened here and that's what you see on your screen. A green Layout Table tab will appear in the upper-left corner indicating that a table has been created. The table cell will appear with a light blue border around it.

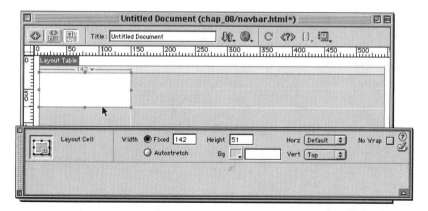

5. Move your cursor over the edge of the layout cell. The border of the layout cell will turn red indicating that you will select that cell if you click. Well, guess what? Click to select that layout cell. ;-)

The Property Inspector will change to display the editable options for the layout cell. Notice that you can numerically adjust the width and height of the cell here.

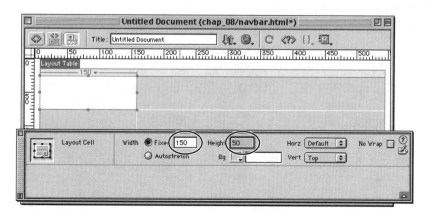

6. In the Property Inspector, change the **Width** to **150** and press **Return/Enter**. Then change the **Height** to **50** and press **Return/Enter.**

7. Click the **Draw Layout Cell** icon in the Objects panel again.

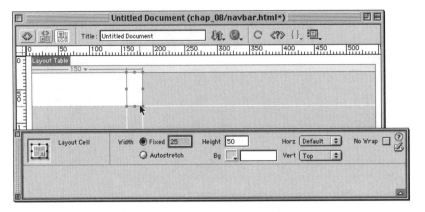

8. Click and drag another layout cell to the right of the first cell. This cell should be **25** x **50** pixels. If you don't get it exactly right, use the Property Inspector to adjust the **Width** and **Height**.

Notice how the cell snaps to the guidelines? This will help ensure that your tables aren't overly complex.

TIP | Drawing Multiple Layout Cells

As you work with the Layout Cells feature, you will find yourself creating several cells at once. However, each time you draw a cell, you need to reselect the Draw Layout Cell object before you can create another one. This can get annoying and slow down your workflow quite a bit. Don't worry, there is a solution! If you hold down the **Cmd** (Mac) or **Ctrl** (Windows) key while you draw a layout cell, you can draw as many cells as you want without having to reselect the Object each time. Nice.

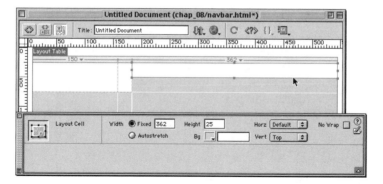

9. Click the **Draw Layout Cell** icon in the Objects panel again and draw a cell to the right that extends to the end of the table. It should have a height of **25** pixels.

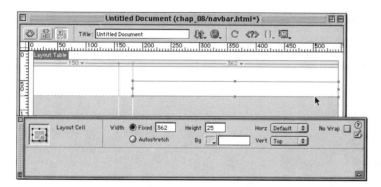

10. Click the **Draw Layout Cell** icon in the Objects panel and draw another cell right below that is the same size.

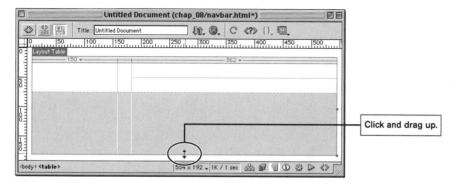

Click and drag up.

11. Click the green **Layout Table** tab in the upper-left corner. Click and drag the middle resize handle at the bottom of the table to bring it up to the bottom of the cells. You don't want the table to be any bigger than necessary.

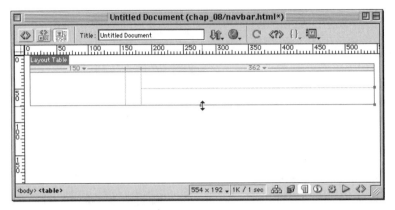

This is what your layout should look like at this point.

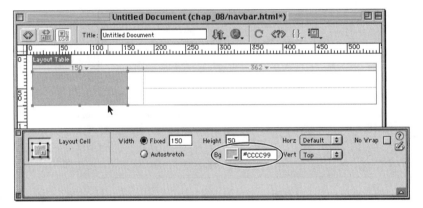

12. Click the border of the large cell on the left to select it. In the Property Inspector, change the background color of this cell to **#CCCC99**.

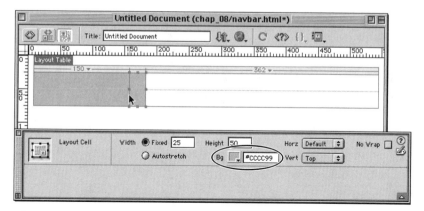

13. Click the border of the middle cell to select it. In the Property Inspector, change the background color of this cell to **#CCCC99**.

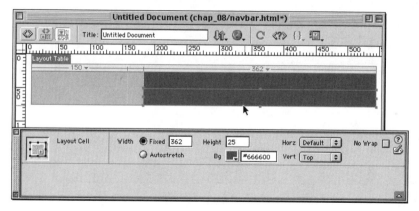

14. Using this same process, change the background of the two long vertical cells to **#666600**.

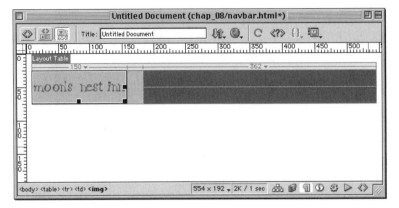

15. Click inside the large cell on the left and insert the **pagetitle3.gif** image into that cell.

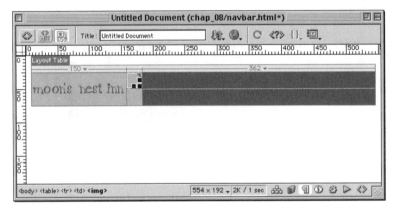

16. Click inside the middle cell and insert the **arch5.gif** image into that cell.

17. Click to select the border of the upper-right horizontal cell. You are going to insert some text into this cell so you will first modify the alignment properties of this cell.

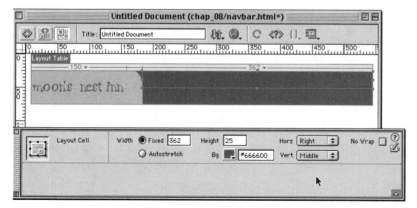

18. In the Property Inspector, change the **Horz** alignment to **Right** and the **Vert** alignment to **Middle**. This will place any text in this cell in the middle and align it to the right side of the cell.

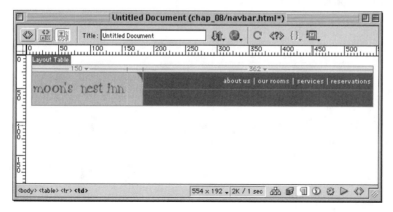

19. Click inside the upper-right cell and create a text navigation like the one shown above. Make sure you change the text color to white or some other light color. We changed the font to Verdana at a size of 1.

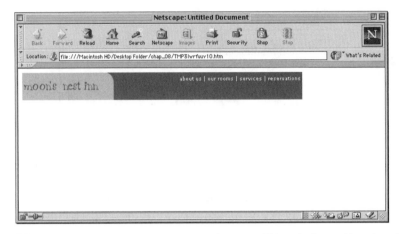

20. Press **F12** to preview your page in a browser. Things look good but the table doesn't stretch with the browser window. The following steps will show you how to make the table stretch with the browser window.

21. Return to Dreamweaver.

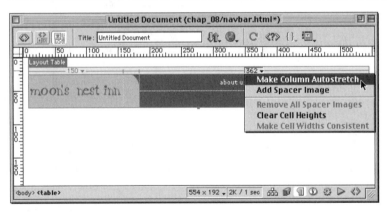

22. Click the green arrow above the middle of the upper-right cell. Select **Make Column Autostretch**. This option will set the right column to 100% so that it stretches with the browser window. Simple huh?

In order to prevent the table from collapsing in some browsers, Dreamweaver needs to insert an invisible GIF inside the cells with no content. Don't worry if you don't have an invisible GIF file, Dreamweaver will even create one for you. The following dialog box displays the different options available to you.

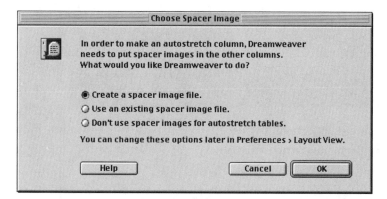

23. Make sure the **Create a spacer image file** is selected and click **OK**. This will cause Dreamweaver to create a spacer.gif file—a transparent GIF image—and insert it into the cells with no content.

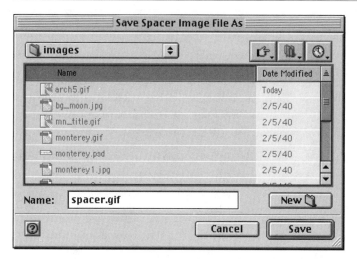

24. Browse to the **images** folder inside the **chap_08** folder and save the **spacer.gif** file there.

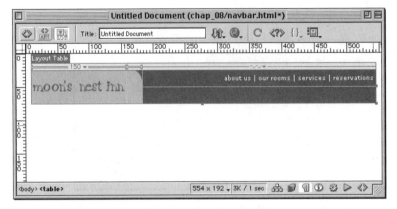

Notice that the tops of all the cells have changed. The following chart explains what each of these different visual cues mean.

Anatomy of Layout Cells	
Item	**Description**
[cell with 133 at top]	A layout cell with a numeric value displayed at the top means that the cell has a specific width value set in pixels. This value can be changed with the resize handles or the in the Property Inspector.
[cell with 133 and thick double line]	A layout cell with a numeric value and a thick double line is an indication that the cell is set to a specific pixel value, and it also contains a spacer.gif. This occurs when another column has been set to Autostretch.
[cell with squiggle at top]	A layout cell with a little squiggle at the top is an indication that this column has been set to Autostretch, which means that it will stretch to fill the remaining horizontal space in the browser window. This setting can be changed to a fixed pixel value in the Property Inspector.

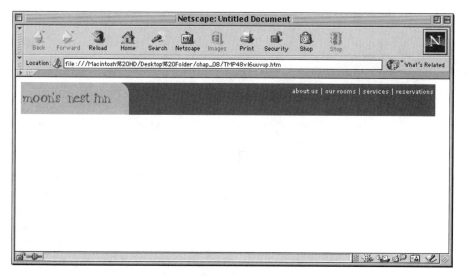

25. Press **F12** again to preview this page in a browser. Wah-lah, your table will now stretch to the width of the browser window.

26. Return to Dreamweaver and close and save this file.

You finished yet another chapter… congratulations, you might want to take a short break before moving onto Chapter 9, "*Frames.*"

MOVIE | layoutview.mov

To see this exercise in action, check out **layoutview.mov** located in the movies folder on the Dreamweaver 4 **H•O•T CD-ROM**.

9.

Frames

| The Pros and Cons of Frames | Saving Frames |

| Coloring Frames | Links and Targets | Adding a Background Image |

| Seamless Background Across Two Frames |

| Frames Objects Panel |

chap_9

Dreamweaver 4
H•O•T CD-ROM

So far in this book, you've learned to insert text, tables, and images into individual HTML pages. The concept of **frames** is a little more challenging since, in effect, a frame is an HTML page inside another HTML page. Why would anyone want to put an HTML page inside another HTML page? So that one part of a page can update independently from another.

Let's say that you've created an image that belonged at the bottom of an HTML page. If your site contained 100 pages, and you wanted to put that same image at the bottom of all of them, you would need to insert that image 100 times into each of those 100 individual pages.

Frames allow you to reuse a single HTML page by nesting it inside another HTML document (otherwise known as a **frameset**). This would make it possible to create that image at the bottom of an HTML page only once, but allow 100 other pages to load up beside it. If it sounds complex, it is. Frames have a high learning curve, but fortunately this chapter is here to walk you through every step of the way.

What Are Frames?

Lynda's husband Bruce, who also teaches classes at our training center, came up with this wonderful metaphor for teaching frames. Imagine a TV dinner. You've got your peas and carrots, an entrée and, if you are really lucky, a dessert. Don't forget, though, about the tray that holds all these food items together! A frameset, if you will, is the TV dinner tray that holds together multiple HTML documents.

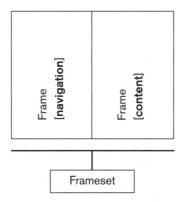

If you were to build a frameset that contained two frames, a left frame for your Web navigation element and a right frame for your content, visitors to your site would see only two frames. What's hidden is that your visitor would actually be working with three documents: a frameset (think TV dinner tray) and two frames (the content HTML page and the navigation HTML page). Every time you come to a page that contains frames, it always includes a frameset that holds the frames in place. If this sounds confusing at all, welcome to frames! Conceptually, they can be a bit of a brain twister.

We promise that the exercises in this chapter will help you unravel these concepts. You'll learn that frames are controversial creatures, and that they are either loved or hated by most people. We'll do our best to fill you in on the pros and cons of using frames, as well as a variety of techniques for using them effectively and creatively. In the end, you will have the honor of deciding if they are right or wrong for your site. Hey, we just teach this stuff!

Frames: A Love-or-Hate Proposition

First, a word from our sponsors (the venerable authors of this book). Frames are controversial—most people either love or hate them. You may want to consider the pros and cons before you use them in your site. Here are two charts to help you if you're weighing the decision to use or not use frames:

Love Frames	
Pro	**Explanation**
Good Workflow	It's easier to update a single page than hundreds, right? If you put a navigation element (all your links) into a single frame of a frameset, and then your site's navigation changes, you only have to update that one page.
Fixed Navigation	The entire page doesn't have to reload each time a link is clicked, only sections of the page. This means that you can anchor a navigation page so it doesn't have to be reloaded with each new page click and always stays consistent throughout your site.
Special Effects	Frames let you do cool special effects, such as putting a single background into multiple *frames* for aesthetic purposes. You'll learn this technique in this very chapter!

Hate Frames	
Con	**Explanation**
Confusing	If not well implemented, frames can create confusing navigation for your audience. However, this chapter will teach you how to implement frames well, of course!
Printing Hassles	It is not possible to print an entire frameset. That would be like printing three or more HTML pages at once. Your end user can print an individual frame, but frames are often transparent to the end user so this can prove challenging. Our suggestion? If you think people are going to print a page from your site, don't put it in a frameset.
Bookmark Hassles	The only part of a framed page that can be bookmarked easily is the frameset. Let's say you have 20 pages that load into a single frameset. If one of your end users wanted to bookmark page 11, he/she would not be able to do so, since only the first page that loads into the frameset could be bookmarked. We have no remedy for this problem, except to say that you should make it very clear how to get to the other 19 pages within that frameset, by adding a simple navigation path on the first page.
Hidden Security Issues	At the *lynda.com* Web site, we once made the mistake of placing a secure order form into an insecure frameset. Some of our customers complained because they couldn't see the lock symbol at the bottom left of their browser that ensures a page is secure. Although the order form page was in fact secure, we eventually took it out of the frameset so our customers would see the lock symbol and feel more confident buying from us.
Too Boxy!	Frames divide an already small amount of screen real estate into smaller regions, which causes a boxy effect. You'll learn how to make framesets without unsightly scrollbars and borders. That will help eliminate the ugly boxy effect.

I. _____Saving Your First Frameset

This chapter is going to build your frame-making skills gradually. This first exercise will show you how to save a set of frames properly. Sound simple? Unfortunately, frames are much harder than anything you've learned so far. By taking you slowly through the process, our hope is that you'll get through these hurdles without a problem

1. Copy **chap_09** to your hard drive. Define your site for Chapter 9 using the **chap_09** folder as the local root folder. If you need a refresher on this process, visit Exercise 1 in Chapter 3, *"Site Control."*

---

2. Start this exercise with a blank untitled document. If a blank untitled document is not already on your screen, choose **File > New** (Mac) or **File > New Window** (Windows). Don't save this page just yet. You may be surprised by this advice, given our past warnings, but saving now will cause Dreamweaver to believe that this is a single HTML page (which it is not!). You are going to divide this into a frameset and frames before you save.

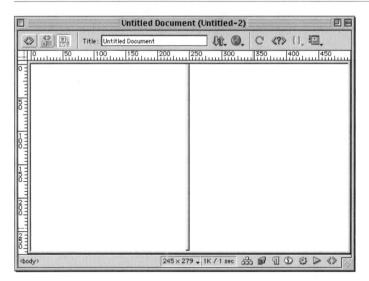

3. Choose **Modify > Frameset > Split Frame Left**. This puts a vertical frame divider through your page. What's more, it switches you from looking at one page to looking at three: the **frameset**, the **left frame**, and the **right frame**.

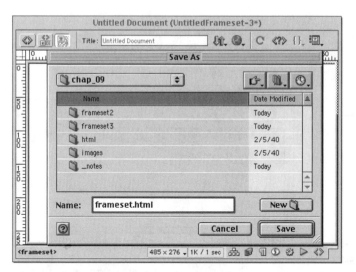

4. Choose **File > Save Frameset As...** and save the file as **frameset.html** inside the **chap_09** folder. The frameset document will be the container for the other HTML files. *Note: If you wanted this frameset to be the first page in your site (sometimes referred to as the home page), you would save the frameset as index.html.*

MOVIE | saving_frames.mov

To learn more about saving frames, check out **saving_frames.mov** located in the **movies** folder on the Dreamweaver 4 **H•O•T CD-ROM**.

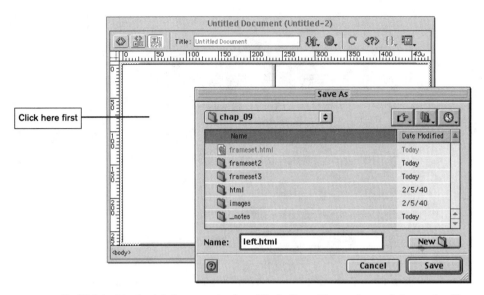

5. Click inside the left frame and select **File > Save Frame As...** and save the file as **left.html**. Make sure you are saving this file in the same location as the frameset.html file.

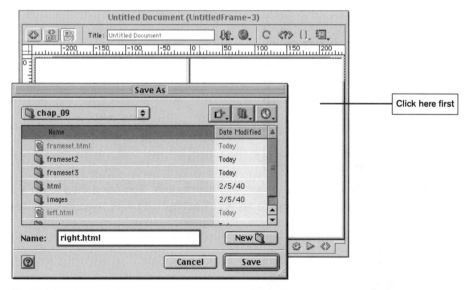

Click here first

6. Click inside the right frame and select **File > Save Frame As...** and save the file as **right.html**. Make sure you are saving this file in the same location as the frameset.html file.

Even though you just saved these files, notice that it says Untitled Document at the top of each document window? What's up with that? As you learned in Chapter 4, "Basics," you've saved and named the HTML document, but have not assigned the title yet. In order to assign the title, follow the exact directions below, because you are juggling three HTML documents and you want to put the title in the outermost page (frameset.html).

7. Select **Window > Frames** to open the **Frames** panel. This panel will give you a preview of your frameset structure and can be helpful for selecting different portions of your frameset.

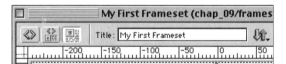

8. Click your mouse on the thick black border around the edge of the Frames panel. This is a quick way to select the frameset. In the toolbar at the top of the document, enter in the **Title** field: **My First Frameset**, and press **Return**. The default untitled document title should be instantly replaced by your new title. **Note:** Press **Return** only after you deselect your new title; otherwise, it will be deleted!

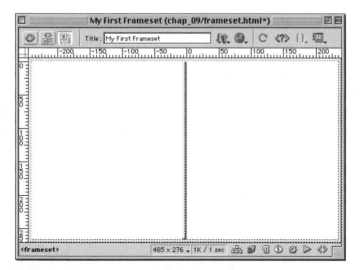

9. Choose **File > Save All Frames**. Once you define the initial frameset and frames, you can perform one simple **Save All Frames** operation to save the changes to all the files and be done. Leave this file open for Exercise 2.

Different Ways to Save Frames

This exercise taught you to save frames by choosing **File > Save As...** There are a few different ways to save them besides this, but the way we already showed you is the best because you always know what file you are saving. All three ways are listed in the handy chart below.

Ways to Save Frames	
Option	**Explanation**
File > Save Frame **File > Save Frame As...**	To save a document inside a frameset, click the cursor in the frame and use this method.
File > Save Frameset **File > Save Frameset As...**	To save a frameset file only, you may choose to use either of these methods.
File > Save All Frames	To save all open files at once, use this method. However, we don't recommend this method. There's a known bug on the Macintosh that doesn't give you a good visual cue about which file is being saved using this method. Using the *File > Save All Frames* method *after* you've saved the first time using the other listed methods is fine. Just don't start the process with a *File > Save All*, or you'll potentially get confused by the process.

2. ——————Coloring Frames

Coloring frames is challenging because you're manipulating multiple HTML documents in one Dreamweaver window. This exercise teaches you how to color two frames independently. You'll also learn how to turn off the borders between them, which can help eliminate that boxy appearance that many people don't like about frames.

1. You should still have **frameset.html** open from the last exercise. In the document window, click on the **left frame** and make sure you see the text-insertion cursor blinking.

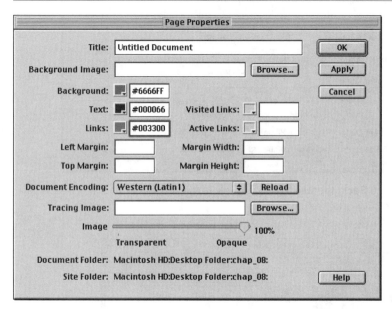

2. Choose **Modify > Page Properties... Cmd+J** (Mac) or **Ctrl+J** (Windows). Make the **Background** a light blue color, the **Text** a dark blue, and the **Links** a dark green. Click **OK**. The left frame should turn light blue.

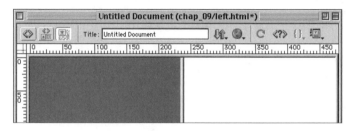

The left frame should be light blue at this point.

3. In order to change the color for the right side, click in the right frame and make sure you see the text-insertion cursor blinking. **Choose Modify > Page Properties...** yet again.

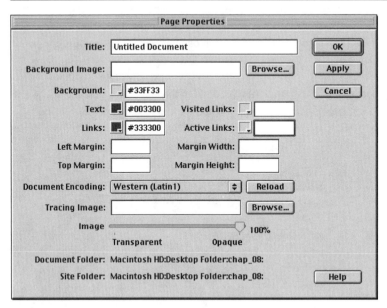

4. Make the **Background** a light green, the **Text** a dark green, and the **Links** a dark yellow. Click **OK**.

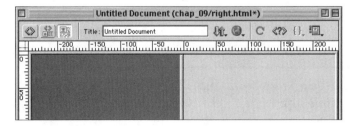

The left side of the document should be blue, and the right side green.

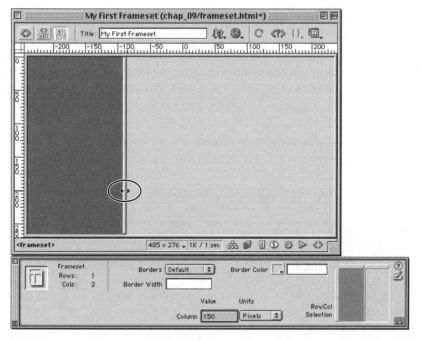

5. Click on the middle dividing frame border and move it over to the left until the Property Inspector reads **Column: 150 Pixels. Tip:** You can enter the value **150** into the **Column** setting instead of dragging, if you prefer. If the Property Inspector's not visible, go to **Window > Properties**.

6. We don't know if you agree with us, but part of what we do not like about frames is their boxy appearance. To turn off the border on the frame divider, select **Borders: No**, and **Border Width: 0** in the Property Inspector. Now the dividing border should be gone. Choose **File > Save All Frames** and leave this document open for the next exercise.

Links and Targets

You've gotten through the hardest part of making a frameset, but there's still more distance to go to the finish. This exercise will show you how to insert a link into the left side page of the frameset. You've learned about making links, so much of this should be familiar. This exercise introduces a new concept, however—using a "target"—which allows you to specify which frame the link will trigger in your frameset.

1. Click inside the left frame and make sure you see the blinking text-insertion cursor. Type the words "**Our Rooms**."

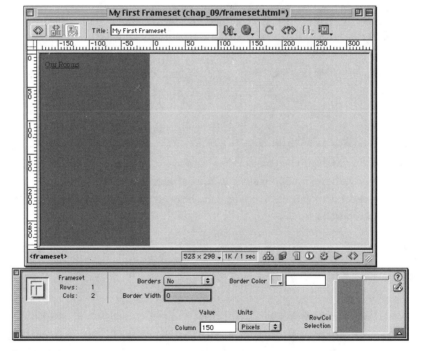

2. Select the words "**Our Rooms**" and click on the folder to the right of **Link** in the Property Inspector. Browse to the **html** folder inside the **chap_9** folder and select **rooms.html**. Click **Open**. "**Our Rooms**" should now appear as an underlined link.

3. You can't preview links in Dreamweaver, so press **F12** to preview in your browser. You'll be prompted to save your files before you preview them in a browser, so click **Save**. **Note:** We suggest that you click the **Don't warn me again** checkbox so you don't see this message every time your test your frameset in a browser.

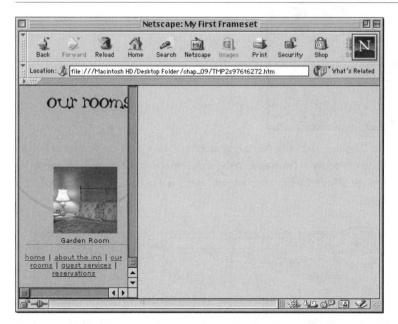

4. Once in the browser, go ahead and click the link "**Our Rooms**." You might be surprised that the "**rooms**" page appears in the left frame, the exact frame where the link was in your Dreamweaver file! Just like in any other Web page, once you click on a link, it's replaced with whatever content to which it was linked. However, in this situation, the narrow left frame isn't where you want that linked page to appear. The left frame should remain stationary, and the linked pages should open on the right. The way to make this happen is by setting up a target for the link.

If you'd prefer (as we do) that the link load in the larger right side of the frameset, you must first name the two frames. Giving a name to an element in HTML is something you haven't done yet, but you'll see that it is necessary in certain instances throughout the exercises in this book. In this situation, you can't target the right frame to receive the results of the link without first giving it a name.

Note: *The directive to give the frame a name, because you've already saved all the documents with file names, frameset.html, left.html, and right.html, might confuse you. You also gave a title, **My First Frameset**, to the frameset.html document. Giving a "name" to an element in HTML, in order to set custom targets in links, is something totally different, however.*

5. Return to Dreamweaver to fix the target problem. Make sure the Frames panel is open. If it's not, choose **Window > Frames** to bring it up. Notice that it reads "**(no name)**" on both the right and left sides? Click on the left side and it will become outlined with a dark line, as shown above.

6. The Property Inspector should now display the setting for the **Frame Name** field. Enter **left**. You could name it anything you want. However, you should name it something meaningful because this name will appear in a menu later on and you'll want to easily remember what it meant.

7. Click on the right side of the Frames panel and look at the Property Inspector again. This time there is no frame name because you haven't given the right side of the frameset a name yet. Enter **right** into the **Frame Name** field. The Frames panel should now read **left** and **right** in faint letters. Leave the Frames panel open as you'll need it shortly.

8. Select the words "**Our Rooms**" in the left frame. Click on the arrow next to the **Target** field to access the pop-up menu. Select **right** from the menu. The word "**right**" should pop into the **Target** field.

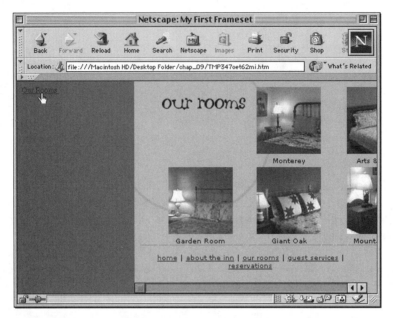

9. Press **F12** to preview the page again. Click on the link. If you're prompted again to save your files, click **Save**. This time the results should appear on the right side. You've just set up your first target in your first frameset. And you're on your way to mastering frames, which is no small accomplishment!

10. Return to Dreamweaver and keep the files open for the next exercise.

Target Names

A further explanation of Target Names is in order, because in the last exercise you used only the **Custom Target** feature.

When you access the pop-up menu for **Target**, you may wonder what do the terms **_blank**, **_parent**, **_self**, and **_top** mean? You created the targets right and left, and those names are in the menu because you added them. The other names, however, are part of the HTML specifications. Below you will find a chart that explains their meanings.

HTML Specifications for Target Names	
Target Name	**Significance**
_blank	Loads the link into a new browser window. This is the target to use if you want to keep someone inside your site, and show them another site at the same time. It opens a new browser window, so that two windows are on the screen at the same time—one containing your site, and the other containing the URL of the site you linked to.
_parent	Used when framesets are nested, to send your end user to the parent of the nested framesets. It's possible to put a frameset inside another frameset, but that's more advanced frameset building than this book will cover. Frankly, we rarely use this target, because we rarely work with nested framesets.
_self	Used when you want the results of the link to load in the same page that the link was in. That's the default behavior of HTML anyway, so we never use this.
_top	Transports the end user from a frameset to a single HTML page. This breaks the frames and loads all of the results into a single page, in the same window. Use this target when you want to exit a frameset.

NOTE | To Scroll or Not to Scroll?

We keep harping on the fact that frames can look boxy, and you've already learned how to remedy this by turning off the border on the frameset. What about scrollbars, which can also make a frameset look boxed in? Scrollbars are necessary if your content is larger than the size of the frame. You can turn scrollbars off completely or allow them to appear automatically, which is the Dreamweaver default. We suggest you leave the program at its defaults. If the content is big enough to warrant scrollbars, they'll appear.

Scrollbars are set in the Property Inspector.

*To access the Property Inspector's **Frame Scroll** options, click on the right or left region of the Frames panel. Scrollbars are set independently for each frame. It is not necessary to do this at all unless you want to force scrollbars on or off via the **Scroll** option.*

4. —————————Adding a Background Image

You've learned how to color the background of each frame, but what about adding a **Background Image**? This is similar to coloring the background of each frame, which you already did in Exercise 2. There can be unexpected alignment problems with this process, however, if the frameset clips the background image on one of the frames. In this exercise, you will learn how to set the left frame to a specific size so that it doesn't cut off the background image unexpectedly.

1. Click inside the **left** frame and make sure you see the text-insertion cursor blinking to the right of the linked words "**Our Rooms.**" Choose **Modify > Page Properties...**

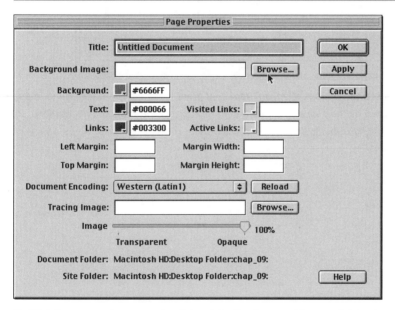

2. Click **Browse...** button to the right of the **Background Image** field to browse to the **images** folder, and select **bg_moon.jpg**. Click **Open**, and then **OK**. The background image should appear in the left side of the frameset.

3. Click inside the frame named **right.html** and make sure you see the text-insertion cursor blinking, then choose **Modify > Page Properties...**

4. Click on the **Browse...** button to the right of the **Background Image** field to locate once again **bg_moon.jpg** in the **images** folder where you just were. Click **Open**, and then **OK**. The background image should appear in the right side of the frameset.

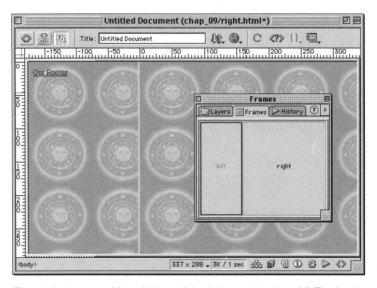

There's just one problem. It doesn't look that great, does it? The background image has been clipped by the size of the two frames. To correct the problem, it's essential to know the dimensions of both the graphic and the frameset. The following steps walk you through this process.

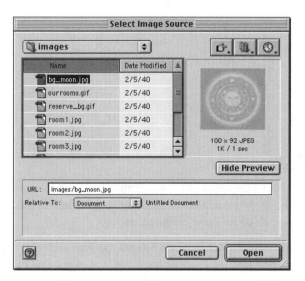

5. To establish the size of the background image, click on the **left.html** frame again and make sure you see the blinking text-insertion cursor. Choose **Modify > Page Properties...** again. Click on the **Browse...** button to the right of the **Background Image** field to locate **bg_moon.jpg**. Make sure that you click the **Show Preview** button in the **Select Image Source** dialog box. Notice that the dimensions **100 x 92** appear in the **Select Image Source** preview window? You now know that the width of the image is 100 pixels. Click **Cancel** twice to return to the document window.

Why cancel? The sole purpose for doing this step was to read the dimensions of the graphic, not to actually reinsert the background image! Often we will insert an image just to learn more about its size or downloading speed, and then cancel out of the process once the information is gathered.

*Next, you'll want to make the left column of the frameset match the size of that background image. Because the background image is 100 pixels wide, you could make the **left.html** column 200 pixels wide, and it would tile twice perfectly. Question is, how do you get to the information about what size the left column is? Frankly, it's a bit tricky and takes some clicking around.*

6. In the Frames panel (if it's not visible, go to **Window > Frames**), click on the outer border of the panel. Your Frames panel might already look like this before you read this step. If so, click on the left side, and then click on the outer border again.

Sometimes you have to toggle the outer border of the Frames panel on and off to get it to show the correct information settings in the Property Inspector. What's the goal of doing this? Changing your Property Inspector to show you the frameset's column size.

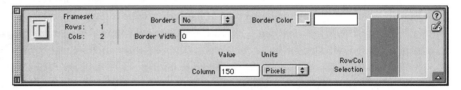

*The goal of clicking on the outer border of the Frames panel is to change your Property Inspector so that it looks like this, which gives you access to the **column value**. With the left column selected in the Property Inspector, you can see the **Column** setting is 150 pixels. That shows the setting that you created way back in Exercise 2. You'll want to change this to accommodate the size of the background image in this exercise. The next steps will walk you through this process.*

 MOVIE | frames_settings.mov

To learn more about frames, check out **frames_settings.mov** located in the **movies** folder on the Dreamweaver 4 **H•O•T CD-ROM**.

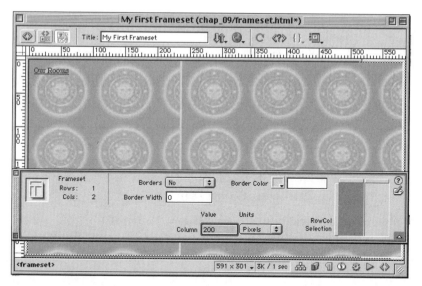

7. Enter the value **Column: 200** into the Property Inspector and press **Return/Enter**. The left column should have just shifted a bit to the right. Things still don't fit properly because there are more steps to follow.

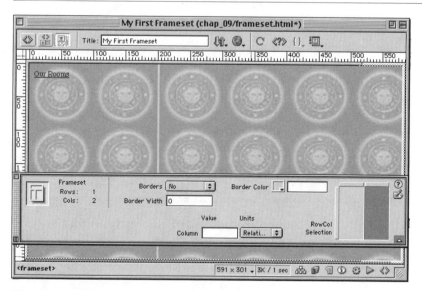

8. In the Property Inspector, click on the right **Column** icon, at the right of the panel. Select **Units: Relative**. Bingo! The background image now tiles perfectly!

9. Select **File > Save All Frames**. Close the file.

If the directions in Exercise 4 seemed odd and/or mysterious to you, it's because they are a little odd and mysterious! Perhaps this review will help: Clicking on the right side of the Property Inspector's **Column** icon allowed you to change the settings for the right column. Choosing **Relative Units** makes HTML allocate to the right column whatever space is left over from the fixed-pixel left column. In Exercise 4, you wanted the left side to be fixed, but the right side to scale proportionately depending on how the size of the end-user's monitor.

TIP | Specifying a Frame Size

The last exercise showed how to specify the left frame to be 200 pixels wide. Here are step-by-step directions to access the frame size settings.

1. Make sure the **Frames** panel is open (**Window > Frames**).

2. Next, click on the outer region of the Frames panel.
Tip: You might have to click on an inner region and then an outer region to jog the Property Inspector to show the correct setting.

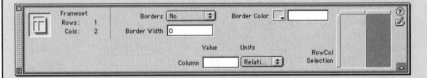

3. Click on the icon to the far right of the Property Inspector to select the appropriate frame. In this instance, it's the right one.

4. Enter the **column value** of your choice. You can select units in either **Pixels**, **Percent**, or **Relative**. See the chart on the next page for a description of each.

Units

Below is a chart that defines the choices you have when specifying a frame size in the Property Inspector:

Frame Size Settings	
Units	**Function**
Pixels	Sets the size of the selected column or row at an absolute value. This option is the best choice for a frame that should always be the same size, such as a navigation bar. If you set one of your frame regions to *Pixels*, then all the other frames will have to yield to that size. In other words, *Pixels* takes priority over all other settings.
Percent	Specifies that the current frame take up a specified percentage of frameset. This causes frames to dynamically resize according to the width or height the end user's browser was opened to. If you mix *Pixels* and *Percent*, *Pixels* will be honored first.
Relative	Allocates space after frames with *Units* set to *Pixels* and *Percent* are satisfied. These frames are designed to take up all the remaining space in the browser window.

NOTE | Frame Properties

What do the frame settings mean in the Property Inspector? On the following page you will find a chart to help you understand them.

Frame Properties In Dreamweaver	
Setting	**Description**
Frame Name	Sets the name of the current frame so you can use targets (remember _blank, _parent _self, and _top?) when setting up links. This name must be a single word or use underscores (my_name) or hyphens (my-name). Spaces are not allowed.
Src	Sets the source document for each frame. Enter a file name or click the folder icon to browse to and select the file. You can also open a file in a frame by clicking the cursor in the frame inside the document window and choosing *File > Open in Frame...*
Scroll	Determines whether scrollbars appear when there is not enough room to display the content of the current frame. Most browsers default to *Auto*. This is a good thing, because you only want scrollbars if they are necessary. Scrollbars aren't pretty, but they are necessary when there's more content than the frameset column size can display.
No Resize	Prevents a frame from being resizable in browsers. *Tip:* If you turn the borders off in your frameset, end users won't be able to resize them even if the *No Resize* option is left off.
Borders	Controls the border of the current frame. The options are *Yes, No,* and *Default.* This choice overrides border settings defined for the frameset. It's important to set the borders to *No* even if you've set them to *0*, because of differences between Netscape and Explorer. Netscape honors *0*, while Explorer honors *No*.
Border Color	Sets a border color for all borders adjacent to the current frame. This setting overrides the border color of the framesets. It's only supported on 4.0+ browsers, so if you choose to use it at all, we don't recommend that you make it an integral part of your design.
Margin Width	Sets in pixels the width of the left and right margins (the space between the frame border and the content). The default is that the frame border and content are aligned, so unless you want an offset, you don't need to adjust this setting.
Margin Height	Sets in pixels the height of the top and bottom margins (the space between the frame border and the content). The default is that the frame border and content are lined up, so unless you want an offset, you don't need to adjust this setting.

5. —————— Seamless Background Across Two Frames

In the previous exercise, you learned to put the identical background image into two frames and how to set a frameset's column width. Next, you'll produce a similar exercise that uses different artwork to further alter the appearance of the frameset. In this example, the background image art was created at a size large enough to fill the entire screen (1024 x 768 pixels), then sliced into two pieces, and then reassembled inside the frameset to appear as a seamless image. This technique successfully hides the unwanted boxy appearance that results so often when creating frames.

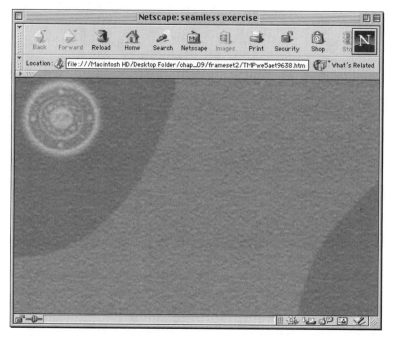

You may not realize that this page is composed of frames. That's because this frameset uses two different background images that have been cut up to appear as a single background image. You'll learn how to accomplish this technique by following the steps in this exercise.

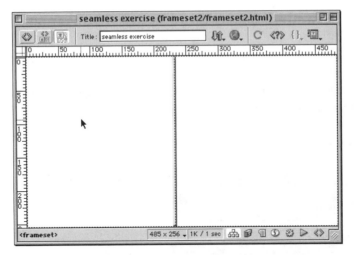

1. Open **frameset2.html** from the **frameset2** folder. This is similar to the document you made before, but a lot of the early steps are already completed. Click on the **left frame**, in the document window. Next, choose **Modify > Page Properties...**

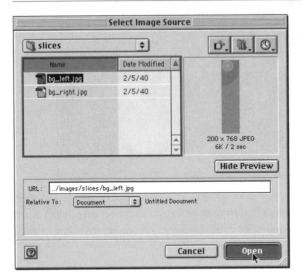

2. Click on the **Browse...** button to the right of the **Background Image:** field and browse to the **images** folder and then the **slices** folder. Select **bg_left.jpg**. Notice that the dimensions appear in the **image preview** of the **Select Image Source** window and that the width of this image is 200 pixels. Click **Open**, then **OK**.

3. Click on the right frame of the frameset and choose **Modify > Page Properties...** Select **bg_right.jpg** (from the **slices** folder you'll find inside the **images** folder) as your background image. Notice that the dimensions appear in the **Image Preview** of the **Select Image Source** window and that this image is 824 pixels wide. Click **Open**, then **OK**.

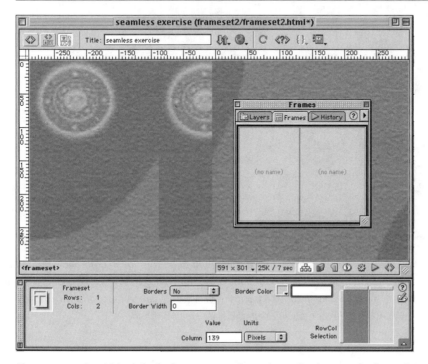

Your screen should look funky because you haven't set the frameset's dimensions yet.

4. Make sure the Frames panel is open (**Window > Frames**), and click on the outer region (if you've forgotten how, check Exercise 4, Step 6) to make your Property Inspector display the frameset's dimensions. Click on the left side of the **Column** icon and select **Borders: No**. Then enter **Border: Width 0, Column Value: 200**, and **Units: Pixels**.

5. Next, click on the right side of the **Column** icon, and enter **Units: Relative**. Press **F12** to preview the results.

If your screen looks like this, you did everything right! If it doesn't, go back and reread all the steps (especially the part about setting the right side to Relative!) It looks like a single page with a single background, does it not? If your audience hates the way frames look, they should have no complaints with this little sleight of hand.

6. —————————**Frames Objects Panel**

The previous examples taught you a lot about the basics of frames. Now that you have that knowledge under your belt and understand the concepts behind frames, you will be able to fully understand the power of the **Frames Objects** panel. This exercise will show you how to use it.

1. Open a new blank document.

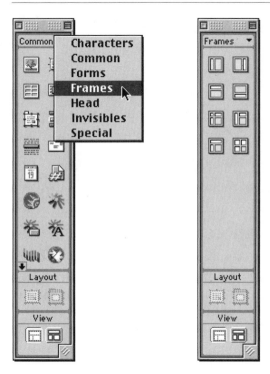

2. Click on the small black arrow at the top of the Objects panel. Select **Frames** from the pop-up list. This will change the icons on the Objects panel.

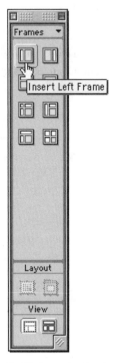

3. Click on the first icon in the top-left column. This will make Dreamweaver create a frameset similar to the icon.

Note: *This step is an alternative method to Step 3 in Exercise 1. You don't have to choose Modify > Frameset Split Frame anymore if you use these handy objects on the Objects panel.*

TIP | What Does the Blue and White Mean?

You might have noticed that the icons in the Frames Objects panel are colored in blue and white. This has significant meaning: it tells you how the different areas have been specified with regard to size. The blue areas are set to a relative size, and the white areas have been set to an exact pixel size.

What you spent several steps establishing in Exercise 4 by setting the frames to be either relative or pixel-based is accomplished automatically by using one of these frames objects from the Objects panel. This is a huge improvement in Dreamweaver. Don't hate us for making you go through all those steps in Exercise 4 though. As teachers, we decided it was good for your education to appreciate the new frames features in Dreamweaver by learning how to do it manually and painfully first. Sorry 'bout 'dat, but not really. Just think, "no pain, no gain." ;-)

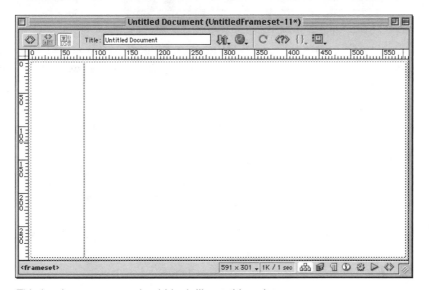

This is what your page should look like at this point.

4. With the frameset still selected, choose **File > Save Frameset As...** This works just like the procedure you learned in Exercise 1.

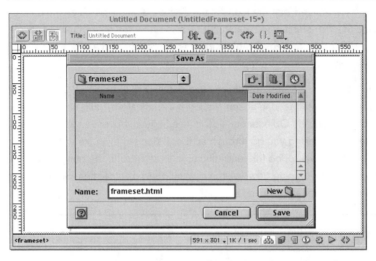

5. The first file you are going to save is the frameset file. It contains all of the information on how the entire structure of the page is set up. Save this file as **frameset.html** inside the **frameset3** folder.

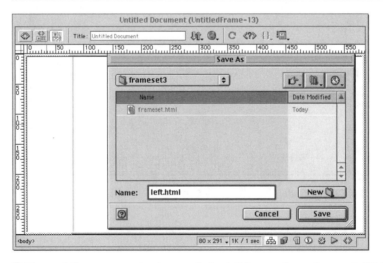

6. The next file you are going to save is the left frame of your frameset. Click inside the left frame of the document window and choose **File > Save Frame As...** Save this file as **left.html** inside the **frameset3** folder.

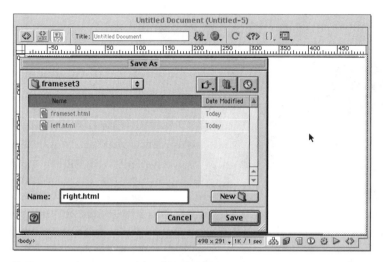

7. The next file you are going to save is the right frame of your frameset. Click in the right frame of the document window and choose **File > Save Frame As...** Save this file as **right.html** inside the **frameset3** folder.

As you can see, using a frames object from the Objects panel is a pretty simple way to create a frameset. But you still need a working knowledge of framesets, so that's why we chose to wait until the end of this chapter to show you this option. Now that you know it's here, use it!

---

8. Close this file. You are done working with it.

Phew, this was a long chapter. Take a quick break, and then it's time to move on to the next chapter.

10.

Rollovers

Creating a Simple Rollover	Animated Rollovers!
Creating Pointer Rollovers	Creating Multiple Event Rollovers
Creating Flash Buttons	Inserting a Navigation Bar Rollover
Inserting Fireworks HTML

chap_10

Dreamweaver 4
H•O•T CD-ROM

One of the key challenges in Web development is to invent artwork that clearly communicates how to navigate through your site. **Rollover** graphics, which change when the end user's mouse goes over them, are great for adding visual cues that ensure your audience knows an image has special meaning or that it is a link. Rollovers are also great if you have limited space, because you can put extra information within the changing graphic. For example, we could make a button that says "Services," and when visitors to our site place their mouse over the word, it could change to list the services we offer, such as training, consulting, videos, books, lectures, etc.

What you might not realize is that rollovers are not written in standard HTML. Instead, rollovers are written in a widely used scripting language invented by Netscape, called JavaScript.

Dreamweaver automatically writes JavaScript rollovers for you without you ever having to write the scripts or even understand how they are constructed. This is great news, because a lot of people, ourselves included, don't know how to write JavaScript from scratch. Alternately, we have trained many programmers who do know how to write JavaScript by hand, but enjoy Dreamweaver for its rollover capabilities because it can literally save days of programming work. For this reason, Dreamweaver's rollover features are helpful to both the designer and the programmer.

Rollover Rules

While this book provides many exercises that teach you how to implement rollovers, it is our hope that you'll move beyond the exercises to create your own custom rollover graphics once you get the hang of this feature. If you plan to make your own rollovers from scratch, you should be aware of a few important concepts.

Rollovers require a minimum of two graphics—an "off" state and an "on" state. Because this is a book on Dreamweaver, it doesn't cover how to make the graphic component of rollovers. You would need an imaging program, such as Fireworks or Photoshop, to make the images.

If you are going to make your own rollover graphics in an image editor, one important rule to understand is that the graphics for the "off" state and "on" state for each of your rollover images must be the same size in dimensions, or you risk that they will look distorted. JavaScript requires **WIDTH** and **HEIGHT** information, which Dreamweaver will add for you automatically. If you have two different-sized pieces of artwork, the JavaScript will scale both to the same width and height, causing distortion. For this reason, all the images that are provided in this chapter's exercises share the same dimensions, as they should. ;-)

 I. —————————Creating a Simple Rollover

This first exercise will show you how to create a simple rollover. These types of rollovers involve two pieces of artwork. The first graphic appears on the screen initially, and the second appears when the mouse "rolls over" it. In JavaScript terminology, this is called a swap image. But you will not be writing any JavaScript from scratch, because Dreamweaver makes creating a simple rollover easier than many other operations you've already learned.

1. Define your site for Chapter 10. If you need a refresher on this process, revisit Exercise 1 in Chapter 3, *"Site Control."*

Before the mouse moves over the star in the Web browser.

After the mouse moves over the star in the Web browser.

2. Open **basicrollfinal.html** in the **html** folder. Move your mouse over the star. Nothing happens, right? Press **F12** to preview the page. When you move your mouse over it in your Web browser, it changes to a yellow star. You can only view a rollover inside a browser because Dreamweaver cannot preview such an effect. Return to Dreamweaver and close the file. You'll get to build this same file from scratch in the following steps.

3. Choose **File > New** (Mac) or **File > New Window** (Windows) to create a new untitled document. It is always a good practice to save a file before you begin working with it, because Dreamweaver will give you error messages if you don't. Choose **File > Save** and name this file **simpleroll.html** inside the **chap_10** folder.

4. Choose **Insert > Interactive Images > Rollover Image** or click the **Insert Rollover Image** object on the **Objects** panel. If the Objects panel is not visible, go to **Window > Objects**.

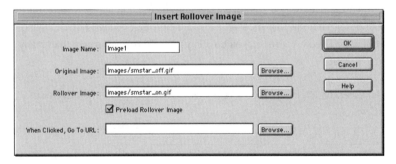

5. The Insert Rollover Image dialog box will appear. For the **Original Image**, click **Browse...** to select **smstar_off.gif** located inside the **images** folder. For the **Rollover Image**, click **Browse...** to select **smstar_on.gif** located inside the same folder. Make sure your dialog box looks just like the one above and click **OK**.

MOVIE | rollover_list.mov

To see this exercise in action, check out **rollover_list.mov** located in the movies folder on the Dreamweaver 4 **H•O•T** CD-ROM.

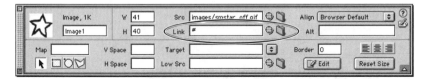

*With the image still selected, notice the hash mark (**#**) inside the **Link** area of the Property Inspector? Dreamweaver inserted this symbol in order to create a link even though you didn't specify one. Why? Because a link is necessary for the JavaScript rollover to work. Putting a hash mark in the Link area inserts a stand-in link that doesn't link to anything. It simply acts as a placeholder so that you can still click it and see the rollover.*

6. In the Property Inspector, click the **folder** icon to the right of the **Link** field, and browse to select **rooms.html** located in the **chap_10** folder. Press **F12** to preview the rollover. Click the star and voilà, **rooms.html** will appear!

7. Return to Dreamweaver and save and close the document.

NOTE | JavaScript and Java: Separated at Birth?

You might wonder if JavaScript bears any relation to the popular programming language Java, developed by Sun Microsystems. Only in name. Netscape licensed the name from Sun in hopes that the Web community would embrace its scripting language more quickly if it had a recognizable name. Ironically, since then, JavaScript has become more widely embraced than Java, and has taken on a life and following all of its own.

One important distinction between JavaScript and Java is that the code for JavaScript is placed inside your HTML pages, while Java is compiled as a separate program, meaning that you can't see the code for it inside an HTML page. This means that you can see JavaScript code inside HTML documents if you view the source code, while the code within a Java applet is hidden. This has made JavaScript immensely popular among Web authors, as many people were able to teach themselves the language by looking at other people's Web-page source and by copying, pasting, and experimenting.

2.————————**Animated Rollovers!**

This next exercise uses the same technique as Exercise 1, only instead of two static images, the rollover image is an animated GIF. You'll be putting the rollover graphics inside a table to ensure that they don't move around once they're in place. Working with animated rollovers may look complicated, but it's just as easy as the last exercise you completed.

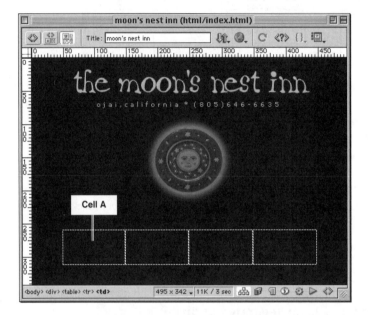

1. Open **index.html** located in the **html** folder. Notice the empty table where the navigation elements belong? This is where you're going to insert rollovers for each button. Click inside **Cell A** (row 1, column 1) and click the **Insert Rollover Image** object on the Objects panel.

 MOVIE | smooshed_table.mov

To see a movie of how to insert these rollovers into the table, check out **smooshed_table.mov** located in the **movies** folder on the Dreamweaver 4 H•O•T CD-ROM.

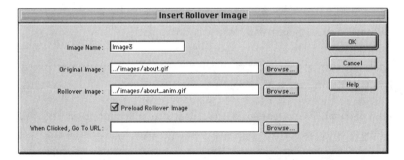

2. The **Insert Rollover Image** dialog box will appear. For the **Original Image**, click **Browse...** to select **about.gif** located in the **images** folder. For the **Rollover Image**, click **Browse...** to select **about_anim.gif** located in the same folder. Click **OK**.

Notice that the table got all smooshed up after you inserted the image? You'll fix that shortly, so don't worry about it just yet.

---

3. Unfortunately, you can't preview the results of what you just did in Dreamweaver, so press **F12** to view it in a browser. Move your mouse over the **about the inn** image. Notice that the rollover state is an animated GIF? Dreamweaver treats the animated GIF as it would any other GIF, yet the result when previewed in a browser is different from that of a rollover created from two static GIFs. This technique produces a simple, novel effect.

---

4. Return to Dreamweaver and click to the right of the **about the inn** (**about.gif**) graphic to make sure it is deselected. Press **Tab** to insert your cursor in the next cell, which is now scrunched up with the other cells on the right-hand side of the table.

---

5. Once your cursor is in **Cell B** (row 1, column 2), click the **Insert Rollover Image** object on the Objects panel. For the **Original Image**, click **Browse...** to select **rooms.gif** located in the **images** folder. For the **Rollover Image**, click **Browse...** to select **rooms_anim.gif** located in the same folder. Click **OK**.

---

6. Click to the right of the **our rooms** (**rooms.gif**) image to deselect it. Press **Tab** to insert your cursor in **Cell C** (row 1, column 3), then click the **Insert Rollover Image** object on the Objects panel. For the **Original Image**, click **Browse...** to select services.gif located in the **images** folder. For the **Rollover Image**, click **Browse...** to select **services_anim.gif** located in the same folder. Click **OK**.

---

7. Click to the right of the **guest services** (**services.gif**) image to deselect it. Press **Tab** to insert your cursor in **Cell D** (row 1, column 4) and click the **Insert Rollover Image** object on the Objects panel. For the **Original Image**, click **Browse...** to select **reservations.gif** located in the **images** folder. For the **Rollover Image**, click **Browse...** to select **reservations_anim.gif** located in the same folder. Click **OK**.

---

8. Press **F12** to preview the results. We hope you agree that this was simple to execute and impressive upon completion. Return to Dreamweaver, then save and close your document.

WARNING | Animated GIF Rollovers and Preload

The previous exercise used animated GIF files for one of the rollover states. Dreamweaver regards these files no differently from static GIFs. If you make your own animated GIF files in an image editor and use them in Dreamweaver as rollover states, there's a problem that we would like to warn you about.

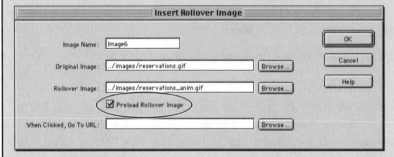

Notice that Dreamweaver automatically checks the **Preload Rollover Image** checkbox in the **Insert Rollover Image** dialog box? What does that mean, exactly? The browser is being instructed to wait until all the graphics for the rollover have been downloaded before the rollover functions.

Animated GIFs can be set to play once, any number of times (2x, 3x, etc.) or loop indefinitely. If when you create your animated GIF files you set them to loop indefinitely, then leaving the Preload Rollover Image box checked will work just fine, as it did here. However, if you have your animated GIF play only one time, it will play when it's preloaded and by the time your end user looks at your rollover it will no longer animate! The rule of thumb is this: leave Preload Rollover Image on for looping GIFs, and uncheck Preload Rollover Image if your GIF is set to play only one time.

3. —————————**Creating Pointer Rollovers**

This next exercise shows you how to create pointer rollovers. Pointer rollovers reuse one piece of artwork (in this example, the star) which follows the mouse as you move over each word. This type of rollover involves making a table to hold all the artwork in place. You'll also get to use the **Behaviors** feature, instead of the **Insert Rollover Image** object from the Objects panel. Are you feeling macho, or what?

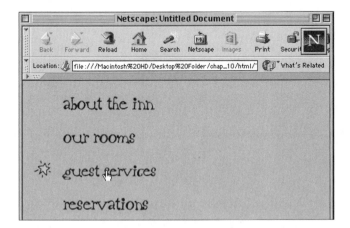

1. View the finished file first. Open **pointerfinal.html** located in the **html** folder and press **F12** to preview it inside a browser. Return to Dreamweaver and close the file. You're going to re-create it from scratch.

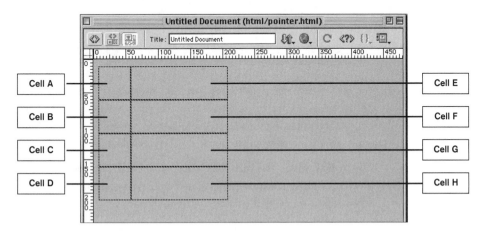

2. Open **pointer.html** in the **html** folder, which already contains an empty table with four rows and two columns. You could have created this table from scratch, but we just wanted to help you get to programming the rollovers faster.

3. Click inside **Cell A** and choose **Insert > Image**. Select **blank_p.gif** from the **images** folder, then click **Open**. The goal of the first part of this exercise is to insert the same **blank_p.gif** image in every location that the pointer will appear. Why? Because rollovers require two images: the original state and the rollover state. In this instance, the original state looks like nothing, because it is a transparent GIF, which lets the background color show through.

4. Repeat this process three times, inserting the same **blank_p.gif** file inside **Cells B**, **C**, and **D**.

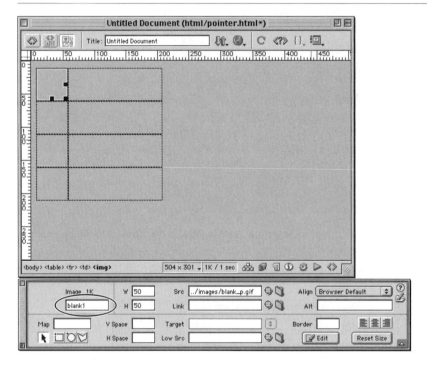

5. After you have inserted the **blank_p.gif** image into these four cells, click inside **Cell A**, as shown above. Inside the Property Inspector, give it the name **blank1**. It is essential that you assign a unique name to each image by selecting each instance of **blank_p.gif** and naming it respectively **blank1**, **blank2**, **blank3**, **blank4**. Make sure to highlight the appropriate **blank_p.gif** image when naming each graphic.

NOTE: In Exercise 1, Dreamweaver gave the rollovers names automatically. When you use the Swap Image behavior, you have to manually give each image a unique name, or the behavior will not work. Be aware that names in Dreamweaver (or HTML) cannot contain any spaces.

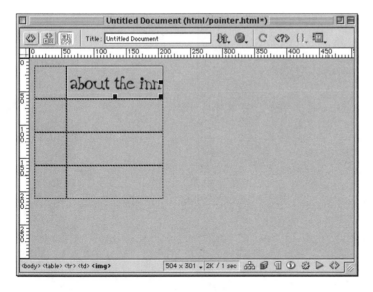

6. Click **Cell E** and choose **Insert > Image**, then browse to **about_p.gif** located in the **images** folder and click **Open**.

7. With **about_p.gif** selected, enter the name **about** inside the Property Inspector.

NOTE: Naming each image is essential to working with rollovers in Dreamweaver. This is because JavaScript requires a unique name for each source graphic in order to perform rollover functions. For this reason, you will need to add a unique name for every image that you insert into this table.

8. Click **Cell F** and choose **Insert > Image**, then browse to **ourrooms_p.gif** located in the **images** folder and click **Open**.

9. While **ourrooms_p.gif** is selected, enter the name **rooms** inside the Property Inspector.

10. Click **Cell G** and choose **Insert > Image**, then browse to **reservations_p.gif** located in the **images** folder and click **Open**.

11. While **reservations_p.gif** is selected, enter the name **reservations** inside the Property Inspector.

12. Click **Cell H** and choose **Insert > Image**, then browse to **services_p.gif** located in the **images** folder and click **Open**.

13. While **services_p.gif** is selected, enter the name **services** inside the Property Inspector.

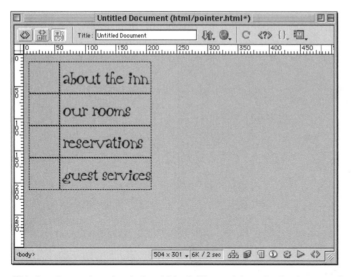

This is what pointer.html should look like at this point in the exercise.

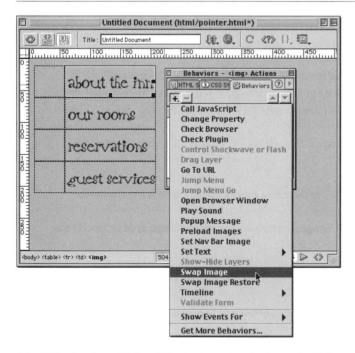

14. Click **about_p.gif** (**about the inn**) to select it. Open the Behaviors panel (if it isn't already open) by selecting **Window > Behaviors** or using the shortcut key (**Shift+F3**).

15. With **about_p.gif** (**about the inn**) selected, click the plus sign above the **Events** column and select **Swap Image** from the pop-up menu.

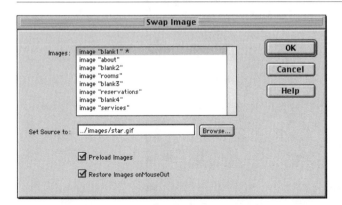

16. In the **Swap Image** dialog box that will open, make sure the "**blank1**" image name is highlighted at the top. Click **Browse...** and select **star.gif** located in the **images** folder. Click **Open**. Back in the **Swap Image** dialog box, click **OK**.

17. Next, select **ourrooms_p.gif** (**our rooms**) and click the **plus** sign, in the Behaviors panel, to select **Swap Image**. Select image "**blank2**" from the **Images:** list and click **Browse...** to locate **star.gif**. Click **Open**. Back in the **Swap Image** dialog box, click **OK**.

18. Repeat this process for **reservations_p.gif**, selecting image "**blank3**," and **services_p.gif**, selecting image "**blank4**."

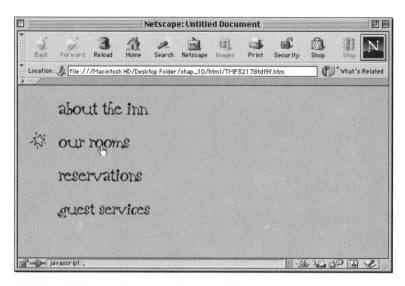

19. Press **F12** to preview in your browser. What you see should look just like the **pointerfinal.html** document you opened and previewed at the beginning of this exercise. To make yourself feel really good, return to Dreamweaver and press the **Code View** button to view the code. Hey, you didn't have to write any of that! Press the **Design View** button to return to the design view. Save and close the file to move on to the next exercise.

This exercise demonstrated the benefit of using a table to hold together multiple graphics. It also reinforced the fact that you need two images for a rollover—the original state and the rollover state. In this instance, the original was a blank image. When you program rollovers from the Behaviors panel, you also must give them a name, which you did several times in this exercise!

Creating Multiple-Event Rollovers

A multiple-event rollover uses more than two pieces of artwork in the Swap Image behavior. In this example, three different pieces of artwork change for every rollover. If that sounds complicated, it is! Assembling this type of rollover can be tedious, but not nearly as tedious as writing all the HTML and JavaScript from scratch.

1. Open **multiple_final.html** located in the **html** folder, and preview this finished exercise in your browser. Roll your mouse over each item in the list and watch the rooms change. This is a very impressive type of rollover, and you (yes you!) are going to know how to do it as soon as you follow along. Close this file.

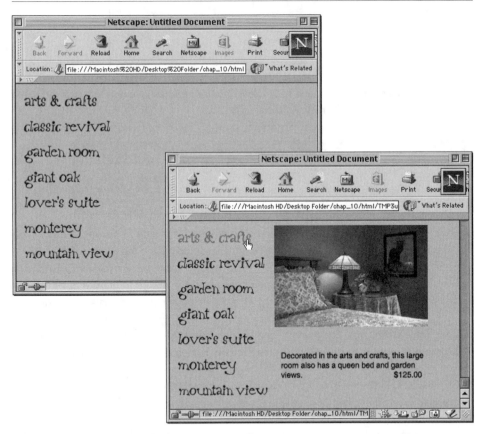

The image on the left shows the page before the rollover. The image to the right shows the page when the mouse rolls over a name on the list, the name turns red and a photograph and description appear at the same time.

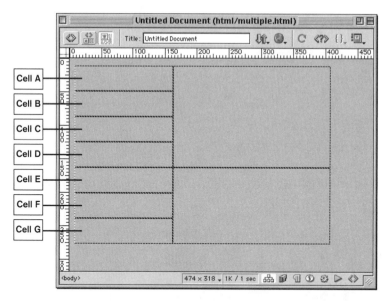

2. Open **multiple.html** located in the **html** folder. This file includes an empty, pre-built table. You learned to make a table like this in Chapter 7, *"Tables."*

3. Click inside **Cell A** (row 1, column 1) and choose **Insert > Image** to browse to **arts.gif** located in the **images** folder, then click **Open**. In the Property Inspector, name the image **arts**.

4. Click inside **Cell B** (row 2, column 1) and choose **Insert > Image** to browse to **classic.gif** located in the **images** folder, then click **Open**. In the Property Inspector, name the image **classic**.

5. Click inside **Cell C** (row 3, column 1) and choose **Insert > Image** to browse to **garden.gif** located in the **images** folder, then click **Open**. In the Property Inspector, name the image **garden**.

6. Click inside **Cell D** (row 4, column 1) and choose **Insert > Image** to browse to **giant.gif** located in the **images** folder, then click **Open**. In the Property Inspector, name the image **giant**.

7. Click inside **Cell E** (row 5, column 1) and **choose Insert > Image** to browse to **lovers.gif** located in the **images** folder, then click **Open**. In the Property Inspector, name the image **lovers**.

8. Click inside **Cell F** (row 6, column 1) and choose **Insert > Image** to browse to **monterey.gif** located in the **images** folder, then click **Open**. In the Property Inspector, name the image **monterey**.

9. Click inside **Cell G** (row 7, column 1) and choose **Insert > Image** to browse to **mountain.gif** located in the **images** folder, then click **Open**. In the Property Inspector, name the image **mountain**.

10. Click in the **top cell** (row 1, column 2) and choose **Insert > Image** to browse to **blank1.gif** located in the **images** folder, then click **Open**. In the Property Inspector, name the image **blank1**.

11. Click in the **bottom cell** (row 2, column 2) and choose **Insert > Image** to browse to **blank2.gif** located in the **images** folder, then click **Open**. In the Property Inspector, name the image **blank2**.

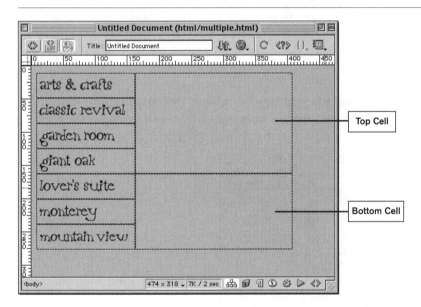

This is what your page should look like now.

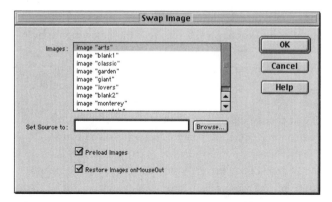

12. Select the image in **Cell A** (row 1, column 1). With the image selected, click the plus sign in the Behaviors panel to select **Swap Image**. If the Behaviors panel is not open, press **Shift+F3** to open it. In the **Swap Image** dialog box that will open, notice that "**arts**" is selected in the **Images** list. Be sure not to click **OK** until we say so.

13. Click **Browse...** to **Set Source** to: **arts_on.gif**, then click **Open**. This sets the rollover for the graphic **arts & crafts (arts.gif)** to turn red when you move your mouse over it. Don't click **OK** yet!

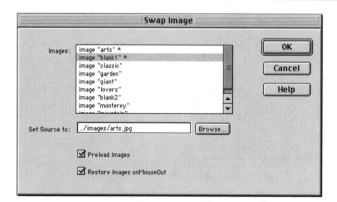

14. Select "**blank1**" from the same **Images** list. Click **Browse...** again to **Set Source** to: **arts.jpg**, then click **Open**. You just instructed the behavior to swap the **blank1 (blank1.gif)** artwork to the picture of the **arts & crafts hotel room (arts.jpg)**. Don't click **OK** yet!

The rollover now triggers two behaviors: the lettering for "arts & crafts" has been instructed to turn red, and an image of the room will appear when the mouse moves over the original image.

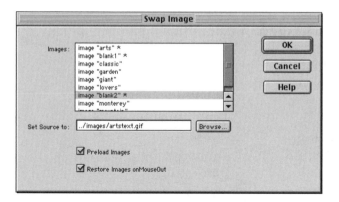

15. Scroll down the **Images** list to select "**blank2.**" Click **Browse...** again to **Set Source** to: **artstext.gif**, then click **Open**. You may now finally click **OK** to end this process.

16. Press **F12** and test your first rollover! Move your mouse over the words "**arts & crafts.**" The lettering should turn red and a picture of the room should appear to the upper right, with its description below. You've just set the rollover for **arts & crafts**.

There are only six more items on the list to go.

17. Return to Dreamweaver and repeat this process for the other images. Start by selecting the image in **Cell B** and clicking the plus sign in the Behaviors panel to select **Swap Image**. When you're done, press **F12** to preview your work in a browser, then close the file and move on to the next exercise. The chart on the next page shows which files go where.

MOVIE | swap_image.mov

This isn't the most intuitive operation in the universe, so don't kick yourself if you don't get it right the first time. If it didn't work, please view the movie **swap_image.mov**, located in the movies folder on the Dreamweaver 4 **H•O•T CD-ROM**.

Swap Image At A Glance		
Cell	**Images**	**Set Source To**
B (row 2, column 1)	classic.gif blank1 blank2	classic_on.gif classic.jpg classictext.gif
C (row 3, column 1)	garden.gif blank1 blank2	garden_on.gif garden.jpg gardentext.gif
D (row 4, column 1)	giant.gif blank1 blank2	giant_on.gif giant.jpg gianttext.gif
E (row 5, column 1)	lovers.gif blank1 blank2	lovers_on.gif lovers.jpg loverstext.gif
F (row 6, column 1)	monterey.gif blank1 blank2	monterey_on.gif monterey.jpg montereytext.gif
G (row 7, column 1)	mountain.gif blank1 blank2	mountain_on.gif mountain.jpg mountaintext.gif

What are Flash Buttons?

Dreamweaver 4 has new feature that lets you create something called **Flash Buttons**. Those buttons have very similar characteristics to other rollovers you have worked with in this chapter. For example, like other rollovers, Flash Buttons have an Up state and Over state. They can be set up to link to other pages, both internal and external. However, unlike other buttons, they are created from within Dreamweaver. This means that they can be quickly changed with just a few clicks, which can save you time. You don't need to use an image editor like Fireworks or ImageReady to work with Flash Buttons.

Creating Flash Buttons is fairly simple, as you will see by following the next exercise. What is different is that Dreamweaver creates the rollover images in the .swf file format, instead of GIF or JPG, once you click **OK** in the easy-to-use Flash Button interface. In other exercises, you have simply worked with existing images and set the behavior to write the necessary JavaScript to enact a rollover. With Flash Buttons, you are creating actual image files from Dreamweaver. This can be wonderfully convenient!

In order to view Flash content on the web, you must have the Flash plug-in installed in your browser. If you don't have this plug-in, you can download it for free at http://www.macromedia.com/software/flashplayer/

Creating Flash Buttons	
Pro	**Explanation**
Font Integrity	With Flash Buttons, you can use any font installed in your system and the visitors to your page don't need to have that font installed. This gives you much more flexibility when you are designing your pages.
Easily Updated	With just a few clicks, you can change the text and entire look of your Flash Buttons. This can save you a lot of time when you need to make changes to your site.
Complex Animations	Some of the Flash Buttons available to you in Dreamweaver have more complex animation than you could easily achieve with animated GIF files.
Design Consistency	Because a navigation system that uses Flash Buttons can be set up in minutes, it's easy to get a consistent look and feel to your site without a spending a lot of time designing your own rollover art. This helps to bring consistency to the overall design of your site.

Using Flash Text	
Cons	**Explanation**
Plug-in Required	All Flash content on the web requires a plug-in in order to be viewed properly. Flash Buttons are no different, and require that the Flash plug-in be installed in the browser.

5. ————————————**Creating Flash Buttons**

Dreamweaver 4 introduced a new feature that enables you to create Flash rollover buttons from a pre-defined set of styles, without ever leaving Dreamweaver. This exercise will show you how to work with this new feature.

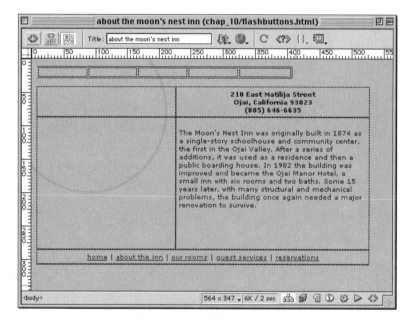

1. Open the **flashbuttons.html** file located inside the **chap_10** folder. This page contains a table at the top that is setup to hold the Flash Buttons you will create this exercise.

2. Click inside the first cell of the table. You should see a blinking cursor inside the cell. This indicates that your content will be inserted in this cell.

WARNING | **Flash Plug-In Required**

One advantage of Flash Buttons is that you can use any font you want and the end user does not have to have that font on their computer. All Flash content on the web requires that the end user have the Flash plug-in installed in their browser. According to Macromedia, about 330 million people have a version of the plug-in installed. That's a lot of people. We will talk about ways to detect if users have this plug-in installed in Chapter 14, *"Behaviors."*

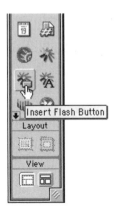

3. In the Common Objects panel, click the **Insert Flash Button** object. This will open the **Insert Flash Button** dialog box.

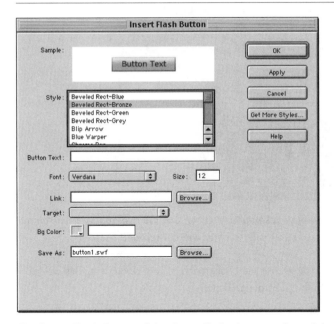

The Insert Flash Button dialog box will display a preview of the button settings at the top of this dialog box. As you select different styles, the Sample area will change. Moving your cursor over the Sample area will display a preview of the rollover effect.

4. Under the **Style** option, select **Beveled Rect-Bronze**. This will change the Sample area at the top.

5. Move your mouse over the Sample area to preview the rollover effect for this style.

6. For the **Button Text** option type **Home**. This option defines the text you want to appear on the button. If you leave this option blank, no text will appear on the button.

7. Make sure the **Font** option is set to **Verdana** and the **Size** option is set to **12**.

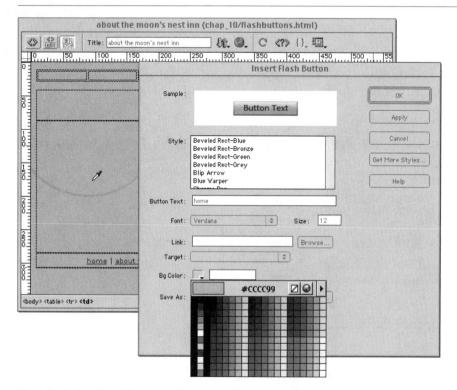

By default, the Flash Buttons will have a white background. You can use the eyedropper to match the background of the buttons with other colors in your site, such as the background color.

8. Click the **Bg Color** box and move your mouse over the background of your document. This will let you sample the light brown color so that both backgrounds match.

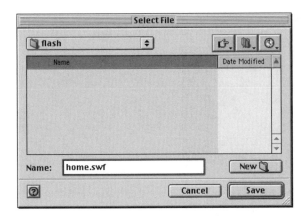

9. Click the **Browse** button to the right of the **Save As** option. Browse to the **flash** folder located inside the **chap_10** folder. Name the file **home.swf** and click the **Save** button.

NOTE: If it seems odd to save this file, let us take a moment to explain what is happening. Not only are you creating settings for the Flash text, but you're actually creating the Flash file from directly within Dreamweaver. The Flash file format is SWF. If you do not manually choose where to save the SWF file, it will be saved in the same location as the HTML document. It will work either way, but we created a flash folder to hold the SWF files for this exercise. While it's not necessary, many developers like to create separate folders for images and content (such as Flash).

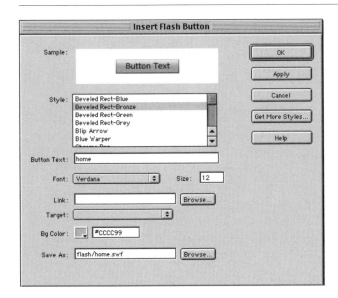

This is what the dialog box should look like at this point in the exercise.

10. Click **OK** to complete this process and create the Flash button.

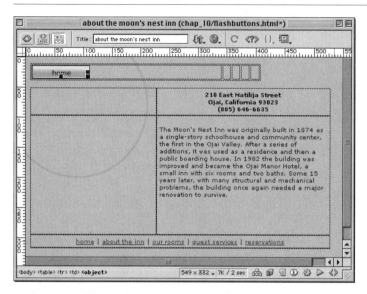

This is what your page should look like when the first button is inserted.

11. Press the **Tab** key to move your cursor to the next table cell.

12. Using the same steps, create a Flash Button for the following options: **about the inn**, **our rooms**, **services**, and **reservations**. Don't forget to save each file, with a unique name, inside the **flash** folder.

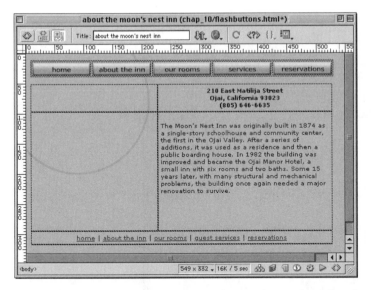

This is what your page should look like after you have added the other Flash Buttons.

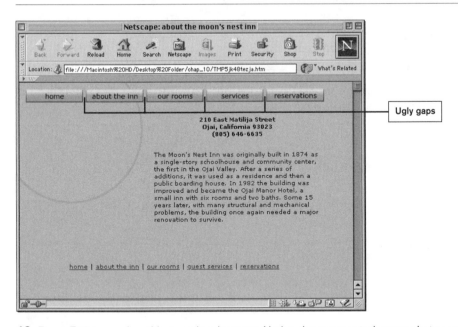

Ugly gaps

13. Press **F12** to preview this page in a browser. Notice the unexpected spaces between the buttons? You will learn how to get rid of those next.

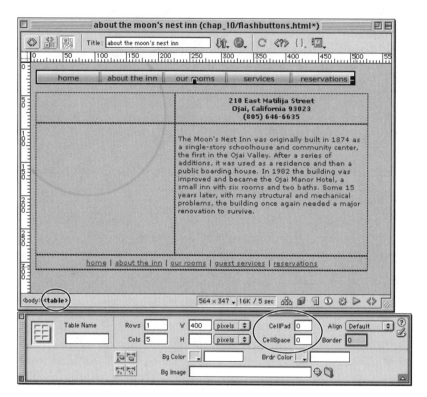

14. Return to Dreamweaver. Select the entire table. In the Property Inspector, set the **CellPad** and **CellSpace** options to **0**. This will remove those spaces in the table.

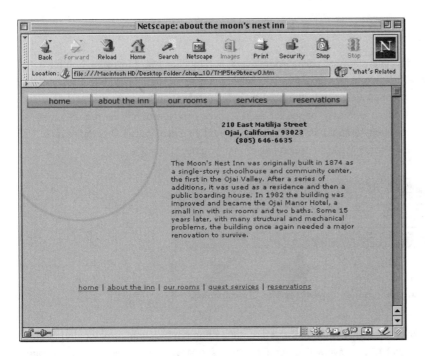

15. Press **F12** to preview the page again in a browser. Look ma, no more spaces! ;-)

16. Return to Dreamweaver. Save and close this file.

MOVIE | flashbuttons.mov

To learn more about Dreamweaver's Flash Buttons feature, check out **flashbuttons.mov** located in the **movies** folder on the Dreamweaver 4 **H•O•T CD-ROM**.

6.————————**Inserting a Navigation Bar Rollover**

So far, you have created simple rollovers, animated rollovers, and multiple-event rollovers. You have one more type of rollover to learn to create before you finish this chapter—the **Navigation Bar** rollover. A navigation bar-style rollover allows each button to display four **states: up**, **over**, **down**, and **over while down.** Instead of working with two images for each rollover, this type of rollover requires that you work with four, one for each separate state. This might sound intimidating, but Dreamweaver's new **Insert Navigation Bar** feature makes it much easier than you might imagine.

1. To view a sample of what you are about to create, open **navbar_final.html** located in the **html** folder. Press **F12** to preview this page in a browser. Move your mouse over the images and click a few as well. Notice there are more than two rollover states? This is what you'll learn to build in this exercise. Pretty neat-o!

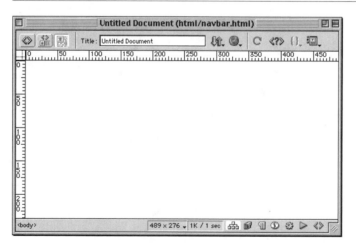

2. Return to Dreamweaver. Close **navbar_final.html** and open **navbar.html** located in the **html** folder. This is simply a blank file that has been saved for you already. You are going to use it as a starting point to create your own navigation bar.

3. Click the Insert Navigation Bar object in the Objects panel. As an alternative, you could select **Insert > Interactive Images > Navigation Bar**. Either way is fine and will open the **Insert Navigation Bar** dialog box (and a big dialog box it is at that!).

Different Rollover States

Keeping track of the different types of rollover states can be a little tricky. Heck, we have a hard enough time keeping track of our car keys, not to mention our rollover states. So, we have included the chart below to help you with this task:

Rollover States	
State	**What It Does**
Up	The graphic that appears on the Web page when it is loaded. This is also referred to as the "static" or "off" state.
Over	The graphic that appears when the end-user's mouse moves over the image. Most often, this image will revert back to the **Up** state when the mouse is moved off of the image. This is sometimes referred to as the "on" state.
Down	The graphic that will appear after the end user has clicked on the **Over** state. This state will not change again until the end-user's mouse moves over this image or clicks on another image.
Over While Down	This appears when the end-user's mouse moves over the **Down** state. It works just like the Over state, except that it works on the Down state only. Because the user's mouse is only depressed on a button for a short time, this state is not used very often.

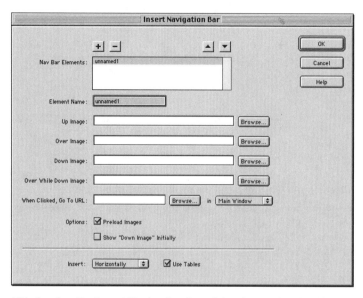

*This is what **the Insert Navigation Bar** dialog box looks like by default.*

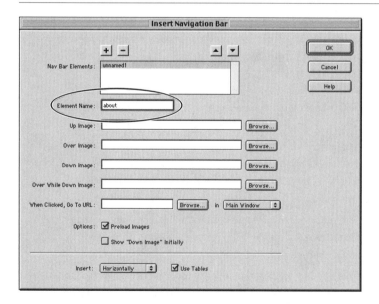

4. Enter **Element Name: about**. This assigns a name to the first rollover image in this navigation bar. Each element (rollover) must have a unique name. We suggest you name them in relationship to their function on the page. The first button will access the **About the Inn** page, so you will name this first element **about**.

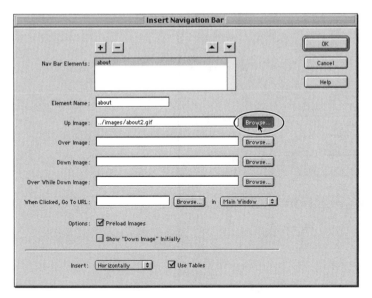

5. Click **Browse...** next to the **Up Image** field. Browse to the **images** folder and select **about2.gif**. Click **Open** to select this image. You've just specified the image for the Up state of the rollover.

---

6. Click **Browse...** next to **Over Image:**. Browse to the **images** folder and select **about_over.gif**. Click **Open** to select this image. You've just specified the image for the Over state of the rollover.

---

7. Click **Browse...** next to **Down Image:**. Browse to the **images** folder and select **about_down.gif**. Click **Open** to select this image. You've just specified the image for the Down state of the rollover.

---

8. Click **Browse...** next to **Over While Down Image:**. Browse to the **images** folder and select **about_overdown.gif**. Click **Open** to select this image. You've just specified the image for the Over While Down state of the rollover.

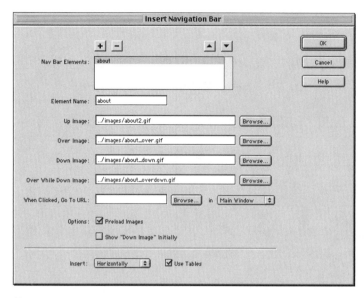

This is what your screen should look like at this point in the exercise.

Now that you have added the first rollover button in your navigation, it's time to add the next one. By the end of this exercise, this will all be second nature to you!

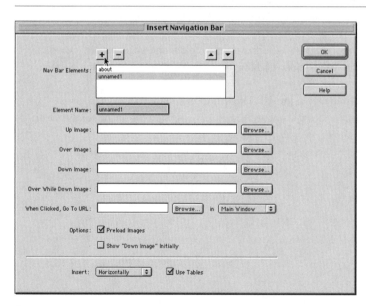

9. Click the plus sign at the top of the dialog box. You will see that a new unnamed element is added. This will let you add the second rollover image to the navigation bar.

10. Enter **Element Name: rooms**. This will assign a name to the second rollover image in this navigation bar. Remember, each element must have a unique name.

---

11. Click **Browse...** next to **Up Image:**. Browse to the **images** folder and **select rooms2.gif**. Click **Open** to select this image. This option lets you specify the image for the Up state of the rollover for the second element in the navigation bar.

---

12. Click **Browse...** next to **Over Image:**. Browse to the **images** folder and select **rooms_over.gif**. Click **Open** to select this image. This option lets you specify the Over state of the second rollover.

---

13. Click **Browse...** next to **Down Image:**. Browse to the **images** folder and select **rooms_down.gif**. Click **Open** to select this image. This option lets you specify the Down state of the second rollover.

---

14. Click **Browse...** next to **Over While Down Image:**. Browse to the **images** folder and select **rooms_overdown.gif**. Click **Open** to select this image. This option lets you specify the Over While Down state of the second rollover.

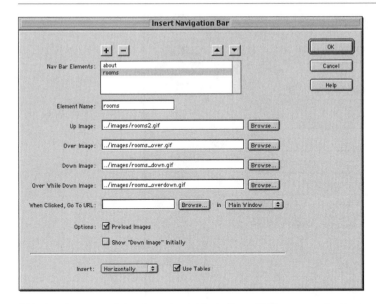

This is what your dialog box should look like with the second rollover settings.

Adding Elements to the Navigation Bar		
Element	**State**	**File**
Guest	Up	guest2.gif
	Over	guest_over.gif
	Down	guest_down.gif
	Over While Down	guest_overdown.gif
Reserve	Up	reserve2.gif
	Over	reserve_over.gif
	Down	reserve_down.gif
	Over While Down	reserve_overdown.gif

15. Now that you know how to add new elements to the navigation bar, go ahead and add two more 4-state buttons, using the chart above.

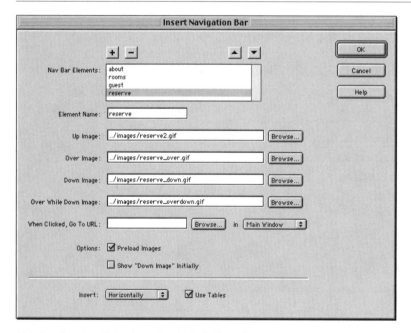

This is what the dialog box should look like when you are finished.

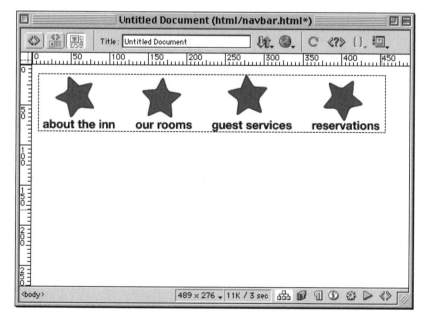

16. After you have added the fourth element, click **OK**. Dreamweaver will automatically create a table, insert the images you specified, and create all of the complex JavaScript necessary for the rollovers to function. It does all of this in about two seconds. We dare any JavaScript programmer to compete with this time!

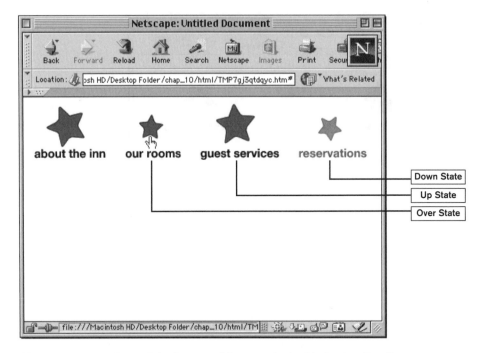

Here you can see three of the four possible states in the Navigation Bar. If you move your mouse over the Down state, you will see the fourth.

17. Go ahead and press **F12** to preview your navigation bar in a browser. Make sure you roll over each of the images, click them, and then roll over them again to see the four different states of each.

18. Return to Dreamweaver. Save and close the file.

7.——————————**Inserting a Simple Rollover from Fireworks**

Like peanut butter and jelly, Dreamweaver and Fireworks were made to go together. But once you've created your rollovers in Fireworks, how in the heck do you get them into Dreamweaver and still have them work? Have you ever tried to copy and paste your rollovers from Fireworks into Dreamweaver, only to end up with a bunch of broken images and JavaScript? This exercise is going to show you how to import Fireworks HTML files; it's as easy as clicking a button.

> **NOTE:** *You do not need to have Fireworks 4 installed to complete this exercise. We have included the exported Fireworks HTML file on the **H•O•T CD-ROM**.*

1. Open **fw_simple.html** located in the **html** folder of **chap_10**. This is simply a blank file that we created for you.

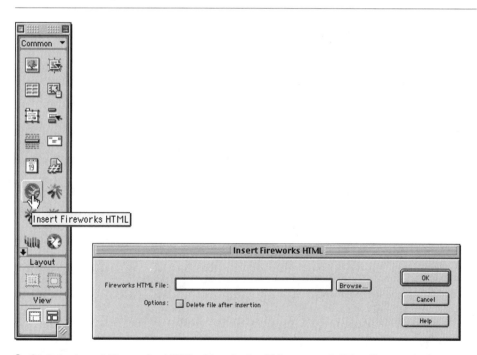

2. Click the **Insert Fireworks HTML** object in the Objects panel. This will open the **Insert Fireworks HTML** dialog box.

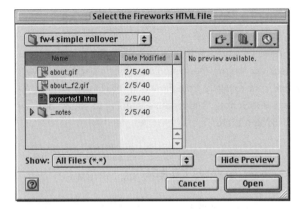

3. Click **Browse...** to select **exported1.htm** located in the **fw4 simple rollover** folder. Click **Open**.

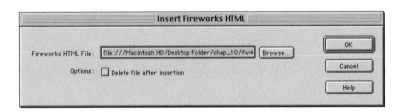

4. You'll be returned to the **Insert Fireworks HTML** dialog box. Click **OK**.

*NOTE: If you check the **Delete file after insertion** checkbox, the original HTML file that you selected will be deleted after it is inserted into your document. We recommend that you don't delete the file unless you are sure you don't want to import it into another page.*

NOTE | Import from Outside Your Local Root Folder

If you try to import an HTML file that is not within your local root folder, you will get the dialog box above. Click **OK** and choose a place inside your local root folder to save them.

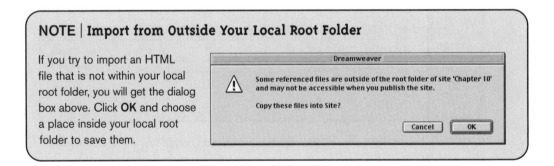

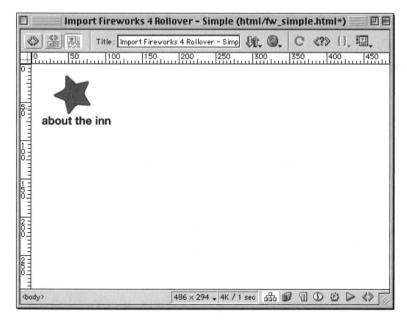

This is what your page should look like now.

5. Press **F12** to test your rollover. With the click of a few buttons, Dreamweaver imported the images, table, and JavaScript.

6. Save and close the file.

Wow, another chapter under your belt, congratulations. We know it was a lot of hard work, but you are well on your way to becoming a Dreamweaver expert.

11.

Cascading Style Sheets

| Redefining HTML with Style Sheets |
| Making Classes | Using Selectors |
| Affecting Links with Selectors |
| Linking to a Style Sheet |
| Converting Style Sheets to HTML |

chap_11

Dreamweaver 4
H•O•T CD-ROM

CSS, which stands for **c**ascading **s**tyle **s**heets, is a standard defined by the World Wide Web Consortium that offers a more flexible and accurate way to define the appearance of your text and formatting than standard HTML. If, for example, you wanted all the text in your document to be blue and all the headlines to be green, with standard HTML you would have to go through the elements on the page one by one and assign those colors to the text. Using **style sheets**, you can redefine all the body elements in the entire document to turn blue with just one instruction and then perform the same single step for the headlines to turn green.

The style sheets specification also offers more control over type than standard HTML. With styles, you can specify the amount of space between lines of type (called the **line height** in Dreamweaver), the size of the type in pixels instead of points, and specific fonts for specific page elements. Anyone yearning for more control over typography is going to be drawn to using styles as opposed to the type attributes discussed in Chapter 6, *"Typography."*

There is a dark side to styles, however—they're supported only by Netscape 4.0+, 6.0+, and Explorer 4 and 5. Even these browsers don't offer full support for the entire CSS1 specification, although Netscape 6 has increased support for CSS1. If someone looked at your styles-based page with an older browser, they would not see any formatting whatsoever beyond the default colors, sizes, fonts, and positions. Of course, Dreamweaver has a great solution to this. It's the only program we know of that can convert styles to HTML tags automatically. Dreamweaver offers the best of both worlds—it allows you to design with styles and convert to backward-compatible HTML. Ya gotta love it!

Style Sheets—A Hard Decision?

This chapter offers exercises in setting up styles and style sheets. Style sheets are collections of rules that define the styles of a document. You will get a chance to redefine HTML using styles, define custom style classes, which can be repeatedly applied to tags, and convert everything you did to HTML.

Many Web developers think highly of style sheets, yet they do not use them often. Until the support for them is more consistent, the decision as to whether to use style sheets will be a challenging one you will have to make. You may want to create two versions of documents—one with style sheets and one without. Using a Dreamweaver behavior, you could deliver the style sheet version to the people with current browsers and an HTML page to those who have older browsers. You will learn how to do that in Chapter 14, *"Behaviors."*

The Cascading Part of Style Sheets

The term "cascading" in style sheets has to do with how browsers interpret the style sheet code. Sometimes, when multiple style sheets are used (such as inline and external, which you'll learn about very soon in this very chapter!), the browser might not know which style sheet to honor. The "cascading" part of CSS has to do with what rules the browser should follow when it encounters conflicting CSS information. The rules are complex and describing them would require more space than we have room for in this book. Furthermore, not all browsers support the cascading aspect of CSS. If you are interested in learning more about the rules for the "cascading" structure, visit http://www.htmlhelp.com/reference/css/structure.html.

Types of Style Sheets

Before you jump right into the exercises in this chapter, we thought you should have some background information about the different type of styles and where you would use each. Knowing the difference between them is important so you can decide which one is best for your Web projects. The table on the next page outlines the different types of style sheets:

Types of Style Sheets	
Style Sheet Type	**Description**

Embedded	This type of style sheet is an internal part of the HTML document. All of the code is written inside the **\<head\>** tag of the document and affects only this one page. Some sample embedded CSS code looks like this:
	
	`<STYLE TYPE="text/css">`
	`<!-`
	`H1 {color:blue; font-family: verdana}`
	`->`
	`</STYLE>`
	
	This type of style sheet is useful if you want to apply this style to only a single page.

External	External style sheets are the most powerful type of style sheet. One single file can be used to format hundreds, thousands, and even millions of pages. Then, with one change, all of those pages can instantly be changed to have a new style. The contents of an external CSS file look just like the embedded code, except that they are not part of the HTML page. Instead, they are stored in a separate file with a .css extension instead of an .html extension. This file simply contains a list of styles, with no other HTML code. Instead of embedding the code in the HTML document, you make a link to the external CSS file. Here's an example: `<LINK REL=stylesheet HREF="mystyles.css" TYPE="text/css">`

Inline	This type of style sheet is useful when you have multiple pages that share the same style(s). Inline styles are similar to embedded styles, in that they are part of the HTML document. However, they are written directly in the **\<body\>** of the page, not the **\<head\>** section. This is what some sample code would look like:
	
	`<BODY>`
	`<H1 STYLE="color: orange; font-family: verdana">This is some sample text.</H1>`
	`</BODY>`
	`</HTML>`
	
	Inline styles are much less powerful than embedded and external style sheets. Why? Because if you ever want to change the style, you would have to do it every place the inline style appeared in your document.
	
	Inline styles do have a purpose, however. For example, they can be used to override styles from an external style sheet.

NOTE: Dreamweaver 4 does not have any way of creating inline styles. You would have to know the correct syntax and enter the code manually.

I. —————————**Redefining HTML with Style Sheets**

As we pointed out, there are multiple ways to implement styles in Dreamweaver. In this exercise, you'll learn how to assign font attributes–such as color and size–by redefining HTML tags. You will also learn how to create an embedded style sheet, where the CSS code is written inside the **<head>** tag of the document.

1. Copy **chap_11** to your hard drive. Define your site for Chapter 11, using the **chap_11** folder as the local root folder. If you need a refresher on this process, visit Exercise 1 in Chapter 3, *"Site Control."*

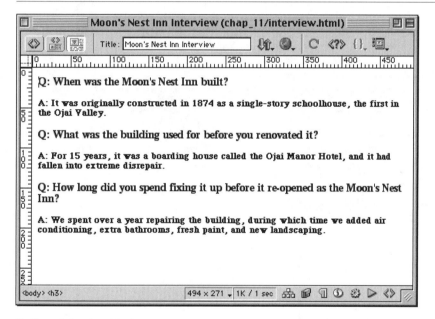

2. Open **interview.html**.

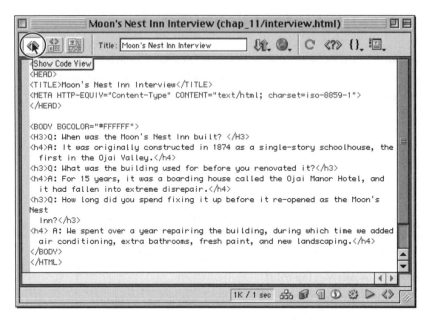

3. Click the **Show Code View** button to look at the HTML code for this document. Notice that it uses a combination of **<h3>** and **<h4>** tags as delineators between the formatting of the interview questions. Click the **Show Design View** button to return to the design view.

4. Make sure your **CSS Styles** panel is open. If it is not, choose **Window > CSS Styles (Shift+F11)**. Click the **New Style** button at the bottom of the panel. The **New Style** dialog box opens.

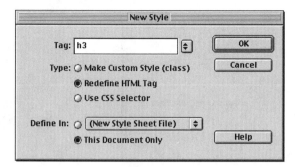

5. Choose **Redefine HTML Tag**. Click the arrow next to the **Tag** option and select **<h3>** as the **tag**, if it's not already selected. Make sure **This Document Only** is selected for the **Define In** option. This option tells Dreamweaver to create an embedded style sheet. Click **OK**.

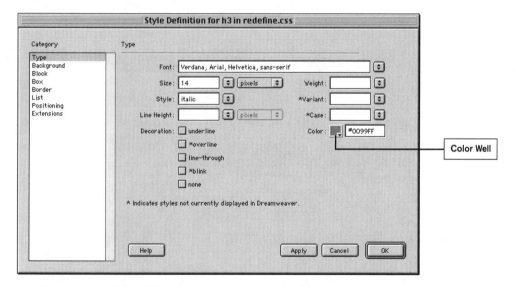

Color Well

6. Select **Font: Verdana, Arial, Helvetica, sans-serif** and **Size: 14 pixels**. Choose **Style: italic**. Change **Color:** to a light blue by clicking on the **Color Well** (shown above) and selecting your own color or by typing in the value **#0099FF**. Click **OK**.

Note: For the Font setting, Dreamweaver defaults to pixels rather than points, because this results in better consistency between the Mac and Windows platforms. Unfortunately, as we discussed in Chapter 7, "Typography," Windows renders type at 96 dpi, while Macs render it at 72 dpi. By default, Internet Explorer 5, on the Macintosh, will display HTML text at 96 dpi too, which causes the fonts on Explorer to be larger than in Netscape. Egads—it's an awful frustration for those of us who want consistent type between browsers and platforms!. Setting the type to pixels eliminates this problem, but only for 4.0+ browsers.

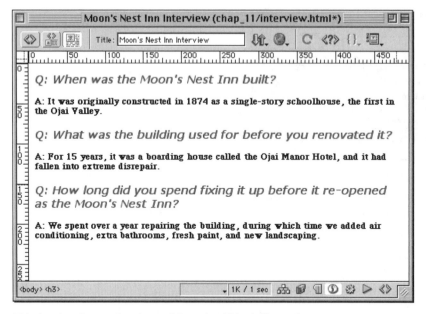

This is what the results of your labor should look like so far.

7. At the bottom of the **CSS Styles** panel, click the **New Style** icon. This opens the **New Style** dialog box.

8. Choose **Redefine HTML Tag** (if it isn't already selected). Use the small arrow to select **<h4>** for the **Tag** option. Make sure that **This Document Only** is selected for the **Define In** option. Click **OK**. This opens another Style Definition dialog box.

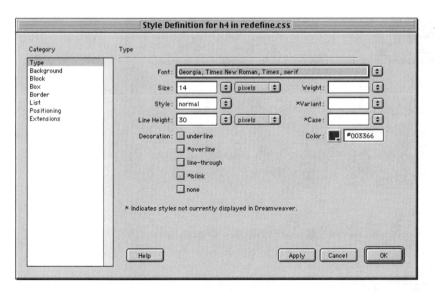

9. Select **Font: Georgia, Times New Roman, Times, serif** and **Size: 14 pixels**. Select **Style: normal**, and enter **Line Height: 30 pixels**. Click **Apply**. Notice how the space between the lines of type just increased? Ya just can't do that in vanilla HTML, folks! Change the **Color** setting to a dark blue by using the **Color picker** or by typing in the value **#003366**, as shown above. Click **OK**.

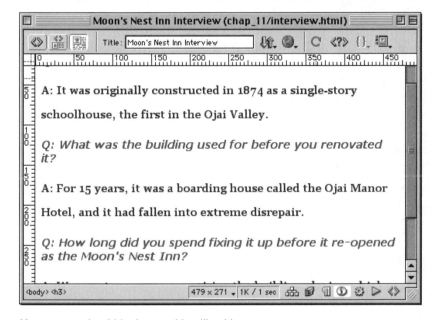

Your screen should look something like this.

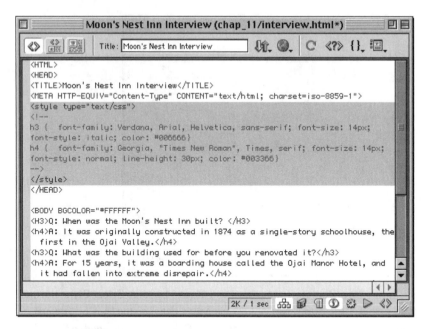

10. Click the **Show Code View** button to check out the code. Notice all the style sheet information that was added to the **<head>** of the document? Pretty darn cool of Dreamweaver to write all of that for you, wasn't it? This is what the code of an embedded style sheet looks like. Save and close this document.

We encourage you to click the Open Style Sheet... icon, at the bottom of the CSS Styles panel, select either <h3> or <h4>, and then click Edit... Make some changes and try some other settings. Knock yourself out, have some fun! When you're finished, close the document. Whether you save your changes is up to you, because this book won't require using the file again.

What was the point of all this, you might ask? Styles offer a different method for formatting your documents. They ensure consistency and can save a lot of time by formatting global changes. As you will soon see, redefining HTML is just one way to apply styles. The next exercises will show you how to make changes that are local (that apply to individual text characters or words instead of entire tags).

2. _____Defining a Custom Class

You just learned to redefine the default formatting of an HTML tag with style sheets. Now it's time to move on to make your own custom class. A style sheet class is a set of specifications that can be applied to any tag on the page. Why would you use a class instead of redefining the formatting of an HTML tag, as you did in the last exercise? Perhaps there's a set of styles, such as a particular color and text size, that you would like to apply randomly without having them automatically applied to every instance of a particular HTML tag. For example, maybe you don't want all the **<h3>** tags to automatically be green, and perhaps you want some **<h4>** tags to be green, as well. Rather than redefining an existing HTML tag, you can use a class to apply the same style to different tags on your page. In other words, a class can be applied to any tag at any time. If this sounds confusing, try the exercise and it will likely make more sense.

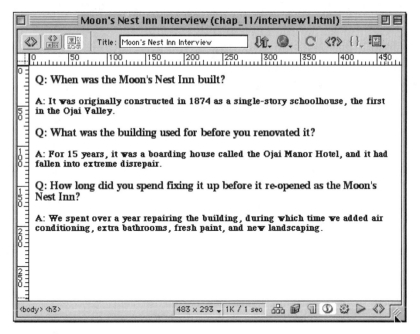

1. Open **interview1.html**. It should look like the file in Exercise 1, because at this point it is identical. It is very important that it does not contain any style sheet information as of yet!

2. Make sure your **CSS Styles** panel is open. If it is not, choose **Window > CSS Styles** (**Shift+F11**). Click the **New Style** icon to open the **New Style** dialog box.

3. You should have **Make Custom Style (class)** selected. Enter **Name: .blue.** Make sure you put a period before the word "blue." All class names must start with a period. Make sure that the **Define In** option is set to **(New Style Sheet File)**. This option creates an external style sheet file, which is where style sheets become really powerful. Click **OK**.

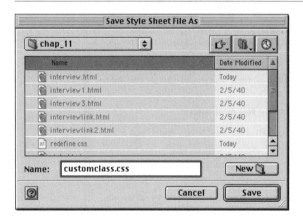

4. Browse to the **chap_11** folder and save this file as **customclass.css**. This creates an external style file that any page within your site can link to.

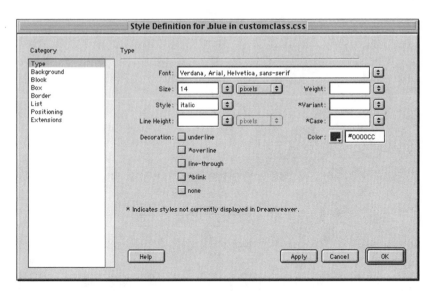

5. Fill out the **Style Definition for .blue** dialog box however you like, but make sure to set the **Color** field to a blue! **Note:** Clicking **Apply** will have no effect in this instance, because you aren't redefining an existing tag. Therefore, click **OK** once you're finished.

Your CSS Styles panel should now contain the word "blue" in it. **Note:** *The proper syntax for a style sheet class is to contain a period in front of the class name, such as .blue. Even though the period is necessary, it doesn't show up in this panel. Dreamweaver is well aware of this, and the needed period will still appear in the code.*

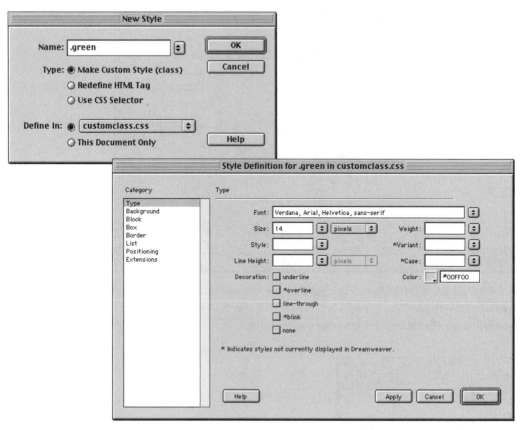

6. Create a class, **Name: .green** by following Steps 2 and 3 and setting the **Color** to green. We don't want to be nags, but remember to put that period in front of the class name **.green**! Click **OK**.

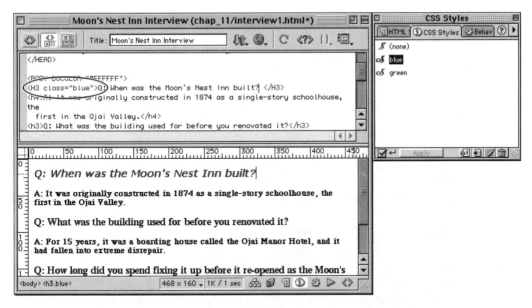

7. Click anywhere in the first line of text, and click the class named **blue** inside the CSS Styles panel. This changes that entire line of text. If you click the **Show Code and Design View** button, as shown above, you can watch Dreamweaver construct the style code before your eyes. Classes can be applied to lines of text or even to individual words or characters. Go ahead and click on different bits of type on your page and click the classes named **blue** and **green** to see what happens. Congrats! You've just created classes and applied them to a document.

8. Save and close the document.

MOVIE | externalclass.mov

To learn more about external CSS, check out **externalclass.mov** located in the **movies** folder on the Dreamweaver 4 **H•O•T CD-ROM**.

Using Selectors to Group Tags

In the last two exercises, you learned how to apply styles to redefine an HTML tag and how to create custom classes and apply them to selective text. What if you want to apply a single style to multiple HTML tags? Let's say you wanted to reformat both the **<h3>** and **<h4>** tags at the same time. **CSS selectors** are the answer, as they allow you to apply styles to multiple HTML tags at once.

1. Open **interview3.html**.

2. Make sure your **CSS Styles** panel is open. If it is not, choose **Window > CSS Styles** (**Shift+F11**). Click the **New Style** icon at the bottom of the CSS Styles panel.

3. Click **Use CSS Selector**. Enter **h3 h4** in the **Selector** field to select tags **<h3>** and **<h4>**. Note that there is a space between the two tags. **Warning:** Do not try to enter commas between these values; they will not work! Click **OK**.

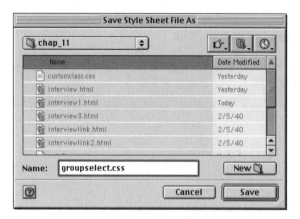

4. Save the file as **groupselect.css** inside the **chap_11** folder. Again, this will save an external style sheet file that other HTML pages could eventually link to.

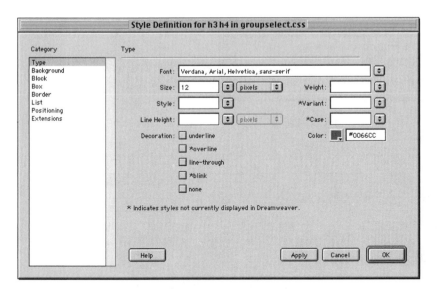

5. Set **Color:** to a **blue** and click **OK**. If you want, you can also change the font and size.

The code that Dreamweaver just created will not work as is and requires a little hand-tweaking in HTML.
Unfortunately, there is no way to directly edit the code of the external style sheet in Dreamweaver.
To do this, you will need a separate text editor. On the Macintosh, you can use SimpleText, and in
Windows you can use NotePad.

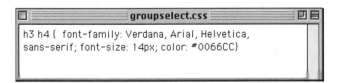

6. Using a text editor (such as SimpleText or NotePad), open the **groupselect.css** file located inside the **chap_11** folder. Notice that there is no comma between the **<h3>** and **<h4>** tags. A comma is required in order for these grouped selectors to function properly.

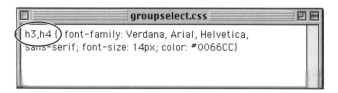

7. Insert a comma between the **<h3>** and **<h4>** tags. Make sure there are no spaces on either side of the comma. Close and save this file.

WARNING | Refresh Problem

There is sometimes a problem with the document window not refreshing after you make changes to an external CSS file with another application. In this exercise, the text should have turned blue in the document window as soon as you made changes and saved the external CSS file. It almost looked as though the exercise didn't work, but it did, we swear. When you press F12, you should see the text turn blue. If you close and reopen the document in Dreamweaver, you will see the changes inside the document window. This is just one of those "undiscovered features" we wanted to tell you about! [grin]

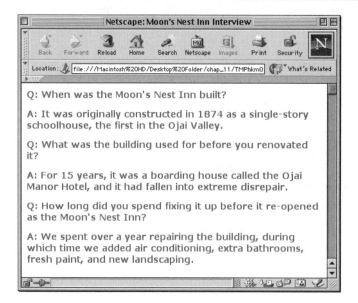

8. Return to Dreamweaver and press **F12** to view this page in a browser. Voilà: your text turned blue.

9. Save and close the file.

4. ——————Affecting Links with Selectors

The default appearance of a link in standard HTML is that it is formatted with an underline. One reason people use style sheets is to turn off this underlining. We're not sure we think this is a good idea, because many people rely on the visual cue of underlined text to know that it is truly a link. Regardless, some of you may want to remove it anyway, so this exercise will show you how. Not only that, you'll get to use the CSS selector feature again! Woo hoo!

1. Open **interviewlink.html**. As you can see by the underlined text, this document contains a link.

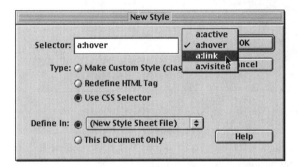

2. Make sure your **CSS Styles** panel is open. If it is not, choose **Window > CSS Styles** (**Shift-F11**). Click the **New Style** icon at the bottom of the CSS Styles panel. The **New Style** dialog box opens. Click **Use CSS Selector** and select **a:link**. This allows you to define the **<a>** (anchor) tag's link properties. Make sure **(New Style Sheet File)** is selected, and click **OK**.

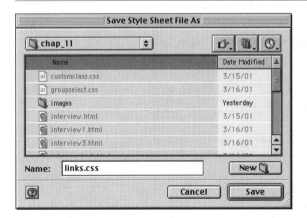

3. Save the file as **links.css** inside the **chap_11** folder.

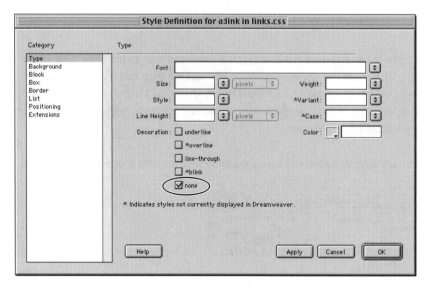

4. Check **Decoration: none** and click **OK**. You are returned to the document window. The term "Decoration" refers to how the link is displayed. In this case, because an underline is not wanted, this option is set to **none**. Notice that nothing looks different on your page. That is because this feature does not preview in Dreamweaver; it must instead be viewed inside a browser.

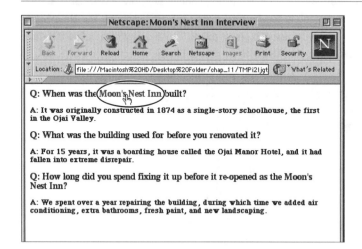

5. Press **F12**, and you'll see that the link is there, but it isn't underlined.

NOTE: This change can be seen only from a 4.0+ browser. If you have an earlier browser, you will not be able to see it even though you made it. Such is life in the not-so-fair world of never-ending browser incompatibility.

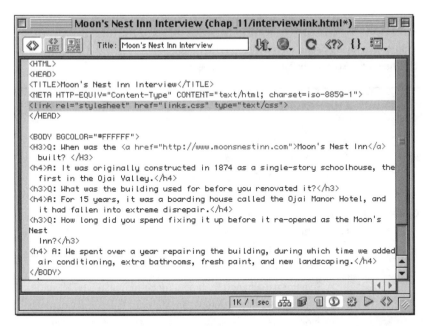

6. Return to Dreamweaver and click the **Show Code View** button to view the HTML code. Notice that the style selector information was added! We don't know about you, but we sure like that we don't have to hand-code this sort of thing.

7. Save and close this file.

NOTE | Changing the Appearance of Links with Selectors

You might have noticed that the pop-up menu for the Selector field had four entries: a:active, a:hover, a:link, and a:visited. Exercise 4 showed you how a:link affects the attributes for links, but what do the other entries stand for? The selection a:active affects the active link, which is the appearance when the mouse is depressed on a link. The selection a:hover affects the appearance of the link when your mouse rolls over it. You could, for example, have the text color change upon rollover. Note that a:hover is honored only by Explorer, not Netscape. The a:visited selection alters the appearance of a visited link or, in plain English, a link that has already been clicked.

Redefine HTML, Custom Class, or Selector?

Now that you've learned to create styles based on redefining HTML, a custom class, and a CSS selector, here is a handy chart that helps to explain when to use which type of style.

Creating Styles in Dreamweaver	
When to Use?	**For What Purpose?**
Redefine HTML Tag	Use when you want to change the appearance of content based on a certain tag. For example, everything with an <h1> tag could be made to look consistent.
Create a Custom Class	Use when you want to change the appearance of your document, but not have it dependent on a tag. Use also when you want to make certain words a particular color—regardless of whether they are in the headline or the body copy.
Selector	A Selector can change the appearance of multiple HTML tags all at once. Use this feature when you want to make appearance changes based on tags, but on more than one tag at a time. Dreamweaver also includes the a:Selectors as a way to change the appearance of linked text (turning off the underline, for example).

5. _____Linking to a Style Sheet

Most of the exercises in this chapter have had you create external style sheets, so at some point different pages in your Web site could share the same style information. We had you do this because external style sheets are very powerful, since you can base all the style information in one document. If you make a change, you only have to change it there, instead of in each individual document that references it. This exercise will show you how to create another external style sheet and then how to link several pages to it once it's created.

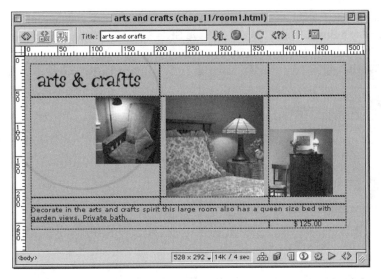

1. Open the **room1.html** file located inside the **chap_11** folder. This page contains a simple layout with some HTML text. You are going to style the text using an external style sheet.

2. At the bottom of your **CSS Styles** panel, click the **New Style** icon. The **New Style** dialog box opens.

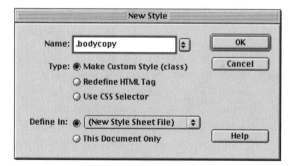

3. Click **Make Custom Style (class)** and enter **Name: .bodycopy**. Make sure that the **Define In** option is set to **(New Style Sheet File)**. Click **OK**. A **Save Style Sheet As** dialog box opens.

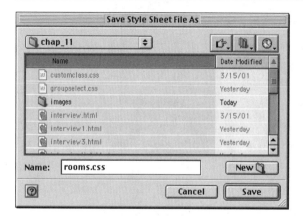

4. Save this file as **rooms.css** inside the **chap_11** folder. This will be the external style sheet file to which you will link the other pages later in this exercise.

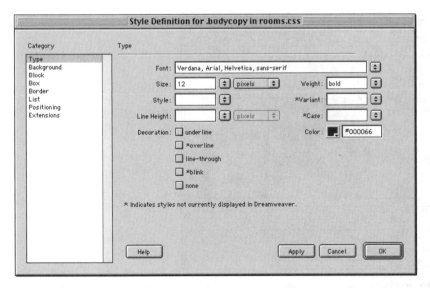

5. Go ahead and define the way you want this style to look. This style will be used to define the room description, so don't make it too big or use any real crazy fonts. Well, OK, go ahead, but don't tell anyone. :-) Click **OK**.

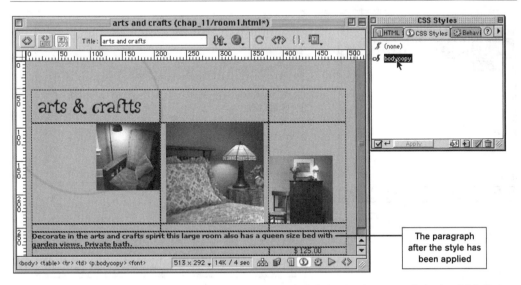

The paragraph after the style has been applied

6. Click anywhere in the room description paragraph, and click the **.bodycopy** style in the CSS Styles panel. This formats all the text in that paragraph.

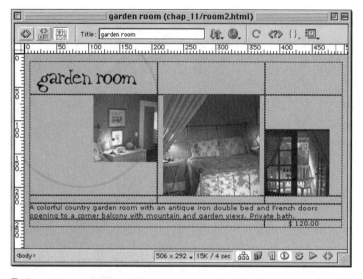

7. Open the **room2.html** file. This page is just like the **room1.html** file. It is formatted exactly as **room1.html** was before you changed it in Step 6. That's fine for now, because next you'll learn how to attach it to the external .css document you made in the last few steps. This will cause both **room1.html** and **room2.html** to share the same style sheet information.

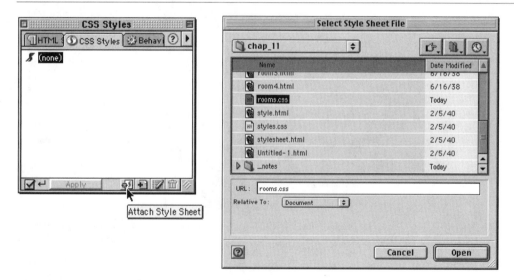

8. In the **CSS Styles** panel, click the **Attach Style Sheet** button. This option lets you attach an external style sheet to the HTML file. Browse to the **chap_11** folder and select the **rooms.css** file. Click **Open**. This attaches the **rooms.css** file to the **room2.html** file.

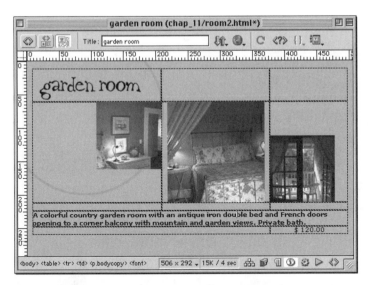

9. Click anywhere in the room description paragraph, and click the **.bodycopy** style in the **CSS Styles** panel. This formats all the text in that paragraph.

So far, you have two HTML files linked to the external style sheet: room1.html and room2.html. You could easily continue this process and link room3.html and room4.html to the same style sheet file. In fact, that's what the next step is going to have you do.

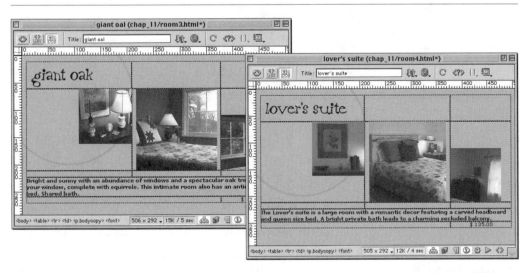

10. Using these same steps, go ahead and link the **rooms.css** file to **room3.html** and **room4.html**. Make sure you format the room description paragraph with the **.bodycopy** class, just as you did in **room1.html** and **room2.html**.

When you are done, **room1.html**, **room2.html**, **room3.html**, *and* **room4.html** *should be linked to the* **rooms.css** *file, and the paragraph at the bottom should be styled using the .bodycopy class. To fully illustrate the power of external style sheets, the following steps will show you how to edit the external CSS file and how those changes will propagate throughout all four HTML files.*

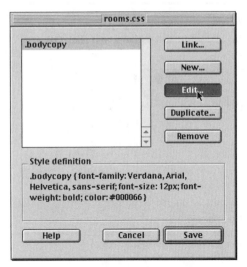

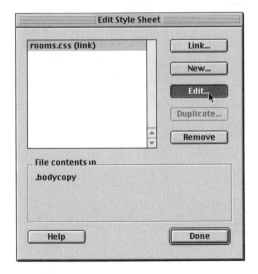

11. From the **CSS Styles** panel, choose the **Edit Style Sheet...** button. This opens up the **Edit Style Sheet** dialog box showing the external CSS file this HTML page has been linked to.

12. Select **rooms.css (link)**, and click **Edit**. This opens the **rooms.css** file and shows you what styles are contained within that file. Select **.bodycopy** and click **Edit**. This opens the Style Definition dialog box so you can make changes to the style.

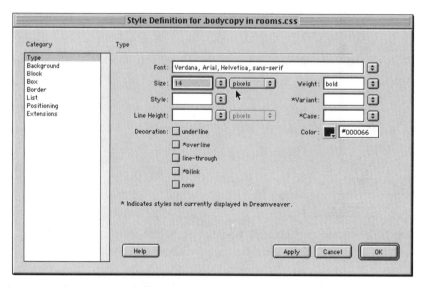

13. You can make any change you want in this dialog box. To make the change really obvious, increase the size of the text to **14 pixels** and click **OK**.

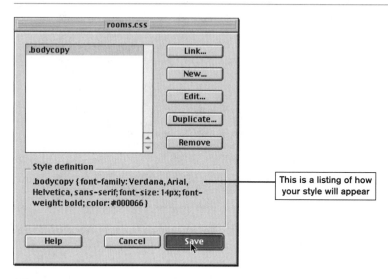

This is a listing of how your style will appear

14. Click **Save** to save the changes you just made to this class. Notice that the bottom of this dialog box lists the different attributes of the selected class.

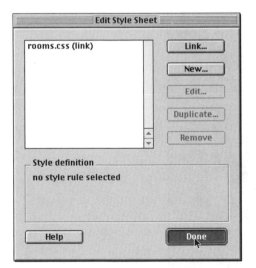

15. Click **Done** in the **Edit Style Sheet** dialog box. This returns you to your document window.

WARNING | Refresh Problem (Again)

As we mentioned earlier, there is sometimes a problem with the document window not refreshing after you make changes to an external CSS file. In this exercise, the text size in the document window should have increased as soon as you made the changes to the external CSS file. It almost looked like the exercise didn't work, but it did. When you press F12, you should see the text size increase. If you close and reopen the document in Dreamweaver, you will see the changes inside the document window.

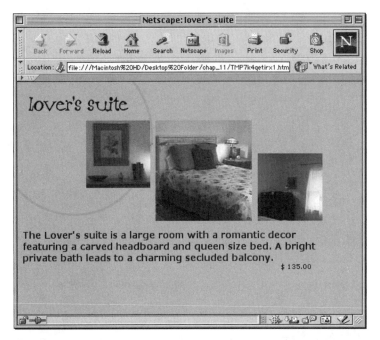

16. Press **F12** to preview **room4.html** in a browser so that you can see the changes you made to the class. Go ahead and preview **room1.html**, **room2.html**, and **room3.html** in a browser. Yup, the changes were made there as well. Cool, huh? This is the true power of external style sheets!

17. When you are done, save and close all of the open files.

MOVIE | externalcss.mov

To learn more about external CSS, check out **externalcss.mov** located in the **movies** folder on the Dreamweaver 4 **H•O•T** CD-ROM.

6. _____Converting from CSS to HTML

Now that you've successfully created internal and external style sheets, you ought to be feeling pretty proud. You may be feeling so good, in fact, that you have forgotten that all browsers don't support style sheets. What's a conscientious Web designer to do? Dreamweaver has a great solution—you can convert the CSS to HTML! The only caveat is that HTML doesn't support certain things, such as links with no underlines or font sizes in pixels. You'll see the conversion process for yourself if you follow this next exercise.

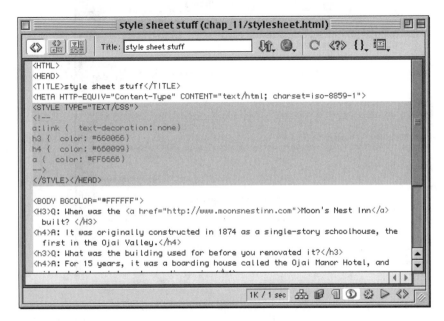

1. Open **stylesheet.html**. Click the **Show Code View** button, and you'll see style sheet code in the document.

2. Choose **File > Convert > 3.0 Browser Compatible…** The **Convert to 3.0 Browser Compatible** dialog box opens.

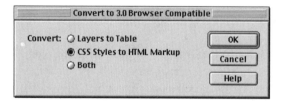

3. Choose **CSS Styles to HTML Markup** and click **OK**. This creates a new document window.

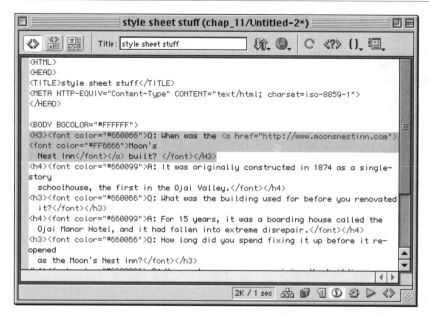

This is what the code looks like for the new document containing only HTML code. As you can see, the CSS code has been converted to regular HTML code, which is compatible with just about any browser.

4. Save this file as **stylesheet2.html**. You should now have two documents in your **chap_11** folder, **stylesheet.html** and **stylesheet2.html**.

Why did Dreamweaver create another document for you? Because you might want to have two pages on hand: one to deliver to your 4.0+ browser audience and another for your audience that can't see the style sheets.

5. Close both files. Phew, this was a pretty intense chapter. You deserve a little break. But, hey, don't let us stop you if you want to move on to the next chapter!

12.

HTML

| Code View | Editing in Code View |
| Using the Quick Tag Editor |
| Cleaning Up HTML | Cleaning Up Word HTML |

chap_12

Dreamweaver 4
H•O•T CD-ROM

At our hands-on courses, we are frequently asked whether it's necessary to know HTML to be a successful Web designer. A few years ago, the answer was a resounding yes, because there were no alternatives to writing HTML code to put Web pages together. With the introduction of WYSIWYG HTML editors like Dreamweaver, Web developers are shielded from writing the HTML code and can create Web pages in a completely visual environment. The invention of the WYSIWYG editor brought Web page publishing within the reach of almost anyone. However, it's still our belief that a basic understanding of HTML is beneficial to anyone planning to work in this field professionally. This book doesn't teach HTML, but you can teach it to yourself by looking at the code while building pages visually within Dreamweaver. This chapter will show you how to do this, of course!

Dreamweaver 4 introduced two new views in the document window, combining the best of both the visual and the code environment. The Code view lets you use Dreamweaver like other full-featured text editors that specialize in HTML, such as BBEdit or HomeSite. The Code and Design view lets you work with both the code and the visual elements of your page within the same document window.

A lot of what is covered in this chapter will appeal to people who already know how to hand-code their pages, but don't be afraid to read on and dig into the exercises in this chapter, even if you are not familiar with HTML. The step-by-step tutorials will walk novices as well as experienced HTML coders through the process of editing HTML.

I. ————————The Code View

The Dreamweaver 4 interface has three new and extremely useful buttons: the Show Design View button, the Show Code View button, and the Show Code and Design Views button. Those of you who have used Dreamweaver before will recall that you used to be able to view and edit the HTML code in a separate window called the HTML window. This window still exists, but it is far easier to use the Show Code View button to easily access code directly from the document window. The ability to toggle quickly between editing your code and working in the visual editing environment has made working with the HTML code simpler than ever. For those of you who are familiar with HTML code, you won't feel so far from home when using Dreamweaver. Those of you who are less familiar with HTML will find that you can watch Dreamweaver create the HTML code as you use the visual editing environment. Observing this process is actually a great way to teach yourself HTML.

This first exercise exposes you to the Design view, the Code view, and the Code and Design view to show you how to edit your HTML code. Even if you don't know a whole lot about HTML, you should still work through this exercise. It's not that hard, and it will show you that learning HTML is truly within your reach.

1. Copy **chap_12** to your hard drive. Define your site for Chapter 12, using the **chap_12** folder as the local root folder. If you need a refresher on this process, visit Chapter 3, *"Site Control."*

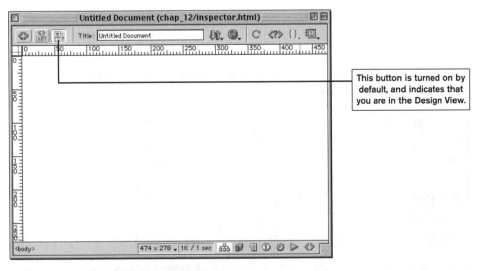

This button is turned on by default, and indicates that you are in the Design View.

2. Open the **inspector.html** file located inside the **chap_12** folder. This is just a blank file that has been saved for you. By default, your page will open in what's known as the Design view.

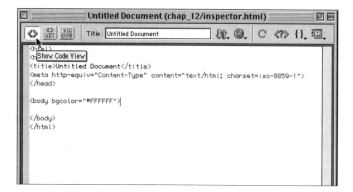

3. Click the **Show Code View** button to the view the HTML of your document window. This window doesn't have much in it, but neither does your page yet!

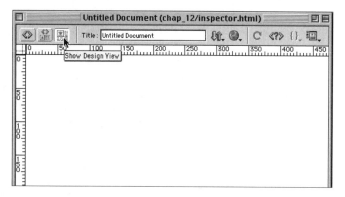

4. To return to the Design view, click the **Show Design View** button. As you can see, it's really easy to switch between the different views.

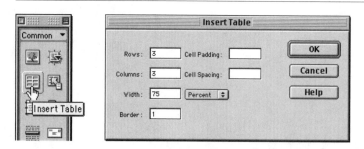

5. Click on the **Insert Table** object in the Objects panel. When the **Insert Table** dialog box appears, make sure the settings match the dialog box above, and then click **OK**.

NOTE | Options in the Code View

Several options are available in the Code view. The following table outlines each of these options.

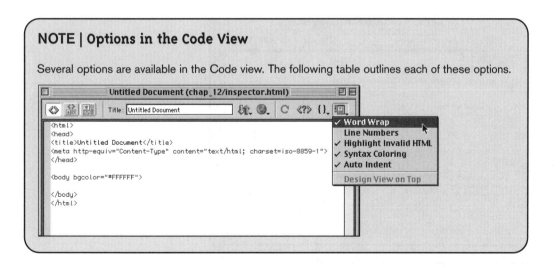

Code View Options

Option	Description
Word Wrap	Wraps code within the window so you don't have to scroll to the left and right, making large amounts of code easier to see.
Line Numbers	Adds line numbers along the left side of the window. This is especially helpful when you need to identify a specific line of code, such as when troubleshooting an HTML error. The numbers won't appear in the final HTML output; they're just there for your own reference.
Highlight Invalid HTML	Invalid HTML code will be highlighted in yellow. This is really helpful when you are looking for errors in your code. When bad code is selected, look in the Property Inspector for ways to correct the problem.
Syntax Coloring	Color-codes parts of your HTML based on your Code Color preferences. This helps you quickly spot the different elements of code.
Auto Indent	Automatically indents code, which helps with readability.
Design View on Top	Available only in Code and Design view, this option inverts the positioning in the document window.

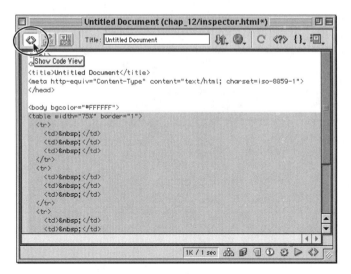

6. Click the **Show Code View** button. Check out all the code that was generated to create the table. Would you like to have to type it all? Your answer most likely is heck, no!

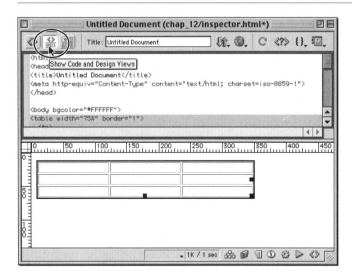

7. Click the **Show Code and Design Views** button so that you can see the code and the table on your page at the same time. This splits your document window so you can see both the code and the visual elements. Pretty neat, huh?

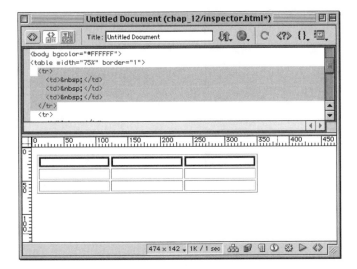

8. Click in the first cell and drag to the right. This lets you select the entire first row. Notice that the associated HTML code is also selected. This level of visual feedback is really great for identifying how the code and the visual results are joined at the hip. Nice!

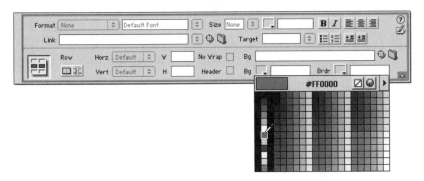

9. In the **Property Inspector**, click the **Bg** option and choose any color of red. This changes the background of the selected row.

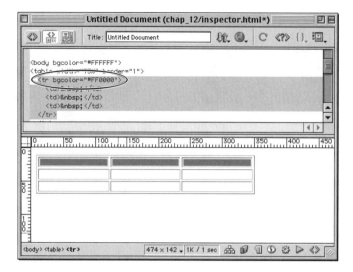

Look at the Code window. See how the HTML code is updated to reflect the changes you just made? This is a great way to learn HTML. You can literally watch the code being generated as you add, modify, and remove content from your page. Go ahead and make some more changes to your page, but leave the Code window open so you can watch all the HTML being created. To think that people used to type all of this by hand! We are sure glad we don't have to do that anymore.

10. When you are finished, save your changes and leave the file open for the next exercise.

2. _____Editing in the Code View

Now that you have an idea of how the Code window works, you will learn how to use it to modify your page. In fact, if you wanted to hand-code a page, you could create your entire page right within the HTML Code window.

In this exercise, you will use the Code window to add content to your page and then make modifications to it. The purpose of this exercise is to make you more comfortable with the Code window.

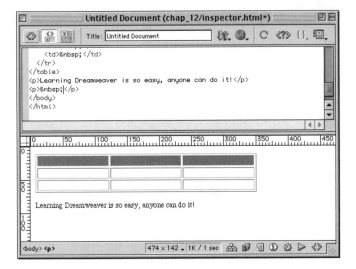

1. Click anywhere below the table and type **Learning Dreamweaver is so easy, anyone can do it**. Look inside the Code window and watch as your text is created. Press **Return** or **Enter** to add a paragraph break when you are finished typing.

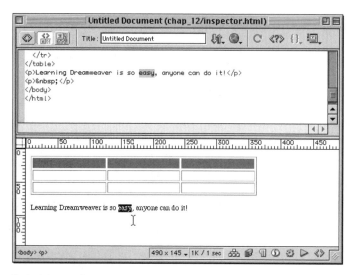

2. Inside the Code window, click and drag to select the word **easy**. Once you have it selected, type **simple**. When you are done typing, click anywhere in the Design view portion of the document window to see the changes updated.

3. In the document window, click and drag to highlight the word **simple**. With the word highlighted, use the Property Inspector to make the word **bold**. Notice that the **<b>** tags were added around the word in the Code window, which shows you the tag required to achieve bolding of text.

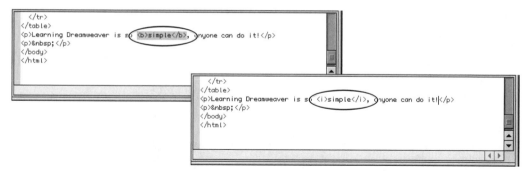

```
</tr>
</table>
<p>Learning Dreamweaver is so ⟨b⟩simple⟨/b⟩, anyone can do it!</p>
<p> </p>
</body>
</html>
```

```
</tr>
</table>
<p>Learning Dreamweaver is so ⟨i⟩simple⟨/i⟩, anyone can do it!|</p>
<p> </p>
</body>
</html>
```

4. In the Code window, change the **<b>** tags so they have an **i** in the middle instead of a **b**. The **<i>** tag will format the text so it's in *italics* instead of **bold**.

TIP | Code Preferences

Dreamweaver gives you several ways to control the view and behavior of the Code view. Under Preferences, you can use the **Code Colors**, **Code Format**, and **Code Rewriting** options to set everything from how the HTML code appears to how it is formatted. So if you find yourself working in the Code view a lot, be sure to look over these different options.

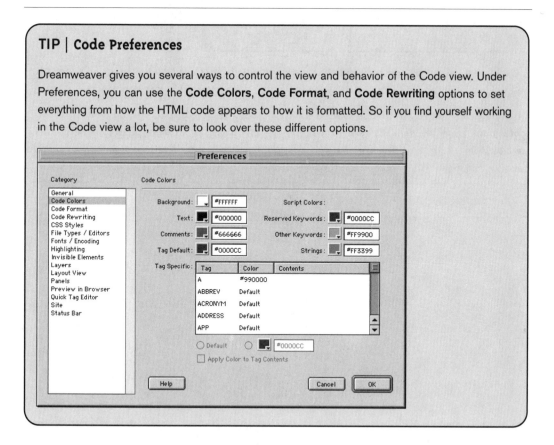

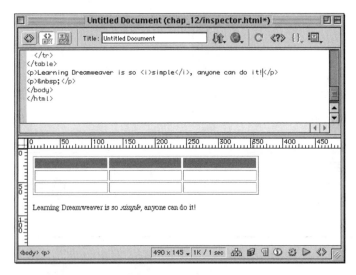

5. Click in the Design window and your changes are updated. You can begin to see how you can use the Design window and the Code window in tandem to create and modify your documents.

*You don't have to know HTML tags, like **<b>** and **<i>**, but if you do know them you can type them right into the code. We think it's easier to use the Property Inspector for this type of formatting. This exercise is here simply to show you that you can edit the code directly if you want to, and it achieves the same result as if you had used the Property Inspector.*

6. When you are finished, save your changes and close this file.

3. —————————**Using the Quick Tag Editor**

The **Quick Tag Editor** gives you instant access to the HTML code on your page without forcing you to access the Code window or an external HTML editor. This is great if you want to make a quick change to a tag or attribute. This exercise will show you how to use the Quick Tag Editor to make changes to a file.

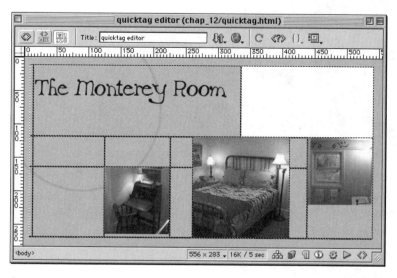

1. Open the **quicktag.html** file located inside the **chap_012** folder.

This file needs a few changes. First, the large cell at the top has a white background and is not allowing the tan background to show through. Second, the image of the window is aligned with the top of the table cell and should be aligned with the bottom of the table cell. These problems can be easily fixed with the Quick Tag Editor.

2. Click inside the large white cell at the top of the table, so that your cursor is blinking inside the cell. Next, click on the **<td>** (table **d**ata) tag in the **Tag selector** at the bottom of the document window. This selects the entire large white cell.

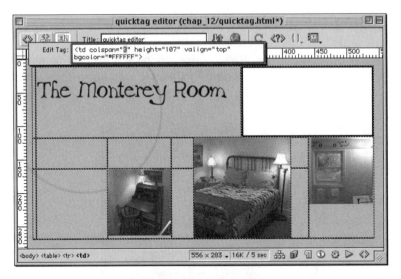

3. Press **Cmd+T** (Mac) or **Ctrl+T** (Windows) to access the **Quick Tag Editor**. (You could also choose **Modify > Quick Tag Editor**.) The Quick Tag Editor appears at the top of the document window. It currently displays the active attribute settings for the selected **<td>** tag. Notice that the **bgcolor** attribute is set to #FFFFFF, which is the hexadecimal value for white.

```
Edit Tag:  <td colspan="3" height="107" valign="top"
           bgcolor="#FFFFFF">
```

Select the tag exactly as shown here.

NOTE | What Are HTML Attributes?

HTML consists of a series of HTML tags. These tags define how your page is formatted in a browser. Attributes attach to these HTML tags to further define the appearance of your page. For example, **<TABLE>** is a standard HTML tag. The **<TABLE>** tag has several different attributes that can be used to further define its appearance, such as **width**, **height**, **bgcolor**, and so on.

For some great references on HTML tags and their associated attributes, make sure you check out the following links:

```
http://www.w3.org/MarkUp/
http://www.htmlhelp.com/
```

4. Click and drag inside the **Quick Tag Editor** to select the **bgcolor** attribute. Be sure to select it exactly as you see here–don't select the last close bracket. Press the **Delete** key to remove this attribute. Press **Return** or **Enter** to accept the changes you made. With the **bgcolor** attribute removed, the tan background is allowed to show through the table cell.

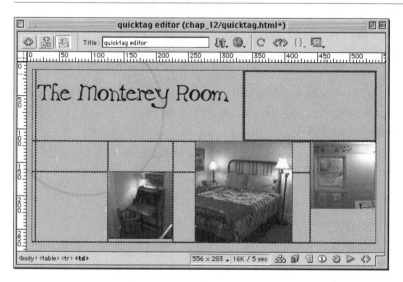

This is what your page should look like with the **bgcolor** *attribute removed.*

5. Click on the window image (on the right), which is currently aligned with the top top of the cell. With the image selected, click on the **<td>** tag in the **Tag selector**, at the bottom of the document window. This selects the cell so you can change the vertical alignment attribute tag by using the Quick Tag Editor.

6. Press **Cmd+T** (Mac) or **Ctrl+T** (Windows) to access the **Quick Tag Editor**. (You could also choose **Modify > Quick Tag Editor**.)

7. The image should be aligned with the bottom of the cell, not the top. Click and drag to select the word **top** in the **Quick Tag Editor**. Be careful to select just the word and not the quotation marks that surround it.

```
Edit Tag: <td rowspan="2" height="151" valign="top">
```

8. Delete the word **top**, then double-click on the word **bottom** in the small pop-up menu that appears. This changes the **VALIGN** (vertical alignment) attribute to **bottom** and moves the image accordingly. Press **Return** or **Enter** to accept your changes.

The Quick Tag Editor is a great tool if you want quick access to the HTML code. As you just saw, you can make changes to the HTML code without ever leaving the visual environment, which is very cool!

9. Save your changes and close this file.

4. ————————Cleaning Up HTML

There might be times when you have to work with HTML that was written by another person or in a program other than Dreamweaver. The HTML may not be the best code you have ever seen and might need to be cleaned up a little. Dreamweaver has a useful command called **Clean Up HTML** that automatically removes empty tags, redundant nested tags, non-Dreamweaver HTML comments, Dreamweaver HTML comments, nested font tags, and any tag you specify. This exercise will show you how to use the feature.

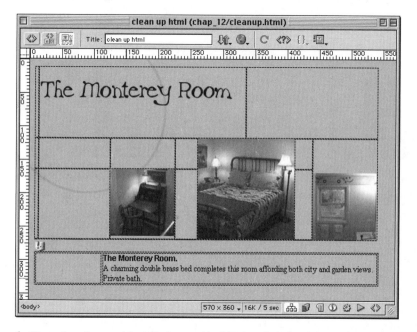

1. Open the **cleanup.html** file located inside the **chap_12** folder. Although the page may look normal, it has a few things that need to be fixed. You will learn what needs to be fixed and how to fix it in this exercise.

---

2. Press **F12** to preview this page in a browser. Everything looks fine, except that the words **Private bath** are blinking. That's because the **<blink>** tag was applied to that text.
Note: The **<blink>** tag will not display in version 5 of Microsoft Internet Explorer.

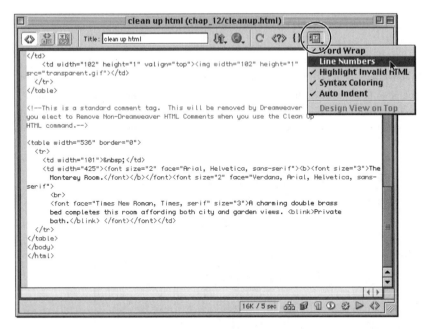

3. Return to Dreamweaver. Click the **Show Code View** button to show the Code window. Click the **View Options** button at the top right of the document window (it's circled above), and select **Line Numbers**, if it isn't already turned on. Look at line **42** (scroll down, if necessary).

```
   src="transparent.gif"></td>
38    <td width="102" height="1" valign="top"><img width="102" height="1"
   src="transparent.gif"></td>
39    </tr>
40 </table>
41
42 <!--This is a standard comment tag.  This will be removed by Dreamweaver if
43 you elect to Remove Non-Dreamweaver HTML Comments when you use the Clean Up
44 HTML command.-->
45
```

A standard comment tag has been added on lines 42 through 44. While these don't take up that much room, you might want to remove them from documents you inherit. This is one of the things you will remove using the Clean Up HTML command.

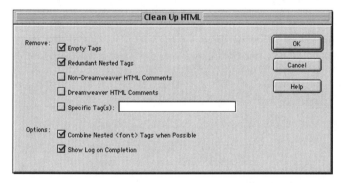

```
50     Monterey Room.</font></b></font><font size="2" face="Verdana, Arial, Helvetica,
sans-serif">
51        <br>
52        <font face="Times New Roman, Times, serif" size="3">A charming double brass
53        bed completes this room affording both city and garden views. <blink>Private
54        bath.</blink> </font></font></td>
55     </tr>
56  </table>
57  </body>
58  </html>
```

4. Scroll down to line **53**. Notice the **<blink>** tag that is surrounding the words **Private bath**. This is what's causing the words to blink on and off. The effect, while novel at first, can get very annoying after a few seconds. You will remove it as well.

5. Click the **Show Design View** button to return to the Design window.

6. Select **Commands > Clean Up HTML** to open the Clean Up HTML dialog box. This is where you can specify what parts of the HTML you want to clean up.

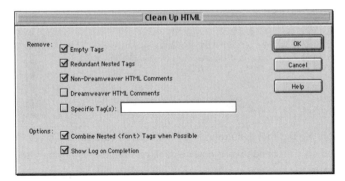

7. Click on the **Non-Dreamweaver HTML Comments** checkbox to put a check there. This will make sure that the comment tag you looked at in the HTML code will be removed.

8. Click on the **Specific Tag(s)** checkbox to put a check there. Type **blink** in the text field to the right of the checkbox. This will ensure that the annoying **<blink>** tag at the bottom of the page is also removed. **Tip:** Be careful to type just the word **blink**, and not the brackets that surround it. Click **OK**.

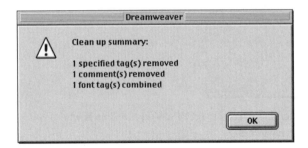

9. Dreamweaver analyzes the HTML code in your document and cleans it up based on the selections you made. It also produces a dialog box with a brief summary of what actions were performed. Click **OK**.

10. Open the Code window again by clicking the **Show Code View** button. Scroll down and look for the comment tag, the nested font tag, or the **<blink>** tag. They have all been removed. As you can imagine, the Clean Up HTML command can be a very useful tool, especially when you get a file that was not written properly.

11. Close and save this file.

Options for Cleaning Up HTML

The following chart lists the different options available in the Clean Up HTML dialog box and outlines what each of them does:

Options in the Clean Up HTML Dialog Box	
Option	**Purpose**
Remove: Empty Tags	Removes any tags that have no content between them. For example, **\<i>\</i>** would be removed because there is nothing between the two tags.
Remove: Redundant Nested Tags	Removes tags that are redundant and not needed. For example, **\<b>**This**\<b>** is a **\<b>**redundant**\<b> \<b>**tag**\</b>**, has two redundant **\<b>** tags that would be removed because they are not needed.
Remove: Non-Dreamweaver HTML Comments	Removes any comment tags that are not specific to Dreamweaver, but does not remove comments that are native to Dreamweaver. **\<!– #EndEditable "image" –>**, for example, would not be removed, because it is used native to Dreamweaver to designate the end of an editable area of a template.
Remove: Dreamweaver HTML Comments	Removes all HTML comments that are native to Dreamweaver. However, it does not remove standard HTML comments.
Remove: Specific Tag(s):	Removes specific tags that you specify in the text field. For example, you could remove all of the **\<blink>** tags in a document or any other tag that you specify.
Options: Combine Nested \<font> Tags When Possible	Combines nested tags when they control the same block of text.
Options: Show Log on Completion	Summarizes how the HTML was modified, in a small dialog box, after the Clean Up HTML command has been applied.

5. _____**Cleaning Up Word HTML**

Dreamweaver lets you import HTML files that were saved in Microsoft Word. This is a nice feature, because more and more business professionals are using Word to author Web pages. However, Microsoft Word has a reputation for generating a lot of unnecessary HTML code. Fortunately, the **Clean Up Word HTML** command will help you remove this extra code to ensure that your pages are written in the most appropriate and concise manner. This exercise will walk you through the process of using the Clean Up Word HTML command.

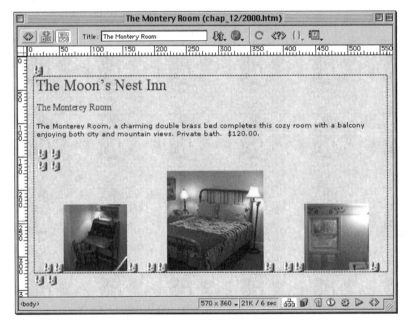

1. Open the **2000.htm** file located inside the **chap_12** folder. This file was created in Microsoft Word 2000 on a Windows machine.

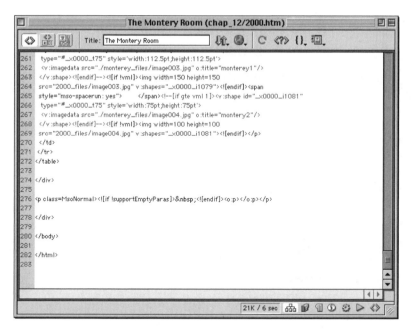

```
        ┌─────────────────── The Montery Room (chap_12/2000.htm) ───────────────────┐
        │ Title: The Montery Room                                                    │
261       type="#_x0000_t75" style='width:112.5pt;height:112.5pt'>
262       <v:imagedata src="./monterey_files/image003.jpg" o:title="monterey1"/>
263       </v:shape><![endif]--><![if !vml]><img width=150 height=150
264       src="2000_files/image003.jpg" v:shapes="_x0000_i1079"><![endif]><span
265       style="mso-spacerun: yes">        </span><!--[if gte vml 1]><v:shape id="_x0000_i1081"
266       type="#_x0000_t75" style='width:75pt;height:75pt'>
267       <v:imagedata src="./monterey_files/image004.jpg" o:title="montery2"/>
268       </v:shape><![endif]--><![if !vml]><img width=100 height=100
269       src="2000_files/image004.jpg" v:shapes="_x0000_i1081"><![endif]></p>
270       </td>
271       </tr>
272       </table>
273
274       </div>
275
276       <p class=MsoNormal><![if !supportEmptyParas]> <![endif]><o:p></o:p></p>
277
278       </div>
279
280       </body>
281
282       </html>
283
        ├────────────────────────────────────────────────────────────────────────────┤
        │ 21K / 6 sec                                                                  │
        └────────────────────────────────────────────────────────────────────────────┘
```

2. Click the **Show Code View** button to display the Code window. Scroll down to the bottom of the window. This page has more than 275 lines of HTML code. That's an awful lot for this very simple page.

3. Click the **Show Design View** button to return to the Design view.

WARNING | Make a Backup

Before you use the Clean Up Word HTML command, make sure you have a backup of the file. When you apply this command, it will make changes to the HTML that will cause it to look different if opened in Microsoft Word. You never know when you might need to refer back to the original Word file.

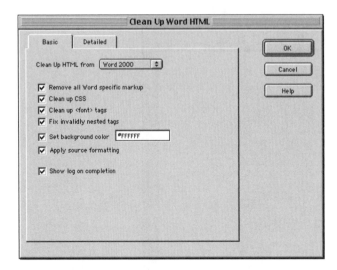

4. Select **Commands > Clean Up Word HTML**. This opens the Clean Up Word HTML dialog box. It might take a few seconds for it to appear. Dreamweaver is trying to detect which version of Word the file was created in.

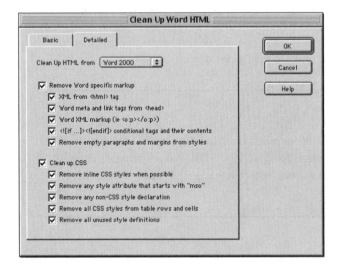

5. Click on the **Detailed** tab at the top of the dialog box. This displays the more advanced options you can control with this command. Unless you are really comfortable with XML and CSS, we suggest you leave these values at their default settings. Click **OK**.

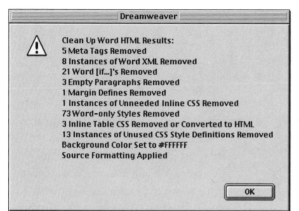

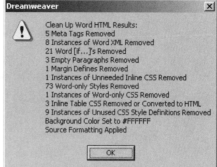

Summary screen on a Macintosh   **Summary screen in Windows**

6. A dialog box appears summarizing the modifications that were made to the page. There summary will differ slightly, depending on whether you're using a Macintosh or a Windows-based machine. When you are finished reviewing this information, click OK.

7. Click the **Show Code View** button to open the Code window. You should see significantly less HTML code now. The HTML was reduced from more than 275 lines down to 37 (Mac) and 34 (Windows). Now, that's something you'll want to show all your friends! Well, maybe only your friends who use Word and know what HTML is in the first place! ;-)

8. Close and save this file.

That's all for now. If you were intimidated by editing HTML before you read this chapter, we hope you are more at ease with it now. Move on to the next chapter if you have the stamina—there's still more to learn! Otherwise, pick this up another day. You've earned your rest!

13.

Forms

| Working with Form Objects |
| Creating a Form | Creating a Jump Menu |

chap_13

Dreamweaver 4
H·O·T CD-ROM

Forms are one of the most important elements of a Web site, because they enable you to ask questions of your end user and receive answers. While forms can be identical to those we're used to in the nonvirtual world (think IRS, car insurance, or loan paperwork), they can also be used for more exciting things, such as voting, guestbooks, or e-commerce. In general, forms-based pages are much more interactive than other types of HTML pages, because they can collect and report information to you.

There are two aspects to creating forms: creating the **Form objects** (text fields, checkboxes, Submit buttons, and so on) and making the forms function properly. This chapter focuses on the creation of Form objects, not on the programming required to make forms transmit data to and from your server. Unfortunately, making the forms operational involves programming that goes beyond the scope of Dreamweaver and this book. Forms might not sound like much fun, but they are at the heart of what makes the Web different from paper and publishing mediums of the past.

The Form Objects Panel

The objects you use to create a form, in Dreamweaver, are referred to as Form objects. These include text fields, checkboxes, images, buttons, and so on. You'll find all the Form objects on the **Objects panel**. Instead of working with the Common objects, as you have in most of the other chapters so far, this chapter will require that you set your Objects panel to Forms. This will display the Form objects, as shown below.

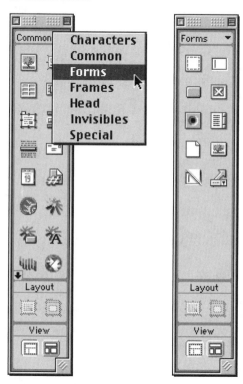

If the **Objects** panel is not visible, go to **Window > Objects**. To access the Forms objects, you need to change your Objects panel from its default setting (**Common**) to **Forms**. You do this by clicking on the arrow at the top of the Objects panel and selecting Forms from the pop-up menu.

Form Objects

The table below outlines the different objects available on the **Form Objects** panel. As you become more familiar with forms, you will not need this table. Meanwhile, it should help you get a better inkling of what each of the Objects does:

\	Form Objects in Dreamweaver	
Icon	**Name**	**Function**
	Insert Form	This is the very first step in creating a form. It inserts the <form> tag into your document. If you do not place all of your objects inside the <form> tag, your form will not work!
	Insert Text Field	Inserts a Text Field object on your form. It can be set to contain single or multiple lines of data.
	Insert Button	Inserts a Submit Button object (Dreamweaver default) on your form. You can also make this a Reset button, or set it to None.
	Insert Checkbox	Inserts a Checkbox object on your form. These check-boxes are used to select an option on a form.
	Insert Radio Button	Inserts a Radio Button object on your form. Radio buttons are used to select one item out of a list of available options.
	Insert List/Menu	Inserts a List object or Menu object on your form. These two objects (list or menu) allow you to make single or multiple selections in a small area of space.
	Insert File Field	Inserts a text box and button that lets the end user browse to a file on his or her hard drive, for uploading.
	Insert Image Field	Inserts an image on a form, which the user can click. This can be used to make graphic-based buttons.
	Insert Hidden Field	Stores information that does not need to be displayed but is necessary for processing the form on the server
	Insert Jump Menu	Inserts a jump menu that allows the user to select a URL from the menu and then jump to that page.

NOTE | Making Forms Function with CGI

Dreamweaver gives you complete control over the layout of your form and the creation of Form objects, but that is just half the battle. Sending the information from the form to your server or database requires more than HTML can do. In order to process forms, it's necessary to use some type of additional scripting beyond HTML. While it is possible to process form data through JavaScript or even Java, most Web developers agree that the most foolproof way to program forms is through CGI, PHP, or ASP.

CGI stands for Common Gateway Interface. In essence, CGI is a protocol to send information to and from a Web server. CGI scripts can be written in a variety of programming languages, ranging from Perl to C to AppleScript. If that doesn't sound complicated enough for you, add that different types of CGI scripts work with different Web servers, ranging from UNIX to Mac OS to Windows NT.

If you have a Web site, chances are very high that your Internet service provider or Web administrator has existing CGI scripts that you can use. Because there are so many variables to CGI, and it is outside the scope of Dreamweaver, it will be up to you to coordinate obtaining the scripts and implementing the processing of your forms.

Here are some online resources for CGI scripts:

FreeScripts.com
http://www.freescripts.com

The CGI Resource Index
http://www.cgi-resources.com/

Free Code
http://www.freecode.com/

I. _____Working with Form Objects

In this exercise, you will get hands-on experience with each of the various form elements. You won't be adding any scripts because doing that would require another book, but you will get everything set up so that when you do want to add a CGI script, your pages will be ready!

1. Copy the contents of **chap_13** to your hard drive, and press **F8** to define the site. If you need a refresher on this process, revisit Exercise 1 in Chapter 3, *"Site Control."*

2. Open the **objects.html** file. It's just a blank page, but at least it has a page title for you.

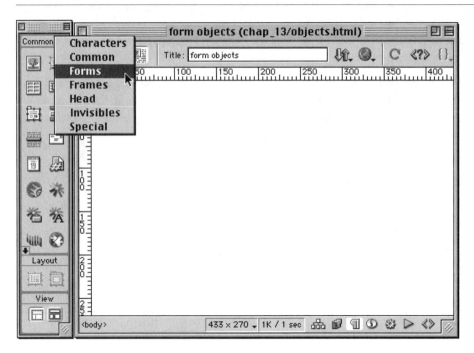

3. Make sure the **Form Objects** panel is visible. If it's not, click on the small black arrow at the top of the **Objects** panel and select **Forms** from the pop-up menu.

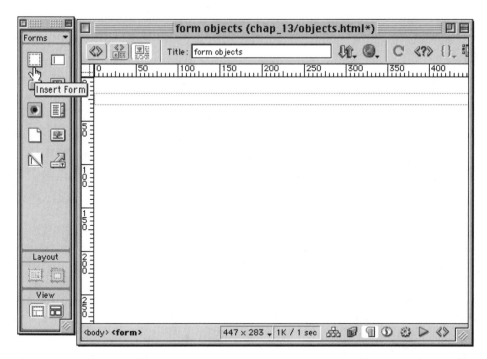

4. Click on the **Insert Form** object in the **Form Objects** panel. This inserts the **<form>** tag into your document. You should see red dashed lines on your page. If you do not see them, select **View >** **Visual Aids > Invisible Elements**.

The visibility of the Insert Form object doesn't matter in terms of its functionality. It's a preference of ours to turn its visibility on so we ensure that it was added properly. You can work with it off or on; just know that it's there for the viewing if you feel more secure seeing it, as we do!

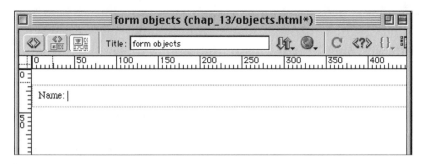

5. Position your cursor inside the red dashed lines, and type **Name:**. Press the **spacebar** once to create a single space.

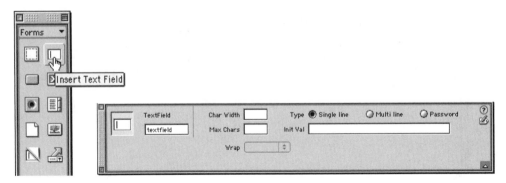

6. Click on the **Insert Text Field** object in the **Form Objects** panel. This inserts a blank text field onto your page. With the text field highlighted, notice that the Property Inspector options change.

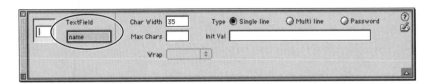

7. In the **TextField** setting in the Property Inspector, replace the existing text with the word **name**. This gives a unique name to the text field. Enter **Char Width: 35**. This sets the length of the text field. It does not limit the amount of text that your user can enter, just how much will be visible in the browser. To limit the amount of text entered, you would enter a value for **Max Chars**. Since we don't want to limit the text, leave **Max Chars** blank.

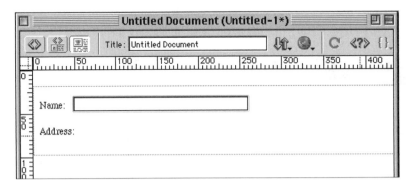

8. Click to the right of the text field in your document and press **Return** or **Enter**. Type **Address:** and press the **spacebar** to create one space.

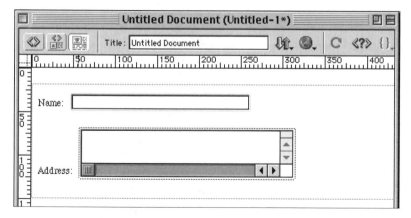

9. Click on the **Insert Text Field** object. This inserts another text field onto your page. In the Property Inspector, enter the word **address** in the **TextField**. Choose **Type: Multi line** and set **Num Lines: 2,** then set **Char Width: 40**. You can see how the **Multi line** attribute works. This is great for larger areas of text when you don't know how much will be inserted.

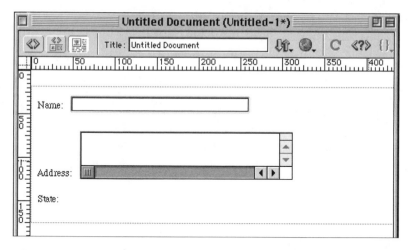

10. Click to the right of the **Multi line** text field in your document, and press **Return** or **Enter**. Type **State:** and insert one space by pressing the **spacebar**.

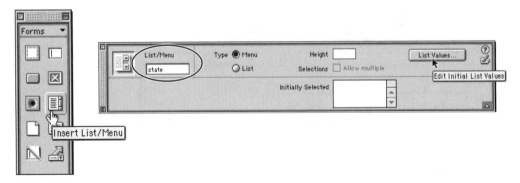

11. Click the **Insert List/Menu** object. By default, this inserts a **Menu object** onto your form. In the Property Inspector, type **state** in the **List/Menu** field. Next, click the **List Values...** button.

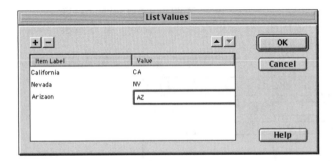

12. For the first **Item Label**, type **California**, and then press **Tab**. For the first **Value**, type **CA**, and then press **Tab**. Repeat this same process for **Nevada** and **Arizona**, using the information from the image above. This Form object will give you a pop-up menu displaying the information in the **Item Label** column. The information in the **Value** column is what a CGI or JavaScript program would process with the Form. Click **OK**.

13. In the Property Inspector, select **Initially Selected: California**. This determines what menu item is visible before the user clicks on the pop-up menu.

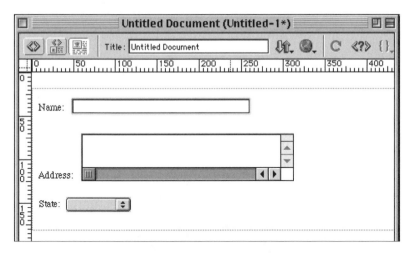

14. Click to the right of the **State** pop-up menu, and press **Return** or **Enter**.

TIP | Initially Selected Values in Menus

Sometimes, when you are creating menus, you would like a default value to appear in the menu. For example, if you were building a menu with a list of all U.S. states, you might want to have California appear in the menu automatically. Selecting the value from the Initially Selected option in the Property Inspector can do this. The value you select here appears as the default value for the menu.

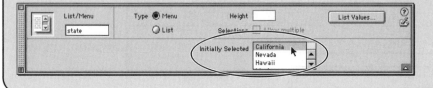

15. Click the **Insert Checkbox** object. This inserts a checkbox onto your page.

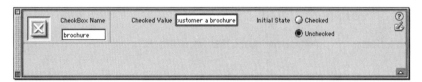

16. In the Property Inspector, name the checkbox **brochure**. For the **Checked Value**, type **Send the customer a brochure**. The Checked Value information will appear next to the checkbox name when a CGI script processes the form. This information is hidden from your end user, but it is useful to a programmer who is setting up the CGI because it tells him or her what the checkbox relates to.

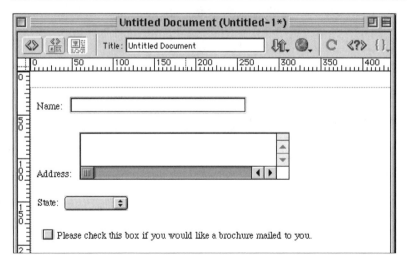

17. Click to the right of the checkbox and type **Please check this box if you would like a brochure mailed to you**. This will help end users understand what information they are requesting by checking this box. Press **Return** or **Enter**.

18. Click the **Insert Button** object. This inserts a **Submit** button on your page, which is Dreamweaver's default button type. Because you need to have a button to submit the form, leave the options at their default values.

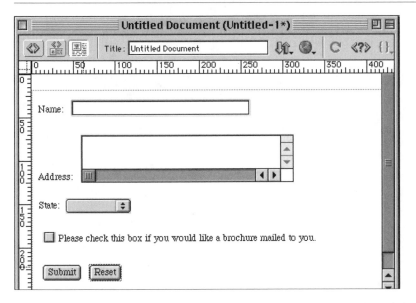

19. Click to the right of the **Submit** button. Click the **Insert Button** object again. This inserts another **Submit** button on your page. In the Property Inspector, change the **Action** to **Reset form**. This creates a button that clears the form, just in case your end user makes a mistake and wants to start over. Change the **Button Name** to **Reset**.

20. Save your file. Press **F12** to preview your form in a browser. Remember, the **Submit** button will not work because you did not attach any CGI scripts.

21. Return to Dreamweaver, save, and close the document.

The purpose of this exercise was to get you comfortable inserting different Form objects and modifying some of their properties. To make a form perform its functions, you would need to attach a CGI or other scripting program to it.

2. ————————————**Creating a Form**

This exercise is designed to help you become more familiar with creating a layout for your forms. Forms can combine other HTML elements such as background images and tables, and by the end of this exercise you should be comfortable combining your new form-creation skills with your existing Web-layout skills.

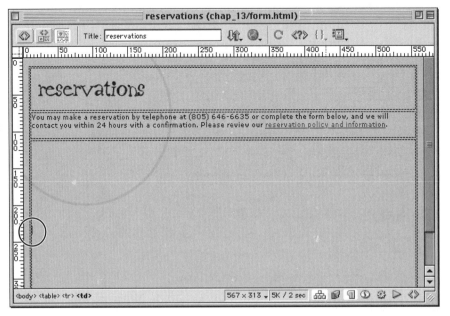

1. Open the **form.html** file. Notice that it already contains a background image, a graphic (reservations), and a table. Click your cursor in the bottom cell of the table.

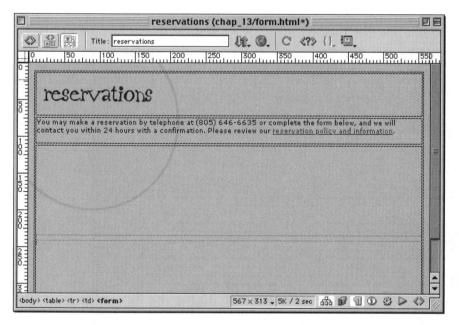

2. Click on the **Insert Form** object in the **Objects** panel. Red dashes should appear in the table cell, indicating that you have inserted a **<form>** tag. If you don't see these red dashes, select **View > Visual Aids > Invisible Elements**.

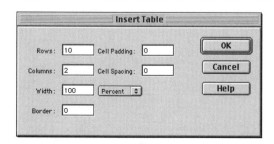

3. Select **Insert > Table**. (If you're used to clicking on the Table object in the **Objects** panel, you would need to switch it back to **Common**. For convenience's sake, just use the Insert menu right now.) Change the settings to **Rows: 10, Cell Padding: 0, Columns: 2, Cell Spacing: 0, Width: 100 Percent**, and **Border: 0**. Click **OK**.

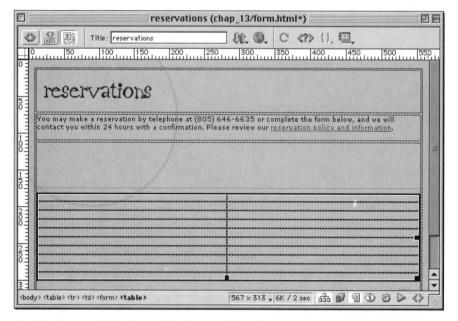

A table appears inside the red dashes, as shown here.

4. Click inside the first cell in column 1 and type **Name**. Click inside the second cell in column 1 and type **Arrival Date**. Click inside the third cell in column 1 and type **Departure Date**. Click inside the fourth cell in column 1 and type **# of Guests**. Click inside the fifth cell in column 1 and type **Phone**. Finally, click inside the sixth cell in column 1 and type **Room Preference**.

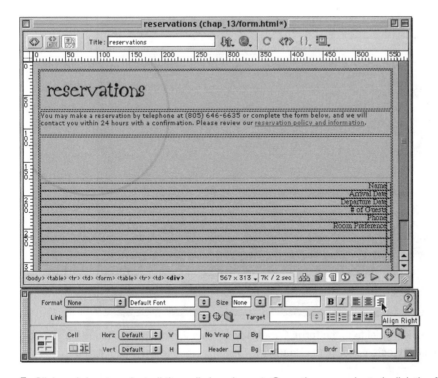

5. Click and drag to select all the cells in column 1. Once they are selected, click the **Align Right** button in the Property Inspector.

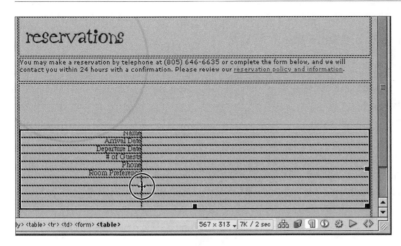

6. Click and drag the middle divider between the two columns to move it over to the left.

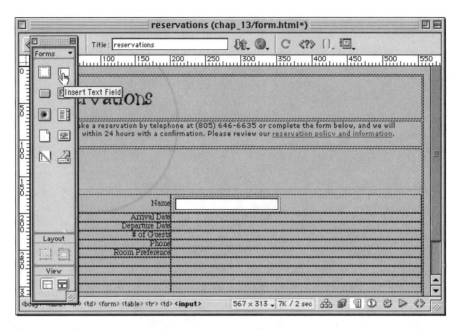

7. Next, you'll add some entry fields to the **form**. Click inside column 2, row 1, and choose the **Insert Text Field** object in the **Objects** panel. In the Property Inspector, name the **TextField: name**.

8. Repeat this same process for the next five cells down. Make sure you give each text field a unique name that describes the associated column.

WARNING | Strange Table Behavior

As you work with forms and tables in Dreamweaver, you might notice that sometimes it looks as though your Form objects are jumping out of their cells. Don't worry; they really haven't moved at all. This is just a little visual glitch in Dreamweaver. You can get them back to their correct places by simply clicking outside the table.

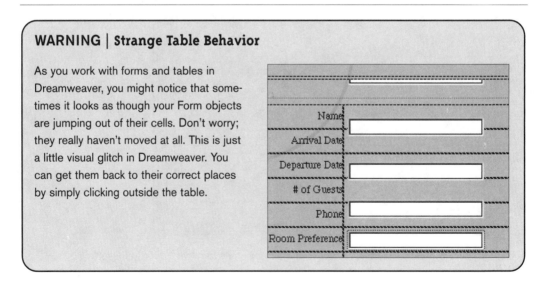

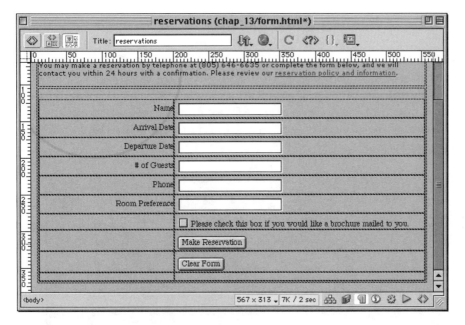

9. Position your cursor inside row 7 in column 2 and click. Next, click on the **Insert Checkbox** object in the **Objects** panel. In the Property Inspector, change the **CheckBox Name** to **mail** and the **Checked Value** to **mail brochure to customer**. Click to the right of the checkbox that just appeared, and type **Please check this box if you would like a brochure mailed to you.** into the document.

---

10. Click in row 8 in column 2, then click the **Insert Button** object in the **Objects** panel. In the Property Inspector, change the **Label** to **Make Reservation**. The **Action** should be set to **Submit form**.

---

11. Click in row 9 in column 2, then click the **Insert Button** object in the **Objects** panel again. In the Property Inspector, change the **Action** to **Reset form**, the **Label** to **Clear Form**, and the **Name** to **Clear**.

Congratulations—you've just designed a custom-formatted form using form and table elements. Save and close this file; you won't be needing it again.

5. ——————Creating a Jump Menu

Dreamweaver's **Jump Menu** object combines a forms element for lists and a JavaScript behavior that causes the menu to go to its target without the use of a Go button. Adding this specialized kind of form can be very useful when you have a small amount of screen real estate in which to place a lot of navigation choices. This exercise will show you how to use Dreamweaver to create a jump menu on **your** page. The jump menu works really well as a navigation tool within framesets, which is what you'll get to try in this hands-on exercise.

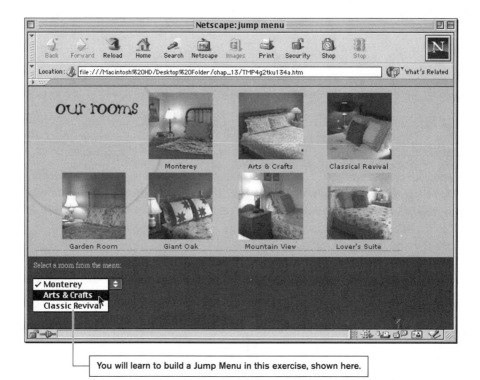

You will learn to build a Jump Menu in this exercise, shown here.

*The **jump menu** is a special kind of Dreamweaver object that combines a form element with JavaScript. It allows the visitor to a page to select a choice and have that choice load without having to first click a Go button.*

1. Open the **frameset.html** file located inside the **chap_13** folder. This is a simple frameset that we have created for you.

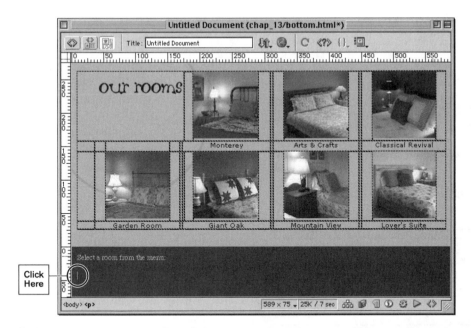

Click
Here

2. Click in the bottom frame. Type **Select a room from the menu:**. This text will help the user understand what the menu contains and what it's used for. Press **Return or Enter**.

3. Select **Insert > Form Objects > Jump Menu**. This opens the **Insert Jump Menu** window. As an
alternative, you could have clicked on the **Insert Jump Menu** object in the **Objects** panel.

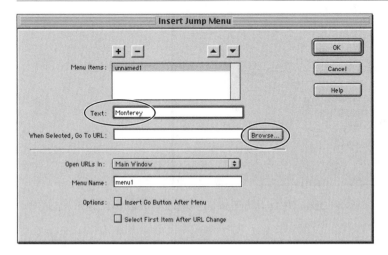

4. In the **Text** field, type **Monterey**. This option sets the actual text that appears in the menu when the
user clicks on it.

5. Click on the **Browse...** button next to the **When Selected, Go To URL** field. This lets you browse to the HTML file you want to jump to when this menu item is selected.

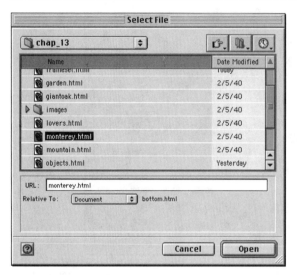

6. Navigate to the **monterey.html** file located inside the **chap_13** folder. Select it and click **Open**.

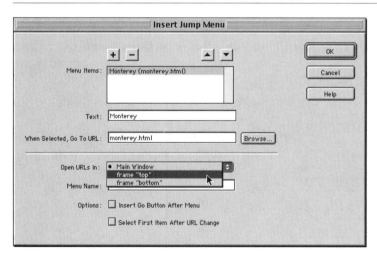

7. Click on the pop-up menu next to the **Open URLs In** option and select **frame "top."** This option determines what frame the Web page will load into.

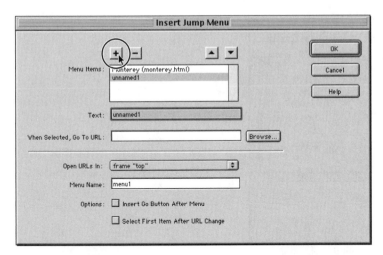

8. Click on the **plus** button at the top of the dialog box to add another item to your jump menu. This interface is very similar to the Insert Navigation Bar dialog box you learned about in Chapter 10, *"Rollovers."* It's nice to see the continuity in the interface; you gotta love it!

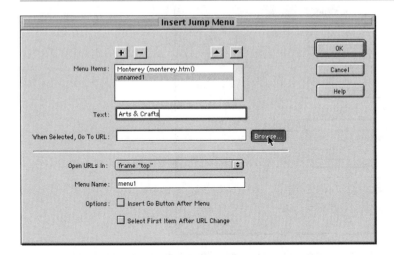

9. Enter **Arts & Crafts** for the **Text** field. Click on the **Browse...** button next to the **When Selected, Go To URL** option.

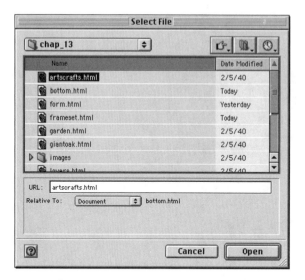

10. Browse to the **artscrafts.html** file located inside the **chap_13** folder. Select it and click **Open**.

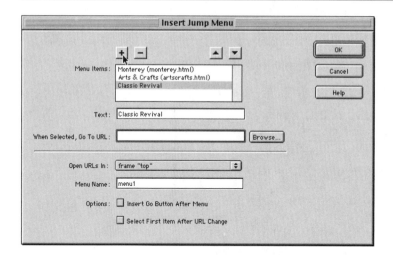

11. Click on the **plus** button at the top of the dialog box. Enter **Classic Revival** for the **Text** field. Click on the **Browse...** button.

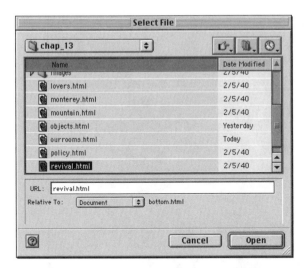

12. Browse to the **revival.html** file located inside the **chap_13** folder. Select it and click **Open**.

13. You've just finished setting up your jump menu. Click **OK**. Notice how Dreamweaver automatically added the **<form>** tag. Nice.

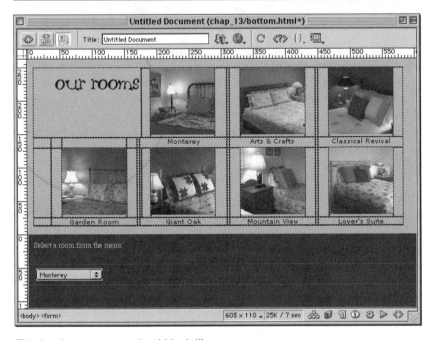

This is what your page should look like now.

14. Save your work. Press **F12** to preview your page in the browser.

15. Click on the menu and select **Arts & Crafts**. This will jump you to the **artscrafts.html** page.

16. Return to Dreamweaver and close the document.

Phew! Another chapter under your belt. Move to the next chapter if you feel ready.

14.
Behaviors

chap_14

Dreamweaver 4
H•O•T CD-ROM

Dreamweaver **behaviors** are scripts written in JavaScript that extend HTML to do things that it can't do on its own. Dreamweaver ships with a variety of behaviors that allow you to do all kinds of cool things, such as open a browser in a smaller window or detect the version of your end-user's browser.

The **Macromedia Extension Manager** is a program that lets you easily install and remove extensions from Dreamweaver. In previous versions of Dreamweaver, you had to download and install the Extension Manager application yourself. In Dreamweaver 4, the Extension Manager is preinstalled for you and ready to be used. However, as new versions of the Extension Manager are released, you might need to install them. To learn how, you can follow the exercise in this chapter that walks you through the process of downloading and installing the Extension Manager. For now, you can skip Exercise 6 and come back to it later.

This chapter will show you how to use some of the behaviors that ship with Dreamweaver right out of the box. You'll also learn how to download additional behaviors from Macromedia Exchange, a free online service bureau that Macromedia provides, which houses hundreds of additional Dreamweaver behaviors that don't ship with the program!

I. ————————Creating a Check Browser Behavior

As you start adding different features and technologies to your site, such as DHTML and JavaScript, you might want to make sure that the people viewing your pages are using a browser that can see these features (4.0 browsers and later). This exercise will show you how to use the **Check Browser** behavior to determine which browser and version the user has and then redirect the user to another page. This technique is very useful if you want to create different versions of your site, one that works with 4.0 or later browsers and one that works with earlier browsers. Even though fewer 3.0 browsers are in use today, knowing how to set up this behavior is still a good thing.

Note: In order to check the success of this exercise, you must have either Netscape Navigator 3.0+ and 4.0+ or Internet Explorer 3.0+ and 4.0+ installed on your computer. If you don't have both versions of one of these browsers and you wish to complete this exercise, please install both of these browser versions before continuing. We've included copies of Netscape Navigator and Internet Explorer 3.0 and 4.0 on the Dreamweaver 4 **H•O•T CD-ROM** in the **Software/Browsers** folder. **Tip:** Windows users should install these browsers into separate directories to avoid accidentally overwriting other previously installed browsers.

1. Define your site for Chapter 14. If you need a refresher, visit Exercise 1 in Chapter 3, *"Site Control."* Browse to **checkbrowser.html** and open it. This file contains some text in a table.

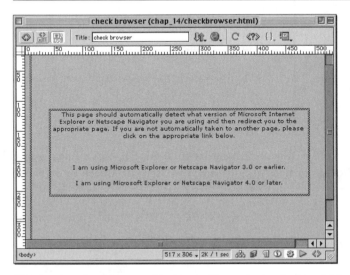

*This is what **checkbrowser.html** looks like at the beginning of this exercise. It's a page with a table that has text in it. You'll add the Check Browser behavior to it, which will determine the user's browser and version then redirect the user to another page.*

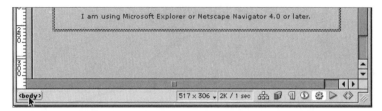

2. Click on the **<body>** tag in the **Tag selector** at the bottom of the document window. If you can't see the **<body>** tag in the Tag selector, simply click anywhere inside the document window. You want to attach the Check Browser behavior to the **<body>** tag of the document so that the behavior can run when the page is first loaded.

3. In the **Behaviors** panel (**Window > Behaviors** or **Shift+F3**), click the **plus** sign and choose **Check Browser** from the pop-up menu. This opens the **Check Browser** dialog box.

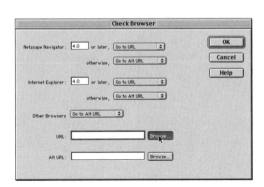

4. Click **Browse...** near the bottom next to the **URL** field. Browse to **version4.html** in the **chap_14** folder and click **Open**. This will be the page your end users will see if they are using Netscape or Explorer 4.0 or later. Don't click OK just yet.

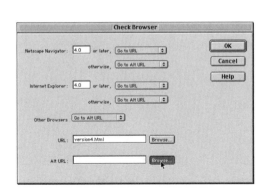

5. Click **Browse...** at the bottom next to **Alt URL** field. Browse to **version3.html** in the **chap_14** folder and click **Open**. The Alt URL is the page your end users will see if they are using something other than Netscape or Explorer 4.0 (i.e., Netscape 3.0, Explorer 2.0, etc.).

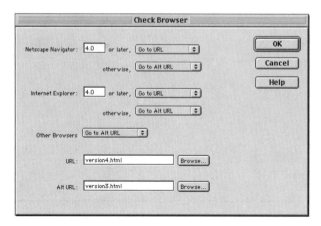

This is what your Check Browser dialog box should look like at this point.

6. Click **OK** to accept these settings. You won't detect any visual changes to your page, but a whole bunch of complex JavaScript was just added to it.

7. Notice that the Check Browser behavior now appears in the **Behaviors** panel. Also, notice that its event is automatically set to **onLoad**. This means that when the Web page is loaded, it will perform the Check Browser behavior. Cool!

TIP | Events and Actions

Each behavior has two components: the **event** and the **action**. Events are defined by a user's mouse state (such as onClick) or a browser's load state (such as onLoad). Actions, on the other hand, are blocks of prewritten JavaScript that are executed when the event occurs. In the context of a rollover, when the event is completed (the user's mouse moves over the graphic), the action takes place (one image is swapped with another). While the terms "event" and "action" might sound like Greek to you right now, once you see how easy behaviors are to use, you'll find the learning curve to be remarkably low.

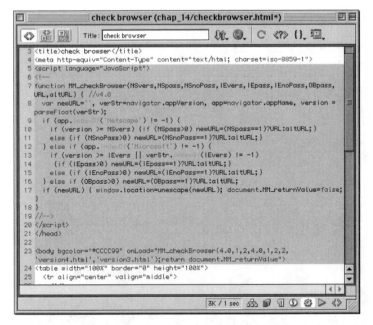

```
3 <title>check browser</title>
4 <meta http-equiv="Content-Type" content="text/html; charset=iso-8859-1">
5 <script language="JavaScript">
6 <!--
7 function MM_checkBrowser(NSvers,NSpass,NSnoPass,IEvers,IEpass,IEnoPass,OBpass,
URL,altURL) { //v4.0
8   var newURL='', verStr=navigator.appVersion, app=navigator.appName, version =
parseFloat(verStr);
9   if (app.indexOf('Netscape') != -1) {
10    if (version >= NSvers) {if (NSpass>0) newURL=(NSpass==1)?URL:altURL; }
11    else {if (NSnoPass>0) newURL=(NSnoPass==1)?URL:altURL;}
12  } else if (app.indexOf('Microsoft') != -1) {
13    if (version >= IEvers || verStr.indexOf(IEvers) != -1)
14    {if (IEpass>0) newURL=(IEpass==1)?URL:altURL; }
15    else {if (IEnoPass>0) newURL=(IEnoPass==1)?URL:altURL; }
16  } else if (OBpass>0) newURL=(OBpass==1)?URL:altURL;
17  if (newURL) { window.location=unescape(newURL); document.MM_returnValue=false;
}
18 }
19 //-->
20 </script>
21 </head>
22
23 <body bgcolor="#CCCC99" onLoad="MM_checkBrowser(4.0,1,2,4.0,1,2,2,
'version4.html','version3.html');return document.MM_returnValue">
24 <table width="100%" border="0" height="100%">
25  <tr align="center" valign="middle">
```

8. Click the **Show Code View** button to open the Code window. Notice all the JavaScript that was added to your page. Could you imagine having to create all of that code from scratch? Part of the power of behaviors is that they shield you from such tedious tasks. Click the **Show Design View** button to return to the Design view.

9. Choose **File > Save** to save the changes you made to **checkbrowser.html**.

Now that you've added the Check Browser behavior to your page, you're ready to check your work by opening this page in both the version 3 and version 4 browsers. Will the correct version load? Stay tuned.

10. Launch Netscape 3.0 (shown above) or Internet Explorer 3.0+. Select **File > Open File...** Browse to the **chap_14** folder, select **checkbrowser.html**, and click **Open**. Notice that you are immediately taken to **version3.html**. Exit the Netscape 3.0 application.

WARNING | JavaScript Potential Problem

There's a potential problem with using this type of browser detection. Because this detection is constructed with JavaScript and users can disable JavaScript in their browser preferences, this script may not always work properly. As a safeguard against this, you'll finish this exercise by learning how to give the user an option to load the appropriate page by clicking a link. This will prevent anyone from being locked out of your site, which is a very good thing.

11. Launch Netscape 4.0 (shown above) or Internet Explorer 4.0+. Select **File > Open > Page in Navigator...** (Mac) or **File > Open Page** (Windows). Browse to the **chap_14** folder, select **checkbrowser.html**, and click **Open**. Notice that you are immediately taken to **version4.html**. Exit the Netscape 4.0 application and return to Dreamweaver.

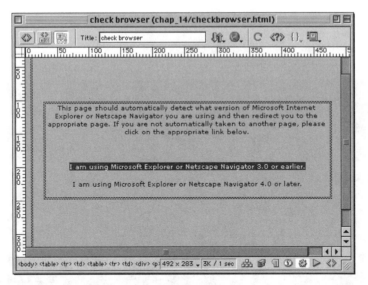

12. In the Dreamweaver **checkbrowser.html** document, click and drag to select the words **I am using Microsoft Explorer or Netscape Navigator 3.0 or earlier.** Now you'll use the Property Inspector to make this text into a hyperlink to **version3.html**.

13. In the Property Inspector (**Window > Properties** or **Cmd+F3**), click the **Browse for File** folder icon to the right of the **Link** field. Browse to **version3.html** and click **Open**.

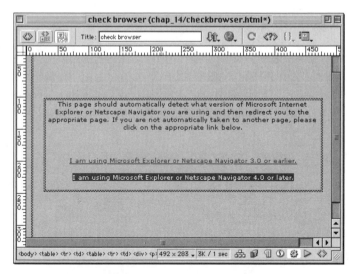

14. In the **checkbrowser.html** document, click and drag to select the text **I am using Microsoft Explorer or Netscape Navigator 4.0 or later.**

15. In the Property Inspector, click the **Browse for File** folder icon again. This time, browse to **version4.html**. Click **Open**.

Setting up these two links is a good idea, because if users don't have JavaScript turned on, they will still have a way to get into the site.

16. Choose **File > Save**, and close this file. You won't be working with it anymore.

2.  Creating a Set Text of Status Bar Behavior

The **status bar** is located at the bottom of a browser window and can display text in addition to what is on the Web page. Using the **Set Text of Status Bar** behavior, you can display any text that you want in the status bar of the browser window. This is often used in conjunction with links to provide additional detail about the destination page. This exercise will show you how to add the Set Text of Status Bar behavior to a page.

This is what text looks like in a browser status bar.

1. Open **statustext.html**, located inside the **chap_14** folder. You will add the Set Text of Status Bar behavior to several of the links on this page, to provide additional feedback to the user.

2. Click the **about the inn** image to select it. In the Property Inspector (**Window >
Properties** or **Cmd+F3**), notice that this image has a hash mark (**#**) in the **Link** field. This is
referred to as a "nowhere" link. It's a link that goes, well, nowhere. The only reason you need
it is that certain behaviors (such as the one you're about to add) must be attached to links.

3. With the image still selected, in the **Behaviors** panel (**Window > Behaviors** or **Shift+F3**),
click the **plus** sign to access the pop-up menu, and choose **Set Text > Set Text of Status
Bar**. This opens the **Set Text of Status Bar** dialog box.

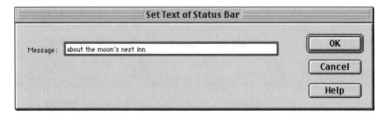

4. Enter **Message: about the moon's nest inn**. Click **OK**.

5. Notice that the **Set Text of Status Bar** behavior now appears in the **Behaviors** panel with the **onMouseOver** event.

6. Repeat this process for each of the other buttons, adding a short description for each one.

7. When you're finished, press **F12** to preview your page in a browser. Move your mouse over any of the four images and look at the text that is displayed in the browser window's status bar.

8. Return to Dreamweaver and choose **File > Save** to save your changes and close this file. You won't need it any longer.

3.————————**Creating a Set Text of Text Field Behavior**

Earlier, in Chapter 13, *"Forms,"* you learned how to create forms. This exercise will show you how to create preset content that will fill specific form fields as the user interacts with your form. It uses the Set Text feature of the Text Field behavior.

1. Open **reserve_done.html**. This is what your file will look like when you finish this exercise. Press **F12** to preview this in a browser.

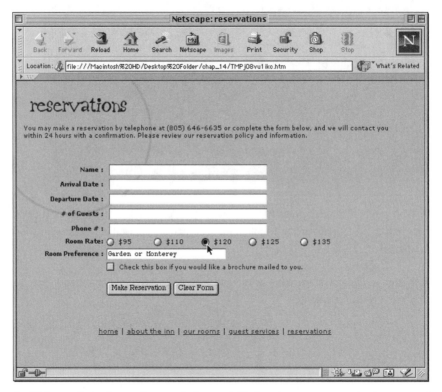

2. Click any of the **Room Rate** radio buttons. Notice that text automatically appears in the **Room Preference** text field. This effect was created using the Set Text behavior, which ships with Dreamweaver. Close this file for now. You will create this effect in the steps that follow.

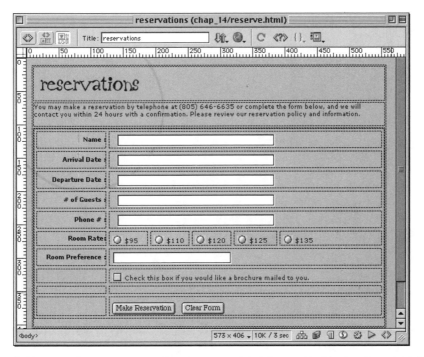

3. Return to Dreamweaver and open **reserve.html**, located inside the **chap_14** folder. This file consists of a form that we created for you. You will learn how to use the Set Text of Text Field behavior to dynamically update this form as the user interacts with it.

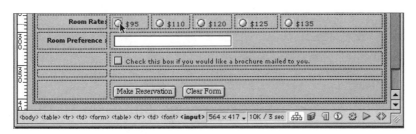

4. Click the radio button next to **$95**. You are going to apply the Set Text of Text Field behavior to this form element so that the Room Preference text field is automatically updated when a user selects this button in the browser.

5. From the **Behaviors** panel (**Window > Behaviors** or **Shift+F3**), click the **plus** sign and choose **Set Text > Set Text of Text Field** from the pop-up menu. This opens the **Set Text of Text Field** dialog box.

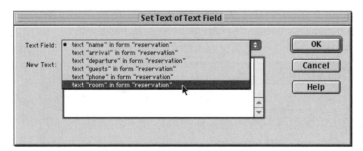

6. Click the **Text Field** pop-up menu at the top and choose **text "room" in form "reservation."** Don't click OK just yet.

The pop-up menu lists each of the form objects with their newly assigned names. As you can see, it's a good idea to use descriptive names that relate to the information being requested so they can easily be found and identified in this dialog box.. The Text Field option determines which text field in the Reservations form will automatically display the text.

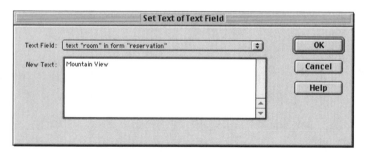

7. Enter **Mountain View** in the **New Text** field. This will replace any text that is in the Room Preference text field when the user clicks the $95 button. Click **OK**, and you're ready to set up the next button.

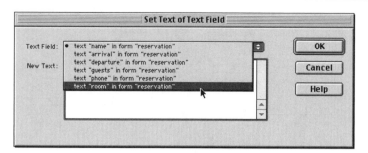

8. Click the radio button next to **$110**.

9. From the **Behaviors** panel, click the **plus** sign and choose **Set Text > Set Text of Text Field** from the pop-up menu. This opens the **Set Text of Text Field** dialog box.

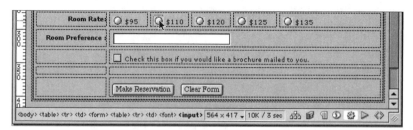

10. Click the **Text Field** pop-up menu at the top and choose **text "room" in form "reservation."** Don't click **OK** just yet.

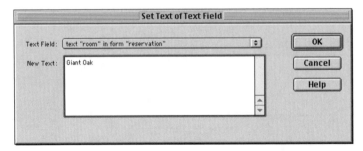

11. Enter **Giant Oak** in the **New Text** field. This will replace any text that is in the Room Preference text field of the form when the user clicks the $110 button. Click **OK**.

Set Text of Text Field Behavior	
Radio Button Text	**New Text**
$120	Garden or Monterey
$125	Arts & Crafts
$135	Classical Revival or Lovers' Suite

12. Using the above chart, add the **Set Text of Text Field** behavior to the other three radio buttons.

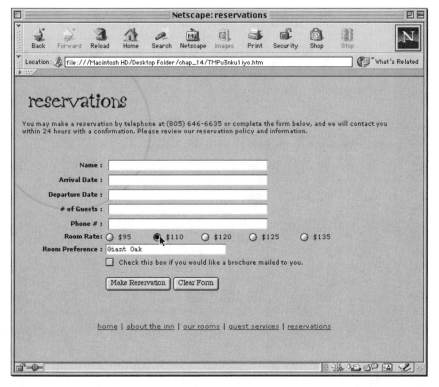

13. When you're finished, press **F12** to preview this page in your primary browser. Click each of the radio buttons and watch the Room Preference text field change automatically.

14. Return to Dreamweaver. Save and close this file. You will not need it for the remainder of the book.

4. —————————Opening a New Browser Window

There are going to be times when you just can't cram everything onto a single Web page. An option that many Web developers use is to open additional yet related information in another window. In this next exercise, you will open a new browser window to display information that wouldn't fit comfortably on a single page.

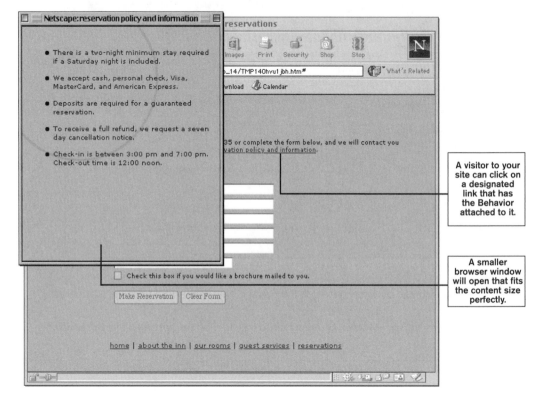

This is the example you will build in this exercise. When you click on a link on the main browser page, this second, smaller browser window will open without any of its own navigation bars.

1. Open **newwindow.html**, located inside the **chap_14** folder.

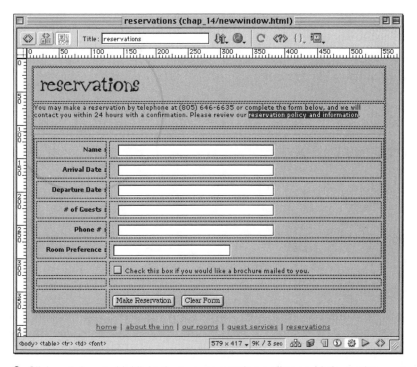

2. Click and drag to highlight the text **reservation policy and information**.

3. In the Property Inspector (**Window > Properties** or **Cmd+F3**), enter a **#** in the **Link** field. You remember why you should do this from Exercise 2, right?

4. From the **Behaviors** panel (**Window > Behaviors** or **Shift+F3**), click the **plus** sign and choose **Open Browser Window** from the pop-up menu. This opens the **Open Browser Window** dialog box.

5. Click **Browse...** and browse to **policy.html**. Click **Open**. This is the HTML file that will be displayed in your new window. The link can be an internal or external link.

Next, you'll specify the size of your new browser window.

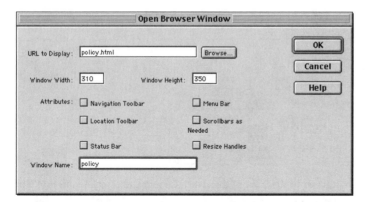

6. Back in the **Open Browser Window** dialog box, enter **Window Width: 310** and **Window Height: 350**. This specifies the pixel size of your window when it opens. At the bottom of the window, type **policy** in the **Window Name** field. Click OK.

*We specified 310 x 350 pixels because those dimensions fit the contents of **policy.html**, the page you are going to display in the second browser window. On other projects, you could specify any size that's appropriate to the content of your second window.*

This is what the Behaviors panel should look like now

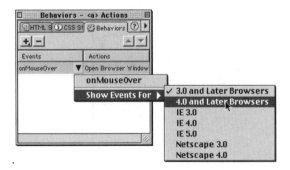

7. Click on the small arrow to the right of the **Events** column and make sure that **Show Events For** option is set to **4.0 and Later Browsers**. This displays the events that are allowed for 4.0 and later browsers **Note:** JavaScript is supported differently by different browsers. You can see a detailed list of what behaviors work in which browsers on page 444 of the Macromedia Dreamweaver 4 manual.

8. Click on the small arrow again and select **onClick** as the event. This option determines what the user must do before the new browser window will open. The **onClick** event means that the user must click on the link in order for the new window to open.

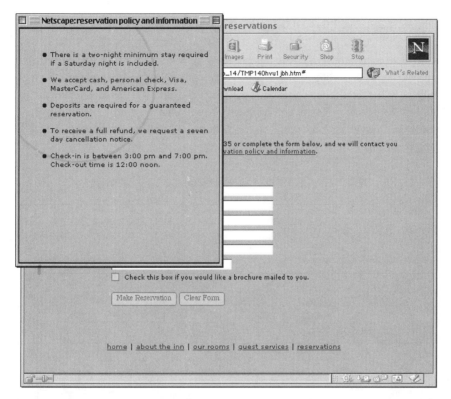

9. Save your page and press **F12** to preview all your hard work. Click the **reservation policy and information** link at the top of the page. Voila! A new browser window opens, displaying **policy.html** in a window set to 310 x 350 pixels.

---

10. Return to Dreamweaver, and save the file. Leave it open for the next exercise.

5.———————**Validating Forms with Behaviors**

Now that you have learned how to create forms and lay them out with tables, it's a good time to show you how to validate the information being typed into the form. What does that mean? Giving users a place to enter information doesn't guarantee that they will enter the information correctly. It also doesn't guarantee that they will enter any information at all. What's a Web designer supposed to do? Well, by using Dreamweaver's behaviors, you can validate, or check, the type and format of the information being provided.

1. The file from the previous exercise should still be open. If it's not, go ahead and open that file now.

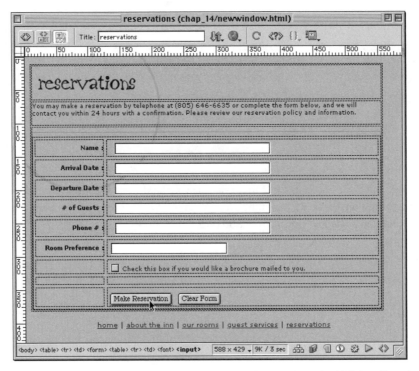

2. Click to select the **Make Reservation** button. By attaching the Validate Form behavior to this button, you can verify that the required information has been entered before a CGI script processes the form.

3. From the **Behaviors** panel, click the **plus** sign and select **Validate Form** from the pop-up menu. This opens the Validate Form dialog box.

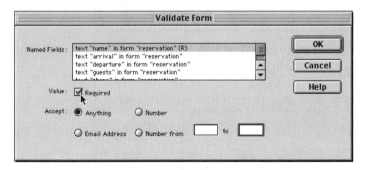

4. Make sure that the **"name" in form "reservation"** option is highlighted. Click the **Required** checkbox to make this field a required entry. A small (R) appears at the end when you do this. This is really important information, and you want to make sure that people don't forget to enter something. **Note:** Make sure the correct field is highlighted in the Validate Form dialog box before you click the Required checkbox.

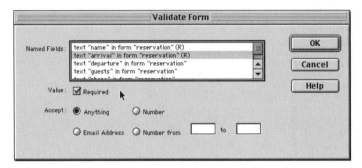

5. Highlight the **"arrival" in form "reservation"** option. Click the **Required** checkbox to make this a required entry.

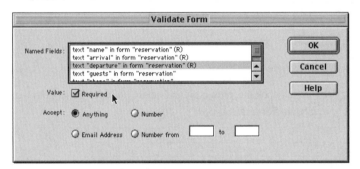

6. Highlight the **"departure" in form "reservation"** option. Click the **Required** checkbox to make this a required entry.

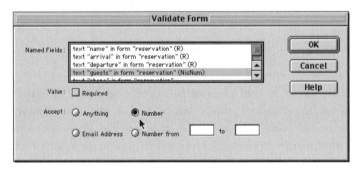

7. Make sure the **"guests" in form "reservation"** option is selected, and click the **Accept: Number** radio button. This ensures that only numbers are entered into this field. Click **OK**.

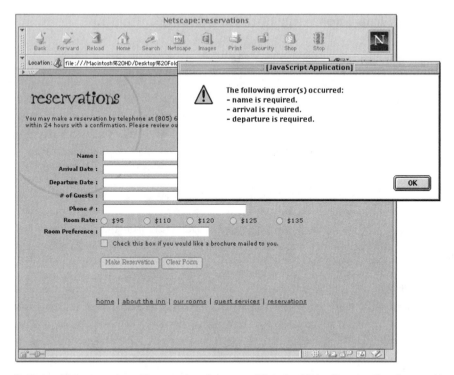

8. Press **F12** to preview this page in a browser. Click the **Make Reservation** button. You will get a JavaScript warning indicating that some fields are required. Click **OK**.

9. Return to Dreamweaver, and save and close this file.

The Macromedia Exchange—Dreamweaver

http://www.macromedia.com/exchange/dreamweaver/

Macromedia has set up a section of its Web site, designed to be a portal for Dreamweaver users, called the **Macromedia Exchange—Dreamweaver**. There you'll find hundreds of free extensions written by third-party users and developers for Dreamweaver that can help you build new features into your Web site. Many of these are advanced features that normally would require the skills of a programmer to create. For example, some of these behaviors can give you the ability to perform complex browser detection, password-protect areas of your site, connect to back-end databases, etc.

The Macromedia site is not just for developers but for any Dreamweaver user who wants to take Dreamweaver to the next level. If you are a developer, this is a great place to learn how to write your own behaviors that take advantage of the Dreamweaver DOM (**D**ocument **O**bject **M**odel). The DOM for Dreamweaver is a specification that enables increased levels of extensibility not afforded by standard HTML and JavaScript.

The Macromedia Exchange for Dreamweaver is also where you can download a free copy of the **Macromedia Extension Manager**. This indispensable add-on for Dreamweaver lets you easily (and painlessly) download, install, and manage your extensions, which is a catch-all phrase for any behavior, command, or object. Installing the Extension Manager is recommended for any serious Dreamweaver user, because it makes it easy for you to add new features to the program. Luckily, in Dreamweaver 4, the Extension Manager is preinstalled. If you don't have the Macromedia Extension Manager already installed on your hard drive for some reason, we've included a copy on the **H*O*T CD-ROM**. If you already have it installed, skip to the next exercise

6.————————Installing the Macromedia Extension Manager

Note: In previous versions of Dreamweaver, you needed to download install the Macromedia Extension Manager yourself. This is no longer necessary. Dreamweaver 4 now has the Extension Manager prein-stalled for you. We have included this exercise so when updates to the Extension Manager are released, you can come back and learn how to download and install the updates yourself. *For now, you can skip this exercise and come back to at a later date.*

This exercise will show you how to install the Macromedia Extension Manager for Dreamweaver. It's very easy to do, especially if someone is giving you step-by-step instructions to follow.

1. If you have Dreamweaver open, quit the application now. Dreamweaver can't be open when you're installing the Extension Manager, or the process won't work.

2. Open the **Macintosh** or **Windows** folder inside the **software** folder to locate the Extension Manager on the **H•O•T CD-ROM**. Copy the Extension Manager installer to your hard drive, preferably to your desktop.

3. Once you have the installer copied to your computer, double-click on the installer's icon to start the installation program.

4. Click **Continue...**

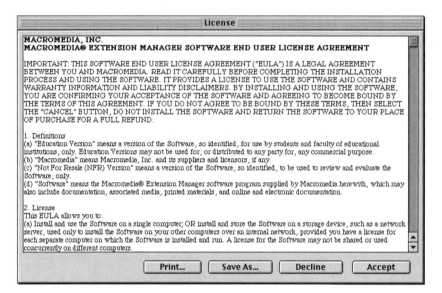

5. When you are ready, click **Accept**.

6. Select the specific folder where you'd like to install the Extension Manager. Because it is a separate application, you can install it into any folder on your hard drive. Click **Install**.

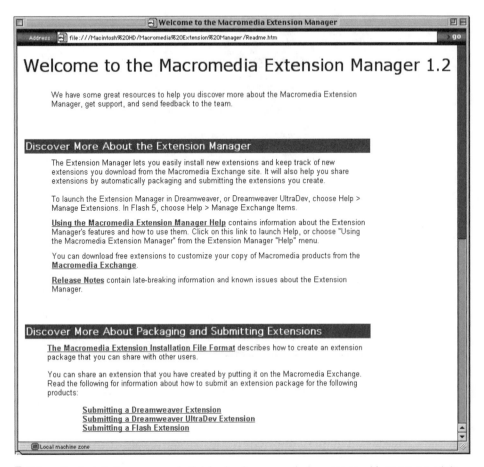

7. When the installation process is finished, a browser window opens with some extra information about the Extension Manager. You can read this if you want. When you are done, exit the browser.

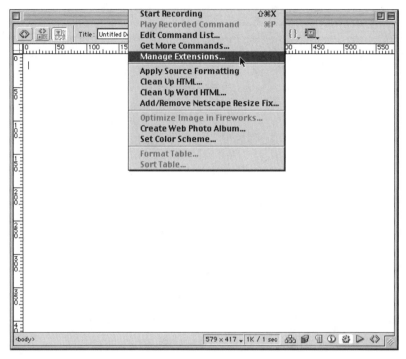

8. Launch Dreamweaver. To confirm that the Extension Manager is installed, select **Commands > Manage Extensions...** This menu command will be available only if you have properly installed the Extension Manager.

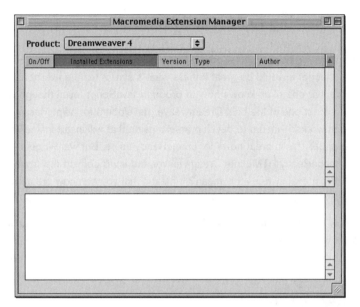

9. Selecting the **Manage Extensions...** menu item will launch the Extension Manager and open the interface. You will learn how to use the Extension Manager with the Macromedia Exchange – Dreamweaver site in the next exercise.

10. Quit the Extension Manager and return to Dreamweaver. Once you quit the Extension Manager, Dreamweaver will be properly configured. You are now ready to move on to the next exercise, which will show you how to install an extension using the Extension Manager.

7. —————————Inserting ImageReady HTML

Dreamweaver has a great feature for inserting Fireworks HTML; however, it works only with HTML files generated by Fireworks. We thought it would be great if there were a similar feature available for users of ImageReady. Well, since neither one of us knows how to program JavaScript (even though Garo is learning!), we decided to contact one of the best Dreamweaver developers for help. Massimo Foti, a top Dreamweaver developer, worked with us to develop an extension that will insert ImageReady HTML in your Dreamweaver page. This is great news for ImageReady users. But wait—it gets even better. Not only will it insert ImageReady HTML into Dreamweaver, but it will convert the JavaScript to Dreamweaver JavaScript. What exactly does this mean? It means that you can now create rollovers in ImageReady and edit the JavaScript in Dreamweaver.

This exercise will show you how to install the **Insert ImageReady HTML** extension using the Dreamweaver Extension Manager. In addition, you will learn how to insert ImageReady HTML into your Dreamweaver page.

1. In Dreamweaver, select **Commands > Manage Extensions...** This launches the Extension Manager so you can install the **Insert ImageReady HTML** extension.

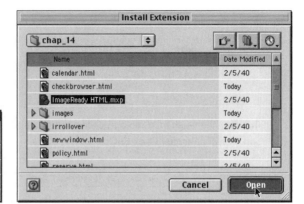

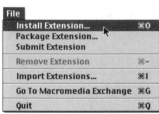

2. From the Extension Manager, select **File > Install Extension...** Browse to the **chap_14** folder and locate the **ImageReady HTML.mxp** extension file. Highlight this file and click **Open**.

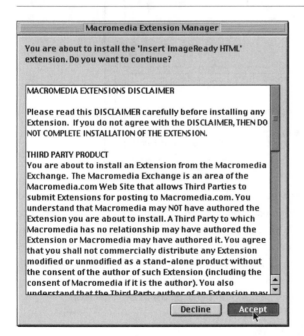

3. A disclaimer appears for you to read. When you are finished, click **Accept** (assuming you agree with the terms). The installation of the Insert ImageReady HTML extension will proceed.

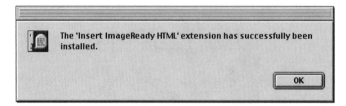

The 'Insert ImageReady HTML' extension has successfully been installed.

OK

4. When it's finished, a dialog box like the one above will display, indicating that the installation was successful. Click **OK**.

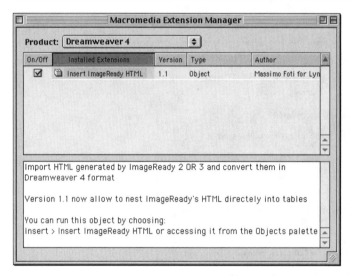

When the extension has been installed properly, it will be displayed in the Extension Manager window. If it is highlighted, a brief description will appear in the bottom portion of the window.

5. To exit the Extension Manager, select **File > Quit** (Mac) or **File > Exit** (Windows).

6. Once the extension has been installed properly, return to Dreamweaver.

7. Quit, and then relaunch Dreamweaver.

Tip: *Each time you use the Extension Manager to install a new extension, you'll need to quit and then relaunch Dreamweaver before you can use your new extension.*

8. From Dreamweaver, select **File > New**. This will create a new blank document. Save this file inside the **chap_14** folder as **insertir.html**.

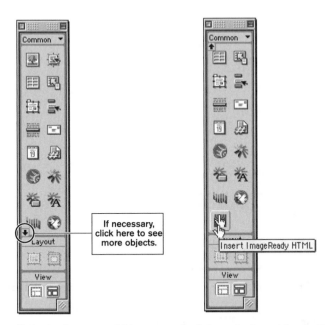

9. In the **Common Objects** panel, click on the **Insert ImageReady HTML** object, the new object that was added to Dreamweaver when you installed the **Insert ImageReady HTML** extension. This opens the **ImageReady HTML** dialog box. **Note:** You might have to click on the small arrow at the bottom to see all of your installed objects.

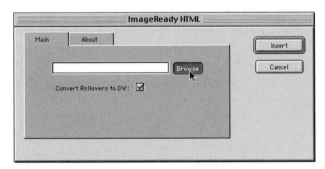

10. Click **Browse**. Locate the **irrollover.html** file inside the **irrollover** folder. This file was created in Adobe ImageReady 3 and contains a rollover button.

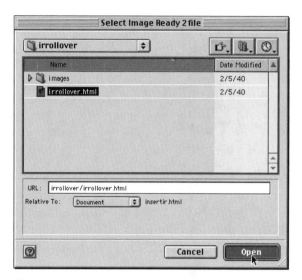

11. Once you locate the **irrollover.html** file, highlight it and click **Open**, then click **Insert**.

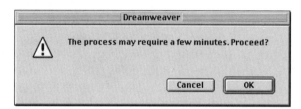

12. A dialog box opens, indicating that it may take a few minutes to convert and import the file. Click **OK**.

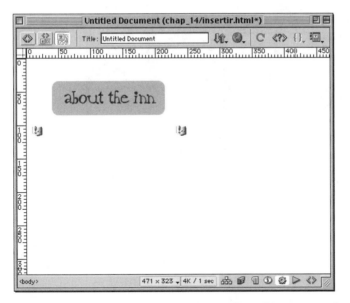

After you click OK, the ImageReady HTML file will be converted and then imported into Dreamweaver. This is what your screen should look like now.

13. Make sure your **Behaviors** panel is open. If it's not, select **Window > Behaviors** or (**Shift+F3**).

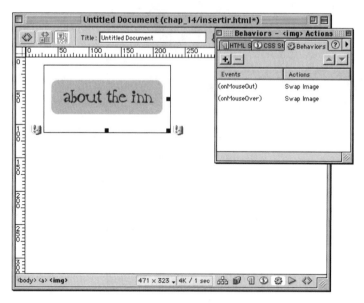

14. Click on the **about the inn** image. In the **Behaviors** panel, notice that this was converted from an ImageReady action, which would appear as an unknown script, to a native Dreamweaver action. Pretty slick, huh?

15. Press **F12** to preview this page in a browser. The rollover is not only written as a native Dreamweaver JavaScript rollover, but it works flawlessly as well.

16. Exit the browser and return to Dreamweaver.

8. —————————— **Downloading from Macromedia Exchange**

As we mentioned earlier, Macromedia Exchange–Dreamweaver is a new site that Macromedia developed to serve as a repository for Dreamweaver extensions. It is literally a gold mine of widgets and add-ons to help you add life to your Web pages. In this exercise, you will learn how to download one of these cool extensions from the Exchange and install it using the Extension Manager.

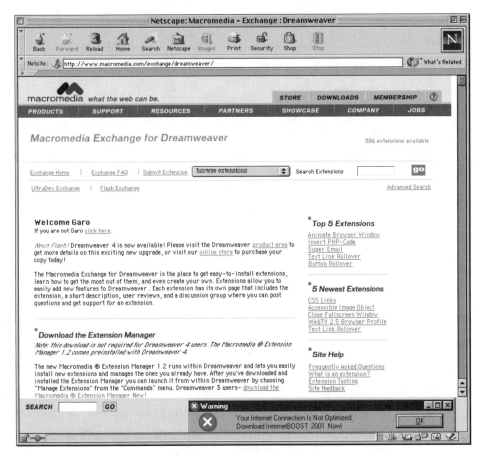

1. Open a Web browser and go to **http://www.macromedia.com/exchange/dreamweaver/**. This takes you to the new Macromedia Exchange–Dreamweaver Web site. If you have not created an account yet (it's free), you will need to do so before downloading any of the extensions. If this is the case, click Membership and follow the instructions for setting up an account before proceeding with the exercise.

> ### NOTE | Behaviors, Commands, and Objects
>
> As you start downloading extensions from the Exchange and other Web sites, you'll
> need to know more about where to find your installed behaviors, commands, and/or
> objects. These are accessed from different places in the Dreamweaver interface.
> Behaviors are accessed from the **Behaviors** panel, commands are accessed from the
> **Commands** menu, and objects are stored in the **Objects** panel and accessed from
> the **Insert** menu.

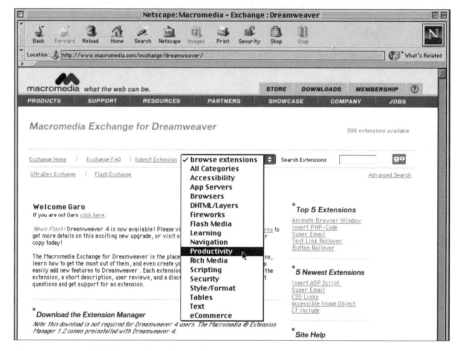

2. Click on the pop-up menu at the top of the screen. As you can see, the extensions have
been neatly organized into various groups for easy access. Select **Productivity**. This takes
you to a page with extensions that relate directly to productivity.

AutoTitle Untitled Documents	Paul Mader	Jul 3, 2000	1.0	4/5	M	12638
Borderless Frame	Massimo Foti	May 4, 2000	2.01	4/5	M	14601
CN Show PopUp Window	CrystalNet – Chris Acton	Dec 14, 2000	1.0.2	4/5	Basic	5491
Calculate Form	Jaro von Flocken	May 25, 2000	3.0.1	3/5	Basic	12865
Calendar Object	Scott Richards	Jun 11, 2000	1.0.5	4/5	Basic	27059
ChromelessWin	Public Domain Ltd	Feb 7, 2001	2.1.3	5/5	M	6473
Clean Up FrontPage HTML	Macromedia	Feb 9, 2001	1.0.5	5/5	M	18859
Close Folders	Brendan Dawes	Apr 17, 2000	1.0.2	No rating	Basic	3966
Comment Suite	Harold Bakker	Aug 18, 2000	1.2	4/5	M	5259

3. Notice that this page gives you a lot of useful information about each extension, such as author, date created, version, rating, approval, and number of downloads. Click on the **Calendar Object** link. This takes you to a page where you can download this extension.

4. In the **Download Extension** section, click on the appropriate download link for the operating system you are using. For example, if you are using a Macintosh, click on the **macintosh** link. This starts the download process.

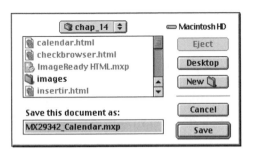

5. When you are prompted to save the extension, choose a location on your hard drive and click **Save**. Remember where you saved this file, because you'll need to access it later. You may want to store it in the same directory as the Dreamweaver 4 application, so you'll know where it is in the future.

6. You're done with the Macromedia Exchange–Dreamweaver site for now, and you can log off before continuing with the exercise, if you wish.

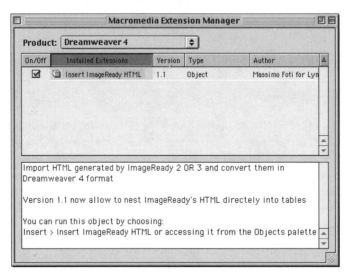

7. Select **Commands > Manage Extensions...** This launches the Extension Manager. As you did earlier, you will use the Extension Manager to install the extension you just downloaded.

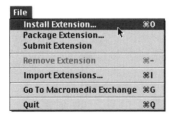

8. In the Extension Manager, select **File > Install Extension...** This opens a dialog box so you can browse to the extension file you just downloaded. **Note:** All extension files you download should have an extension of .mxp.

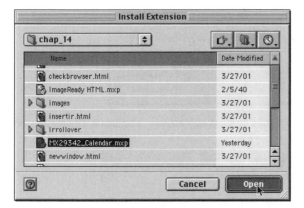

9. Locate the file on your hard drive and click **Open**.

10. The disclaimer that appears is the one you have seen before. Click **Accept**, and the installation will continue.

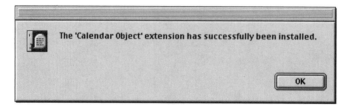

11. When the installation process is finished, the above dialog box is displayed. Click **OK**.

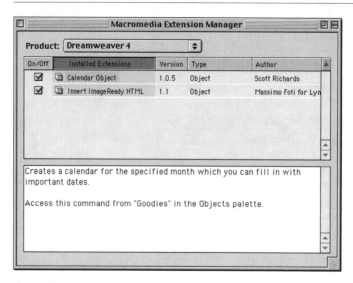

Once the installation is complete, your new extension appears in the Extension Manager window.

12. Select **File > Quit** (Mac) or **File > Exit** (Windows) to exit the Extension Manager.

13. Return to Dreamweaver. Quit, and then relaunch so you can check out your new extension.

14. Return to Dreamweaver. From the Site window (**F8**), open the **calendar.html** file. This is nothing more than a blank file that we created for you.

15. From the **Objects** panel, select **Goodies**. This is a new group that was added when you installed the Calendar Object extension; it's not part of the normal installation. Aren't you glad we told you that?

16. Click on the **Insert Calendar** icon in the **Goodies Objects** panel. This opens the **Insert Calendar** dialog box.

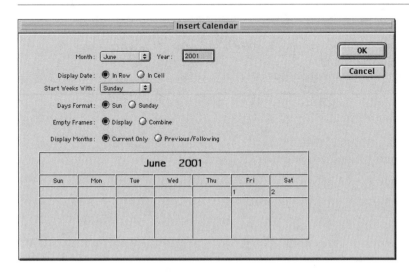

17. If you want to modify some of the options, you can. Click **OK**.

TIP | Extending Dreamweaver

If you're well versed in JavaScript, you can learn to write your own custom extensions, and you'll find plenty of great resources on the Macromedia Exchange – Dreamweaver. If you want, you can download a PDF version of the Extensibility Manual from the Macromedia Web site and/or subscribe to their Extensibility newsgroup. Both are great resources for extensibility authors.

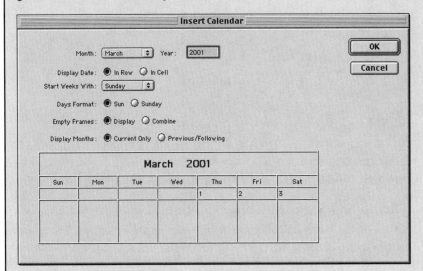

This extension, complete with the great interface, was designed by Scott Richards. Creating extensions requires a working knowledge of JavaScript and the Dreamweaver DOM.

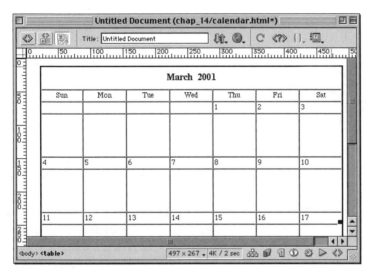

*This is what the calendar looks like within Dreamweaver. Pretty slick, huh? Can you imagine having to create that table and insert all the correct dates yourself? Now any time you want to add a calendar to a Web page, it's as simple as clicking a button object in the Objects panel. This is definitely a very handy and useful extension to Dreamweaver. **Note:** If you modified some of these options, your calendar may look different than this one.*

18. Save and close this file.

This is just one example of the many cool extensions you can download from the Macromedia Exchange. It is definitely one of those sites you should bookmark and check back with on a daily or weekly basis, since new extensions are constantly being added.

If you have the energy, move on to the next chapter. If not, that's OK; it will be waiting when you are ready.

15.
DHTML

| Dragging Layers | Using the Timeline for Animation |
| Playing, Stopping, and Resetting the Timeline |
| Creating a DHTML Pop-Up Menu |

chap_15

Dreamweaver 4
H•O•T CD-ROM

The "D" at the beginning of DHTML stands for "dynamic," as in **D**ynamic **H**yper**T**ext **M**arkup **L**anguage. DHTML was introduced several years ago to offer more dynamic content, such as animation and interactivity, than basic HTML affords. DHTML combines multiple technologies, such as HTML, JavaScript, style sheets, absolute positioning, plug-ins, and DOM. For a definition of these technologies, revisit Chapter 1, *"Background."*

Unfortunately, most of the content produced by using DHTML is not supported on all browsers. Browser versions that present problems with DHTML include Netscape 6.0 and Internet Explorer 5.0. The exercises in this chapter were tested with and work well in Microsoft Internet Explorer 4.5 and Netscape Navigator 4.7 for both the Macintosh and Windows operating systems.

DHTML is usually reserved for entertainment-based sites, where games and/or dynamic presentations are expected and embraced. If you plan to use techniques presented in this chapter, it's best to put them on interior pages so visitors with older browsers can see your first page and important content. Alternatively, you could offer DHTML content only to those end users who can see it, by using the browser-detection techniques discussed in Chapter 14, *"Behaviors."*

WARNING | Prevent Overlaps

This chapter includes exercises that use layers, which you also worked with in Chapter 8, *"Layout."* Before you begin the exercises, open your Layers window (F2) and make sure that Prevent Overlaps is not checked. If this option is left checked, the exercises in this chapter will fail.

When you are converting layers to tables, as you did in Chapter 8, it's necessary to put a check in the Prevent Overlaps checkbox. That's because table cells can't overlap, and the layers information was being used to produce tables.

In this chapter, however, you want the layers to overlap, since you will be creating animations in which objects fly one on top of another. It's easy to change this setting by simply deselecting the Prevent Overlaps setting in the Layers window.

In order to successfully complete this chapter's exercises, make sure you do not have the Prevent Overlaps setting checked.

I. ————————**Dragging Layers**

When Lynda was in Dallas speaking at a Macromedia seminar, her husband, Bruce, sat on the sidelines and drew this little game for their daughter. We thought the example was delightful, though Lynda's daughter did complain that the monkey had no shoes! Regardless of her criticism, it's a fun example of what you can do with DHTML, and so it leads this chapter.

Note: There are some known problems with the Drag Layer behavior that ships with Dreamweaver 4 in Netscape 6. Macromedia has released updated behaviors to fix this problem. You can download the updated behaviors at: **http://www.macromedia.com/support/dreamweaver/ts/documents/ netscape_6.htm**. This page contains complete instructions for downloading and installing the files. Before trying to complete this exercise, you should be familiar with using the Extension Manager and downloading and installing extensions. If you aren't, be sure to review the exercises in Chapter 14 before continuing. If you have downloaded the 4.01 update to Dreamweaver 4, this update is already included in that fix.

1. Define your site for Chapter 15. Copy the contents of **chap_15** to your hard drive and define it (**F8**). If you need a refresher on this process, revisit Exercise 1 in Chapter 3, *"Site Control."*

2. Open **dress_final.html** and press **F12** to preview it in a browser. Take any item and drag it onto the monkey. Notice that the items snap into place if you position them close to where they belong. This game was created using Dreamweaver's **Drag Layer** behavior, which you're about to learn. Return to Dreamweaver and close the file.

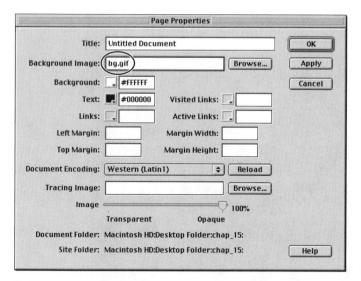

3. Choose **File > New** (Mac) or **File > New Window** (Windows) and then save the document as **monkey2.html** in the **chap_15** folder. Choose **Modify > Page Properties...** and enter **Title: Monkey Drag Layer Exercise**. **Note:** You can add the title in the Page Properties dialog box or in the document window; either method works well. But while you're in this dialog box, you might as well fill in the title. To the right of the **Background Image** field, click **Browse**, and then browse to **bg.gif**. Click **Open**. Click **OK**.

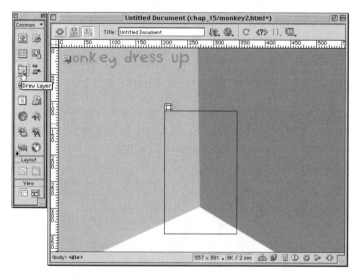

4. In the **Common Objects** panel, use the **Draw Layer** object and drag a layer on the page. **Note:** If the **Draw Layer** object is not available, make sure you are in Standard view.

5. Make sure the cursor is inside the layer, and choose **Insert > Image**. Browse to lilmonkey.gif, and click **Open**.

6. Click on the top handle of the layer to select it. In the **Layer ID** area of the Property Inspector, type the name "**monkey**." It's best to name your layer something that relates to the image.

Tip: *Resizing each layer to fit the dimensions of its artwork will help keep your work area clean. You can do this by clicking and dragging the lower-right resize handle to the upper-left corner. Once the layer is the same size as its content, you won't be able to make it any smaller.*

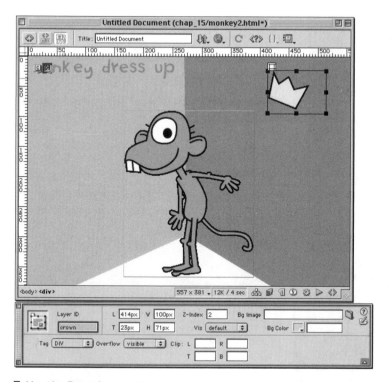

7. Use the **Draw Layer** object again to drag another, smaller layer on the page. With the pointer inside the layer, choose **Insert > Image**. Browse to **crown.gif**, and click **Open**.

8. Select the layer by its handle and name it **crown** inside the **Layer ID** area of the Property Inspector.

9. Move the **crown** layer by its handle to the top of the monkey's head. **Tip:** With the layer selected, you can use the arrow keys on your keyboard to nudge it into place.

10. Click inside the layer to select the image of the crown. Three resizing handles will appear around the image once it's selected. It's essential that the image is selected, not the layer. This has to do with the fact that the JavaScript behavior of the **Drag Layer** command must be attached to the **<img>** tag, not the **<layer>** tag.

11. Open the **Behaviors** panel (**Window > Behaviors** or **Shift+F3**). Click the **plus** sign and select **Drag Layer**.

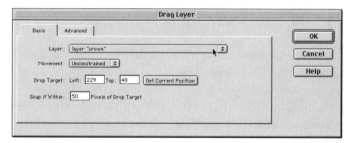

12. The **Drag Layer** dialog box opens. Switch to **Layer: layer "crown."** Leave the setting **Movement: Unconstrained**, and click on the **Get Current Position** button. This inserts numbers into the **Drop Target** fields. These numbers indicate the exact position of the crown on the page. (**Note:** These numbers will vary because you might have positioned your monkey and crown differently than we did.) Leave **Snap if Within: 50 Pixels of Drop Target** and click **OK**.

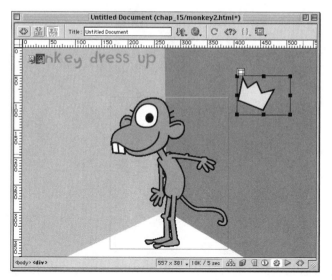

13. Select the layer handles of the **crown** layer to move it away from the monkey. **Note:** Wherever you place it is where it will appear in the browser when the HTML is published. It's important to drag it away from the monkey so your end user can drag it back on!

14. Press **F12** to preview the results. Move the crown back onto the monkey. If it snaps into place when it gets close to the monkey's head, you've successfully followed the steps so far.

15. See if you can complete the exercise with the rest of the dress-up artwork found in the **chap_15** folder. You'll probably be grateful that Bruce didn't make shoes, as it would be more objects to set up! When you're finished fooling around with this exercise, close the file to move on to the next exercise.

2. _____Using the Timeline for Animation

You've probably noticed the item **Timelines** in the Dreamweaver Launcher interface and wondered what it stood for. You'll finally get to find out with this exercise. This time, you'll use the same artwork, but instead of creating a drag-and-drop game, you'll create an animation of the clothes flying onto the monkey's body. Even if this isn't the sort of content you think you'll be adding to your site, you'll still be learning the principles of Dreamweaver animation and have a smile on your face while doing so.

1. Open **dress_timeline1.html** in Dreamweaver, and press **F12** to preview it. This gives you the opportunity to see what you will build by completing the exercise.

2. Close **dress_timeline1.html**, and open **dress_timeline2.html**. This document has been partially built for you.

3. Make sure the **Timelines** panel is open (**Window > Timelines** or **Shift+F9**). Using its handle, drag the layer with the **pants** in it into **Channel 1**. It appears inside the Timeline, as shown above.

4. When this dialog box appears, just click **OK**. It merely lets you know the different ways in which you can animate layers.

MOVIE | keyframe.mov

To learn more about using keyframes, check out **keyframe.mov**, located in the **movies** folder on the Dreamweaver 4 **H•O•T CD-ROM**.

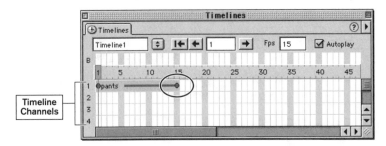

*You will see two dots in the Timeline for the pants. These are called **keyframes**. (The term "keyframe" means an extreme point of movement.) The first keyframe establishes where the pants are at the beginning of the animation. The second one establishes where they will be at the end.*

5. Right now, both keyframes are set to the same position, because you have not programmed any motion yet. Click on the **second keyframe** (the second dot) of the **pants** element in the Timeline. In this case, since both extremes (or keyframes) are set to the same position, nothing happens.

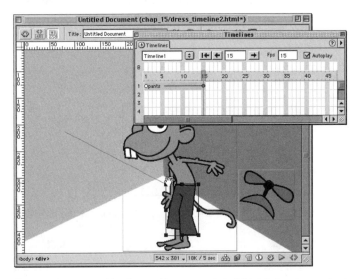

6. With the second keyframe (the second dot) highlighted, use the layer handle of the **pants** layer in the document window to move the pants to where they belong on the monkey. Make sure you are moving the entire layer, not just the image. **Tip:** Once you select the handle of the pants layer to activate it, you can use the arrow keys to nudge the pants into place. *See the light gray line that appears on the screen, from the spot where the pants were originally to where you just moved them? This indicates that you've set up the motion properly.*

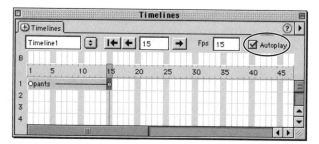

7. Make sure that the **Autoplay** checkbox is checked in the **Timelines** Inspector. This tells Dreamweaver to play the animation when it is viewed from a browser.

8. Press **F12** to see the results of your labor. Unfortunately, you cannot preview animation from within Dreamweaver, only from a browser. You'll see that the pants now fly onto the body. The hat and T-shirt remain stationary, because you haven't programmed the animation of these yet. That's coming up next, so return to Dreamweaver.

9. Using its layer handle, drag the **hat** into **Channel 2**. Now click on its second keyframe (the second dot), and move the hat by its layer handle to the top of the monkey's head. Move the **playback head** back to **Frame 1**. You want to make sure the playback head is on Frame 1 before you add new content to the Timeline.

10. Using its layer handle, drag the **T-shirt** into **Channel 3**. Click on its **second keyframe** (the second dot), and move the T-shirt by its layer handle to the monkey's torso.

11. Press **F12**, and voila! You've got animation.

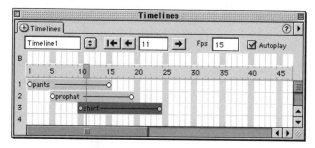

12. Return to Dreamweaver, and move the layers in the channels as shown above. Press **F12** to see the results. You can adjust the timing of these layers by moving them around on the Timeline. You can also extend the number of frames of any layer by clicking on its second keyframe and then dragging it to the right. When you're done playing, save and close the document.

TIP | The Timeline Explained

The **Timeline Inspector** is used to control animation in Dreamweaver. To understand the Timeline interface better, see the image and chart below.

Behaviors Channel   Command Buttons

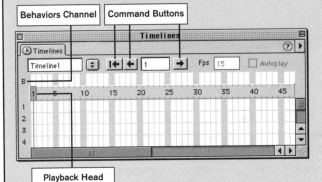

Playback Head

Dreamweaver Timeline Features	
Feature	**Explanation**
Command buttons	Three controls, Rewind (moves to Frame 1 of the Timeline), Back (moves back one frame), and Play (moves forward one frame, hold down mouse button for continuous play), let you control your Timeline.
Playback head	Dragging the playback head allows you to preview your animation and move between frames. This is a great way to preview your animation, especially when you are animating multiple objects.
Behaviors channel	Shows any behaviors that are attached to specific frames. Learning how to add behaviors to the Timeline can be useful for creating slide shows and complex animations and navigation systems.

3. ————————Playing, Stopping, and Resetting the Timeline

Let's say you wanted some links you could click on to play, stop, and reset the Timeline. The next exercise shows you how to set this up.

1. Open **anim_button.html**, and press **F12** to preview it in the browser. Remember that you can't see this DHTML stuff from within Dreamweaver. Click on the link that says **GO** and watch the animation play. Click **STOP** and **RESET** to see them in action, too.

2. Return to Dreamweaver and close the file. Open **anim_button1.html**. This page has been partially built for you; you'll be adding the behaviors.

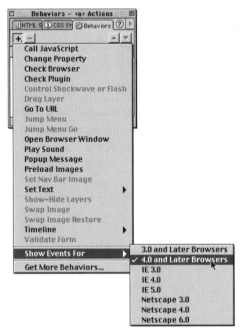

3. Make sure the **Behaviors** panel is open, click the **plus** sign, and select **Show Events For: 4.0 and Later Browsers**.

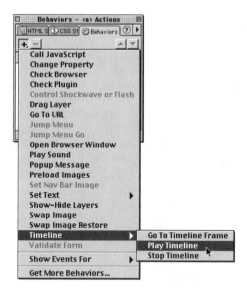

4. Click and drag to highlight the word **GO**. In the **Behaviors** panel, click on the **plus** sign and choose **Timeline > Play Timeline**.

Note: In the Property Inspector, you'll see that the word "GO" contains a link with a hash mark (#) in it. The hash mark sets up a link that doesn't go anywhere, which can be very useful. Many behaviors have to be applied to links, but often you don't want a link to work, just to exist.

5. The **Play Timeline** dialog box appears. It should be set to **Play Timeline: Timeline1**, so click **OK**.

6. Highlight the word **STOP**, click on the **plus** sign in the Behaviors panel, and choose **Timeline > Stop Timeline**. The **Stop Timeline** dialog box appears. Select **Stop Timeline: Timeline 1** (the only Timeline you have defined in this file). Click **OK**.

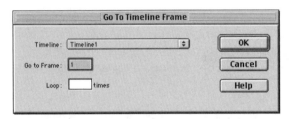

7. Highlight the word **RESET**, click on the **plus** sign in the Behaviors panel, and choose **Timeline > Go To Timeline Frame**. Enter **Go to Frame: 1**, and click **OK**. This tells the RESET link to move the Timeline back to Frame 1.

8. With **RESET** still highlighted, click on the **plus** sign in the Behaviors panel again, and choose **Timeline > Stop Timeline**. The **Stop Timeline** dialog box appears. Select **Stop Timeline: Timeline 1**. Click **OK**. This will add a second behavior to the RESET link. As you can see, it is sometimes necessary to add more than one behavior to a single link. Now, when the user clicks on the RESET link, it will go to Frame 1 and then stop the Timeline.

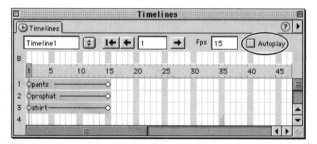

9. In the **Timelines** window, make sure you deselect **Autoplay**. In this exercise, you want the links to control whether the animation plays or not, so Autoplay is no longer necessary.

---

10. Save your work, and press **F12** to see the fruits of your Timeline labor.

When you're finished, you can tell all your friends, family, and coworkers that you just made your first DHTML animation page! Don't forget to tell them where you learned it ;-).

---

4. _____Creating a DHTML Pop-Up Menu

Pop-up menus are popular among Web designers as a means to create more robust navigation systems. These kinds of menu systems let users see what subnavigation categories lie beneath main navigation categories. There are multiple ways to create pop-up menus, many of them extremely complex and too advanced for this book. This pop-up menu exercise is going to show you how to use the **Set Text of Layer** behavior. We refer to the pop-up menu in this exercise as a DHTML pop-up menu because it uses an amalgamation of HTML, CSS, and JavaScript. For this reason, the pop-up menu is this exercise will only work in 4.0 or later browsers. So let's start popping.

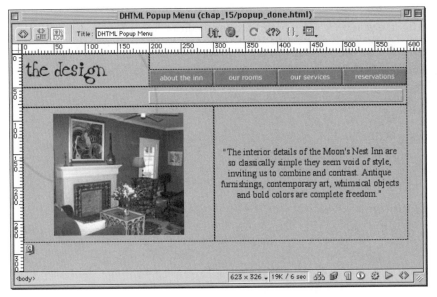

1. Open the **popup_done.html** file located inside the **chap_15** folder. This is the completed version of this exercise.

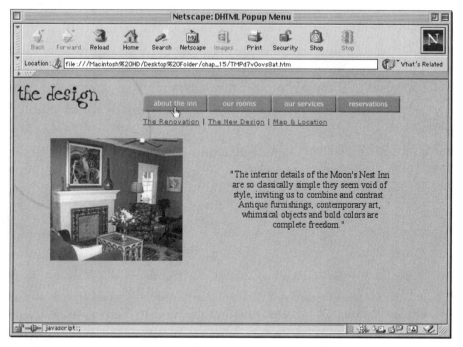

2. Press **F12** to preview this page in a browser. Move your pointer over the buttons at the top. Notice that a submenu appears beneath these buttons. This submenu was created using a combination of layers, CSS, and DHTML. You are going to recreate this example.

3. Exit the browser and return to Dreamweaver. Close the **popup_done.html** file.

4. Open the file **popup.html** located inside the **chap_15** folder. This page has been partially completed for you. In the following steps, you will learn how to create the submenu.

Click and drag to draw a layer on the screen that extends to the end of the table.

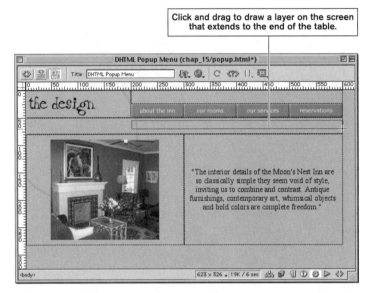

5. Using the **Draw Layer** object, click and drag to draw a layer beneath the buttons and that extends to the end of the cell. Your layer will automatically snap to the edge of the table cell. **Note:** You can disable this snapping feature by holding down the Opt or Alt key as you draw the layer.

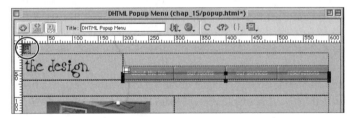

With the Invisible Elements option on, the layout shifts down to make room for the marker at the top.

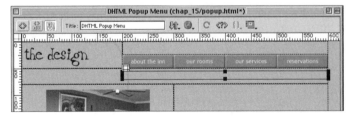

With the Invisible Elements option turned off, the layout appears without any unexpected shift.

6. Make sure the **View > Visual Aids > Invisible Elements** option is not selected. Having this option turned on will cause an unexpected shift in your layout.

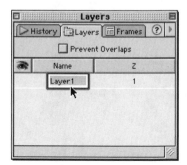 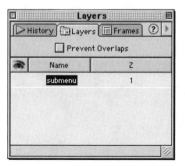

7. Make sure your **Layers** panel is visible. If it's not, select **Window > Layers** to make it appear. In the Layers panel, double-click on **Layer1** so the layer name becomes editable. Rename this layer "**submenu**." Press **Return** or **Enter** to accept the new layer name.

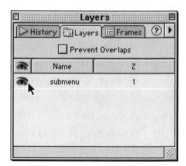

8. Click in the **eye** column until you see an open-eye icon. This sets the layer to be visible when the page loads.

9. Make sure your layer is selected; if it's not, click on the layer name in the **Layers** panel to select it.

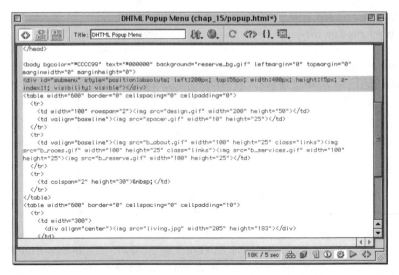

10. With the **submenu** layer selected, click the **Show Code View** button. This displays the code for the page and automatically highlights the code of the selected layer.

11. Select **Edit > Cut** to cut this code and paste it to the Clipboard. You are going to paste the code manually into another part of the document to make the menu work better across different browsers. Some browsers, like Microsoft Internet Explorer on the Macintosh, have problems drawing layers that are inside of table code. Some unexpected and unwanted shifting can occur and really mess up the layout of your pages. You can fix this by moving the **<div>** tag of the layer outside the **<table>** tag. Because the **<div>** tag is using absolute positioning, it doesn't really matter where the code is within your page. The following steps show you how to move the code and where to place it.

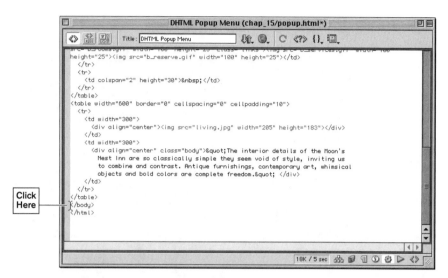

12. Scroll down to the bottom of your Code view and click to the left of the **</body>** tag. This places your blinking cursor to the left of this tag.

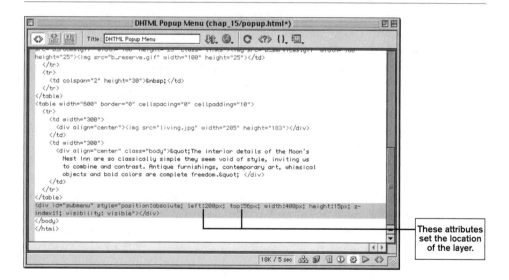

13. Select **Edit > Paste** to paste the layer code at the bottom of your document. Remember, doing this will help avoid display problems in some browsers, like Internet Explorer on the Macintosh.

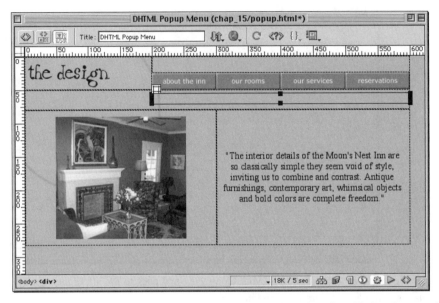

14. Click the **Show Design View** button to switch back to that view. Notice that your layer is still in the same location even though you copied and pasted the code to a different part of the document. Why? Because the location of the layer is specified in the **<div>** tag. You don't change the location of the layer on the page by moving the **<div>** tag in the code, you change it by changing the values of the **left** and **top** attributes of the **<div>** tag. This happens inside the code automatically when you move the layer by its handle.

Now that you have created a layer in which the submenu will appear, you need to determine what content will appear inside the submenu. You do this by adding the Set Text of Layer behavior to the four main buttons. Since this submenu is going to contain HTML formatted text, we have set up another page that contains the submenu options for each of the four buttons, already formatted with CSS. Using CSS to format the text lets you specify the type in pixels, which will not change in size between the Macintosh and Windows operating systems. We strongly recommend that you do this to avoid any unexpected changes in the size or layout of your submenu. Formatting this HTML code in another document makes it easier to copy and paste into the submenu. Sound a bit confusing? Don't worry; we'll will walk you through it, one step at a time.

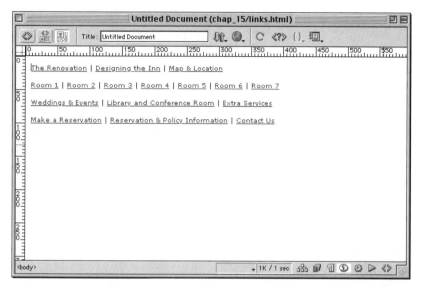

15. Open the **links.html** page located inside the **chap_15** folder. This page contains some links for the submenu that have been formatted with an external CSS. Remember, by using CSS, you can set the text in pixel units, which will prevent it from changing between the Macintosh and Windows operating systems.

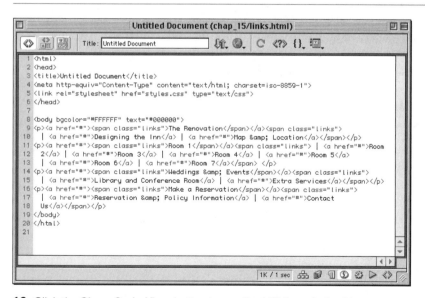

16. Click the **Show Code View** button to see the HTML code for this page.

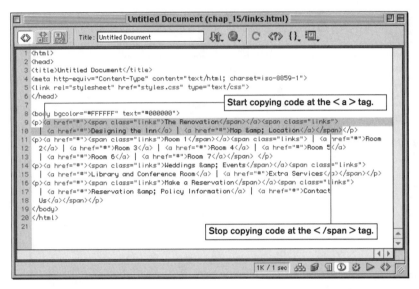

17. Click and drag to select the code as shown in the image above. Make sure you start copying at the **<a>** tag immediately following the **<p>** tag and stop at the **</span>** tag immediately before the **</p>** tag. This selects the first set of submenu links, including the necessary CSS reference.

18. Select **Edit > Copy**. This copies the selected HTML code to the Clipboard so it can be easily pasted into another document.

19. Select **Window > popup.html** to return to the original page.

20. Make sure your **Behaviors** panel is visible; if it's not, select **Window > Behaviors** to make it appear.

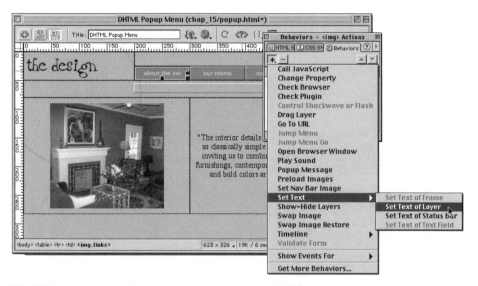

21. Click to select the **about the inn** button. From the Behaviors panel, select **Set Text** > **Set Text of Layer**. This opens the **Set Text of Layer** dialog box.

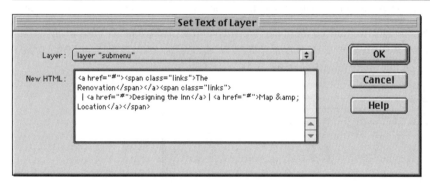

22. Make sure the **Layer:** option is set to **layer "submenu."** Click inside the **New HTML** text field and press **Cmd+V** (Mac) or **Ctrl+V** (Windows). This pastes the HTML and CSS code, copied from the **links.html** page, into the dialog box. Click **OK**.

23. Repeat Steps 15 through 22 for the other three buttons. When you are finished, all four of your buttons should have a submenu. If you get stuck, you can refer back to the **popup_done.html** file for assistance.

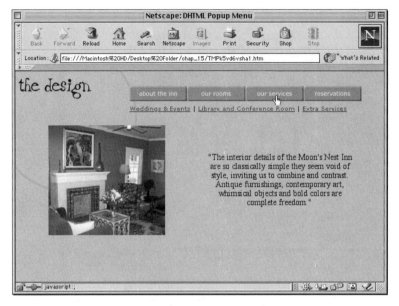

24. Press **F12** to preview your work in a browser. Move your mouse over each one of the buttons. A submenu will appear with different options for each button. Pretty cool!

You might have noticed that once the submenu appears, it never goes away. What if you want the submenu to disappear if the user decides to stay on this page? You'll see how to do this in the following steps.

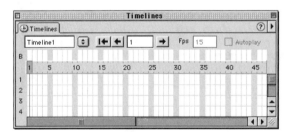

25. Return to Dreamweaver and make sure your **Timeline Inspector** is visible; if it's not, select **Window > Timeline** to make it appear.

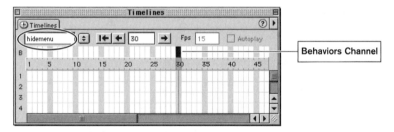

Behaviors Channel

26. Set the name of the Timeline to "**hidemenu**". Click on **Frame 30** of the **Behaviors** channel. The Behaviors channel is where you add behaviors to the Timeline. The purpose of using the Timeline is to trigger the behavior automatically when the playback head reaches that frame of the Timeline.

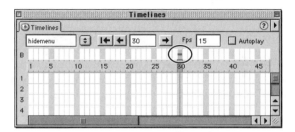

27. In the Behaviors panel, select **Set Text > Set Text of Layer**. When the **Set Text of Layer** dialog box opens, click **OK**. This writes a blank layer, and causes the submenu to seemingly disappear. A small dash appears in the Behaviors channel, indicating that Frame 30 now contains a behavior.

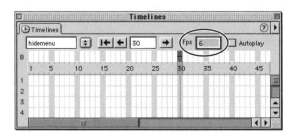

28. Set the **FPS** (**F**rames **P**er **S**econd) option to **6**. This sets how fast the Timeline moves. At a setting of 6, it will move 6 frames for every second of time that passes. Placing the behavior on Frame 30 and setting the FPS to 6 means that it will take 5 seconds for the submenu to disappear. You can enter any amount of time you want for the submenu to stay visible; we are simply recommending 5 seconds.

29. Click and drag the **playback head** back to Frame 1. Be careful to move only the playback head; you do not want to change the location of the behavior in Frame 30.

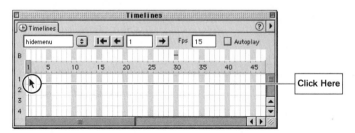

30. Click in **Frame 1** of the Timeline. This deselects the Behaviors channel of the Timeline so you can add additional behaviors to the images on the page.

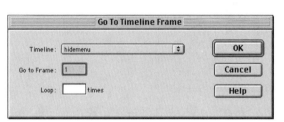
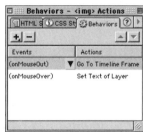

31. Select the **about the inn** button. In the Behaviors panel, click on the **plus** sign and select **Timeline > Go To Timeline Frame**. Since your document has only one Timeline, called hidemenu, click **OK**. In the Behaviors panel, change the event to **(onMouseOut)**. This moves the playback head to the beginning of the Timeline each time you move the pointer away from the button.

32. In the Behaviors panel, click the **plus** sign and select **Timeline > Play Timeline**. Click **OK**. In the Behaviors panel, change the event to **(onMouseOut)**. This makes the Timeline play after it's been reset by the previous behavior.

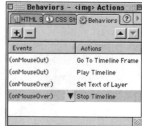

33. In the Behaviors panel, click the **plus** sign and select **Timeline > Stop Timelime**. Select **hidemenu** from the Stop Timeline drop-down menu. Click **OK**. In the Behaviors panel, change the event to (**onMouseOver**). This stops the hidemenu Timeline each time you move the pointer over the button.

34. Repeat Steps 30 through 33 for the other three buttons.

35. Press **F12** to preview your page in a browser. Move the pointer over the buttons, and then move it away from the submenu. Notice that after a few seconds the submenu disappears. It had better after all that hard work. ;-)

36. Select **File > Save** to save the changes you made to this file. You can close this file; you won't be using it anymore.

MOVIE | dhtmlpopup.mov

To learn more about creating DHTML pop-up menus, check out **dhtmlpopup.mov** located in the **movies** folder on the Dreamweaver 4 **H•O•T CD-ROM**.

Wow, you have just finished another chapter. Congratulations! If you feel up to it, keep on going to the next chapter.

16.

Automation

| Using the History Panel for Undo/Redo |

| Copying and Pasting History |

| Creating Custom Objects |

| Creating a Web Photo Album | Optimizing Images in Fireworks |

---

chap_16

Dreamweaver 4
H•O•T CD-ROM

If you design Web pages, you will quickly notice that it can involve an abundance of incredibly repetitive and boring tasks. Fortunately, Dreamweaver has several features that can help you automate many of these boring tasks—such as the History panel and the use of custom objects and commands. In this chapter, you'll learn about the **History panel**, which memorizes and replays steps you've performed while you're creating a Dreamweaver document. This panel can be scripted to replay these steps, which is one great way to automate repetitive tasks. Additionally, you will learn to create a **custom object** that will be stored on the Toolbar. This will allow you, with the click of the mouse, to complete several tasks at one time.

Commands are another way to automate different actions in Dreamweaver. The term "commands" refers to the creation of a replayable script or macro. Once you create a command, it will appear on the Commands menu. You can also use preexisting commands that ship with Dreamweaver right out of the box. **Note:** The term "extension" is a catch-all phrase that refers to any behavior, command, or object that you can use in Dreamweaver as one collective body of features.

What Is the History Panel?

The History panel displays all of the steps that you have performed since you created or opened your file. This gives you a nice visual overview of the different steps you've completed. You can use the slider to quickly undo and redo these steps. This visual approach to stepping backward and forward through your document gives you more feedback than pressing Ctrl+Z and Ctrl+Y or (Cmd + Z and Cmd+Y). The steps in the History panel can be copied from one document to another, which is helpful when you want to share information between documents. You can also copy steps from the History panel and save them as commands, which allows them to be replayed at a later time, in any document, with a just single click.

I. _____Using the History Panel for Undo/Redo

This first exercise will get you comfortable working with the History panel. You will learn how to use this panel to repeat or delete operations you've performed. Working with the History panel can be much easier than choosing Undo and/or Redo multiple times.

1. Copy **chap_16** to your hard drive. Define your site for Chapter 16, using the **chap_16** folder as the local root folder. If you need a refresher on this process, visit Exercise 1 in Chapter 3, *"Site Control."*

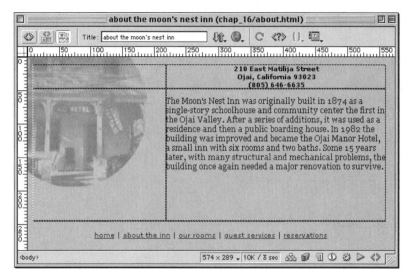

2. Open **about.html**. The large block of text in the middle of the screen would be easier to read in a different font, so you will change it.

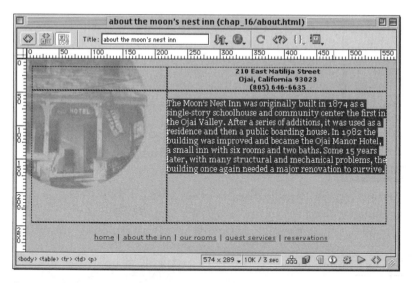

3. Click and drag so that the entire paragraph of text is highlighted. **Note:** You can also click on the **<p>** tag, in the Tag selector, to select the entire paragraph.

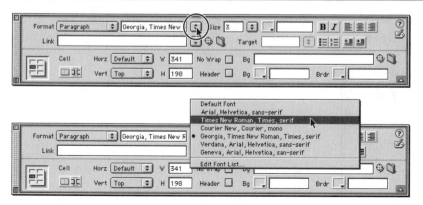

4. In the Property Inspector, click the font pop-up menu and select **Times New Roman, Times, serif**. This changes the font used to display this text.

5. Make sure your **History** panel is open. If it is not, choose **Window > History (Shift+F10)**.

The History panel displays the change you made to the block of text in Step 4. As you continue to make additions and changes to your document, your steps will be displayed here.

6. With the block of text still selected, change the font to **Verdana, Arial, Helvetica, sans-serif**. Notice that the History panel records this step as well.

7. In the History panel, click and drag the **History** slider up so that the first step is highlighted. This will undo the last formatting you applied to the text, just as though you had used the **Undo** command. Click and drag the History slider down to the bottom of the list to reapply the text formatting.

This is a nice way to step through the changes you have made to your document. It beats having to press Cmd+Z (Mac) or Ctrl+Z (Windows) because it gives you feedback about what change you are undoing.

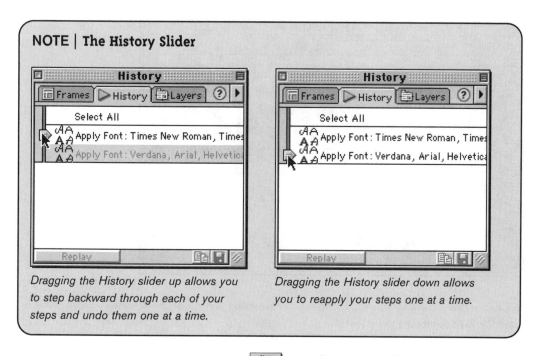

Dragging the History slider up allows you to step backward through each of your steps and undo them one at a time.

Dragging the History slider down allows you to reapply your steps one at a time.

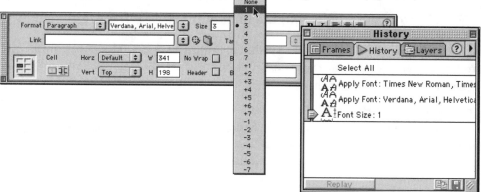

8. With the block of text still selected, reduce the **Size** to **1**. This too is recorded in the History panel.

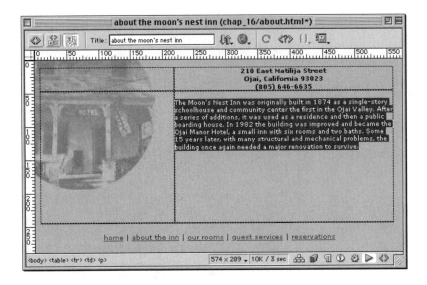

9. Choose **File > Save** to save the changes you have made to this document. When you are finished, leave this file open for the next exercise.

> ## NOTE | Saving Files and Clearing the History Panel
>
> The History panel is not cleared automatically when you save a file. This is great if you want to utilize it to make changes even after you have saved the document. However, if you close the file and reopen it, the history will be removed.
>
> It is possible to clear the History panel at any time. For instance, if you want to save memory (RAM), clear the history by clicking the arrow in the upper right of the History panel and choosing Clear History from the pop-up menu. This action cannot be undone, so be careful when using it.

2. ——————————Copying and Pasting History

Now that you have a grasp of the basic functions of the History panel, you will learn how to use it to automate some of your workflow. In this exercise, you will learn how to copy and paste information from the History panel into another document. This allows you to easily take what you have done in one document and replicate it inside another.

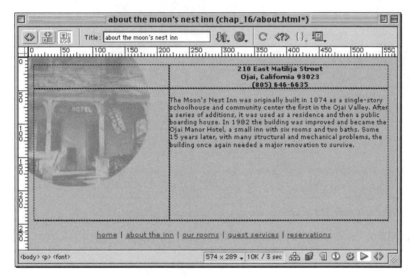

1. Make sure you have **about.html** open from the previous exercise.

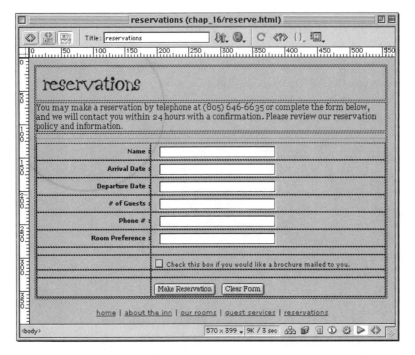

2. Open **reserve.html**. Notice that the text at the top of this page doesn't match the other text on the page, but don't worry: you'll fix that in a jiffy.

3. Choose **Window > about.html** to make it your current document.

4. In the History panel, click the last entry. Next, **Shift+click** the top entry in the panel. This selects all of the steps in the History panel. You want to make sure that they are all selected before you copy them.

Copy selected steps to the clipboard

5. Click the **Copy selected steps to the clipboard** icon at the bottom of the History panel. This copies everything you have selected to the Clipboard so that it can be pasted into the History panel of another document.

6. Choose **Window > reserve.html** to bring **reserve.html** forward and make it your current document.

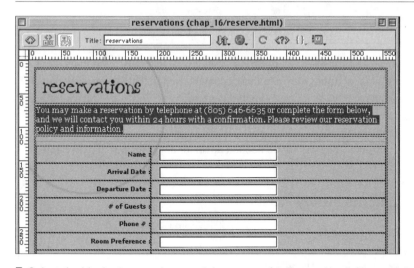

7. Select the block of text at the top of the **reserve.html** page by clicking and dragging.

Make sure that the selection represents everything you want reformatted when you paste the steps from the other document into the History panel.

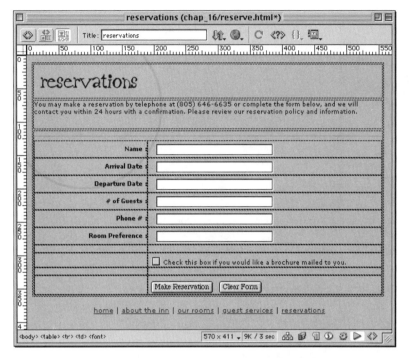

8. Choose **Edit > Paste**, or press **Cmd+V** (Mac) or **Ctrl+V** (Windows). This pastes the three steps you copied from the History panel of **about.html** into this document. Notice that Dreamweaver has formatted the text you selected the same way it was formatted in **about.html**. This is because it followed the steps you copied from the History panel of that file.

9. Save and close both documents. They will not be needed again for any exercises in this chapter.

NOTE | Paste Steps in the History Panel

Any time you paste steps from the History panel of one document into another, they will appear in the History panel as a single step, called **Paste Steps**. Regardless of how many steps you copied, they will always be pasted as one single entry in the History panel. In addition, pasted steps will have the Paste icon (a clipboard with a small piece of paper) next to them in the History panel.

Creating Custom Objects

Throughout this book, you have been using the Objects panel to add different objects to your page, such as images, tables, rollovers, etc. For the most part, all you have to do is click a button. Guess what? You can also create your own custom object, which can save a lot of time for repetitive tasks. In this exercise, you'll learn to make a custom object of an email link that contains specific information. This could be very handy for a site that used this email address over and over on many pages. While this exercise might seem a bit advanced, it's worth learning because as you become the Dreamweaver power user you were destined to be, learning things like this can really save you time!

1. Select **File > New** to create a new blank document. You will use this file to create the object, the HTML element that you want to add to the Objects panel.

2. Click the **Insert Email Link** button in the **Common Objects** panel. This opens the **Insert Email Link** dialog box.

3. Enter your name and email address. Hey, if you want to, you can pretend you are Garo Green and enter his. ;-) Click **OK**.

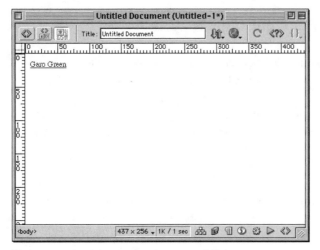

Your page should now contain an email link.

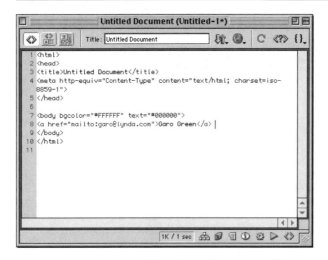

4. In the Toolbar, click the **Show Code View** button. This displays the HTML for the page.

In the following steps you will make an object from this code. Objects are nothing more than HTML documents that have been stripped of their **<html>**, **<head>**, **<title>**, *and* **<body>** *tags. The only thing that should be in this document is the code for the object itself, and that will be what you add to your page when you choose this object in the Toolbar. The next few steps show you how to delete some of the extra HTML code.*

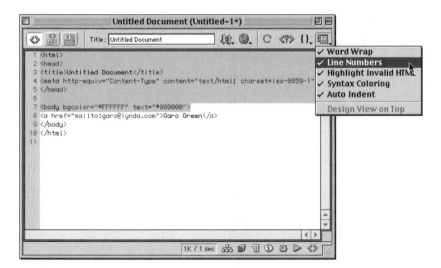

5. Click and drag to select lines 1 through 7. Press **Delete/Backspace**. This part of the document is not needed to create this object. **Note:** If you don't see any line numbers in the Code view, you can turn them on using the View Options drop-down menu.

6. Click and drag to select lines 3 through 4. Press **Delete** again. This is also extra code that can be deleted.

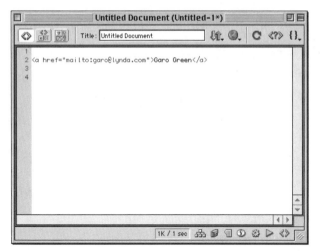

This is what your page should look like now. The document should now contain only the line of code necessary to create the email link.

You have just created the code that is necessary for the custom object. Now you need to know where to store it so that it can function in Dreamweaver. All objects are stored inside the Objects folder, which is inside the Configuration folder for the Dreamweaver 4 application. Inside the Objects folder, you will see other folders: Characters, Common, Forms, Frames, Head, Invisible, and Special. You might already have other folders if you have installed some extensions from the Macromedia Exchange. You can save your object into one of these folders to have it appear on the corresponding Objects panel, or you can create a new folder and make a new panel. The following steps show you how to create a new panel.

---

7. Hide Dreamweaver for now. Don't close the application—just minimize the window so you can see your desktop.

8. Look in the **Objects** folder located inside the **Configuration** folder within the Macromedia Dreamweaver 4 folder. These folder names should look familiar. They are the same options that are available at the top of the Objects panel.

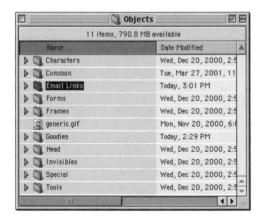

9. Create a new folder inside the **Objects** folder titled **Email Links**. You are going to save the object you created inside this folder. This will also give you a place to add more email objects later, if that need should ever arise.

10. Return to Dreamweaver.

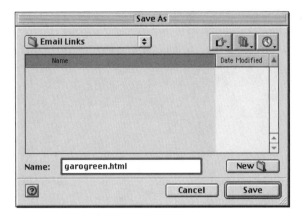

11. Select **File > Save** and save this file as **yourname.html** (make sure you use your own name, with no spaces, for the file name) inside the **Email Links** folder you just created.

Once you add a new object, you need to reload your extensions before you can use it. You can reload them by quitting and restarting Dreamweaver, or you can use the Reload Extensions command, as described next.

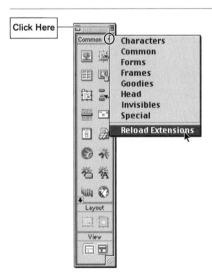

12. Option+click (Mac) or **Ctrl+click** (Windows) at the top of the Objects panel. This causes a new option, Reload Extensions, to appear at the bottom of the pop-up menu. Select **Reload Extensions**.

13. Select **File > New** to create a new blank document.

14. Click at the top of the Objects panel and choose **Email Links** from the pop-up menu. This new option appears because you created a folder of the same name inside the Objects folder. Are you starting to feel like a power user yet?

A single generic icon, a blue box with a question mark, appears in the Objects panel. That's your object! By now, you should have a pretty good grip on what objects are, how they are created, and where they are stored.

15. Move your pointer over the little blue icon. A small tag will appear revealing the name you gave the file. In our example we used **garogreen.html**, so that's what appears, minus the .html extension.

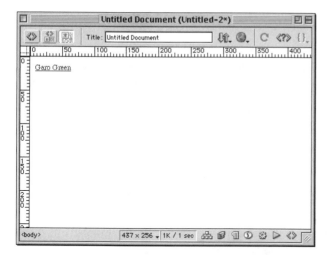

16. Click on this icon and an email link is added to your page. Cool, huh? That's all there is to it.

17. If you want, go ahead and see if you can create two more email link objects for other people. Make sure they are saved inside the Email Links folder so they appear in this panel.

18. When you are done, close all windows. You can save any changes you made, but you don't have to because you won't be using these files any more.

NOTE | What Is a Command?

A command is a small JavaScript file that records specific functions performed in Dreamweaver. These files are stored inside the Commands folder within the Configuration folder. Some commands come with Dreamweaver, like the Create Web Photo Album command, while others can be downloaded from a number of different Web sites, as we'll describe later. You can even create your own custom commands, using the History panel, or write them from scratch with JavaScript. For example, you can copy steps from the History panel and save them as a command. Dreamweaver will convert the selected steps into JavaScript so that they can be replayed again from any document. As you can see, commands can be very powerful and can save you a lot of time.

Getting More Commands

It is possible to create commands that are far more complicated than the ones this chapter describes, such as ones that script complex interactions between Dreamweaver and Fireworks. However, creating this type of command requires very strong JavaScript skills, which are way beyond the scope of this book.

The good news is that the JavaScript jocks who can create more complicated custom commands often distribute these from their own sites. There is actually a sizable third-party market for Dreamweaver commands. You'll find information below on the Macromedia Dreamweaver Support Center and a couple of the third-party sites we've found most useful. Make sure you also check out Appendix B, *"Online Resources,"* for a listing of these sites. In addition, you can choose **Commands > Get More Commands...** to access Dreamweaver Exchange, the online community for extensibility developers.

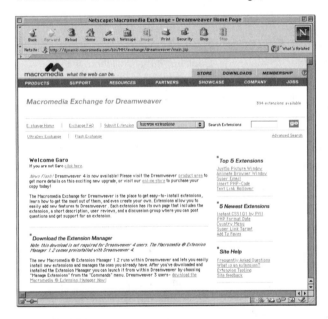

Dreamweaver Support Center

If you are proficient in HTML and JavaScript, the Macromedia site offers a great resource for developers who plan to create custom commands and other extensions for Dreamweaver. Macromedia has prepared a comprehensive document that gives detailed information on the extensive Dreamweaver API (**A**pplication **P**rogramming **I**nterface), which you can also download at the URL listed below. The API refers to the methods a programmer can use to make requests of the application.

`http://www.macromedia.com/support/dreamweaver/extend.html`

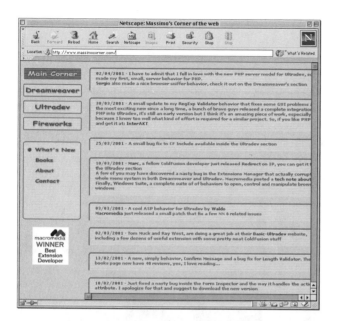

Massimo's Corner

Massimo's is a great site for getting some really useful commands.

`http://www.massimocorner.com`

Yaromat

This is another great repository for Dreamweaver behaviors, commands, and objects.

`http://www.yaromat.com/dw/`
`index.php`

What Is a Web Photo Album?

The Create Web Photo Album command is a great feature in Dreamweaver that lets you quickly create a small Web site–based catalog of images. If you are a designer, photographer, or just some-one who has a bunch of images to share with friends and family, you will really appreciate this feature. This command, which comes with Dreamweaver, works in conjunction with Macromedia Fireworks 4 to batch-process a collection of images and create a set of Web pages that links them all together. You simply tell Dreamweaver where your source images are located, and it will launch Fireworks to optimize them and create thumbnails (smaller versions of your images), then use Dreamweaver to create a page for each and link them all together. In the end, you have a great way to share your image collections with the rest of the world.

The Web photo album is created automatically from a folder of images. Dreamweaver will create a catalog page of thumbnail images (shown on the left) as well as individual pages for larger images. You'll learn to make this photo album yourself in the next exercise.

4. ——————————Creating a Web Photo Album

The Create Web Photo Album command automatically creates a complex Web site that displays your images. An online photo album is great way for artists to display their work, for architects to show renderings to clients, for photographers to show proofs to clients, for families to share personal photos, and for other purposes too numerous to list here. All you need is a folder of images on your hard drive, and the Create Web Photo Album command will convert them into an elaborate Web site, complete with thumbnails and larger images and links to navigate between them. You'll be impressed by how easy it is to create this complex site with just a folder of images and the Dreamweaver Create Web Photo Album command.

Note: Before completing this exercise, you must have Fireworks 3 or 4 installed on your computer. If you don't own a copy of Fireworks, don't worry. There is a free, 30-day trial demo copy in the **software** folder of the **H•O•T CD-ROM**.

1. Choose **File > New** to create a new blank document.

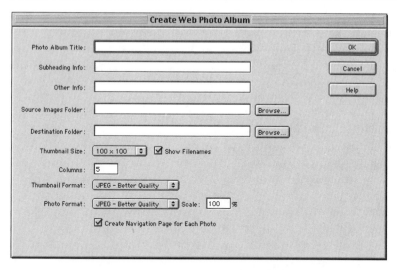

2. Choose **Commands > Create Web Photo Album**. This opens the **Create Web Photo Album** dialog box. If you don't have Fireworks installed yet, Dreamweaver will display a **Download Fireworks trial** button.

3. Enter **Photo Album Title: The Moon's Nest Inn**. This text, along with the other information you enter on this page, will appear at the top of the home page of your completed Web album site once you've completed this exercise.

4. Enter **Subheading Info: Ojai, California**. This text will appear immediately below the **Photo Album Title** field on your Web album site.

5. Enter **Other Info: (805) 646-6635**. This text will appear immediately below the **Subheading Info** field.

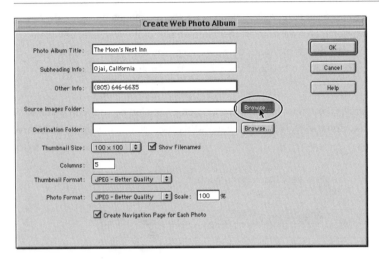

6. Click **Browse...** to the right of the **Source Images Folder:** field. Browse to the **source images** folder inside the **chap_16** folder.

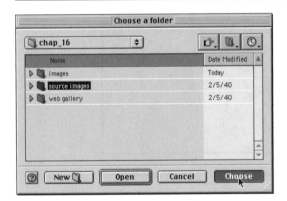

7. Click **Choose**. This option determines which folder contains the source files you want to use to create your Web photo album.

Tip: *The Create Web Photo Album command can process only whole folders of images.*

> ## TIP | Web Photo Album Source Files
>
> The source files for your Web photo album must be saved in the .gif, .jpg, .jpeg, .png, .psd, .tif, or .tiff file format. The files must have the proper extension in order to be included in the Web photo album. If they are in another file format, you will get an error message that says no files exist in your source folder.

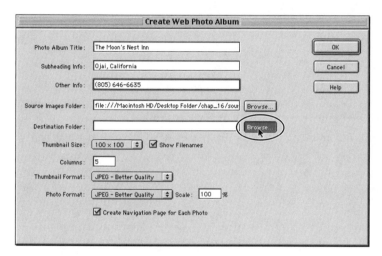

8. Click **Browse...** to the right of the **Destination Folder:** field. Navigate inside the **chap_16** folder to select the **web gallery** folder. This is an empty folder we made for you that will be the destination folder for the Web photo album once Dreamweaver is finished executing this command.

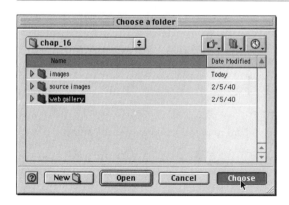

9. Click **Choose**.

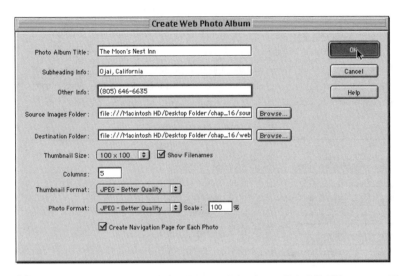

10. Inside the **Create Web Photo Album** dialog box, click **OK**. This causes Fireworks to launch and start processing the images.

You will see a window like this while Fireworks is processing the images in your source folder.

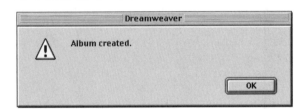

11. When Fireworks is done processing the images, you are returned to Dreamweaver, and you see this dialog box. Click **OK**.

This is what your Dreamweaver page should look like after the photo album has been created.

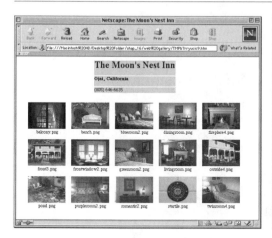

12. Press **F12** to preview your page in a browser. Click any of the images to see the larger version. Dreamweaver and Fireworks worked together to modify your images, create several Web pages, insert the images, and create links to all of the pages. It all happened in just a few seconds! Sweet.

13. Save and close all open files.

5. _____Optimizing Images in Fireworks

In the previous exercise, you saw the power of Dreamweaver and Fireworks working together to create a Web photo album. This power is also available for editing single images in a document. The **Optimize Image in Fireworks** command allows you to reoptimize an image without leaving Dreamweaver. This can save you a lot of time when you are trying to make your file sizes as small as possible.

Note: This exercise also requires that you have Fireworks 4 installed on your computer. If you don't own a copy of Fireworks 4, don't worry; we stole a copy for you! Just kidding, there is a free, 30-day trial demo copy in the **software** folder of the **H•O•T CD-ROM**. ;-)

1. Open **optimize.html**, located inside the **chap_16** folder. This file contains a really large image, **monterey.jpg**, that is well over 80K. You are going to use the **Optimize Image in Fireworks** command to reduce the file size of this image directly from Dreamweaver.

2. In the document window, click the image of the bed to select it.

3. Choose **Commands > Optimize Image in Fireworks...** This launches Fireworks if you don't already have it open.

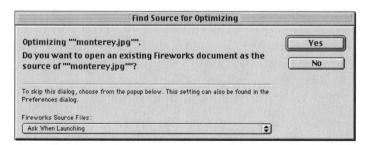

4. Fireworks will ask if you want to open an existing Fireworks document as the source of **monterey.jpg**. Click **Yes**. We have included a copy of the **monterey.png** source file for you to work with.

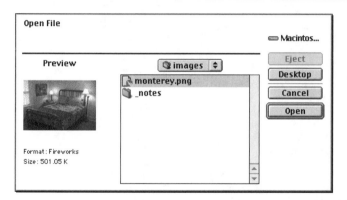

5. Browse to **monterey.png**, located inside the **images** folder, and click Open.

NOTE | The Significance of PNG in Fireworks

Fireworks uses the PNG file format as its native source format. A PNG file that was generated by Fireworks includes proprietary information, such as vector, layer, effects, frames, and optimization settings. This type of PNG file is also uncompressed, so it is a true master file, which is the best thing to start with when you plan to optimize for the Web. (If you are familiar with Photoshop, the same is true for a .psd file there.) If you save a GIF or JPEG from Fireworks and do not save the source PNG file, you will not have an original uncompressed file to use as a resource.

What does it mean to click Yes or No in the Find Source for Optimizing dialog box? Basically, if all you have is a GIF or JPEG, click No in this dialog box; if you possess a Fireworks PNG, then click Yes. Although it can be done, it's not a good idea to recompress an existing GIF or JPEG image, because the image quality of your end result will not be as good.

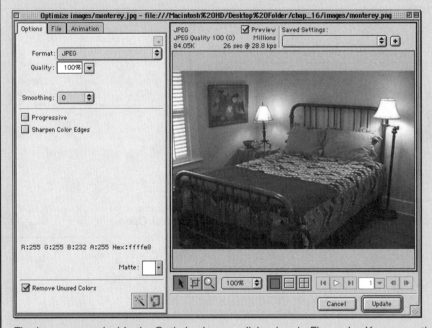

The image opens inside the Optimize Images dialog box in Fireworks. You can optimize this image just as if you had opened it in Fireworks yourself.

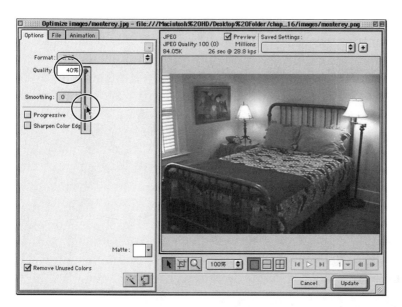

6. Notice that the image is over 80K in size. Click the **Quality:** slider and drag it down to **40%**.

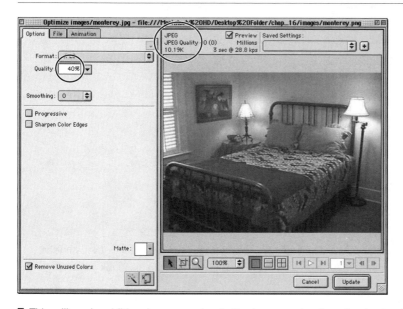

7. This will apply additional compression to the image and reduce its size to about 10K, an 88% reduction in file size! You can experiment with some of the other settings if you want. When you are happy with your changes, click **Update**.

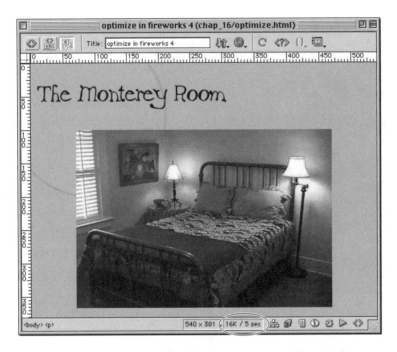

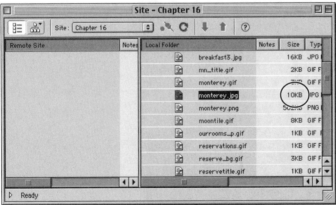

8. Fireworks reoptimizes and saves a new .jpg file. You are then returned to Dreamweaver, and the new, much smaller image, is inserted automatically inside your page. You can also look inside the **images** folder to see the smaller .jpg file.

9. Save your changes and close this file.

TIP | Refresh Problems

You might notice that the page size information at the bottom of your Dreamweaver document window does not update properly all of the time, especially after using the Optimize Image in Fireworks command. If that happens, you might have to save your work, quit, and then restart Dreamweaver to see the lower page size.

Woo-hoo, another chapter under your belt. Congrats! If you feel up to it, keep on moving to the next chapter.

17.

Templates/Libraries

| Templates in Action |
| Creating a New Template | Modifying a Template |
| Library Items in Action | Creating a Library Item |
| Modifying a Library Item |

chap_17

Dreamweaver 4
H·O·T CD-ROM

Two of the biggest challenges that face Web designers are making pages look consistent and updating changes throughout a site. **Templates** and **Library items** can help you meet both challenges successfully, because they make it easy to create consistent pages and page elements and to automatically update multiple pages when changes are made.

Templates are useful for entire page designs. They can lock in colors, fonts, tables, or images while leaving other parts of the document editable. When you create a template, you use it by requesting a copy of it. Instead of creating a new untitled document, you request a new page based on a template that you have designed.

Library items are useful for page-design elements, such as a navigation bar or copyright notice. They are little pieces of HTML or text that can be dropped anywhere within a page. You will soon learn the differences between these two Dreamweaver features by following the hands-on exercises in this chapter.

I. ——————Templates in Action

The best way to understand templates in Dreamweaver is to observe them in action. For this first exercise, you will modify an existing template, which will show you how quickly they can update across multiple pages in your site. You will also see how, with just a few clicks, you can use templates to change your color scheme across several pages.

1. Copy **chap_17** to your hard drive. Define your site for Chapter 17 using the **chap_17** folder as the local root folder. If you need a refresher on this process, visit Exercise 1 in Chapter 3, *"Site Control."*

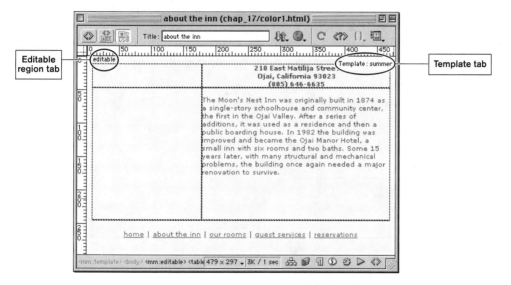

When you open a file that has a template applied to it, you will see a tab in the upper right corner that identifies the name of the template file and a tab around each of the template's editable areas. The colors of these areas are set in the Highlighting category of the Preferences dialog box.

2. Open **color1.html**. This file, and several others inside the **chap_17** folder, including **color2.html**, **color3.html**, and **color4.html**, have a color scheme template called **summer** already applied to them. If you want, go ahead and open these other files and notice that they all share the same color scheme.

TIP | Templates and Library Folders

You might have noticed that there are two folders inside the **chap_17** folder, called **Templates** and **Library**. Dreamweaver automatically creates these folders for you on any site that uses templates or Library items. If you do not use templates or Library items, Dreamweaver will not put these folders in your directory structure. These folders (Templates and Library) do not need to be uploaded to your Web site if you publish it to the WWW. They are for internal purposes only. If Dreamweaver sees that these folders are present in your directory structure, it knows to insert any new templates or Library items that you create into the appropriate folder (Templates or Library) without your having to do so.

3. When you are working with templates in Dreamweaver, you will typically want to have the **Assets** panel open. Choose **Window > Templates** to open it. This opens the **Assets** panel with the **Templates** category selected.

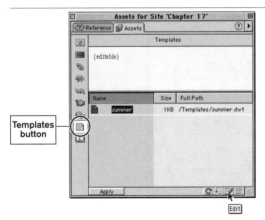

4. Highlight the template called **summer** in the **Assets** panel, and then click the **Edit** icon at the bottom of the panel. This opens the template so you can start editing, or modifying it. **Tip:** As an alternative, you can switch to the Site window to open **summer.dwt** from the Templates folder.

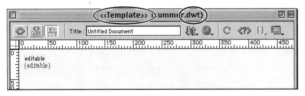

It's easy to tell when you are editing a template because the title bar displays <<Template>>, the template file name, and a .dwt extension.

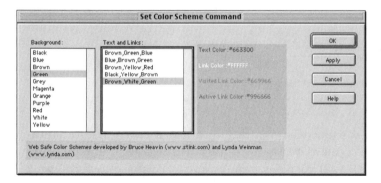

5. To change the color scheme of this template, you will use some of the preset color schemes that ship with Dreamweaver. Choose **Commands > Set Color Scheme...** This opens the **Set Color Scheme Command** dialog box. Select **Background: Green** and **Text and Links: Brown, White, Green**. Click **OK**.

6. Close the **summer.dwt** template and save your changes when prompted.

NOTE | Templates, Library Items, and HTML

Dreamweaver's template format (.dwt) and Library format (.lbi) are internal file-naming conventions only. These files do not mean anything to other HTML editors, nor are they meant to be viewed on the Web from a browser. Templates and Library items are used internally in Dreamweaver and function only in Dreamweaver. If you base an HTML page on a template or use Library items in it, it will appear as a normal page in the browser, the same as any other HTML page. It will be regarded differently in Dreamweaver only, in that it will be updated if the original template or Library items are changed.

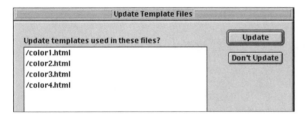

7. Once you have closed and saved the modified template, you are notified that you have modified a template and asked if you want to update all the files in your site that use this template. Because you want to apply the new color scheme to all four pages, click **Yes**. If you are presented with the **Update Template Files** dialog box, click **Update**.

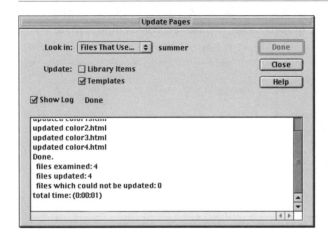

8. Dreamweaver will scan your site to determine whether any files are using this template. It will update any files that it finds during the scan. In this case, there are four such files. A dialog box will list which files were updated. Once you are finished reviewing this screen, click **Close**.

Note: *If you have* **color1.html** *open while performing this operation, the color scheme will be updated, but if you close the file without saving the changes you'll lose them. Make sure you save your changes when you close any open files.*

TIP | Templates and Page Properties

Once a template has been applied to a page, you can no longer edit any of the Page Properties options, with the exception of the page title. Therefore, the only way to change the color scheme is by opening and editing the template itself, as you just did in this exercise.

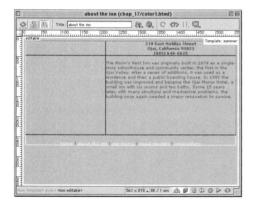

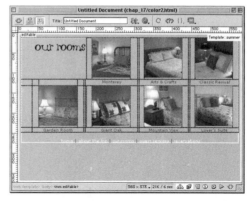

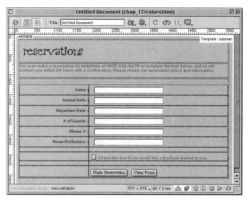

9. Open **color2.html**, **color3.html**, and **color4.html**, and you will see that each now has the new color scheme.

Imagine how much time this could save you if you had hundreds or thousands of pages that were created using a template and share the same color scheme.

---

10. Close all the files. You will learn how to make a template from scratch in the next exercise.

Working with templates is an excellent technique to ensure design consistency. The only caveat is that you must work from a template file to begin with. How do you do that? Check out the next exercise to find out.

2. ——————————**Creating a New Template**

In this next exercise, you are going to create a new template from an existing document and then make parts of your template editable and other parts non-editable. Once you have this skill under your belt, you will understand the capabilities and limitations of templates much more clearly.

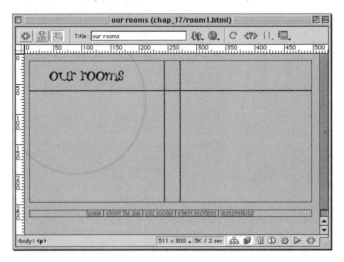

1. Open **room1.html**. This document was created for you, but the following steps would also work on a document of your own creation.

Once you have created the basic layout of your document, the next step is to save it as a template.

2. Choose **File > Save As Template...**

3. When the **Save As Template** dialog box opens, make sure this template is named **room1**. Dreamweaver will automatically enter the name of the HTML file in the **Save As** field. You can see that your other template, summer, is already listed in this box. Click **Save**.

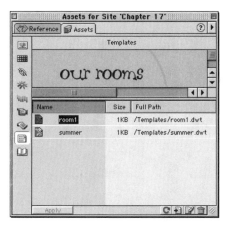

Your new template appears in the Templates category of the Assets panel. The top portion of the Assets panel displays a preview of the template.

Now that you have created your template, you need to decide which areas you want to be able to modify and which areas you want to lock. By default, the entire document is designated as non-editable. This means that if you were to close the file now, it would be impossible for anyone to modify it later. We'll walk you through this process in the next couple of steps.

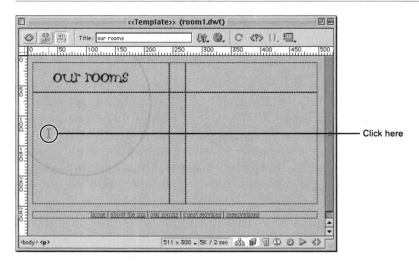

Click here

4. Click inside the large cell directly under the words **our rooms.** Choose **Modify > Templates > New Editable Region...** to designate this area as an editable region so that you or other members of your design team can enter the description of the room here.

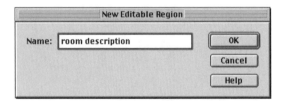

5. When the **New Editable Region** dialog box appears, enter **"room description"** and click **OK.**

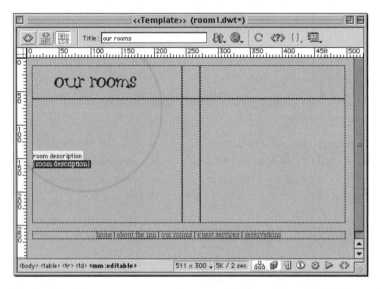

Notice that the name you entered appears in that cell, surrounded by curly braces. This indicates that this area of the template is editable—you or other members of your team can enter information inside this cell. By naming this region **room description**, *you can help others know what information should be entered there.*

6. Click inside the large cell on the far right. Choose **Modify > Templates > New Editable Region...** When the **New Editable Region** dialog box appears, type **"room image"** and click **OK.**

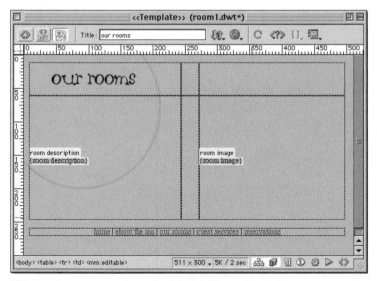

This is what your template should look like at this point.

---

7. Now that you have designated the necessary areas as editable, go ahead and close this file. When prompted, make sure that you save your changes.

Congratulations—you have just created a custom template. Next, you will create a new page based on your newly created template.

---

8. Choose **File > New from Template...**

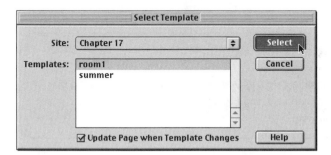

9. Highlight **room1** in the list and click **Select**. This creates a new document based on the **room1** template.

---

10. Choose **File > Save As...** and save the file as **montereyroom.html** into your **chap_17** folder.

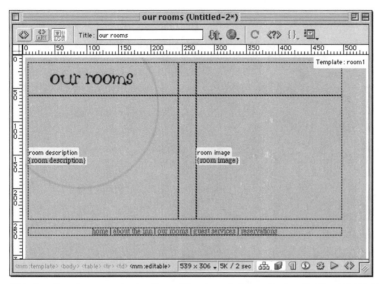

This is what the page looks like with a template applied to it. The highlighted areas are non-editable. The two areas you designated as editable are highlighted and are ready to be edited.

TIP | I Don't See Any Highlighting!

If you don't see any highlighting on your screen, make sure that you have the **View > Visual Aids > Invisible Elements** option enabled. If you disable this feature, you will not see any highlighting. You can choose **View > Visual Aids > Invisible Elements** to disable/enable this feature.

TIP | Highlighting Preferences

You can modify your document's highlighting colors in Dreamweaver's Preferences dialog box. By choosing **Edit > Preferences...** and then selecting Highlighting under Category, you can set the highlighting colors to any color you want.

---

11. Highlight the text **room description** and its surrounding curly braces, press **Delete** to make sure the text and curly braces disappear, and type **The Monterey Room. A charming brass double bed completes this cozy room with a balcony affording both city and mountain views. This room has a private bath.**

12. Highlight the text **room image** on the right and its surrounding curly braces, then press **Delete** to make sure the text and curly braces disappear. Click the **Insert Image** object in the **Common Objects** panel.

13. Browse to the **images** folder inside the **chap_17** folder to locate **monterey1.jpg**. Click **Choose**. This inserts the image into this editable region.

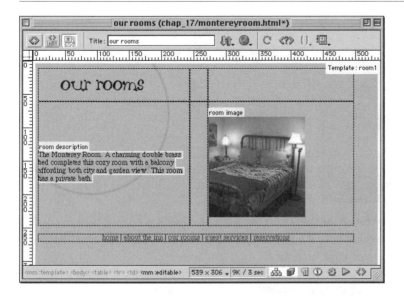

14. Save and keep this file open. You'll be using it in the next exercise.

TIP | Detaching a Template

There may come a time when you want to modify sections of a page that have a template applied to it. Because some areas are locked, this is impossible to do with the template still applied to the page. By choosing **Modify > Templates > Detach from Template**, you can detach the template from the page and make the entire document editable.

3. ─────────Modifying a Template

Now that that you have created your first template; you are ready to learn how to update it. In this exercise, you will change the alignment of the text and image in your layout, causing the text and the image to move to the center. Then, all you have to do is sit back and watch Dreamweaver update all the pages in your site that use this template!

1. Make sure that **montereyroom.html** from the previous exercise is open. Before you can modify a template, you must open it from the **Assets** panel. Double-click the **room1** template in the **Assets** panel to open that template.

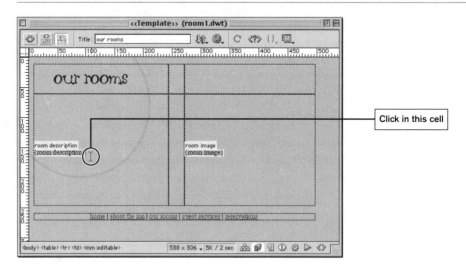

2. The actual template file opens for you to edit. Click inside the **room description** editable region.

3. In the Property Inspector, click the **Horz** pop-up menu and choose **Center**. This moves the text to the center of the cell.

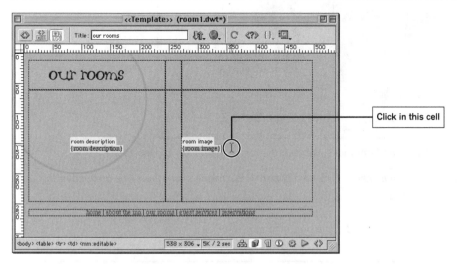

4. Click in the **room image** editable region.

5. Again, from the **Horz** pop-up menu in the Property Inspector, choose **Center**. This moves the text to the center of the cell and also centers any images that are inserted into this cell.

6. Go ahead and close this template file. When prompted, make sure that you save your changes. A dialog box appears, asking if you wish to update the files in your site that use this template. Click **Yes**. If you are presented with the **Update Template Files** dialog box, click **Update**. Any files using this template (in this case, **montereyroom. html** file) will be updated, and a dialog box will list which files were updated. Click **Close**.

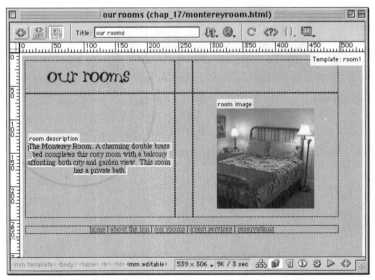

*This is what **montereyroom.html** looks like with the revised template applied to it.*

Note: Templates used in this fashion are helpful only if the pages share the same layout and the same editable region names.

7. Save and close all open files and move on to the next exercise.

WARNING | Template Beware!

Once you have applied a template to a page, you can no longer edit any information in the **<head>** tag. This means you can't add any JavaScript, styles, behaviors, or anything else that would be contained within a **<head>** tag. If you do need to add this type of code to a page that is based on a template, you need to break the template by choosing **Modify > Templates > Detach from Template**. This removes the page's link to the original template and allows you to edit anything within the **<head>** element. The downside to this, of course, is that if you make changes to the template, this unlinked copy will not be able to refer to it.

4. _____**Library Items in Action**

Library items and templates are somewhat similar in function. Both are used to apply changes to multiple pages with ease. The difference is that templates affect the entire page design, while Library items are used for individual page elements. You will start by working with an existing Library item. You'll quickly see how cool these Library things are and how much time they can save you!

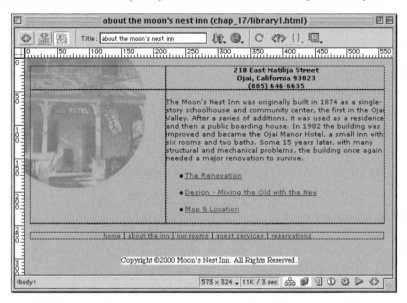

1. Open **library1.html**. At the bottom of this page, you will see a copyright notice that is highlighted in yellow. The yellow highlight is an indication that this text is a Library item.

2. In order to modify the Library item, you need to open the **Assets** panel. Choose **Window > Library**, if it's not already open. You will see that one Library item already exists. This is what you will modify.

3. Highlight the **copyright** Library item and click the **Edit** icon at the bottom of the panel.

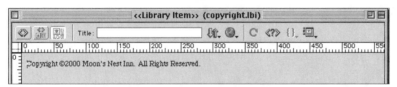

Just as with templates, it's easy to tell when you are editing Library items. The title bar displays <<Library Item>> and the file name with an .lbi extension.

4. Highlight the text **2000** and type **2001**. Can you believe another year has gone by? Sheesh.

5. Close this file. If you are prompted, make sure to save your changes.

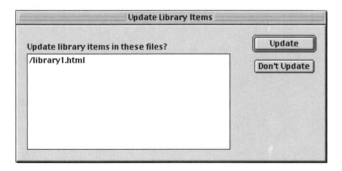

6. When you are asked to update the pages in your site that use this Library item, click **Yes**. If you see the **Update Library Items** dialog box, click **Update**.

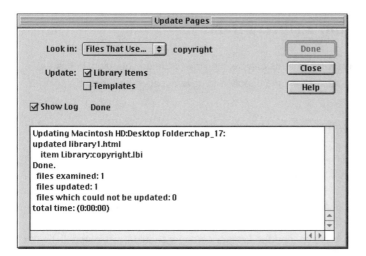

7. The **Update Pages** dialog box appears. Just as with templates, this dialog box gives you all the details of how many and which files were updated in your site. Click **Close** when you are finished reviewing this screen.

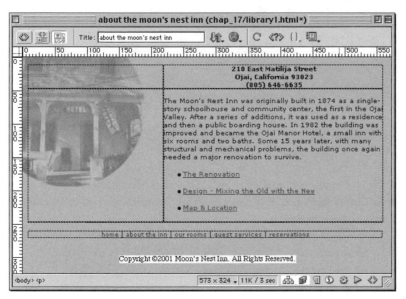

This is what your page should look like with the updated Library item. Can you imagine how long it would take to update this text on a hundred pages? Library items can offer incredible time savings.

8. Save your changes and close this file. You will not need it for the next exercise.

5. ———————Creating a Library Item

Now that you understand how efficient Library items can be, it's time to create your own. In this exercise, you will create a text navigation bar. You will then apply it to several pages by simply dragging it onto a page.

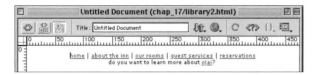

1. Open **library2.html**. This is a just a simple file with text navigation already created.

2. The **Assets** panel should be open, and the **Library** category should be selected. If it's not, choose **Window > Library**.

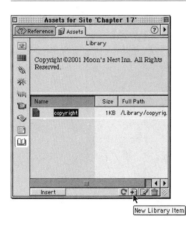

3. In the **library2.html** file, highlight both lines of text. In the **Library** category of the Assets panel, click the **New Library Item** icon. Your new Library item instantly appears in the category. It needs a name, so type "**textnav**."

4. Click inside the document window. Click **Update** when the **Update Files** dialog box opens. Because you changed the name of this Library item, Dreamweaver wants to make sure any links are updated.

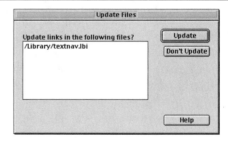

5. Now that you have created your Library item, you can apply it to a page. Create a new blank document by choosing **File > New**. Then choose **File > Save** and save this file inside the **chap_17** folder as **mypage1.html**.

6. In the **Assets** panel, highlight the **textnav** Library item and click **Insert** at the bottom of the panel.

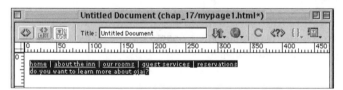

Pow! The Library item is applied to the page. Notice that it did not retain the center alignment you applied when creating it. You'll fix that next.

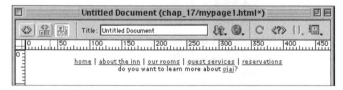

7. Click to the right of the **?** and then, in the Property Inspector, click the **Center Align** button to center-align both lines of text.

8. Save **mypage1.html** and leave it open. Leave **library2.html** open as well. You will be working with both files in the next exercise.

6. _____Modifying a Library Item

Now that you know how to create Library items, you are going to modify the one you just created and then watch Dreamweaver quickly update your page. Can you imagine how joyous you would be if this were a change that needed to be made over hundreds or thousands of pages?

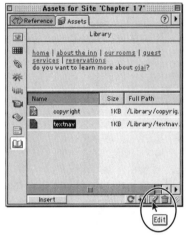

1. With **library2.html** open and **textnav** highlighted in the **Assets** panel from the last exercise, click the **Edit** icon. This opens the Library item for editing.

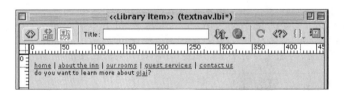

2. Highlight the word **reservations**, and type **contact us**. This should replace the type but maintain the link.

3. Close this file, and when you are prompted make sure you save and update your changes. If you see the **Update Library Items** dialog box, click **Update**. Close the **Update Pages** dialog box when you are done reviewing it.

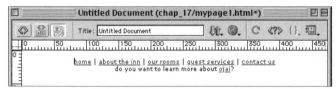

*Check out what **mypage1.html** looks like now with the new Library item applied to it.*

4. Close all documents and save your changes.

You've just conquered making and modifying a Library item. It's all very simple, once you know how. If you feel up to it, move on to the next chapter. If not, don't worry; it will be there tomorrow ;-).

18.

Plug-Ins

| Linking to Sounds | Embedding Sounds |
| Inserting Flash Content | Inserting Director (Shockwave) Content |
| Inserting QuickTime Content |

chap_18

Dreamweaver 4
H•O•T CD-ROM

Hey, you're almost through the book! There's still another important feature of Dreamweaver to learn about, though—how to work with **plug-in**-based content. What are plug-ins, you might ask? Plug-ins are special program extensions installed in your end user's browser that allow the user to view plug-in-based content, such as Flash, Shockwave, Real Audio, QuickTime, etc.

It's good to understand how to work with plug-ins in Dreamweaver because you may want to publish multimedia effects to your page that require plug-ins, such as sound, Flash content, Director content (Shockwave), or QuickTime content. In this chapter, you'll learn how to add this kind of content in Dreamweaver via a variety of objects, and you'll learn how to set parameters in the Property Inspector to control how and when your plug-in-based content will play.

Exciting as this sounds, it's also the area of Web development where compatibility issues between browsers really get intense. Not everyone has the same plug-ins loaded, and some of the plug-ins work differently on Macs than in Windows. Dreamweaver does a great job of letting you put this content on your site. It's the rest of the Web's limitations that you'll more likely have to struggle with!

NOTE | What Is a Plug-In?

In the early days of the Web, any file that wasn't an HTML file had to be downloaded and required a separate "player" for the content to be seen. This was a hassle for most Web surfers, because it meant that you had to break the flow of a good "surf" to view material in an external application. In response to this problem, Netscape introduced the idea of plug-ins, which extended the capability of HTML pages to display content that wasn't HTML based. Today, certain plug-ins ship with most browsers. These include QuickTime, Flash, and RealPlayer. This chapter focuses on techniques to insert plug-in-based content into HTML pages so it can be viewed as an "inline" element, without requiring the use of an outside player application.

Plug-Ins Require Viewer Participation

As you are working through these exercises, you might find yourself being directed to download plug-ins from the Internet or reassign them in your browser preferences. If this seems like a hassle, remember that you are asking your audience to do the same thing when you present plug-in-based content to them!

URLs for Downloading Plug-Ins	
Plug-Ins	**URL**
QuickTime	http://www.apple.com/quicktime
Flash	http://www.macromedia.com/software/flashplayer/
Shockwave	http://www.macromedia.com/software/shockwaveplayer/
Acrobat	http://www.adobe.com/products/acrobat/readstep.html
Real Player	http://www.real.com/player/

I. _____Linking to Sounds

There are multiple ways to add sound to your page. In this first exercise, you will learn to add sound to your page simply by creating a link to a sound file. As you will see, there are some nuances to consider when you are working with sound files. For example, there is no standard format for sounds on the Web. Sounds are handled differently between browsers and operating systems (as if designing Web pages was not difficult enough). But have no fear! By the time you finish the hands-on exercises in this chapter, you'll have a much better understanding of how to add sound to your site.

1. Define your site for Chapter 18. Copy the contents of **chap_18** to your hard drive and press **F5** to define it. For a refresher on this process, revisit Exercise 1 in Chapter 3, *"Site Control."*

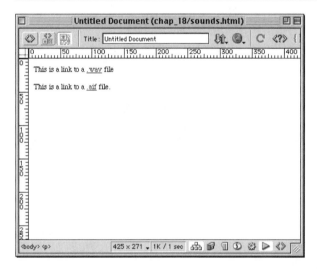

2. Open **sounds.html**. You will see two links at the top of the page. These two links point directly to two different sound files. The first link points to a .wav file, and the second link points to an .aif file.

3. Click on the **.wav** link at the top of the page. In the Property Inspector, notice that this links to the **tell-me-about.wav** file. That's all there is to it. When the user clicks on this link in a Web browser, the sound plays. You'll need to preview this file in a browser in order to play the sound.

4. Click on the **.aif** link. Notice that this link points to the **sound.aif** file. Nothing too complicated about this so far. You are simply creating a link, but instead of pointing to an HTML document, you are pointing to a sound file.

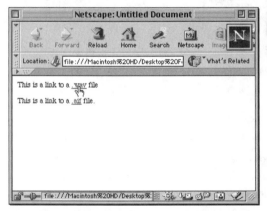

*When the page is previewed in Netscape Navigator 4.7 on the Mac, clicking on the .wav link should play the sound with the Netscape Audio player, the default setting. If you have QuickTime installed, it will play the sound with the QuickTime player. **Note:** Be sure that you have the most current version of QuickTime by visiting **http://www.apple.com/quicktime/**. For your convenience, we have included a full copy of QuickTime 5 on the **H•O•T CD-ROM**.*

TIP | Different Sound Players

Both Netscape Navigator and Internet Explorer let you choose what application or plug-in will play audio files found on Web pages. In fact, you can set a different one for each type of audio format. For example, you might choose to have the QuickTime plug-in play .aif and .wav files and have the Flash plug-in play .swf files. You can control this by modifying your browser preferences. Check these settings if you experience any problems while trying to play sound files. For instructions on how to change these settings, refer to your browser's Help feature.

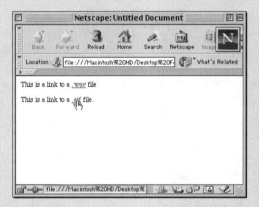

Clicking on the .aif link launches the QuickTime plug-in, if you have set the QuickTime Player as the audio player for all .aif files. You can do this in the Netscape Preferences, under Applications. **Note:** *This works identically on the Mac and Windows operating systems.*

5. Press **F12** to preview this page in a browser. Click on each of the links. Clicking on the **.wav** link plays the sound of a man saying, "Tell me about your childhood." Clicking on the **.aif** link plays a beeping sound. You will have to use the **Back** button in the browser after clicking on the first link. Depending on how your browser preferences are set up and what operating system you are using, clicking on the links might launch different audio players—or none at all!

6. Return to Dreamweaver and close the file.

Different Sound Formats

One of the problems in adding sound to your Web page is deciding which format to use. Most Web publishers use either .aif or .wav files—the two native sound formats for the Mac and Windows operating systems. It is a good idea, however, to be familiar with the other formats that you might run into on the Web. The chart below gives you an idea of what's out there:

Sound Formats	
Extension	**Description**
.au	This format was one of the first introduced on the Internet. It was designed for NeXT and Sun Unix systems.
.aiff/.aif	The .aif (**A**udio **I**nterchange **F**ormat) was developed by Apple and is also used on SGI machines. It is the main audio format for Macintosh computers.
.midi/.mid	The .midi (**M**usical **I**nstrument **D**igital **I**nterface) format was designed to translate how music is produced. MIDI files store just the sequencing information (notes, timing, and voicing) required to play back a musical composition, rather than a recording of the composition itself, so these files are usually small, but playback quality is unpredictable.
.MP3	The .MP3 (**MP**EG-1 Audio Layer-**3**) format is the hottest audio file format on the Web. It offers superior compression and great quality.
.ra/.ram	The .ra (**R**eal **A**udio) format was designed to offer streaming audio on the Internet.
.rmf	The .rmf (**R**ich **M**usic **F**ormat) was designed by Headspace and is used in the Beatnik plug-in. This format offers good compression and quality.
.swa	The .swa (**S**hock**w**ave **A**udio) format was developed by Macromedia and is used in Flash.
.wav	The .wav audio format was developed by IBM and Microsoft. This is the main audio format for the Windows operating system, but .wav files play on Macs and other systems as well.

2. _____Embedding Sounds

In addition to linking to a sound file, there is another, much better approach to adding sound to your Web pages. You can choose to embed the sound so that it plays from your page, instead of linking to it (as in the last exercise). Embedding sounds gives you much more control over them, since they actually appear inside your HTML files, along with the other content. By modifying specific parameters, you can control when the sound plays and how it appears on the page, whether it loops (replays continuously) or not, and several other settings. So if you embed your sounds, you get more control, and hey, that's what most people want in life, right?

1. Open **embed.html** inside the **chap_18** folder. This is simply a blank file that we created for you.

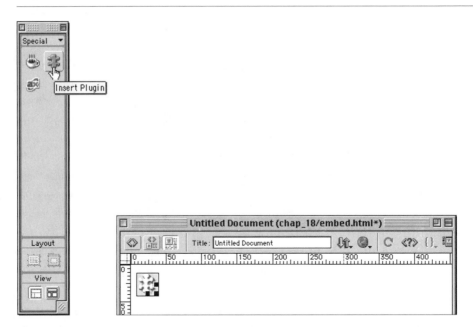

2. Click on the **Insert Plugin** object in the **Special Objects** panel. Browse to the **chap_18 folder** and highlight **sound.aif**. Click **Open**. This inserts a small plug-in icon on your page.

In this example, it does not matter where the sound file is placed physically on the page. If you had a page where you wanted the sound controllers (Play, Stop, and Rewind buttons) to appear, you would simply position this element like any other image or text component of any page.

3. With the sound still selected, click on the **Parameters...** button in the Property Inspector. This opens the **Parameters** dialog box, which is where you would insert any parameters and values you needed. We've listed some URLs at the end of this exercise that will give you more information about parameters and values; there are way too many to list in this book.

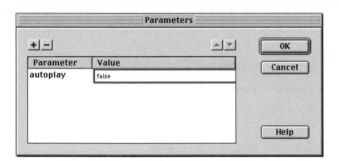

4. Under **Parameter** in the **Parameters** dialog box, type **autoplay**, then press **Tab**. Type **false**, and then click **OK**. This prevents the sound file from playing automatically and instead causes it to wait until the user clicks on the Play button. This is a very useful parameter!

5. Press **F12** to preview your page in a browser. Click on the **Play** button to hear the sound. Here you can see that QuickTime is being used to play .aif files in Netscape Navigator 4.7 for the Macintosh. **Note:** If you get a broken image icon, you might have to download the plug-in from **http://www.apple.com/quicktime**.

6. Return to Dreamweaver to save and close the file.

NOTE | What's a Parameter?

Most plug-in content is controlled by a variety of parameters, which are different for each kind of plug-in. A parameter is an option passed to the plug-in that tells it how to behave. In this exercise, you learned how to set the autoplay parameter to off. That parameter is part of the QuickTime specification.

This chapter covers sound, Flash, Shockwave, and QuickTime, but there are many other types of plug-ins on the Web as well. In order to learn what all the parameters are for a plug-in, it's best to visit the site from which it can be downloaded. Here's a list of sites with more information on plug-in parameters from a variety of vendors.

LiveAudio Plug-In
http://developer.netscape.com/docs/manuals/js/client/jsguide/liveaud.htm

Apple's QuickTime Plug-In
http://www.apple.com/quicktime/authoring/embed2.html

Macromedia's Flash Plug-In
http://www.macromedia.com/support/flash/ts/documents/tag_attributes.htm

Macromedia's Shockwave Plug-In
http://www.macromedia.com/support/director/how/shock/objembed.html

Netscape's Plug-In Registry
http://www.home.netscape.com/plugins

3.————————**Inserting Flash Content**

Because both Dreamweaver and Flash are Macromedia products, it is not entirely surprising that Dreamweaver's support for Flash is superb. Instead of the generic Insert plug-in object that you used in the last exercise, Dreamweaver has an Insert Flash object all its own.

1. Create a new document and save it as **flash.html** inside the **chap_18** folder.

2. Click on the **Insert Flash** object in the **Common Objects** panel, and browse to **splash.swf**. Click **Open**. This Flash piece was donated courtesy of Greg Penny of Flower Records (**http://www.flowerrecords.com**) and was designed by Richard Joffray (**http://www.joffray.com**).

3. Notice that the Property Inspector has a Play button. You should be able to play the content right in Dreamweaver, unlike DHTML or generic plug-in content. Press **F12** to view the content in your browser, to check it again. It's that simple.

4. Return to Dreamweaver. Because Flash is vector-based, it can scale. Change both the **W** and **H** properties to **100%**, and press **F12** again. Now change the size of your browser. The content in your browser scales, too! This happens only if you set the width and height information to percentages.

5. Save and close the file.

The next exercise will explain how to embed Shockwave content.

4. ──────────Inserting Director (Shockwave) Content

Next, you'll get a chance to work with some Director (Shockwave) content. Once again, because this is a Macromedia product, you'll have the advantage of using an Insert Shockwave object instead of the generic Insert Plugin object.

1. Create a new document and save it as **director.html** inside the **chap_18** folder.

2. Click on the **Insert Shockwave** object in the **Common Objects** panel, and browse to **leroy.dcr**. Click **Open**.

3. Notice that the Property Inspector has **W 32** and **H 32** as the dimensions. These are the default dimensions that you'll see for Director or QuickTime content, because Dreamweaver can't detect the size of these two formats automatically. You'll need to plug in the correct dimensions to get this object to work.

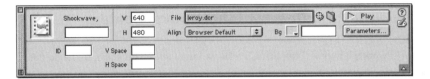

4. Enter the values **W 640** and **H 480**, and press **F12** to preview the content. How did we know that the width and height of the piece were 640 x 480? Because Bruce, Lynda's husband, created it! Sadly, you must know the dimensions of the Shockwave piece before you enter the values, because Dreamweaver doesn't detect them for you.

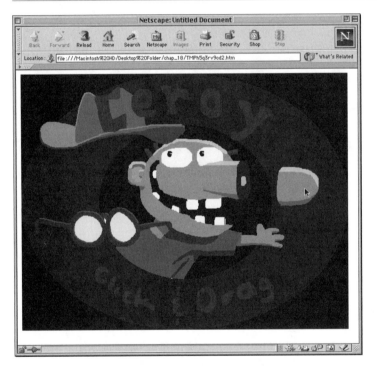

5. Try pulling Leroy's eyeglasses off. Lots of parts come off, so keep pulling on things. This is very similar to the drag-and-drop exercise you completed in Chapter 16, *"DHTML,"* only it was created in Macromedia Director.

6. Return to Dreamweaver. Save and close the file.

NOTE | What Is Shockwave?

Shockwave is a plug-in that allows a Web audience to view Macromedia Director content online. The plug-in is over 1MB in size, while the Flash plug-in is under 200K. Macromedia Director, like Flash, is an authoring tool that supports better animation, sound, and interactivity than HTML pages do. The differences between Flash and Director relate to how the authoring tool is structured, how the interactivity is programmed, and how images are formatted for the Web. Flash is installed in more browsers than Shockwave, and many more people know and use the authoring tool. Director is by far a more powerful authoring tool with much more sophisticated programming capabilities, but because of the larger download and smaller amount of Director content on the Web, it doesn't have the installed user base of Flash. For more information about the two, visit **http://www.macromedia.com** to read the specifications and features.

What Is QuickTime?

QuickTime is a both a file format and a plug-in that includes sound and movies. It is one of the most versatile file plug-ins on the Web, because it is able to play all of the formats listed in the chart below.

What QuickTime Supports:		
3dMF	Image Sequence movie exporters	PLS
AIFF	JPEG/JFIF	PNG
AU	Karaoke	QuickTime Image
AVI	MacPaint	QuickTime Movie
BMP	Macromedia Flash	SGI
Cubic VR	MIDI	System 7
DLS	MPEG1	Sound
DV Stream	MP3	Targa
Flash Pix	Photoshop	Text
FLC	PICT	TIFF
GIF	Picture	WAV

5. ——————————Inserting a QuickTime Movie

QuickTime content is inserted in Dreamweaver using the **Insert Plugin** object. This exercise shows you how to embed the content and preview the results.

1. Create a new document and save it as **quicktime.html** inside the **chap_18** folder.

2. Click on the **Insert Plugin** object in the **Special Objects** panel, and browse to the file **testing.mov**. Click **Open**.

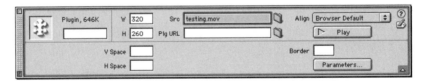

3. Change the width and height information to **W 320, H 260** in the Property Inspector. Note that Dreamweaver could detect the dimensions of a Flash movie but not the dimensions of QuickTime or Director content.

It's important that you know the dimensions of the file before you embed it into Dreamweaver, so you can insert the correct values into the Property Inspector. In this instance, the movie was 320 x 240, but we've added an extra 20 pixels to make room for the controller below the movie, as shown above.

4. Press **F12** to preview the movie in your browser. **Note:** If you get a broken image icon, you might have to download the plug-in from **http://www.apple.com/quicktime**.

5. Return to Dreamweaver. Save and close the Dreamweaver file.

Phew; another chapter bites the dust. Good work! If you feel up to it, go ahead and move on to the next and final chapter.

I9.

Getting It Online

| Setting Up a GeoCities Account |
| Setting the FTP Preferences | Putting Files onto the Web Server |
| Getting Site Reports |

chap_19

Dreamweaver 4
H•O•T CD-ROM

It's one thing to design a Web page, and it's an entirely different thing to get it online. One of the features we felt was missing from other books was concrete instructions covering how to access, upload, and update files to a Web server. Until now, you were forced to struggle through this process on your own, which can prove frustrating. Well, fear not, we are here to walk you through the process of uploading your pages to a real live Web server. This means that you, your family, and your friends will be able to see the results of whatever you publish on the Web.

This chapter will show you how to create a free Web hosting account with GeoCities and then use Dreamweaver to upload a Web site so that it can be viewed live on the Internet. You do not have to sign up for the GeoCities account unless you want to follow along with the exercises. If you already have a Web hosting account, you can use that information to complete the following exercises. Either way, this chapter will show you how to set up your FTP preferences and upload your site using Dreamweaver.

Free Web Hosting with GeoCities

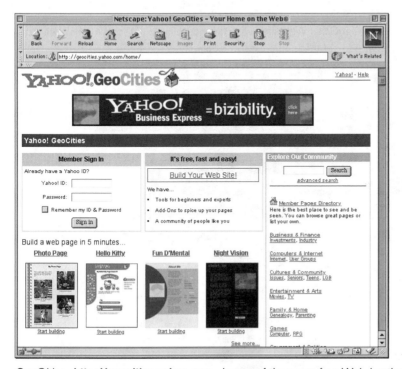

*GeoCities—**http://geocities.yahoo.com**—is one of the many free Web hosting services available on the Internet.*

There are several services on the Web that offer free Web hosting. Of these free services, GeoCities is probably the most famous. GeoCities was one of the first Web services to offer free Web hosting to anyone who wanted to sign up. Within just a few minutes, you can have a place to upload your files to on the Web.

You will be pleasantly surprised by how much you get for free. The GeoCities free Web hosting package includes a lot of extras. All you need to complete the exercises in this chapter are the 15 megabytes of free disk space and FTP access that are provided with the free Web hosting account.

If you already have a hosting service of your own, feel free to use it in the exercises, rather than GeoCities. For the FTP information, just substitute the info you've received from your own hosting service.

Signing Up with GeoCities

The first step in getting your free GeoCities Web site online involves filling out a form on their site. This exercise will show you what parts of the form need to be completed.

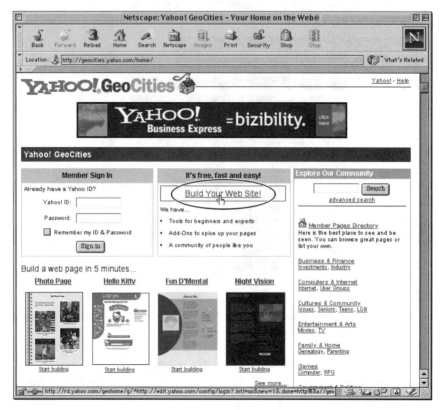

1. Launch your preferred Web browser and browse to the GeoCities home page at **http://geocities.yahoo.com/home/**. Here you'll find a complete rundown on their services.

2. Click on the **Build Your Web Site!** link. This takes you to another Web page where you can choose to sign up for your own account.

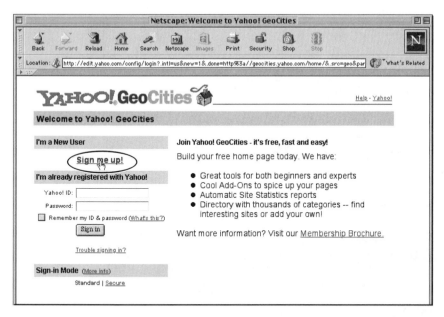

3. Click the **Sign me up!** link. This takes you to a page where you will complete a brief questionnaire, which is required before you can create an account.

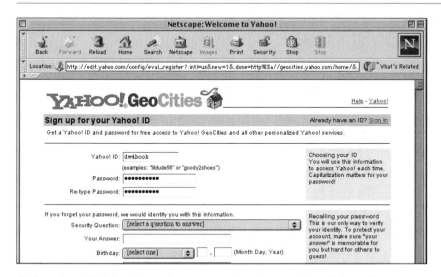

4. Complete all of the information requested on the form. Your **Yahoo! ID** will appear as part of your GeoCities URL. Our Yahoo! ID is **dw4book**; therefore, our URL is:
http://www.geocities.com/dw4book/.

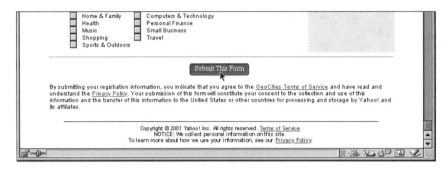

5. When you are finished entering your information, click the **Submit This Form** button at the bottom of the page. This submits your information for processing.

6. For item **1**, choose a category that is appropriate for your site. For Item **2**, enter the confirmation code displayed on your screen. Don't use the one displayed in this book. Click **Submit This Form**. This finalizes the activation process.

NOTE | Privacy Policies

Any time you provide personal information about yourself on a Web site, you should be familiar with the recipient's privacy policy. Some sites gather personal information and then sell it to marketing companies. This can result in some extra and unsolicited emails in your inbox. If this is of serious concern to you, make sure you review GeoCities' privacy policy before you provide them with information. You can review their privacy policy at: **http://docs.yahoo.com/info/privacy/**.

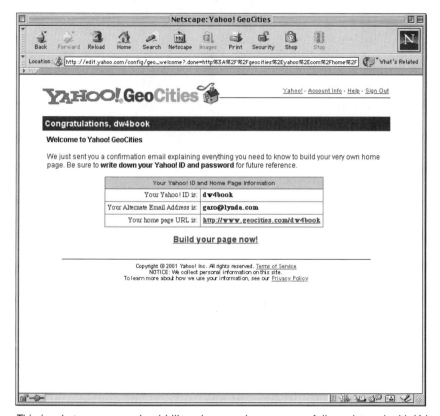

This is what your page should like when you have successfully registered with Yahoo!

7. When GeoCities has finished processing your application for free Web space, you'll be taken automatically to the Welcome page, where your Yahoo! ID, email address, and URL are confirmed. Click the **Build your page now!** link to complete the configuration of your Web site. It might take as long as 24 hours to process your account.

8. You should quickly receive a confirmation email (or two) that repeats your user info and URL and provides more information on GeoCities Web services.

9. You are now ready to set up your FTP preferences in Dreamweaver and begin uploading your site. Exit the browser; you will come back to it later after you have uploaded your site from Dreamweaver.

2. _____Setting the FTP Preferences

In order for your site to be seen on the World Wide Web, your files need to be uploaded to a live Web server. Most Web developers and designers build pages on their hard drive (as you have done in this book) before transferring their files to a live Web server. In Dreamweaver terminology, the files on your hard drive are referred to as **local** files, and the files on a live Web server are referred to as **remote** files. You can upload your files from Dreamweaver by using the **Site Definitions** FTP settings.

The information that you need to fill out in the FTP settings of Dreamweaver will be contained in the email you receive from GeoCities. They include the FTP host, host directory, login (user name or ID), and password. In this exercise, you will enter this necessary information into Dreamweaver's settings, so that you can upload your Web site to a Web server.

1. Copy **chap_19** to your hard drive. Define your site for Chapter 19, using the **chap_19** folder as the local root folder. If you need a refresher on this process, visit Exercise 1 in Chapter 3, *"Site Control."*

2. Select **Site > Define Sites**. In the **Define Sites** dialog box, choose **Chapter 19** and click **Edit...**

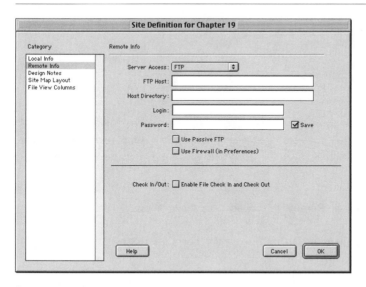

3. In the **Site Definition** dialog box, click on **Remote Info** in the **Category** list, and then choose **FTP** from the **Server Access:** pop-up menu. This will give you access to the various FTP settings you will need to modify before you upload files to your site.

FTP Information

FTP Host:	ftp.geocities.com
Host Directory:	(leave this blank)
Login:	(your Yahoo! ID)
Password:	(your password)

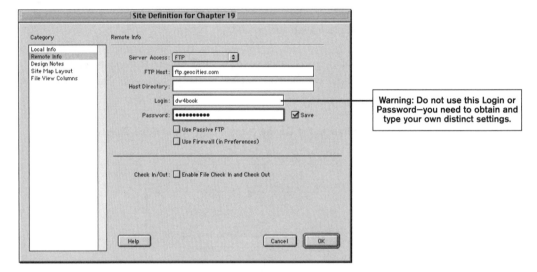

If you signed up for the free GeoCities account, your FTP information should be similar to the information shown above. You can get more information about these settings from the email that you receive from GeoCities. However, if you are using your own Web hosting service, you would enter that information instead.

4. Enter the information for the **Remote Info** options, as shown above.

5. Click **OK**. This returns you to the **Define Sites** dialog box. Click **Done**.

What Is FTP?

FTP stands for **F**ile **T**ransfer **P**rotocol. This term is usually associated with the process of uploading Web files to a live Web server. You will hear this term used as a noun ("I used an FTP program to upload my files") and as a verb ("I am going to FTP all of my files now!").

It is important to note that you do not have to use Dreamweaver to exchange files with the remote server. You can use other FTP applications as well, such as Fetch (Mac) or WS_FTP (Windows). There are advantages to using Dreamweaver over these applications, however, such as file synchronization and site management. You'll learn about these advantages shortly.

Here is a handy chart that describes the FTP settings in Dreamweaver.

FTP Settings in Dreamweaver	
Setting	**Description**
FTP Host	This will typically be an address similar to the URL of your Web site. In some cases it may begin with the prefix FTP.
Host Directory	If you have a specific directory on the server where you are supposed to place your files, you would enter it here. This option is not always used.
Login	You will be given a user name or ID to use to access the remote server. It is important that you enter this information exactly as it is given to you; otherwise you will have problems connecting.
Password	In addition to a user name or ID, you will also be given a password to use when accessing the remote server. If you don't want to enter the password every time you connect to the remote server, select the Save checkbox, and then Dreamweaver will remember your password! **Note:** The password you enter here is just stored in a text file on your hard drive, so anyone can read it. Don't check this if security is a concern at your location.

Putting Files onto the Web Server

Now that you have set up your FTP preferences, you are ready to use Dreamweaver to connect to a Web server and upload your files. Once you have completed this exercise, you will be able to see your Web site live on the internet. Woo-hoo! **Note:** It may take up to 24 hours before your Geocities account is activated. If you get a connection error, wait an hour and then try again.

1. Before you try to upload your files to the Web server, make sure you have established a connection to the internet. For most people, this simply involves connecting through an ISP with a modem.

2. Make sure your Site window is open; if it is not, press **F8**. Notice that the **Connect** button, at the top of the window, is no longer dimmed. Once you enter your FTP preferences, you will have access to this feature.

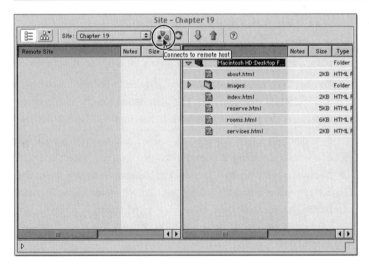

3. Click the **Connect** button. This will connect Dreamweaver to your Web server. If you have not established a connection to the Internet with your modem or network, you will get an error message.

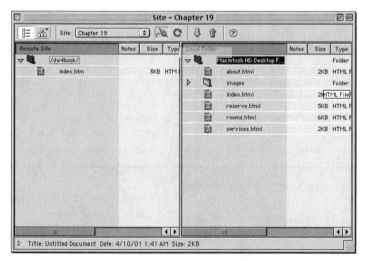

*After making a successful connection to the Web server, your Site window should look like this. The contents of the Web server are displayed in the left side of the window. The **index.html** file was put there automatically by GeoCities. You can remove this file by clicking to select it and then pressing the Delete key.*

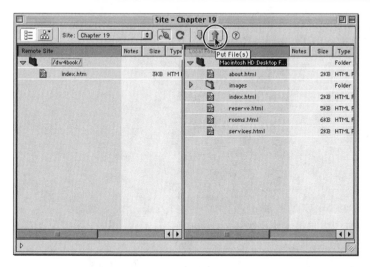

4. With the local root folder selected, you are ready to upload your site. Click the **Put Files** button.

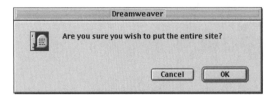

5. You are asked whether you want to upload your entire Web site. Since this is the first time you are uploading your site, click **OK**.

NOTE | The Difference Between Getting and Putting

There are two different ways to transfer files between the local site and the remote site (the Web server). The Get command copies the selected files from the remote site to your local site. This process is referred to as **downloading**. In addition, if you are using the Check-In and Check-Out options, the Get command copies the file to the local site as a read-only file, leaving the original on the Web server for others to download. The Put command copies the selected files from the local site to the remote site. This process is referred to as **uploading**.

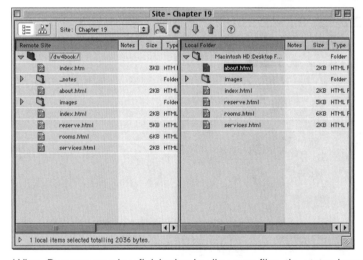

When Dreamweaver has finished uploading your files, the status bar will no longer display any upload status. **Note:** *If an error occurs during the transfer process, Dreamweaver maintains a log of FTP errors that you can review to help troubleshoot the problem. You can access this log by selecting* **Site > FTP Log** *(Mac) or* **Window > FTP Log** *(Windows).*

6. Open a browser. Browse to the URL provided in the emails from GeoCities. Since we are using Garo's account, the URL will be **http://www.geocities.com/dw4book/.** Of course, your URL will be different. Voila, your Web site is live on the Web! Congratulations! Make sure you show all your friends. ;-)

Getting Site Reports

As your sites get larger, you will find it increasingly difficult to manage all of the files. Trying to locate files with missing **<alt>** tags, untitled documents, redundant nested tags, etc. can prove to be a very time-consuming task. Dreamweaver 4 introduced site reports, a feature that lets you identify and locate files that meet specific criteria. This feature can save you time hunting for the files manually, and will make sure your files are in good shape.

This exercise has you run a report on a finished site and fix some of the problems identified in the report.

1. Select **Site > Reports**. This opens the Reports dialog box, where you can specify the type of report you would like to generate.

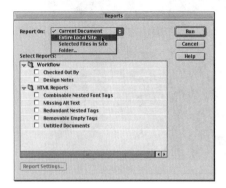

2. From the **Report On** drop-down menu, select **Entire Local Site**. This ensures that all of the files within the local root folder are processed.

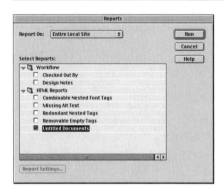

3. Click the **Untitled Documents** checkbox. This option causes all of the page titles of the documents within your site to be examined to make sure each has a unique name. This is a good thing because some search engines use the page title as part of their listings.

The Reports Dialog Box

The Reports dialog box has several features that offer you a wide range of options and flexibility. The table below outlines these options and offers a brief description of each.

Reports Dialog Box Options	
Option	**Description**
Report On:	
Current Document	Checks only the active document.
Entire Local Site	Checks every file within the local root folder.
Selected Files in Site	Checks only the files that are selected within the Site window. You must have the files selected before choosing this option.
Folder	Checks a specific folder. When you choose this option, you can browse to the specific folder you want to process.
Workflow:	
Checked Out By	Identifies files that have been checked out by a specific user. When this option is selected, you can specify the name by clicking on the Report Settings button.
Design Notes	Searches all of the Design Notes in your documents. The Report Settings button will give you access to specific search criteria
HTML Reports:	
Combinable Nested Font Tags	Combines all possible nested font tags. For example `<font color="#CC3366"><font size="1">Hello</font></font>` would be reported.
Missing ALT tags	Identifies all images that do not have an `<alt>` tag applied to them. This is good option to run to make sure you site has good accessibility.
Redundant Nested Tags	Reports nested tags that can be cleaned up. For example `The Moon's Nest Inn <i> is</i> a great place to stay</i>` would be reported. This option helps clean up your HTML.
Removable Empty Tags	Removes any empty tags, which can help clean up your HTML. This is another option that will help clean up unnecessary HTML code.
Untitled Documents	Searches the document to see if it has a page tile of Untitled Document. It's always best to give your documents page titles that reflect their content.

4. Click **Run**. Dreamweaver will begin to scan all of the files in your site, looking for ones that have Untitled Document as their page title.

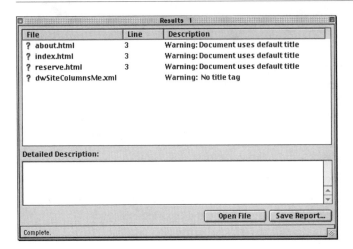

When Dreamweaver is finished scanning your site, it will produce a Results dialog box that displays the files that meet the criteria you specified. In this case, you are looking for files that have Untitled Document as their page title.

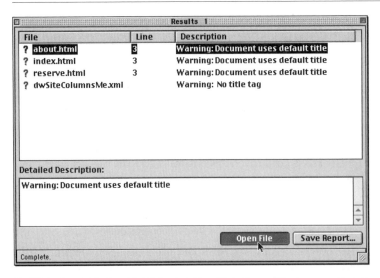

5. Click **about.html** to highlight that file. Click **Open File** to open that file so you can correct the problem. It's really nice that you can open the files directly from this dialog box.

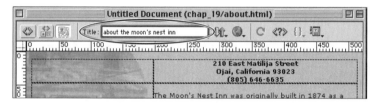

6. Notice that the **Title:** option is set to **Untitled Document**. Change the **Title:** option to "**about the moon's nest inn**." Save and close this file.

---

7. Go ahead and fix the page titles for the **index.html** and **reserve.html** pages. Don't worry about the **dwSiteColumnsMe.xml** file; nobody will ever see that file so it doesn't need a page title. It is an internal document used by Dreamweaver only.

---

8. When you are finished, you can save and close all of the open documents.

Congratulations! You certainly deserve it! You've made it through all the chapters!! We hope that this book helped you get up to speed with Dreamweaver quickly, and that you now feel ready to use your skills to create just about any Web site project. We wish you the best of luck with all of your future projects. Rock on!

Troubleshooting FAQ

| Appendix A |

H·O·T

Dreamweaver 4

If you run into any problems while following the exercises in this book, this F.A.Q. is intended to help. This document will be maintained and expanded upon at this book's companion Web site: **http://www.lynda.com/products/books/dw4hot**.

If you don't find what you're looking for here or there, please send an email to: **dw4faq@lynda.com.**

If you have a question related to Dreamweaver, but unrelated to a specific step in an exercise in this book, visit the Dreamweaver site at: **http://www.macromedia.com/support/dreamweaver/** or call their tech support hotline at 415.252.9080.

Q: How do I call up the Property Inspector?

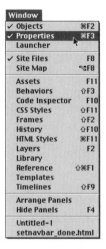

A: If you can't see the Property Inspector or, for that matter, any of Dreamweaver's panels, pull down the **Window** menu and click on the one you want to open. A list of shortcut keys that will help you quickly access all of Dreamweaver's panels can be found at the end of Chapter 2, *"Interface."*

Q: I defined my site for a chapter, but files that are listed in the exercises aren't there. What happened?

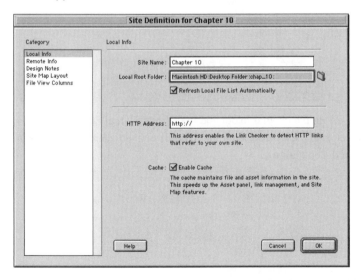

A: This could be because when you were defining the site you specified a folder that was inside the chapter folder, instead of the chapter folder itself. Go ahead and redefine the site. (If you need to revisit these steps, visit Exercise 1 in Chapter 3, *"Site Control.")* **Note:** Selecting the correct folder is done differently on Mac and Windows, as shown below.

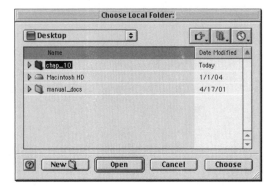

Mac: When you're browsing to define the chapter folder and the **Choose Local Folder** dialog box pops up, notice how there's both an **Open** and a **Choose** option. Highlight the chapter folder, and click **Choose**. Don't click **Open**, because you would then define as your site an interior folder, instead of the main folder. This is opposite to the way Windows users define their sites.

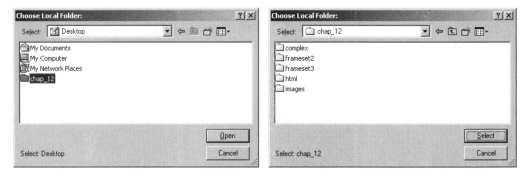

Windows: When you're browsing to define the chapter folder and the **Choose Local Folder** dialog box pops up, select the chapter folder. First click **Open**. After the folder is opened, click **Select**. This is opposite to the way Macintosh users define their site.

Q: Where's the Color panel?

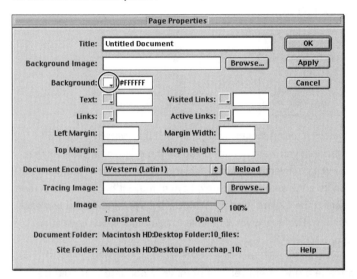

A: Because it's context sensitive, the Color panel only appears when you click in one of Dreamweaver's color wells. Color wells appear inside the Property Inspector and the **Page Properties** dialog box.

Q: I just specified a Tracing Image in my Page Properties window, but I can't see it when I preview the page in my browser. Panic is starting to set in!

A: The **Tracing Image** is a template to be used for layout in Dreamweaver. It is invisible in the browser window, so if you don't see it, that's the whole point! It's there for your reference only, and your end users will never see it.

Q: I put one layer on top of another! How do I delete it?

A: To delete a layer, select it by the handle at its top and hit **Delete**. You can also use the Layers panel to select the layer, which might be easier in some cases where they overlap. Of course, there's always the universal undo command, **Cmd+Z** (Mac) or **Ctrl+Z** (Windows).

Q: When I convert layers to tables, I get an error message stating that one of the layers is off-screen. How did this happen, and how do I fix it?

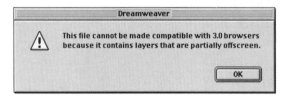

A: It is possible to create a layer and move it, using the arrow keys, so that it is partially or fully off-screen. This is actually handy for images that you want to have bleed off the edge, or animations that begin outside the document window. When converting layers to tables, however, it won't work! If you can locate the offending layer, click on its edge and use the arrow keys to move it back into the screen area. If you can't find the layer, try opening the **Layers** window (**Window > Layers**) and selecting each layer name that appears inside the window. Eventually, you'll be able to figure out which layer is on or off the screen by process of elimination.

Q: Why do I get the message, "To make a document-relative path, your document should be saved first"? I can't figure out what this gibberish means!

A: Hey, we're with you. It would be nice if the dialog box simply stated, "Save your file now, or Dreamweaver can't keep track of your files," because that's all it's asking you to do. Sigh. If only developers knew how to speak in non-technical terms at times, eh? All you need to do is click **OK** and save your file (inside the defined site), and Dreamweaver won't bark any more.

Q: Why do I get the message that my file is located outside of the root folder?

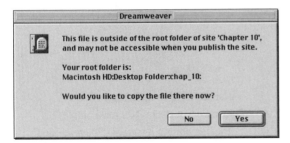

A: Dreamweaver is asking you to move the file into the root folder that you've defined as your site. If you work with files outside your defined root folder, Dreamweaver cannot keep track of your links or manage your site, which is counterproductive to the way the program is structured and to your workflow. Though this message is annoying, it is actually helping you maintain a healthy site without experiencing broken links and problems uploading your files when you publish it. **Note:** There are different ways to handle this message, depending on the system you are running.

Macintosh: You should click **Yes**, and then browse to the correct folder. At that point you will be prompted to save, which you should do.

Windows: You should click **Yes**, and Dreamweaver will automatically pop you into the correct folder. Click save, and the file will be moved.

Q: Why aren't my templates working?

A: If you leave a template file open and work on another site (such as another chapter in this book that you've defined as a different site), Dreamweaver can't keep track of your templates. It's best to work on a single site at a time, and not flip between sites while leaving files open from another defined site. This is true with all Dreamweaver documents, although templates and libraries are particularly sensitive to site-definition confusion.

Q: When I try to locate class files, why can't I see the file extensions at the end of file names, such as *.gif*, *.jpg*, and *.html*?

A: On Windows, you will need to change your Preferences to view file name extensions. Instructions to do this are inside the *"Introduction."*

B

Online Resources

| Appendix B |

The Web is full of great resources for Dreamweaver users. You have ample choices among a variety of newsgroups, listservs, and third-party Web sites that can really help you get the most out of the new skills you've developed by following the exercises in this book. This appendix lists some of the best resources for learning and extending Dreamweaver.

H•O•T

Dreamweaver 4

Lynda.com Discussion Groups

At Lynda.com we have a whole section of our web site dedicated to the discussion of various web design principals and tools, including Dreamweaver, Fireworks, and Flash. You can get more information about this free resource at:

`http://www.lynda.com/discussions/Macromedia Discussion Groups`

Macromedia has set up several discussion boards (newsgroups) for Dreamweaver. This is a great place to ask questions and get help from thousands of Dreamweaver users. The newsgroup is composed of beginning to advanced users, so you should have no problem finding the type of help you need, regardless of your experience with the program. In order to access these newsgroups, you will need a newsgroup reader, such as Microsoft Outlook or Free Agent.

Dreamweaver
`news://forums.macromedia.com/macromedia.dreamweaver`

Course Builder for Dreamweaver
`news://forums.macromedia.com/macromedia.dreamweaver.coursebuilder`

Dynamic HTML
`news://forums.macromedia.com/macromedia.dynamic.html`

Other Dreamweaver Discussion Groups

Intranet Design Magazine (idm.com)
`http://idm.internet.com/ix/`

Internet Related Topics (irt.org)
`http://www.irt.org/discus/`

Listservs

A listserv is different from a newsgroup, and offers another way people can ask questions and get help with Dreamweaver. Questions and answers are exchanged through the email application of your choice. Blueworld, the developers of Lasso for Dreamweaver for example, maintain an active and very useful listserv for Dreamweaver.

Blueworld Listserv:
`http://www.blueworld.com/blueworld/lists/dreamweaver.html`

A Few Third-Party Dreamweaver Web Sites

Massimo's Corner

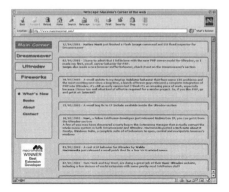

http://www.massimocorner.com/

Dreamweaver Depot

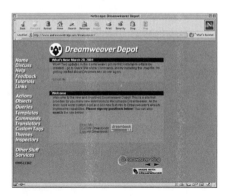

http://www.andrewwooldridge.com/dreamweaver/

Yaromat

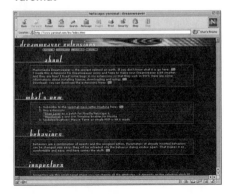

http://www.yaromat.com/dw/index.php

Dreamweaverfever.com

http://www.dreamweaverfever.com/grow/index.htm

Project VII

http://www.projectseven.com

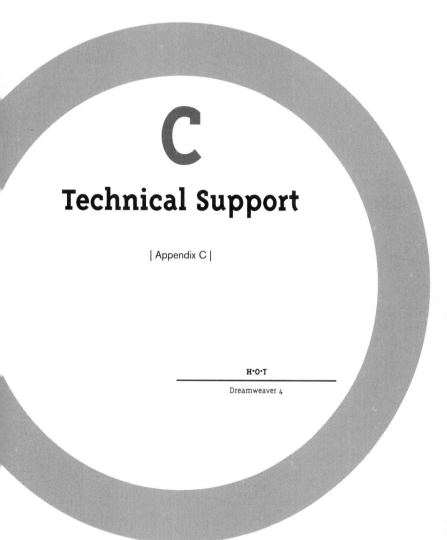

C

Technical Support

| Appendix C |

H•O•T

Dreamweaver 4

Macromedia Technical Support

http://www.macromedia.com/support/

415.252.9080

If you are having problems with Dreamweaver, please contact Macromedia Technical Support at the number listed above. Macromedia staff will be able to help you with such typical problems as: the trial version has expired on your computer; your computer crashes when you try to launch the application; etc. Please note that lynda.com cannot help troubleshoot technical problems with Dreamweaver.

Peachpit Press

customer_service@peachpit.com

If your book has a defective CD-ROM, please contact the customer service department at the above email address. We do not have extra CDs at lynda.com, so they must be requested directly from the publisher.

lynda.com

http://www.lynda.com/products/books/dw4hot/

dw4faq@lynda.com

We have created a companion Web site for this book, which can be found at http://www.lynda.com/books/dw4hot/. Any errors in the book will be posted to the Web site, and it's always a good idea to check there for up-to-date information. We encourage and welcome your comments and error reports to dw4faq@lynda.com. Both Lynda and Garo receive each of these emails.

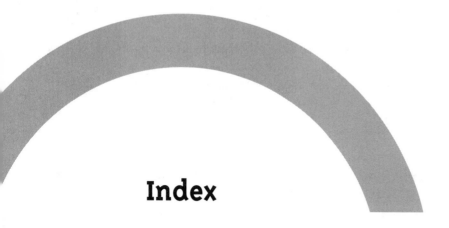

Index